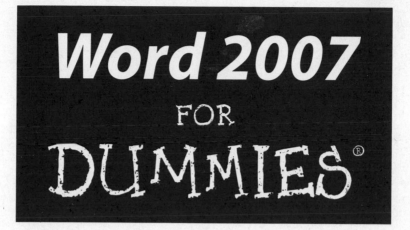

Word 2007
FOR
DUMMIES®

Word 2007 For Dummies®

Cheat Sheet

Word 2007 screen

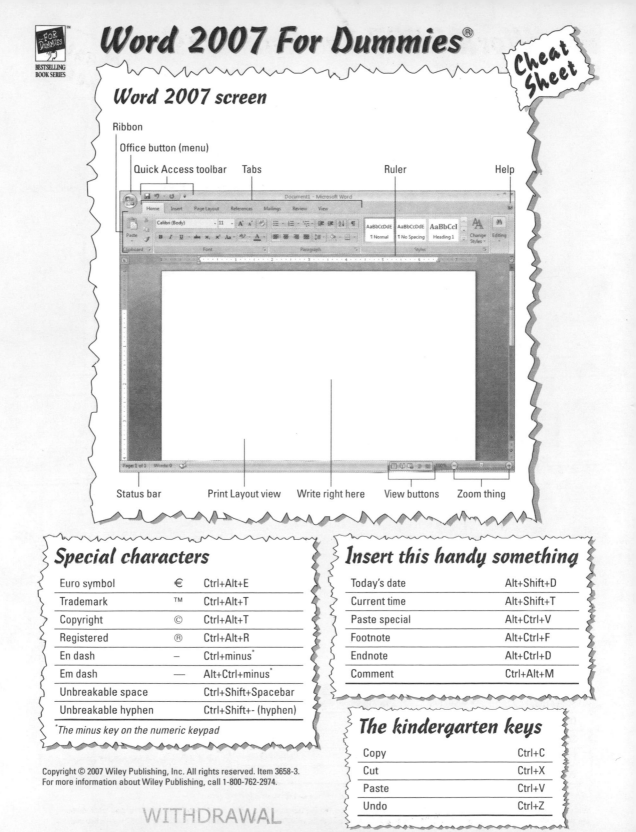

Ribbon

Office button (menu)

Quick Access toolbar   Tabs   Ruler   Help

Status bar   Print Layout view   Write right here   View buttons   Zoom thing

Special characters

Euro symbol	€	Ctrl+Alt+E
Trademark	™	Ctrl+Alt+T
Copyright	©	Ctrl+Alt+T
Registered	®	Ctrl+Alt+R
En dash	–	Ctrl+minus*
Em dash	—	Alt+Ctrl+minus*
Unbreakable space		Ctrl+Shift+Spacebar
Unbreakable hyphen		Ctrl+Shift+- (hyphen)

*The minus key on the numeric keypad

Insert this handy something

Today's date	Alt+Shift+D
Current time	Alt+Shift+T
Paste special	Alt+Ctrl+V
Footnote	Alt+Ctrl+F
Endnote	Alt+Ctrl+D
Comment	Ctrl+Alt+M

The kindergarten keys

Copy	Ctrl+C
Cut	Ctrl+X
Paste	Ctrl+V
Undo	Ctrl+Z

WITHDRAWAL

For Dummies: Bestselling Book Series for Beginners

Word 2007 For Dummies®

Cheat Sheet

Getting around in a document

Key	Moves Insertion Pointer . . .
↑	Up one line of text
↓	Down one line of text
→	Right to the next character
←	Left to the next character
Ctrl+↑	Up one paragraph
Ctrl+↓	Down one paragraph
Ctrl+→	Right one word
Ctrl+←	Left one word
PgUp	Up one screen
PgDn	Down one screen
End	To end of current line
Home	To start of current line
Ctrl+Home	To top of document
Ctrl+End	To bottom of document

Text formatting key commands

Bold	Ctrl+B
Italic	Ctrl+I
Underline	Ctrl+U
Double underline	Ctrl+Shift+D
Word underline	Ctrl+Shift+W
Small caps	Ctrl+Shift+K
Superscript	Ctrl+Shift++
Subscript	Ctrl+=
Erase formats	Ctrl+Spacebar
Grow font	Ctrl+Shift+>
Shrink font	Ctrl+Shift+<
ALL CAPS	Ctrl+Shift+A
Font	Ctrl+Shift+F
Point size	Ctrl+Shift+P
Font dialog box	Ctrl+D

Paragraph formatting key commands

Center text	Ctrl+E	Justify	Ctrl+J
Left align	Ctrl+L	Indent paragraph	Ctrl+M
Right align	Ctrl+R	Unindent	Ctrl+Shift+M
One-line spacing	Ctrl+1	Hanging indent	Ctrl+T
1½-line spacing	Ctrl+5	Unhang indent	Ctrl+Shift+T
Two-line spacing	Ctrl+2		

Common Word key commands

Help	F1
Cancel	Escape
Go back	Shift+F5
New document	Ctrl+N
Open	Ctrl+O
Print	Ctrl+P
Close	Ctrl+W
Quick save	Ctrl+S
Repeat	Ctrl+Y
Find	Ctrl+F
Find and Replace	Ctrl+H
Manual page break	Ctrl+Enter

Uncommon (but useful) Word key commands

Go To	F5	Print Layout view	Ctrl+Alt+P
Show/Hide	Ctrl+Shift+8	Draft (normal) view	Ctrl+Alt+N
Office button menu	Alt+F	Outline view	Ctrl+Alt+O
Styles Task Pane	Ctrl+Shift+Alt+S	Split window	Alt+Ctrl+S
Print Preview	Ctrl+Alt+I	Symbol font	Ctrl+Shift+Q
Word Count	Ctrl+Shift+G		

For Dummies: Bestselling Book Series for Beginners

Word 2007 FOR DUMMIES®

by Dan Gookin

BICENTENNIAL
1807
WILEY
2007
BICENTENNIAL

Wiley Publishing, Inc.

Word 2007 For Dummies®

Published by
Wiley Publishing, Inc.
111 River Street
Hoboken, NJ 07030-5774
www.wiley.com

Copyright © 2007 by Wiley Publishing, Inc., Indianapolis, Indiana

Published by Wiley Publishing, Inc., Indianapolis, Indiana

Published simultaneously in Canada

No part of this publication may be reproduced, stored in a retrieval system or transmitted in any form or by any means, electronic, mechanical, photocopying, recording, scanning or otherwise, except as permitted under Sections 107 or 108 of the 1976 United States Copyright Act, without either the prior written permission of the Publisher, or authorization through payment of the appropriate per-copy fee to the Copyright Clearance Center, 222 Rosewood Drive, Danvers, MA 01923, (978) 750-8400, fax (978) 646-8600. Requests to the Publisher for permission should be addressed to the Legal Department, Wiley Publishing, Inc., 10475 Crosspoint Blvd., Indianapolis, IN 46256, (317) 572-3447, fax (317) 572-4355, or online at http://www.wiley.com/go/permissions.

Trademarks: Wiley, the Wiley Publishing logo, For Dummies, the Dummies Man logo, A Reference for the Rest of Us!, The Dummies Way, Dummies Daily, The Fun and Easy Way, Dummies.com, and related trade dress are trademarks or registered trademarks of John Wiley & Sons, Inc. and/or its affiliates in the United States and other countries, and may not be used without written permission. All other trademarks are the property of their respective owners. Wiley Publishing, Inc., is not associated with any product or vendor mentioned in this book.

For general information on our other products and services, please contact our Customer Care Department within the U.S. at 800-762-2974, outside the U.S. at 317-572-3993, or fax 317-572-4002.

For technical support, please visit www.wiley.com/techsupport.

Wiley also publishes its books in a variety of electronic formats. Some content that appears in print may not be available in electronic books.

Library of Congress Control Number: 2006934826

ISBN-13: 978-0-470-03658-7

ISBN-10: 0-470-03658-3

Manufactured in the United States of America

10 9 8 7 6 5 4

1B/QV/RS/QW/IN

WILEY

About the Author

After physically destroying three typewriters, **Dan Gookin** bought his first computer in 1982 at the urging of the guy in the typewriter repair shop. Contrary to his prejudices, Dan quickly discovered that computers were about more than math, and he quickly took to the quirky little devices.

Twenty-five years later, Mr. Gookin has written over 100 books about computers and high tech and gone through more than 50 computers, including a dozen or so laptops and portables. He has achieved fame as one of the first computer radio talk show hosts, the editor of a magazine, a national technology spokesman, and an occasional actor on the community theater stage.

Dan still considers himself a writer and computer "guru" whose job it is to remind everyone that computers are not to be taken too seriously. His approach to computers is light and humorous, yet very informative. He knows that the complex beasts are important and can do a great deal to help people become productive and successful. Dan mixes his vast knowledge of computers with a unique, dry sense of humor that keeps everyone informed — and awake. His favorite quote is "Computers are a notoriously dull subject, but that doesn't mean I have to write about them that way."

Dan Gookin's most recent books are *PCs For Dummies,* 10th Edition, *Laptops For Dummies,* 2nd Edition, and some new titles he can't yet discuss under threat of death. He holds a degree in communications/visual arts from UCSD. Dan dwells in North Idaho, where he enjoys woodworking, music, theater, riding his bicycle, and spending time with the lads.

Publisher's Acknowledgments

We're proud of this book; please send us your comments through our online registration form located at www.dummies.com/register/.

Some of the people who helped bring this book to market include the following:

Acquisitions, Editorial, and Media Development

Project Editor: Paul Levesque

Acquisitions Editor: Greg Croy

Copy Editor: Rebecca Whitney

Technical Editor: Lee Musick

Editorial Manager: Leah Cameron

Media Development Specialists: Angela Denny, Kate Jenkins, Steven Kudirka, Kit Malone

Media Development Coordinator: Laura Atkinson

Media Project Supervisor: Laura Moss

Media Development Manager: Laura VanWinkle

Editorial Assistant: Amanda Foxworth

Sr. Editorial Assistant: Cherie Case

Cartoons: Rich Tennant (www.the5thwave.com)

Composition Services

Project Coordinator: Adrienne Martinez

Layout and Graphics: Lavonne Cook, Denny Hager, Stephanie D. Jumper, Clint Lahnen, Barbara Moore, Barry Offringa, Lynsey Osborn, Erin Zeltner

Proofreaders: Laura Albert, Christine Pingleton, Techbooks

Indexer: Techbooks

Anniversary Logo Design: Richard Pacifico

Special Help: Mary Lagu

Publishing and Editorial for Technology Dummies

Richard Swadley, Vice President and Executive Group Publisher

Andy Cummings, Vice President and Publisher

Mary Bednarek, Executive Acquisitions Director

Mary C. Corder, Editorial Director

Publishing for Consumer Dummies

Diane Graves Steele, Vice President and Publisher

Joyce Pepple, Acquisitions Director

Composition Services

Gerry Fahey, Vice President of Production Services

Debbie Stailey, Director of Composition Services

Contents at a Glance

Introduction 1

Part I: Hello, Word! 9
Chapter 1: Word Hokey-Pokey 11
Chapter 2: Making Friends with the Keyboard 25
Chapter 3: A Quick Guide to Word (For the Impatient) 35

Part II: Word Processing Basics 45
Chapter 4: Moving Around a Document Hither, Thither, and Yon 47
Chapter 5: Editing Text 55
Chapter 6: Find and Replace 65
Chapter 7: Text Blocks, Stumbling Blocks, Writer's Blocks 79
Chapter 8: Proofing Your Document (Spelling and Grammar) 95
Chapter 9: Documents and Files 111
Chapter 10: The Printer, the Paper, the Document Maker 125

Part III: Formatting 137
Chapter 11: Formatting Text 139
Chapter 12: Formatting Paragraphs 153
Chapter 13: Setting Tabs 167
Chapter 14: Formatting Pages 183
Chapter 15: Formatting Documents 197
Chapter 16: The Styles of Word 211
Chapter 17: Themes and Templates 227
Chapter 18: Misc. Formatting Stuff 239

Part IV: Making Your Document All Fancy-Schmancy 251
Chapter 19: Borders, Boxes, and Background Color 253
Chapter 20: Turning the Tables 261
Chapter 21: Carousing with Columns 273
Chapter 22: I Love Lists 279
Chapter 23: Going Graphical 289
Chapter 24: Stick *This* in Your Document 301

Part V: What Else Is Left? 309

Chapter 25: Multiple Documents, Multiple Windows,
 Multiple Formats, Multiple Madness 311
Chapter 26: Other Ways of Viewing a Document....................321
Chapter 27: Working This Out Together 331
Chapter 28: Merrily We Mail Merge....................339
Chapter 29: Labels of Love....................351
Chapter 30: Customizing Word 357

Part VI: The Part of Tens 365

Chapter 31: The Ten Commandments of Word....................367
Chapter 32: Ten Cool Tricks....................371
Chapter 33: Ten Odd Things 379
Chapter 34: Ten Avuncular Suggestions 385

Index 389

Table of Contents

Introduction *1*

What's New in Word 2007? 1
About This Book..2
How to Use This Book 3
Foolish Assumptions 4
How This Book Is Organized..4
    Part I: Hello, Word!...5
    Part II: Word Processing Basics 5
    Part III: Formatting 5
    Part IV: Making Your Document All Fancy-Schmancy.....5
    Part V: What Else Is Left?.....................................5
    Part VI: The Part of Tens 5
What's Not Here 6
Icons Used in This Book..6
Where to Go from Here..7

Part 1: Hello, Word! *9*

Chapter 1: Word Hokey-Pokey 11

How Do I Start Word? Let Me Count the Ways. 11
    The good, yet unimaginative, way to start Word 12
    The better and best ways to start Word....................13
    Starting Word by opening a document 15
Behold Word! 16
    Maximize Word's window size 16
    Look! Up on the screen! 18
    The blank place where you write 19
    The mouse pointer in Word 20
Cajoling Word to Help You 21
When You're All Done 22
    Quitting Word...22
    How to quit what you're doing without quitting Word...........23
    Putting Word away for a spell 24

Chapter 2: Making Friends with the Keyboard 25

Behold the PC Keyboard! 25
Typing (Or, the Old Hunt-and-Peck) 27
Follow the blinking cursor 28
When to press that Enter key 28
When to whack the spacebar 29
Backing-up and erasing keys..30
Mind your 1's and 0's and L's and O's 30
Things to Notice Whilst You Type 31
The left end of the status bar 31
Life between pages..32
Spots and clutter in your text 33
Strange underlines and colored text......................................33
Word can type that for you 34

Chapter 3: A Quick Guide to Word (For the Impatient) 35

The Overview 36
Starting Out with a New Document 37
Typing the Text...38
Formatting a Document...38
Save Your Stuff!..39
Finishing a Document 41
Proofing your work..42
Previewing a document 42
Printing a document..42
Wrapping Things Up 44

Part II: Word Processing Basics..................................45

Chapter 4: Moving Around a Document Hither, Thither, and Yon 47

Scrolling a Document..47
The vertical scroll bar 47
One paragraph on the horizontal scroll bar 49
Mouse scrolling tricks..49
Moving the Insertion Pointer...50
Commanding the insertion pointer with the mouse.............50
Moving in small increments (basic arrow keys)...................50
Moving from beginning to end..51
The peculiar cases of PgUp and PgDn 51
Using Browse Buttons to Navigate...52
Getting Lost and Going Back 53
Go to Wherever with the Go To Command...................................53

Chapter 5: Editing Text **55**

Deleting Stuff 55
The delete keys: Backspace and Delete 56
Deleting single characters 56
Deleting a word 57
Deleting more than a word 57
Splitting and Joining 59
Making two paragraphs from one 59
Making one paragraph from two 60
Splitting lines with a soft return 60
Mistakes? Mistakes? Undo Them with Haste 60
Now mark me, how I will undo myself 61
Redo, the Undo-Undo command 61
Redo, the Repeat Typing command 62

Chapter 6: Find and Replace **65**

Text Happily Found 65
O villainous text tidbit! Seek it out! 66
The Super Find command 67
Finding stuff you can't type in 70
Finding formatting 72
Replacing What's Been Found 74
The miracle of the Replace All button 76
Finding and replacing formatting 76

Chapter 7: Text Blocks, Stumbling Blocks, Writer's Blocks **79**

What Is a Block of Text? 80
Marking a Chunk of Text As a Block 81
Using the keyboard to select text 81
Marking a block with the mouse 82
Using the F8 key to mark a block 84
Blocking the whole dang-doodle document 85
Deselecting a Block 86
You've Marked the Block — Now What? 86
Copying a block 87
Moving a block 88
Options for pasting text 88
Special pasting 89
Copying or moving a block with the mouse 90
Copying and moving with the F2 key 91
The Miracle of Collect-and-Paste 91
Looking at the Clipboard 91
Pasting from the Clipboard task pane 92
Cleansing the Clipboard task pane 93

Chapter 8: Proofing Your Document (Spelling and Grammar) ...... .95

Hun Dewing Yore Mist Aches...96
Check Your Spelling...96
The red zigzag of shame...96
What to do when the spell checker stupidly assumes
that a word is misspelled but in fact it isn't...............................98
Undoing an Ignore All command 99
Un-adding words to the dictionary 100
Instant Text-Fixin' with AutoCorrect 101
AutoCorrect in action 101
Do your own AutoCorrect entries 102
Undoing an AutoCorrect correction 103
Grammar Be Good...104
Proofing Your Entire Document at Once......................................104
Customizing Proofing Options..106
Improving Your Word Power...106
A thesaurus is not a colossal prehistoric beast 107
The Research task pane...108
Making Every Word Count 109

Chapter 9: Documents and Files .... .111

All About Files...111
Making a New Document..112
Quick! A blank sheet of paper!...113
Using a template 114
Saving a Document...115
Saving a new document to disk the first time........................115
Problems with saving a document to disk 117
Saving or updating a document...118
Saving when you're done..119
Not saving a document 120
Opening a Document 120
Using the traditional Open command......................................120
A handy way to open a recent file...122
Opening one document inside another 122

Chapter 10: The Printer, the Paper, the Document Maker .... .125

Preparing the Printer...125
Preview Before You Print 126
Printing a Whole Document..128
Printing backward 130
Printing a document quickly..131
Choosing another printer..131

Printing Part of a Document 132
Printing a specific page 132
Printing a range of pages..133
Printing a block..134
Printing More than One Copy of Something................................134
Canceling a Print Job (Omigosh!)..135

Part III: Formatting 137

Chapter 11: Formatting Text 139

How to Format Text 139
Basic Text Formatting..140
Changing the font 141
Character formats (bold, italic, and so on)................................142
Text Transcending Teeny to Titanic 144
Setting the text size..145
Nudging text size 145
More Colorful Text Makes Not for More Colorful Writing................146
Undoing All This Text-Formatting Nonsense................................147
Fun and Formatting in the Font Dialog Box................................148
Changing the CASE of Text..151

Chapter 12: Formatting Paragraphs 153

How to Format a Paragraph..153
Where the Paragraph Formatting Commands Lurk................................155
Paragraph Justification and Alignment 156
Line up on the left!..157
Everyone center!..157
Line up on the right!..157
Full justification! (Full justification — aye, sir!)................................158
Making Room Before, After, or Inside Your Paragraphs................158
Traditional line spacing..158
More line spacing options 159
That space between paragraphs 160
Paragraph Indentation..161
Indenting the first line of a paragraph................................161
Making a hanging indent 162
Indenting a whole paragraph..163
Setting the paragraph margins 163
Who Died and Made This Thing Ruler?................................164

Chapter 13: Setting Tabs 167

The Story of Tab..167
The Tab Stops Here..168
The Standard Left Tab Stop 170
    The tabbed list...170
    The tab-tab-paragraph thing..172
The Center Tab Stop 173
The Right Tab Stop...174
    Right stop, left stop list 175
    Tab, right stop list 176
The Decimal Tab...177
The Bar Tab..178
The Tabs Dialog Box 178
    Setting a tab in the Tabs dialog box.............................179
    Setting leader tabs...180
    Default tab stops 181
Unsetting a Tab Stop..182

Chapter 14: Formatting Pages 183

Describe That Sheet o' Paper 183
    A page is a sheet of paper about "this" big...................184
    Page orientation (landscape or portrait) 185
    Marginal information 186
    Behold the Page Setup dialog box................................187
Page Numbering 189
    Where to stick the page number? 190
    Starting off with a different page number 191
    Numbering with Roman numerals 192
    Removing page numbers 192
New Pages from Nowhere 192
    Starting afresh on a new, blank page 192
    Inserting a whole, blank page 193
Page Froufrou 194
    Color your page 194
    The distinguished watermark......................................195

Chapter 15: Formatting Documents 197

The Oft Misunderstood Yet Useful Concept of Sections 197
    Understanding sections...198
    Creating a section...199
    Using a section..200
    Deleting a section break 201
Adding a Cover Page (Sneaky and Quick)..............................201

Hats and Shoes for Your Pages (Headers and Footers) 202
Adding a header 203
Editing a header...204
Making odd and even headers...206
"But I don't want a header on my first page!"......................207
Headers and document sections..207
Removing a header...209

Chapter 16: The Styles of Word **211**
The Big Style Overview 211
Types of styles 212
Styles quick and custom..213
Using a style 213
Effortless Formatting Fun with Quick Styles 214
Applying a Quick Style to your text 214
Employing the Styles task pane 216
The Styles task pane lite...218
Discovering which style you're using...................................218
Switching to another style set 219
Unapplying a style 219
Do-It-Yourself Styles 220
Creating a style based on text you've already formatted 220
Creating character, list, and other types of styles 223
Modifying a style 223
Giving your style a shortcut key 224
Deleting a style 225
Managing All Your Various Styles...225

Chapter 17: Themes and Templates **227**
Formatting Fast and Fancy with a Theme....................................227
Applying a document theme...228
Modifying or creating a theme...229
Whipping Out Similar Documents Based on a Template 230
What is a template?..231
Creating a template based on a document you already have 231
Making a new template from scratch....................................234
Modifying a template you created 234
Attaching a template to a document 235
Understanding NORMAL.DOTM..236

Chapter 18: Misc. Formatting Stuff **239**
Automatic Formatting...239
Enjoying automagical text 240
Paragraph formatting tricks...241
Undoing an AutoFormat 242
Disabling the @#$%&! AutoFormat.......................................243

Become an Expert in Your Fields 244
    Inserting a field into your document 244
    Playing with fields 246
Center a Page, Top to Bottom 248
Steal This Format! 249

Part IV: Making Your Document All Fancy-Schmancy 251

Chapter 19: Borders, Boxes, and Background Color 253
This Border Situation 253
    The Border command button 254
    The Borders and Shading dialog box 255
Lines and Boxes Around Your Text 255
    Drawing a fat, thick line 256
    Making rules 256
    Boxing text or paragraphs 257
    Boxing a title 257
    Putting a border around a page of text 258
    Removing borders 259
Background Colors 259

Chapter 20: Turning the Tables 261
Furnish Forth the Tables 261
    Starting your table-creation fun 262
    Creating a table yay-by-yay big 263
    Drawing a table 264
    Transmuting tabbed text into a table 266
    Turning a table back into plain text 266
It's Your Turn to Set the Table 267
    Using the mouse with a table 267
    Putting text into a table 268
Table Craftsmanship 269
    Designing a table 269
    Adjusting the table 271
    Deleting a table 272

Chapter 21: Carousing with Columns 273
All About Columns 273
Here Come the Columns! 275
    Making more than three columns 275
    Mixing column formats 276
    Adjusting the columns in the Columns dialog box 276
The End of the Column 277

Chapter 22: I Love Lists 279

Basic Bullets and Numbers 279
Making a bulleted list 280
Numbering a list 280
Numbering lines of text 281
Lists of Things in Your Document 281
Creating a table of contents 282
Building an index 283
Footnotes and Endnotes 286

Chapter 23: Going Graphical 289

Here Come the Graphics! 290
Inserting a picture from a file on disk 290
Inserting a clip art image 291
Slapping down an AutoShape 292
Inserting a picture or text into an AutoShape 293
Deleting an image or artwork 294
Images and Text Can Mix 294
Wrapping text around the image 295
Moving an image hither and thither 296
Image Editing 297
Changing an image's size 298
Cropping an image 298
Rotating the image 299
Arranging multiple images 299

Chapter 24: Stick *This* in Your Document .301

Characters Fun and Funky 301
Nonbreaking spaces and hyphens 301
Typing characters such as Ü, Ç, and Ñ 302
Adding a dash of en or em 303
Inserting special characters and symbols 303
Say It in WordArt 304
Spice Up Your Document with a Text Box 306
Instant Graphical Goodness with SmartArt 307

Part V: What Else Is Left? *309*

**Chapter 25: Multiple Documents, Multiple Windows,
Multiple Formats, Multiple Madness** 311

Multiple Document Mania 311
Managing multiple documents 312
Viewing the same document in multiple windows 314
Using the old split-screen trick 315

Working with Non-Word Document Formats 316
 Using the Files Type drop-down list....................................317
 Loading an alien document...317
 Saving a file in a horridly strange and unnatural format..............319
 Updating older Word documents 319

Chapter 26: Other Ways of Viewing a Document 321

Organize Your Thoughts 322
 Entering Outline view 322
 Adding topics to your outline..323
 Demoting a topic (creating subtopics)..................................324
 Promoting a topic..325
 Adding a text topic 326
 Rearranging topics 326
 Expanding and contracting topics 326
 Printing an outline..328
Sit Back and Read..328

Chapter 27: Working This Out Together 331

Here Are My Thoughts 331
 Adding a comment 332
 Hiding comments 333
 Reviewing comments 333
 Printing comments (or not) 334
 Deleting comments 334
Whip Out the Yellow Highlighter..334
Look What They've Done to My Text, Ma 335
 Comparing two versions of the same document...........................335
 Reviewing the changes 337
 Tracking changes as you make them.....................................338

Chapter 28: Merrily We Mail Merge 339

All About Mail Merge 339
Mail Merge Ho!...340
 Creating the main document (Task 1 of 5)..............................341
 Assigning fields (Task 2 of 5) 343
 Building records (Task 3 of 5)..345
 Inserting fields into the main document (Task 4 of 5).................347
 Merging it all together (Last task)...................................348

Chapter 29: Labels of Love 351

The Label Thing..351
Here's a Sheet of Identical Labels 352
Print That Address List 353
A Label Trick with Graphics 355

Chapter 30: Customizing Word **357**

All the Better to See You, My Dear 357
The Status Bar Configuration Menu..359
The Quick Access Toolbar 360
    Finding the toolbar...360
    Moving the toolbar...361
    Adding command buttons to the toolbar............................361
    Removing commands from the toolbar 363
    Restoring the Quick Access toolbar 363

Part VI: The Part of Tens..*365*

Chapter 31: The Ten Commandments of Word **367**

Thou Shalt Remember to Save Thy Work 367
Thou Shalt Not Use More Than One Space..................................368
Thou Shalt Not Press Enter at the End of Each Line 368
Thou Shalt Not Neglect Thy Keyboard..368
Thou Shalt Not Manually Number Thy Pages 369
Thou Shalt Not Use the Enter Key to Start a New Page 369
Thou Shalt Not Click OK Too Quickly...369
Thou Shalt Not Forget Thy Undo Command 369
Honor Thy Printer...370
Thou Shalt Have Multiple Document Windows Before Thee 370

Chapter 32: Ten Cool Tricks **371**

Automatic Save with AutoRecover 371
Keyboard Power!...372
Build Your Own Fractions 372
Electronic Bookmarks 373
Document Inspection..374
The Drop Cap...374
The Document Map..375
Add an Envelope to Your letter 376
Sort Your Text...376
Text That Doesn't Print 377

Chapter 33: Ten Odd Things **379**

Equations 379
Math 380
Document Defense Options 381
Hyphenation 381
Document Properties..381
The Developer Tab..382

Cross-References...382
Smart Tags...383
Click-and-Type...383
Word and the Internet 384

Chapter 34: Ten Avuncular Suggestions **385**
Keep Printer Paper, Toner, and Supplies Handy 385
Get Some References 386
Keep Your Computer Files Organized 386
Know a Little Windows..386
Back Up Your Work 387
Use AutoCorrect 387
Use Those Keyboard Shortcuts...387
Try New Things 388
Let Word Do the Work 388
Don't Take It All Too Seriously 388

Index...*389*

Introduction

· ·

Are you nervous? Intimidated? Befuddled and confused beyond all recourse? *What* did they do to Word? Just when you thought you finally had a leg up on the program, just as you finally remembered that the Sort command is on the Tables menu, they've gone and changed . . . everything! What a headache!

Welcome to *Word 2007 For Dummies,* which is a better solution to your word processing pains than taking two aspirin and calling tech support in the morning. This book is your friendly, informative, and entertaining guide to the newfangled way of processing words that is Word 2007.

I'm not telling you that this book will make you all cozy and pleased with the new ways of Word. No, I'm merely promising that this book eases the pain everyone feels with Word 2007. Let other authors apologize for the program! I'm here to kick Word in the butt and, hopefully, you'll enjoy watching that.

What's New in Word 2007?

Earlier versions of Word all looked alike. They had menus, toolbars, task panes, and other pop-up, drop-down, leak-out nonsense. With Word 2007, all that stuff is gone, nailed shut in a box and wheeled away into that huge warehouse where the U.S. government keeps the Ark of the Covenant. Word 2007 sports no menus. It has only one tiny toolbar.

Replacing the menus and toolbars is a tabbed Ribbon system. The tabs are like the menus of old, but their commands are grouped into graphical command buttons. Some buttons are commands, some buttons are menus. This setup can be overwhelming at first, but I must admit that it makes it possible to do some tasks in fewer steps than with the old Word interface. Knowing that, of course, doesn't make the thing less intimidating.

Beyond the interface, Word is a bit stricter on styles and formatting. The benefit here is *instant previews,* or the ability to instantly see how changes affect your document as you browse a menu. Part III of this book explains more.

Word's main mode of operation is Print Layout view. If you were a fan of Normal or Draft view in previous versions of Word, I highly recommend that you switch to Print Layout view, if you haven't already.

Finally, many commands didn't survive the transition from older versions of Word to Word 2007. You won't find any of the following in Word 2007:

AutoFormat	Save All
Close All	Save As Web Page
Character Animation	Speech
File Search	Wizards
Frames	WordPerfect Help
Office Assistant	

These items were either dropped entirely or replaced with something better.

About This Book

I don't intend for you to read this book from cover to cover. It's not a novel, and if it were, it would be a musical novel and you'd be required to sing the songs and go through the dances with all the characters in a book and, quite honestly, I don't think that the people near you would let you get away with it.

This book is a reference. Each chapter covers a specific topic or task that Word does. Within a chapter, you find self-contained sections, each of which describes how to perform a specific task or get something done. Sample sections you encounter in this book include:

- Saving your stuff
- Moving a block of text
- Quickly finding your place
- Aligning paragraphs
- Cobbling a table together quickly
- Creating a table of contents
- Adding topics to your outline

There are no keys to memorize, no secret codes, no tricks, no videos to sleep through, and no wall charts. Instead, each section explains a topic as though it's the first thing you read in this book. Nothing is assumed, and everything is cross-referenced. Technical terms and topics, when they come up, are neatly shoved to the side, where you can easily avoid reading them. The idea here isn't for you to learn anything. This book's philosophy is to help you look it up, figure it out, and get back to work.

How to Use This Book

You hold in your hands an active book. The topics between this book's yellow-and-black covers are all geared toward getting things done in Word 2007. Because nothing is assumed, all you need to do is find the topic that interests you and read.

Word uses the mouse and keyboard to get things done. Still, the program looks different from traditional Windows programs, so pay attention!

This is a keyboard shortcut:

Ctrl+P

This shortcut means that you should press and hold the Ctrl (control) key and type a P, just as you would press Shift+P to get a capital P. Sometimes, more than two keys need to be pressed at the same time:

Ctrl+Shift+T

In this line, you press Ctrl and Shift together and then press the T key. Release all three keys.

Commands in Word 2007 exist as *command buttons* on the Ribbon interface. This book may refer to the tab, the command group, and then the button itself to help you locate that command button — for example, the Page Layout tab, Page Background group, Page Color button. Or, I might say "the Page Color button found in the Page Layout tab's Page Background group.

Often times, command buttons are shown in the margin, which can help you locate them.

Menu commands are listed like this:

Table⇨Insert Table

This command means that you choose the command named Insert Table from the Table menu. Note that Table is most likely a button on the Ribbon.

The File menu from previous versions of Word now exists as the Microsoft Office Button menu, which I refer to as the Office Button menu. You still press Alt+F to access this menu, and it contains items similar to the old File menu.

When I describe a message or something you see on-screen, it looks like this:

```
Why should I bother to learn about compound interest when
robots will eventually destroy the human race?
```

If you need further help operating your computer or a good general reference, I can recommend my book *PCs For Dummies,* published by Wiley Publishing, Inc. The book contains lots of useful information to supplement what you find in this book.

Foolish Assumptions

Though this book was written with the beginner in mind, I still make a few assumptions. Foremost, I assume that you're using a computer. You use Windows as the computer's operating system, either Windows Vista or Windows XP or any other version of Windows that can run Word 2007. There are no specific issues between Word and Windows as far as this book is concerned, but keep in mind that this book isn't about Windows.

Your word processor is Microsoft Word 2007. It is *not* Microsoft Works. It is not an earlier version of Word. It is not WordPerfect. It is not a version of Word that runs on a Macintosh.

Throughout this book, I use "Word 2007" and "Word" interchangeably. Both refer to the same thing. (Word 2007 may also be referred to as Word 12 in some instances, although not in this book.)

Word 2007 is a part of the Microsoft Office 2007 suite of programs. This book doesn't cover any other part of Microsoft Office, nor do I assume that you even have the Microsoft Office suite installed.

How This Book Is Organized

This book contains six major parts, each of which is divided into several chapters. The chapters themselves have been sliced into smaller, modular sections. You can pick up the book and read any section without necessarily knowing what has already been covered in the rest of the book. Start anywhere.

Here's a breakdown of the parts and what you can find in them:

Part I: Hello, Word!

This part provides a quick introduction to Word and word processing. Information is offered on how best to use your keyboard, plus a simple overview of the typical word processing day. Part I contains lots of good, basic information.

Part II: Word Processing Basics

The chapters in this part of the book cover the 7 basic tasks of any word processor: moving around a document, editing text, search and replace, working with blocks of text, document proofing, saving and opening, and finally printing.

Part III: Formatting

This part deals with formatting, from the smallest iota of text to formatting commands that span an entire document and more. Formatting is the art of making your document look less ugly.

Part IV: Making Your Document All Fancy-Schmancy

This part is formatting dessert, or things you can do beyond regular formatting to help make your document look like more than a typical, boring document. It covers lines, borders, tables, columns, lists, graphical goodness, and all sorts of stuff that makes Word more than a typical word processor.

Part V: What Else Is Left?

This part covers a few dangling details that I consider myself fortunate to write about, such as outlining, collaboration, mail merge, label-making, and other interesting things that Word does.

Part VI: The Part of Tens

The traditional last part of any *For Dummies* book contains chapters with lists of ten items. You'll find lots of helpful stuff here, some weird things you may not know about, plus even more useful tips, tricks, and good suggestions.

What's Not Here

Word is one heck of a program. Covering the entire thing would take a book several thousand pages long. (I kid you not.) My approach in this book is to cover as much basic word processing as possible. Because of that, some advanced features did get pushed off the table of contents.

You won't find any information here on macros in Word. Although they can be useful, it's tough to get into macros without broaching the more technical topic of Microsoft Office Visual Basic, which is a true programming language — definitely not beginner stuff.

Some of the more esoteric features are touched upon lightly here. For example, I could spend about 70 pages detailing what can be done with graphics in Word, but I limited myself to only a dozen pages.

Finally, this book doesn't cover using Word to do anything on the Internet. That includes using e-mail, making a Web page, blogging, online publishing, creating forms, or doing that kind of stuff. This is a word processing book, and Word is a word processor.

Icons Used in This Book

This icon flags useful, helpful tips or shortcuts.

This icon marks a friendly reminder to do something.

This icon marks a friendly reminder *not* to do something.

This icon alerts you to overly nerdy information and technical discussions of the topic at hand. The information is optional reading, but it may enhance your reputation at cocktail parties if you repeat it.

Where to Go from Here

Start reading! Observe the table of contents and find something that interests you. Or, look up your puzzle in the index.

Because Word 2007 has changed, whether you're new to the program or not, you should start reading at Chapter 1.

Read! Write! Let your brilliance shine on a sheet of paper.

My e-mail address is dgookin@wambooli.com. Yes, that's my real address. I try to reply to all the e-mail I get, although sometimes I'm not that speedy. And, although I enjoy saying "Hi" or answering questions about this book, please do not e-mail me with technical support questions or problems with your computer. For that, I can recommend reading my book *Troubleshooting Your PC For Dummies* (Wiley).

You can also visit my Web page for more information or as a diversion: www.wambooli.com. Be sure to check out the Wambooli Forums while you're there.

Enjoy the book. And enjoy Word. Or at least tolerate it.

Part I
Hello, Word!

The 5th Wave · By Rich Tennant

"I wrote my entire cookbook in Word. The other programs I saw just didn't look fresh."

In this part . . .

Blame it all on Homer. One day, he was telling his epic poem *The Iliad* to a crowd of eager Greeks. The Greeks were thrilled. One Greek in particular was so enamored with the tale that he blurted out, "This stuff is great! If only we could remember it all!"

Irritated at being interrupted, Homer replied, "Why not write it down?"

The Greeks collectively went "Huh?"

Homer explained, "Me? I'm blind. I had to memorize the whole thing. You — you have sight. You can write it down. Of course, it would be nifty if you had a word processor, which would make typing the thing easy, as well as formatting and printing it. But you're thousands of years too early for that. So my advice is to start by creating an alphabet. Better still, you're Greeks: Steal an alphabet."

And so the long quest began. From the Greek alphabet to reading and writing for the masses to moveable type to the fountain pen and the typewriter, and now . . . this, this word processor, which I introduce to you in the chapters that comprise this part of the book.

Chapter 1

Word Hokey-Pokey

In This Chapter

▶ Starting Word

▶ Reading the Word screen

▶ Getting help from Word

▶ Exiting Word (or not)

Cheer up! Word processing is one of the best things that a computer can do. It's much better than trying to compose your thoughts on a typewriter. It's better than worrying about good penmanship. It's much more efficient than using Gutenberg's moveable-type machine. It's cheaper than paying a scribe to scribble hieroglyphics on a papyrus roll. And it's certainly better than chipping a stone tablet with a rock. Keep that rock handy, though: You may still need something to smash the computer when it frustrates you.

This chapter provides an overview of Microsoft Word 2007. It's your introduction to the newfangled way that people are word processing during this, the breakfast of the 21st century. So, sit back, relax, grab a refreshing beverage, and definitely put down that rock! You'll be on your way to writing words electric in no time.

How Do I Start Word? Let Me Count the Ways. . . .

Anyone using a computer suspects that there's probably a better, faster, or more serious way to get things done. There are so many options! Who knows when someone will amble up to you and point at how you start your word processor. "You do *that?*" they'll snicker and walk away. Oh, no. What now?

The question isn't really how to start Word, but rather how *best* to start Word. In Windows, there are a bazillion ways to start any program. Other books drag out every last method, but for starting Word (or any program that you use often), there are definitely good, better, and best ways. Before going there, consider taking some general steps before you begin your word processing odyssey:

1. **Ensure that your computer is on and toasty.**

   Any computer that's on is, in fact, toasty. The only way to make it toastier is to insert bread, which I don't recommend.

2. **Prepare yourself physically.**

   Make sure you're seated, with a nice, upright, firm posture. They tell me that your wrists should be even with your elbows and that you shouldn't have to tilt your head forward. Shoulders are back and relaxed.

   Close your eyes. Unwind. Breathe in, breath out.

3. **Prepare yourself mentally.**

   Yes, you can do this! Hail the muse *scribborrhea,* the forest nymph of electronics and typing. Think calm thoughts. Concentrate on letting the thoughts flow from your brain and rush down your arms and into your fingers as they dance upon the keyboard. Remember that you are the master. Mutter that over and over: "I am the master. . . ."

If you need help starting your computer, refer to my book *PCs For Dummies* (Wiley Publishing) for quick and accurate turning-on-the-computer instructions.

You can stop muttering "I am the master" now.

The good, yet unimaginative, way to start Word

Without fail, the place to start any program in Windows is at the fabled Start button. It may not be the coolest way to start a program, but it's consistent and reliable — good things to have in a computer. Obey these steps:

1. **Click the Start button.**

   Use your computer mouse to click the Start button, which is often found on the left side of the taskbar, at the bottom of the screen, adorned with the Windows logo and often (cleverly) the word *Start*.

   Clicking the Start button displays the Start menu.

2. **Choose Word from the All Programs menu.**

   Now, you may be lucky and see the Word program icon on the Start menu. If so, click the Word icon to start Word. If not, you have to click the All Programs menu and look for Word in that vast labyrinth.

TECHNICAL STUFF

Automatically starting Word every ding-dong time you start Windows

To get your computer to start Word whenever you start Windows, you need to move the Microsoft Word item from its current location on the All Programs menu to the All Programs⇨Startup folder. The items in the Startup folder start up automatically when Windows begins its day. As with all things in Windows, there exists a multitude of ways to accomplish the move. Refer to your favorite Windows reference for the details, or just grab someone who looks like a Windows nerd and have them perform the task for you. Suggestion: Bribe them with something salty and crunchy.

Behold! Word starts! Watch in amazement as your computer whizzes and whirs. Before too long, Word appears on the computer's monitor, trying to be friendly and inviting but failing utterly.

Don't let Word's appearance overwhelm you! I describe what you're looking at later, in the section "Behold Word!"

✔ If you can't find Word on the All Programs menu, look for a submenu named Microsoft Office or Office 12 or even Office 2007. Word may be lurking on that submenu.

✔ The Start menu contains a list of many interesting things, including programs, recently used programs, and fun locations to visit in Windows. One of those Start menu things is the All Programs menu, which may also be called Programs (without the word *All*).

✔ Supposedly, every program ever installed on your computer has installed its icon in a spot somewhere on the All Programs menu.

✔ I refer to the program as Word, though the icon may be labeled Microsoft Word, Microsoft Office Word, Word 2007, or some other clever variation on that theme.

The better and best ways to start Word

When you use Word a lot, it helps to have quick access to its icon — that icon is the way you start Word — and then start your work. A better way than keeping Word hidden on the All Programs menu is to create a Word shortcut icon on the desktop. Heed these steps:

1. **Locate the Word icon on the All Programs menu.**

   Don't start Word now! Just point the mouse at the Word icon on the Start button's All Programs menu or wherever else it may be found.

2. Right-click the Microsoft Word menu item.

A pop-up menu appears.

3. Choose Send To⇨Desktop (Create Shortcut).

Whew! The scary part is over. You haven't changed anything, but you have added a new icon to the desktop, an icon you can use to start Word, if you like. To prove it:

4. Click the mouse on the desktop.

The *desktop* is the background you see when you use Windows. Clicking the desktop hides the Start menu.

5. Locate the Microsoft Word shortcut icon.

It looks like the icon shown in the margin. That's your shortcut to Word.

You can now use that icon to start Word: Just double-click, and you "open" the program. Then you can start clack-clack-clacking away at the keyboard. That's faster than using the All Programs menu.

The *best* way to start Word, and the way I do it every day, is to place the Word icon on the Quick Launch Toolbar.

The *Quick Launch Toolbar,* found right next to the Start button on the taskbar, is a row of icons representing programs, which you can start with a single click of the mouse. And, unlike the desktop, the Quick Launch bar is always handy.

To put the Word icon on the Quick Launch bar, you need to drag and drop, so it helps to have a Word icon already on the desktop, as described in the preceding set of steps. From the desktop, use the mouse to drag the Word icon to the Quick Launch bar, and then release the mouse button to "drop" the icon, as shown in Figure 1-1.

Starting Word from the Quick Launch bar is the best way to go: Just point the mouse at the Word icon and click, and Word is summoned to the screen.

✔ The Quick Launch Toolbar may not be visible on your computer. Refer to my book *PCs For Dummies* for more information or if the Quick Launch bar is too narrow and you cannot see the Word icon.

✔ Another way to have the Word icon always handy is to pin it to the Start menu directly. In Step 3 (a few paragraphs back), choose the item named Pin to Start Menu.

✔ Making these multiple copies of the Word icon does not consume extra hard drive space. You're merely copying *shortcuts* to the Word program, not copies of the entire program itself.

Word shortcut icon on the desktop

Figure 1-1:
Putting
Word on the
Quick
Launch bar.

Drag the Word icon here.

Starting Word by opening a document

Word is a computer program. You use that program to create *documents*, which are stored on your computer in much the same way as people pile junk into boxes and store them in their garages. But that's not important. What is important is that you can use those documents to start Word: Opening a Word document causes Word to start *and* to display that document for editing, printing, or just giving others the impression that you're doing something.

Here's one way you can start Word by opening a document:

1. Open the Documents folder.

The Documents folder, also called My Documents in some versions of Windows, is where Word, as well as other applications, stores the stuff you create. You can find this folder on the desktop, or you can get at it from the Start menu.

The Documents folder opens and displays its content, which is the stuff you've already created and saved to disk.

2. Locate a Word document.

A Word document appears, as shown in the margin.

3. Double-click the Word document icon.

Word starts and loads the document for editing, reading, modifying, perusing, cussing, mangling, and potentially fouling up beyond all recognition.

You can open any Word document by following these steps. The document can be on the desktop, in the Documents folder, or in any other folder or location where a Word document icon can lurk.

  ✔ The document name appears beneath or to the right of the icon. You can use the name to determine the document's contents — as long as the document was properly named when it was saved to disk. (More on that later.)

- If you have one document you open consistently, consider putting a shortcut to that document on the desktop for quick access: Right-click the document's icon and choose Send To⇨Desktop (Create Shortcut).

- Word is capable of opening other types of documents, including documents from previous versions of Word, Rich Text Format documents, and others. Each of these documents has its own icon, though the icon looks similar to the standard Word document icon. See Chapter 25 for more information on opening alien documents in Word.

- You can see a list of the recent documents you've worked on by choosing the Recent Items or My Recent Documents submenu from the main Start menu. Choose your document from that list to open it.

Behold Word!

Word appears on your computer's monitor just like any other program, nestled within its own window. Look on the screen and at Figure 1-2. There's more to Word and word processing than an electronic version of the blank sheet of paper.

The details of what you see on the screen are covered elsewhere in this book. Because you may not know what each doodad and greeblie is called, I've labeled some of the important things in Figure 1-2. Use this book's index to help you find stuff you might be curious about.

- Word 2007 represents a new approach to word processing. Gone are the menus and toolbars that have dominated computer programs for a decade or more. Replacing them is a new, tabbed, Ribbon interface. Although it may be intimidating at first, don't let it overwhelm you. Just keep reading this book and you'll be fine.

- The *very* first time you start Word, you may be asked some questions: Enter your name and initials, set up Word security, and set Microsoft update options. I recommend the updates.

Maximize Word's window size

Unless your computer system has one of those huge monitors, you probably want to maximize the Word program window just before you start working. To run Word in full-screen mode, click the Maximize button (the middle one) in the upper-right corner of the window.

Maximizing forces a window to fill the entire screen. If Word is already maximized, two overlapping boxes appear on the button; you don't need to click anything in that case.

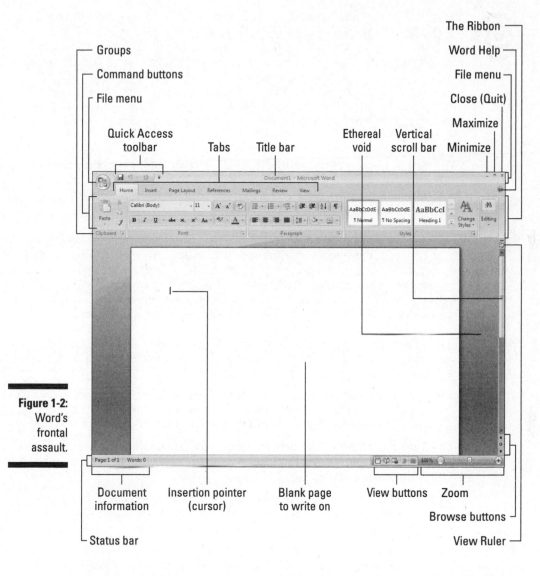

Figure 1-2:
Word's
frontal
assault.

Just in case your computer system is blessed with a giant monitor, you can resize the Word window without maximizing it; drag any of the window's edges in or out.

Word's window size affects what you see in the Ribbon's command groups. On smaller screens, fewer buttons show up, or they may show up in three rows. On larger screens, you see more buttons, usually in two rows.

Look! Up on the screen!

Everything in the Word window is designed to help you write. No, I'm serious! Well, I don't mean *write* in the sense of Ernest Hemingway or Jane Austen, although that's possible. Word wants you to manage, organize, and create things with words. That's the essence of word processing. What you see on the screen, on Word's *interface*, is designed to make writing an easy and effortless task.

The largest portion of the Word screen is for composing text. It's blank and white, just like a fresh sheet of paper. (Refer to Figure 1-2.) That's where you compose and format your text, and I cover that area specifically in the next section.

Surrounding the text-composing area is a host of goobers that are as bewildering as an exhibit in a modern art museum, as intimidating as the cockpit of a jet fighter, and almost as dangerous as a plate of sushi. Despite their overwhelming appearance, the things that cling to the Word program window are there to help you write. The following list gives you the quick top-to-bottom explanation. Use Figure 1-2 for reference. And, please: Do not memorize anything!

- **The title bar** lists the document's title, or merely `Document 1` until you give the document a title by saving it to disk. (See Chapter 9 for information on saving documents — very important!)

- **The Office button replaces the traditional File menu of most Windows programs.** Clicking the Office Button displays the Office Button menu, a list of commands that deal with files and documents.

- **Tabs** organize Word's various and sundry commands into groups based on word processing activities. Tabs appear and disappear depending on what you're doing in Word.

- **Groups and command buttons** help keep commands for the various tabs organized. Each group contains command buttons that do specific things to your text.

- **The Ruler** may or may not be visible. When the Ruler is visible, it helps you set margins and tabs. The View Ruler button (refer to Figure 1-2) shows and hides the Ruler.

Below the writing area dwells the status bar. This informative strip of graphical goodness contains trivial information about your document as well as the following ornaments:

- **Document information** lists optional data specific to your document.

- **The View buttons** specify how the blank page appears in the window (also refer to the next section).

- **The Zoom thing** sets how large or small your document appears inside the window. (See Chapter 30 for more information on zooming.)

Don't fret over these things! What's important now is that you recognize the names of things so that you don't get lost later.

- ✔ The tabs, groups, and command buttons change as you take on various activities in Word. Although this may seem disruptive, it's in fact quite handy.

- ✔ You can hide the Ribbon if you would rather have more room to write: Right-click anywhere on the Ribbon and choose the Minimize Ribbon command from the pop-up menu. To restore the Ribbon, right-click any tab and choose the Minimize Ribbon command again.

- ✔ Another part of the window, not shown in Figure 1-2, is the *task pane*. It shows up when it's needed, to offer more choices, options, or information.

- ✔ A Document Recovery task pane may show up when Word starts, telling you that Word has saved a document that may have been lost because of a power failure or computer crash. Refer to Chapter 32 for information on the AutoRecover feature.

- ✔ The Windows taskbar, located at the bottom of the screen, is a part of Windows itself and not Word. However, as you open documents in Word, buttons representing those documents appear on the Windows taskbar.

- ✔ Unlike in previous versions of Word, the tabs, groups, and command buttons *cannot* be customized, moved, or resized. You can customize the Quick Access toolbar (refer to Figure 1-2), but that's about it.

The blank place where you write

The words you write appear in the center part of Word's program window, in that blank area shown in Figure 1-2. That pallid vista is the equivalent of a blank sheet of paper, and the documents you create on that electronic sheet of paper look just the way they will when they're eventually printed on a real sheet of paper. Such is the magic of word processing.

Word lets you view the blank sheet in five different ways. Two of the views are the most popular for wordsmiths:

- ✔ **Print Layout:** Activate this view by clicking the status bar's Print Layout button. In Print Layout view, you get to see the entire page, just as it prints. Graphical images, columns, and all sorts of other fancy items show up on the page fully visible. You can see the edge of the page and a blank space between pages (the "Ethereal void" in Figure 1-2).

- ✔ **Draft:** Set this view by clicking the Draft button on the status bar. Draft view is favored by writers who don't really want to clutter the page with anything other than text. In Draft view, you see your text and not the fancy graphics, columns, headers, page breaks, and other things that clutter Print Layout mode.

There are three other ways to view your document: Full Screen Reading, Web Layout, and Outline. None of these views has anything to do with basic word processing. Refer to Chapter 26 for more information on these different views.

- Word automatically switches to Print Layout view from Draft view when necessary. So, when you're working in Draft view and you want to edit a header or insert a picture, Print Layout view is activated. You need to manually switch back to Draft view, if that's your preferred way of using Word.

- One thing that's visible in Draft view that you don't find in Print Layout view is a thick, horizontal bar on the left side of the page, just below a document's last line of text. That heavy bar marks the end of your document. You cannot delete the bar — unless you switch from Draft view to Print Layout view.

- Draft view may also be referred to as *Normal view,* as it was in previous versions of Word.

- Writing (or typing, depending on how good you are) is covered in the next chapter. That would be Chapter 2.

- Any weird stuff you see onscreen (a ¶, for example) is a Word secret symbol. Chapter 2 tells you why you may want to view those secret symbols and how to hide them if they annoy you.

The mouse pointer in Word

Word processing is a keyboard thing, although the computer's mouse comes in handy. In Word, you use the mouse to choose commands and to move the insertion pointer around as you edit text.

The mouse pointer changes its look as you work in Word:

For editing text, the mouse pointer becomes the I-beam.

For choosing items, the standard eleven o'clock mouse pointer is used.

For selecting lines of text, a one o'clock mouse pointer is used.

In Print Layout view, the mouse pointer may change its look when *click-and-type* mode is active: Lines appear to the left and right of, and below, the I-beam mouse pointer. Refer to Chapter 33 for more information on using click-and-type.

Memorizing these mouse pointer types isn't important, but remember that the mouse pointer changes as you use Word.

✔ You can use the mouse to see what some of the little buttons and things with pictures on them do in Word. Just hover the mouse pointer over the button, and — voilà! — it's like Folgers instant information crystals.

✔ Chapter 4 discusses how to use the mouse pointer to move the insertion pointer, allowing you to edit different parts of your text.

Cajoling Word to Help You

There are many ways to extract help from Word, the most common of which is to press the F1 key. That key not only works in Word's main window, but can also summon specific help for when you're doing certain things, such as when you're performing some obscure task way inside some dialog box or task pane.

Summoning Word Help displays a separate program window labeled Word Help, as shown in Figure 1-3. You can type a topic, command name, or question into the box in the upper-left corner of the window, or you can browse the table of contents for help.

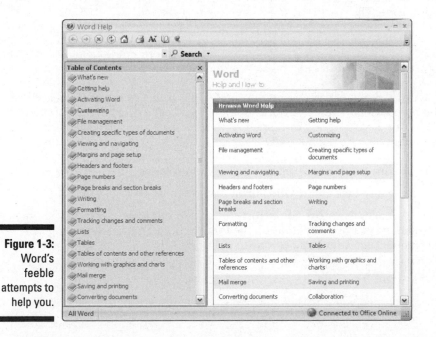

Figure 1-3: Word's feeble attempts to help you.

✔ You can also summon help by clicking the wee round question mark button near the upper-right corner of the Word window.

✔ Word's help works best when you have an Internet connection, especially a high-speed, or *broadband,* connection.

✔ If you've used previous versions of Word, note that there's no more Office Assistant in Word 2007. You can mourn or rejoice as appropriate.

✔ Of course, this book can be your handiest and most useful source for Word help. Sadly, I don't have room here to document *everything,* so Microsoft relented and decided to provide *everything* in its Word Help window.

When You're All Done

It's the pinnacle of etiquette to know when and how to excuse oneself. Leaving can be done well or poorly. Experience taught me this lesson when I was dining with royalty and suddenly all conversation stopped. I had to meekly raise my hand, mutter "It was me," and then run off all red-faced and ashamed. I hope that such a thing never happens to you.

Just as there are many ways to start Word, there are several ways to quit. You can quit the program outright, you can pause and start over, or you can set Word aside. These options are covered in this section.

Quitting Word

When you're done word processing and don't expect to return to it anytime soon, you need to quit the Word program. Quitting a computer program is like putting away a book on a shelf. In the electronic world of the computer, this is how you do such a thing:

1. **Choose Exit Word from the Office Button menu.**

2. **Save any files when Word prompts you to do so.**

   Word always warns you before it leaves; if you have any unsaved documents, you're prompted to save them to disk. You see a warning displayed on the screen, as shown in Figure 1-4.

   Click Yes to save your file. You may be asked to give the file a name, if you haven't yet done so. (Chapter 3 tells you how to do it.)

   If the slop you typed isn't worth saving, click No.

   You can click Cancel to "quit" the Exit Word command and return to Word for more word processing delight.

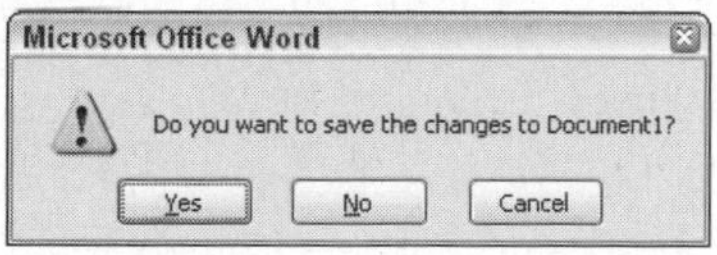

Figure 1-4:
Better click
that Yes
button!

Microsoft Office Word

⚠ Do you want to save the changes to Document1?

[Yes] [No] [Cancel]

If you elect to quit, Word closes its window. Poof! It's gone. You return to Windows or some other program, such as FreeCell, which you know you shouldn't be playing anyway.

✔ You don't have to quit Word just to start editing another document. Refer to the next few sections for helpful, time-saving information!

✔ Do not quit Word by resetting or turning off your computer! It's a *bad thing*. Trust me on this one.

How to quit what you're doing without quitting Word

It's not always necessary to quit Word. For example, if you're merely stopping work on one document to work on another, quitting Word is a waste of time. Instead, you can close one document and then open another. Or, better still, you can simply open the new document and keep the old one active; you can then easily switch between the documents.

To close a document in Word, choose the Close command from the Office Button menu. This doesn't quit Word, but it removes the document from the screen, allowing you to stay in Word or work on another document.

Likewise, you can start up a new document in Word, just like sticking a blank sheet of paper into a typewriter. See Chapter 3, the section about starting out with a new document.

Bottom line: There's no point is quitting Word when all you want to do is start editing a new document.

✔ Closing a document in Word is similar to ripping a sheet of paper out of your typewriter — but without the satisfying *SSHHHHHTHWP!* sound it makes.

✔ There's no need to close a document, really. In fact, I work on a document over a period of days and keep it open (and my PC on) the entire time. Doesn't hurt a thing. (I do occasionally save it to disk, which *is* important.)

✔ When you try to close a document before it has been saved, Word displays a warning dialog box. Click the Yes button to save your document. If you want to continue editing, click the Cancel button and get back to work.

✔ The keyboard shortcut for the Close command is Ctrl+W.

Putting Word away for a spell

There's no need to quit Word if you know that you will be using it again soon. In fact, I've been known to keep Word open and running on my computer for *weeks* at a time. The secret is to use the *Minimize* button.

 Clicking the Minimize button shrinks the Word window to a button on the taskbar. Thwoop! It's gone! With the window out of the way, you can do other things with your computer. Then, when you're ready to word-process again, click the Word button on the taskbar to restore the Word window to the screen.

The Minimize button is the first of the three buttons in the window's upper-right corner. Refer to Figure 1-2.

Chapter 2

Making Friends with the Keyboard

In This Chapter

▶ Knowing the PC keyboard

▶ Typing tips

▶ Using the Enter key

▶ Using the spacebar

▶ Backspacing and deleting

▶ Observing the status bar

▶ Marking the space between pages

▶ Seeing stuff in your text that isn't there

▶ Living with colored underlines and text

Despite the mouse, despite the graphics, Word exists as a program requiring a lot of keyboard input. To best enjoy Word, you should know your computer's keyboard. This means knowing not only where and how to press the keys, but also how certain keys on the keyboard are used in a word processor. This chapter unlocks those secrets that would otherwise linger inside your computer keyboard — along with all those potato chip crumbs, nail clippings, and gross strands of hair.

Behold the PC Keyboard!

Despite all the fancy keyboard extras, as far as word processing is considered, you use only the core keys on the keyboard, keys commonly found on every computer keyboard, as illustrated in Figure 2-1.

Take a look at your own keyboard. If you're lucky, it may be color-coded to help you identify the separate areas.

Depressing the keys

You don't actually depress a key on a computer keyboard. Nope. Instead, you press and release. Any swift tapping motion will do. Some keyboards even generate a pleasing *click* when a key is pressed.

Now, if you really want to depress a key, just stare at it and say "You're one ugly, good-for-nothing key!" If that doesn't work, keep up with the insults. Eventually, any well-adjusted key will succumb to your verbal taunts and find itself sufficiently depressed.

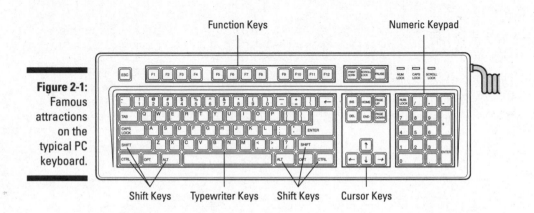

Figure 2-1: Famous attractions on the typical PC keyboard.

When you use Word, you use the keys in groups, either alone or in combination with other keys. Here are the names by which the computer nerds know these things:

- ✔ **Function keys:** The function keys are labeled F1 through F12. You can use them alone or in cahoots with the Ctrl, Alt, and Shift keys.

- ✔ **Typewriter keys:** These are the standard alphanumeric keys that the computer inherited from the antique typewriter: *A* through *Z* and the number keys, plus symbols and other exotic characters.

- ✔ **Cursor keys:** Also called the *arrow keys,* these keys control the cursor. Also included are the non-arrow keys: Home, End, PgUp (or Page Up), PgDn (or Page Down), Insert, and Delete.

- ✔ **Don key:** A domesticated ass.

- ✔ **Numeric keypad:** These keys are sometimes cursor keys and other times number keys. The split personality is evident on each key cap, which displays two symbols. The Num Lock key and its corresponding light are on if the numeric keypad (1, 2, 3) is active. If the cursor keys (arrows, Home) are active, Num Lock is off.

- ✏ **Shift keys:** These keys don't do anything by themselves. Instead, the Shift, Ctrl, and Alt keys work in combination with other keys.

Here are some individual keys worth noting:

- ✏ **Enter:** Marked with the word *Enter* and sometimes a cryptic, curved arrow-thing: ↵. You use this key to end a paragraph of text.
- ✏ **Esc:** The "escape" key, which doesn't really do anything in Word. However, pressing the Esc key in a dialog box is the same as clicking the Cancel button with the mouse.
- ✏ **Spacebar:** The only key with no symbol; inserts spaces between the words.
- ✏ **Tab:** Inserts the tab "character," which shoves the next text you type over to the next tab stop; an interesting and potentially frustrating formatting key (and nicely covered in Chapter 13).
- ✏ **Backspace:** Your backing-up and erasing key — very handy.
- ✏ **Delete:** Also labeled Del; works like Backspace but doesn't back up to erase. Read more on that in Chapter 5.

Every character key you press on the keyboard produces a character on the screen, on the blank part where you write. (Check out Figure 1-2, over in Chapter 1.)

- ✏ The Shift key is used to produce capital letters, just like on a typewriter (in case you've ever used one of those).
- ✏ Ctrl is pronounced "control." It's amazing the variety of names people give to the Ctrl key before they know it as *the control key*.
- ✏ The Caps Lock key works like the Shift Lock key on a typewriter. After you press Caps Lock, the Caps Lock light on your keyboard comes on, and everything you type is in ALL CAPS.

Typing (Or, the Old Hunt-and-Peck)

Words electric march across the screen because you type those words on the keyboard. Despite all the commands and graphical goobers, the thing you do most often in Word is type.

> *Clackity-clack-clack-clack.*

Everything you type on the keyboard appears on the screen, even the typos and mistakes and bad grammar: It all falls into place on the screen regardless of your intent, posture, or good looks.

Follow the blinking cursor

The key to writing in Word is to look for the *insertion pointer* in your text. It's a flashing vertical bar:

|

Text you type appears *before* the insertion pointer, one character at a time. After a character appears, the insertion pointer hops to the right, making room for more text.

For example, type this line:

```
Why blame the computer?
```

The insertion pointer moves to the right, marching along as you type. It's called *insertion* pointer for a reason: Press the left-arrow key a few times to move the insertion pointer back before the word *blame*.

Type the word *not* and a space. The word (and the space) are inserted into your text. The text to the right is pushed off to make room for the new text. Now the sentence should read:

```
Why not blame the computer?
```

Chapter 4 covers moving the insertion pointer around in more detail.

When to press that Enter key

In word processing, you press the Enter key only when you reach the end of a paragraph. Not the end of a line, the end of a *paragraph*. You do this thanks to a neat-o feature called *word wrap*. When the text you type reaches the right margin, the insertion pointer automatically hops down to the next line of text, taking any incompletely typed word along for the ride.

To witness word wrap for yourself, start Word and type the following text, without pressing the Enter key:

```
When the times were hard, we knew what had to be done.
Eatin' was necessary. So as we all sat down to the meal,
and that sweet aroma of roasted meat hit our nostrils for
the first time in months, we held firm. It was especially
hard when little Dana innocently asked where her pet bunny
Fluffy had gone.
```

As you type, and as words grow precariously close to the right margin, Word magically picks up an incomplete word and places it on the following line. That's word wrap in action. It's automatic, and it means that there's no need to press the Enter key until you reach the end of a paragraph.

✔ Some people end a paragraph with two presses of the Enter key; others use only one press. If it's extra space you want between paragraphs, refer to Chapter 12, the section about putting space between paragraphs, to see what to do.

✔ There's no need to use the Enter key when you want to double-space your text. Double-spacing is a formatting command in Word. See Chapter 12 for more information.

✔ If you want to indent a paragraph, press the Tab key after pressing Enter. This can also be done automatically; refer to (you guessed it) Chapter 12.

When to whack the spacebar

The spacebar isn't the same thing as the right-arrow key on the keyboard. Pressing the spacebar doesn't just move the insertion pointer; it inserts a *space character* into the text. Spaces are important between words and sentences. Withoutthemreadingwouldbedifficult.

The most important thing to remember about the spacebar is that you need to whack it only once. In word processing, as in all typing done on a computer, only *one* space appears between words and after punctuation. That's it!

✔ I'm serious! If you're an old-timer, you're probably used to putting two spaces after a period, which is what they taught in typing class. This extra space is wrong on a computer. Type only one space!

✔ Anytime you feel like using two or more spaces, what you really need is a tab. Tabs are best for indenting text as well as for lining up text in columns. See Chapter 13 for more information.

✔ The reason you need only one space between sentences is that computers use proportionally spaced type. Old-fashioned typewriters used monospaced type, and so pressing the spacebar twice after a sentence was supposed to aid in readability (though that's debatable). Computer type is more like professionally typeset material, and both typesetters and professional-document folk put only one space after a period or a colon. So there!

Backing-up and erasing keys

When you make a typo or other typing error, press the Backspace key on the keyboard. The Backspace key is used to back up and erase. The Delete key can also be used to erase text.

✔ Refer to Chapter 5 for more information on deleting text with Backspace and Delete.

✔ The Backspace key is named Backspace on your keyboard, or it may have a long, left-pointing arrow on it: ←.

✔ Backspace doesn't work like the Backspace key on a typewriter. The difference is that when you press Backspace in Word, the cursor backs up and *erases.* (The Word equivalent of the typewriter's Backspace key is the left-arrow key.)

Mind your 1's and 0's and L's and O's

If you're a former typewriter user, you're probably pushing 40! Man, you're old! Seriously, my geriatric friend, the typewriter is merely inspiration for the computer keyboard. Beyond that, the similarity is purely superficial. Please heed these advice nuggets:

✔ Do not use the little L or the big I in place of the number one. Use the 1 key. That's what it's there for.

✔ Do not use the O (oh) key for the number zero. Use the 0 (zero) key.

These habits may be hard to break, but the computer is keen on being exact. Oh, and Geritol now comes in cherry flavor.

Curse you, StickyKeys!

As your mind wanders, your fingers absently press and release the Shift key. Suddenly, you see the warning: StickyKeys! By pressing the Shift, Ctrl, or Alt key five times in a row, you activate the Windows XP StickyKeys function, a tool designed to help disabled people more easily use a computer keyboard. Rather than be glad for the help, you're annoyed at the intrusion.

Don't panic! It's easy to turn off the StickyKeys thing: Open the Control Panel's Accessibility Options icon to display the Accessibility Options dialog box. In that dialog box, remove the check mark by the item labeled Use StickyKeys. Click OK, and you'll never be bothered again!

Things to Notice Whilst You Type

The text you type appears on the computer screen, in the blank, page-like area in the middle of the Word window. But that's not all! As you type, you may notice other things going on. These aren't bugs crawling on the screen, nor are they signs that you need to have your eyes checked. These side effects of typing may puzzle you or annoy you; either way, this section explains things.

The left end of the status bar

The reason it's called the *status* bar is that it can show you the status of your document, lively updating the information as you type, as shown in Figure 2-2.

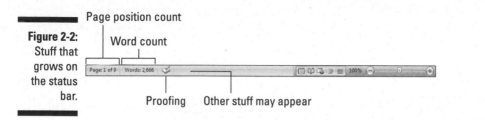

Figure 2-2: Stuff that grows on the status bar.

Page position count

Word count

Page: 1 of 9 | Words: 2,666 | 100%

Proofing   Other stuff may appear

The type of information that's displayed, as well as how much information is displayed, depends on how you've configured Word. Chapter 30 explains which features the status bar can display.

✔ The status bar also displays information when you initially open a document, giving the document's name and character count. That disappears quickly, however.

✔ When a document is saved, the status bar displays information about the save, though often the information appears too fast to see.

Life between pages

Word not only shows you on the screen your text as it will be printed, but also tries its best to show you where one page ends and another page begins. This feature is most helpful because often times you want to keep things on one page, or it could just be that folks like to know when they're moving from one page to the next.

The status bar helps you discover which page you're working on, as discussed in the previous section. Visually, Word also helps you by graphically showing you where one page ends and another begins.

In Print Layout view, you see virtual pages and a space between them, as shown in Figure 2-3. That's your best visual clue to where one page ends and another begins.

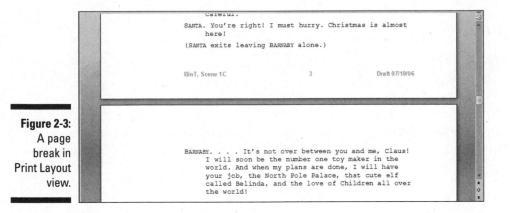

Figure 2-3:
A page
break in
Print Layout
view.

> careful.
>
> SANTA. You're right! I must hurry. Christmas is almost here!
>
> (SANTA exits leaving BARNABY alone.)
>
> BinT, Scene 1C   3   Draft 07/10/06
>
> BARNABY. . . . It's not over between you and me, Claus! I will soon be the number one toy maker in the world. And when my plans are done, I will have your job, the North Pole Palace, that cute elf called Belinda, and the love of Children all over the world!

In Draft mode, the visual break between pages is shown as a faint line of dots, like ants marching across the page:

Text appearing above the line of dots is on one page, and text below is on the next page.

  ✔ Refer to Chapter 1, the section "The blank place where you write," for more information on Print Layout and Draft views.

  ✔ Technically, the page break is a *soft* page break, meaning that one page full of text and Word must start putting text on a new page. See Chapter 14 for information on forcing page breaks and other types of page breaks in Word.

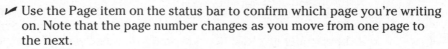

✔ You can adjust the gap between pages in Print Layout view. Point the mouse at the gap. When the mouse pointer changes, as shown in the margin, press the Ctrl key and click the mouse to remove or set the gap.

✔ Use the Page item on the status bar to confirm which page you're writing on. Note that the page number changes as you move from one page to the next.

Spots and clutter in your text

There's no cause for alarm if you see spots — or dots — amid the text you type, such as

```
This·can·be·very·annoying.¶
```

What you're seeing here, and potentially on the screen, are *nonprinting characters*. Word uses various symbols to represent things you normally wouldn't see: spaces, tabs, the Enter key, and more.

To turn these items on or off, click the Show/Hide button on the Home tab in the Paragraph group. Click once to show the goobers; click again to hide them.

The keyboard shortcut for the Paragraph button is Ctrl+Shift+8.

Why bother? Sometimes it's useful to see the marks to check out what's up with formatting, find stray tabs visually, or locate missing paragraphs, for example. (WordPerfect users: This is as close as you can get to Reveal Codes in Word.)

Strange underlines and colored text

Adding underlining to your text in Word is cinchy; Chapter 11 tells you all about that character format. Yet, sometimes Word may do some underlining on its own, with colorful zigzags or dots. What Word is doing is alerting you to certain special aspects of that underlined text.

Red zigzag: Spelling errors in Word are underlined with a red zigzag. See Chapter 8.

Green zigzag: Grammatical errors in Word are underlined with a green zigzag. See Chapter 8.

Blue zigzag: Word-choice errors are really grammatical errors, but Word flags them with a special blue zigzag regardless. The blue underlined word is most likely not the best word to use given the sentence structure. Again, see Chapter 8.

Purple dots: Word's Smart Tags feature uses purple dots to highlight information such as names, dates, places, and similar data that can be shared with other programs in Microsoft Office. Smart Tags are briefly discussed in Chapter 33.

Blue underlines. Word courteously highlights Web page addresses using blue, underlined text in your document. You can Ctrl+click that blue underline text to visit the Web page.

Colored text and underlines: When your text appears in color and underlined, or with strikethrough, and assuming that you haven't specifically set those formatting options, it means you have *revision marks* turned on. Refer to Chapter 27 for more information on revision marks and how to turn them off.

Generally speaking, ignore all squiggly lines until you move into the editing phase for your document. (Well, unless you become obsessive, but that tends to slow down the writing process.) Later chapters in this book describe how to deal with the various underlines I just mentioned.

Word can type that for you

Sometimes when you're typing and in the middle of something, you see a pop-up bubble appear above your text, as shown in Figure 2-4. That's the AutoComplete feature in action. Basically, AutoComplete is Word guessing at what you're typing.

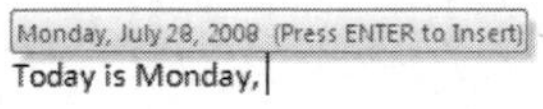

Figure 2-4:
Word
assumes
that it
knows what
you're about
to type.

Monday, July 28, 2008 (Press ENTER to Insert)
Today is Monday, |

When Word has guessed correctly, press the Enter key, and Word inserts the rest of the text. If Word is out of its mind, keep on typing, and the bubble goes away.

Chapter 3

A Quick Guide to Word
(For the Impatient)

In This Chapter

▶ Understanding word processing

▶ Beginning a new document

▶ Typing your thoughts

▶ Formatting chores

▶ Saving the document

▶ Proofing, previewing, and printing

▶ Closing the document

As far as word processing software goes, Word is like a wardrobe full of clothing: Word's closet of clothes includes a selection of formal wear, office attire, casual and "golf" clothing, beach and boating wear, gardening attire, semiformal evening wear, and everything else from shorts to slacks, socks to spats, and cuff links to top hats. Given all that Word offers, most folks spend only two seconds in the Word wardrobe, donning every time the same old pair of jeans and ratty T-shirt.

It's estimated that most people use less than one-tenth of Word's features. There's nothing wrong with that; the power and variety are there when you need them. For most word processing chores, though, getting by with the simple steps outlined in this chapter is about all you need. The rest is fluff, there when you need it — or when you want your work to look better than the mediocre junk made by the masses, who only scratch the surface of what Word can do.

The Overview

The word processing routine works like this:

1. **Start a new document.**
2. **Type.**
3. **Format.**
4. **Save.**
5. **Review or preview (optional).**
6. **Print.**
7. **Save and close.**

Everyone follows these steps in one way or another. A good Word user repeats Steps 2, 3, and 4, sometimes varying the order. Overall, most of the time you're typing in Word.

When you've saved a document and want to work on it again, replace Step 1 with "Open a document on disk." A lot of word processing involves working on stuff you've already started or on things started by others. Refer to Chapter 9 for more information on opening documents.

Formatting, at this level, merely involves selecting a font or two, perhaps applying some character formatting (italics or bold), and maybe adding page numbering. This is really "formatting as you type," as opposed to the more-formal formatting used by the pros. See Part III of this book for chapters on formatting various parts of a Word document.

Skipping Step 4 is one of the biggest mistakes beginners make. Save your stuff! Even trivial stuff. Deleting trivial stuff later is easier than re-creating it from scratch. See Chapter 9 for information on saving.

Steps 5 and 6 are necessary only when you're done and plan on printing your work. Refer to Chapter 8 for a discussion on how to proof your document. Chapter 10 covers printing.

When you're done, of course, you need to properly quit Word or merely close and save the document you created. Then you're ready to do something else with the computer. Quitting Word is covered at the end of Chapter 1.

Starting Out with a New Document

When you start your word processing day, Word automatically presents you with a blank sheet of paper — a blank *document* — on which you can start writing. That's what most folks do, making this the easiest step of your word processing day.

If you're ready to start typing, skip to the next section.

When you're already using Word and need to start a new document, follow these steps to summon that blank sheet o' paper:

1. **Choose the New command from the Office Button menu.**

   The New Document window appears, giving you too many options for creating a new something-or-other, as shown in Figure 3-1. What you want is a *blank document*.

2. **Click the Create button to choose Blank Document.**

   The blank document option is preselected for you. All you need to do is click the Create button, or press the Enter key, to make the New Document window go away, and you see your blank page, ready for typing.

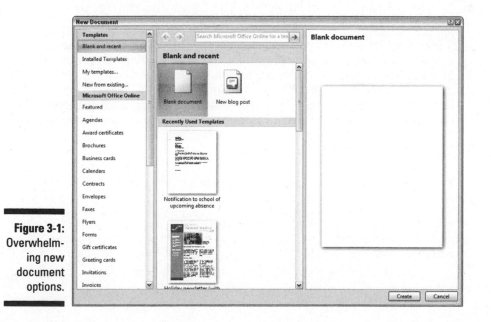

Figure 3-1:
Overwhelming new document options.

You can repeat these steps as often as you need new documents; Word lets you work with many documents at a time. (See Chapter 25 for information on multiple-document mania.)

- ✔ Ah, the shortcut: Press Ctrl+N to quickly summon a new blank document in Word.

- ✔ Another way to start your work is to open a document on disk. To do this, use the Open command form the Office Button menu, which is covered in Chapter 9.

- ✔ The New Document window contains many options for starting something new in Word. Rather than use the Blank Document choice, lots of folks use templates to start documents. *Templates* help save time by predefining document layout and formatting (and sometimes even text). See Chapter 17 for more information on the handy-dandy template.

Typing the Text

Of all the wacky things you can do with a computer, typing makes the most sense. In Word, the text you type at the keyboard appears on the screen. It's easy. In fact, there are few hang-ups regarding typing in Word.

- ✔ Refer to the section in Chapter 2 about typing (or the old hunt-and-peck) for typing tips and suggestions.

- ✔ A big part of typing in Word includes moving the insertion pointer, or cursor, around inside your document. Although some people find moving the cursor an easy thing, I recommend checking out Chapter 4 to help hone your insertion pointer prowess.

Formatting a Document

Formatting makes your documents look professional and not like you're using an abused typewriter from a smelly thrift store. And formatting is more than just making some text italic or bold or adding a heading to your document. In Word, formatting includes lines, styles, colors, textures, pictures — all sorts of fun stuff.

In Word, you can format the following parts of a document:

- ✔ Characters
- ✔ Paragraphs
- ✔ Tabs

✔ Pages

✔ Columns

✔ Headers and footers

✔ The entire document

Word lets you manipulate each of these items in a variety of interesting and creative ways: margins, boxes, spacing, indents, lines, shading, page orientation, and on and on. But remember the following admonishment:

Your primary duty in word processing is to get down the text.

Text comes first! Get your ideas down. After that, you can go back and format and change the text style or adjust the margins. Speaking from experience here, when you get hung up on formatting, you lose your train of thought and your document suffers. Write first; format afterward.

✔ Most folks format text as they type, by adding italic or bold or whatever. That's fine, and this book shows you some keen shortcuts that make such character formatting easy and not distracting to your chain of thought.

✔ You can also format paragraphs as you write, although I still recommend keeping the major formatting chores for *after* you write your text.

✔ Word also lets you format your document by adding drawings, pictures, lines, tables, columns, or other elements that can really make things look snazzy. Parts III and IV covers those topics.

Save Your Stuff!

The biggest mistake made by computer users is *not* saving their stuff. In Word, you must soon, regularly, and often save your documents to disk. Only when a document has been saved on disk can you use it again later or retrieve it after a power outage or when you forgetfully quit Word without saving.

There are two ways to save a document:

✔ The first time

✔ Every time after the first time

The first time you save a document, you must assign the document a name, or *filename*. That's the name by which you can recognize the document when you see its icon in Windows. The name also helps you determine the file's contents.

After initially saving a document to disk, you merely need to update it. So, as you're working, you save again. There's no need to choose the filename at this point; the computer merely overwrites the old file on disk with your new, updated document.

To save a document to disk the first time, choose the Save command from the Office Button menu. The first time you save a document, the Save As dialog box appears. It looks different between Windows Vista and Windows XP, as shown in Figures 3-2 and 3-3, yet both dialog boxes work the same: Type a name for your document in the File Name area. (The name "The Forest" is shown in Figures 3-2 and 3-3.) If you make a mistake typing, press the Backspace key to back up and erase. Click the Save button to save your document.

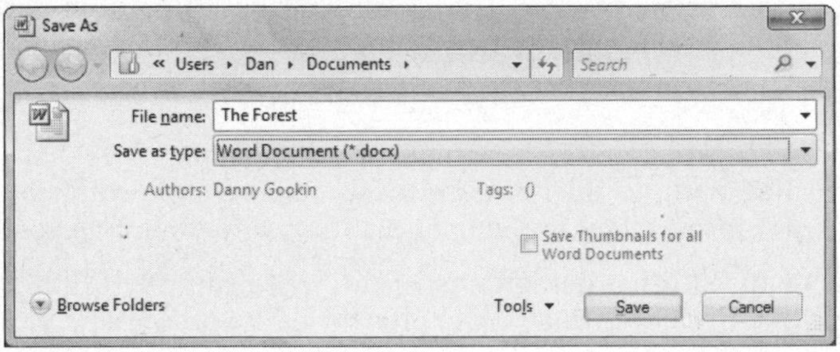

Figure 3-2: The Save As dialog box, Windows Vista.

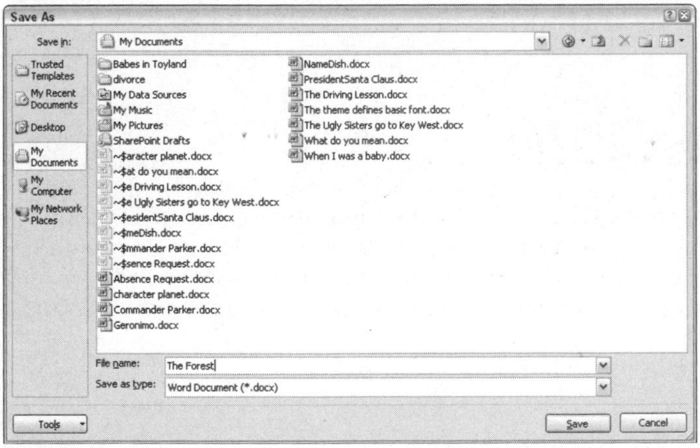

Figure 3-3: The Save As dialog box, Windows XP.

To save a document as you're working on it, just keep choosing the Save command from the Office Button menu. It updates the document on disk with your most recent changes.

✔ Refer to Chapter 9 for more details about saving your document.

✔ Computers are forgetful beasts. Saving a document to disk is like making a permanent copy of the document and storing it in a file cabinet. In fact, the computer refers to documents saved on disk as *files*. Understanding the concept of the file is important in using a computer. If you need more information, I recommend my book *PCs For Dummies* (Wiley Publishing, Inc.).

✔ If you've opened a document already on disk, there's no need to save it for the first time; in fact, the document has already been saved once! You merely need to choose the Save command from the Office Button menu to update the document as you make changes.

✔ Rather than choose the Save command from the Office Button menu, you can click the Save button on the toolbar. Or, from the keyboard, you can press the Ctrl+S keyboard shortcut.

✔ When you save a document, watch the status bar — it temporarily displays a message telling you that Word is saving your document (or *fast saving*, for our frequent fliers).

✔ After the document is saved to disk, you see its name displayed on the window's title bar. That name is your clue that your document has been saved to disk.

Finishing a Document

The last thing you need to do is finish your work. Mostly, that involves printing your document. In fact, you may not think of printing simply because until the word processor came about, every other writing device in history was also its own printer: the rock, the stylus, the pen, the typewriter — each of those writing implements printed as the author wrote. With word processing, printing becomes a necessary, if not final, step.

I recommend three steps to the printing process:

✔ Proof
✔ Preview
✔ Print

Each of these steps is covered in this section.

Proofing your work

Just because you're writing on a word processor and the text looks really neat and graphics and nifty things are right up there on the screen doesn't mean that what you wrote is perfect. I highly recommend that you proof your document before you print.

Proofing means *reading*. Read and review your documents. It also means checking spelling and grammar, which Word does automatically. Refer to Chapter 8 for more information.

Previewing a document

Before you print, I recommend previewing what the final document looks like. Yeah, even though what you've written is supposed to look the same on the screen as it does on the paper, you may still see surprises: missing page numbers, blank pages, or half pages, for example. The best way to find those surprises before printing is to use the Print Preview feature.

Choose Print⇨Print Preview from the Office Button menu. The Print Preview command changes the way Word looks on the screen, as shown in Figure 3-4. You can review your document one page at a time or as multiple pages. You can zoom in and out, and you can even edit, although I don't recommend it.

Click the Close Print Preview button to leave Print Preview mode, in case you need to return to your document for editing and touch-ups. Otherwise, you can print directly from Print Preview mode by choosing the Print command button in the Print group (shown in Figure 3-4).

Printing a document

Printing the document is easy to do:

1. **Make sure that the printer is on and ready to print.**

2. **Choose the Print command from the Office Button menu, or click the Print button when you're using the Print Preview feature.**

   The Print dialog box opens. In this busy place, printing and related activities happen.

3. **Click the OK button.**

   The document comes out of your printer.

Print
the
document

Leave
Print
Preview

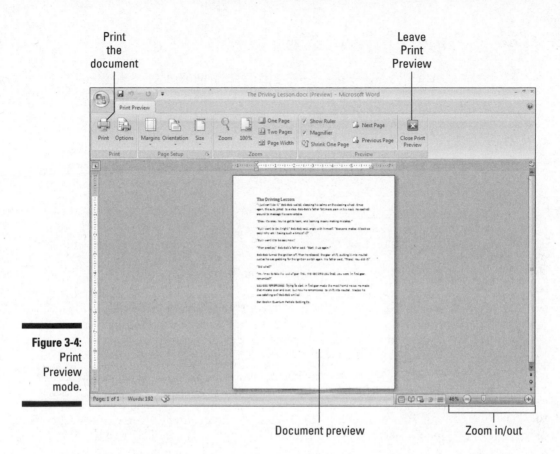

Figure 3-4:
Print
Preview
mode.

Document preview

Zoom in/out

Printing is often a source of woe for computer users. That's because the printer really is its own, specialized computer, one that's designed for printing stuff. Getting your computer and the printer/computer to work well together can be an art form.

- See Chapter 10 for additional information about preparing the printer if you need to.

- You can also summon the Print dialog box by pressing Ctrl+P on the keyboard.

- I highly recommend that you save your document before you print — just in case! I'm a stickler for saving, saving, saving your document.

Wrapping Things Up

When you're done writing, you need to do the electronic equivalent of putting a document away. That electronic equivalent is the Close command: Choose the Close command from the Office Button menu, or use the handy Ctrl+W keyboard shortcut.

If you haven't saved your document recently, Word prompts you to save before you close; click the Yes button and the document is saved. (If it hasn't yet been saved — shame on you! — you see the Save As dialog box; refer to Chapter 9).

When the document has been saved, closing it simply removes it from view. At that point, you can quit Word, start up a new document, open a document on disk, or just put away Word and hit another game of Spider Solitaire.

- ✔ Also refer to Chapter 1 for more quitting options.

- ✔ You don't have to choose the Close command. You can choose the Exit Word command from the Office Button menu if you're all done with Word, which is almost the same thing: You're prompted to save your document if it needs saving; otherwise, the Exit Word command quits Word rather than keeps the window open.

- ✔ If you're working on only one document and you close it, Word looks like it has vacated the premises: Tabs and command buttons dim, and other screen debris goes away. Don't panic; you've just closed a document, and Word has little else to do. Word sits patiently and waits for your next command: Start a new document, open a document on disk, or quit Word.

Part II
Word Processing Basics

The 5th Wave   By Rich Tennant

RICHTENNANT

"I'm just having trouble dating a guy whose name defaults to "Loony Fruitcake" on my Spell Checker."

In this part . . .

Although it never made the papers, for the past 25 years a word processing revolution has been taking place. The primitive, steam-powered computers of the 1970s had word processors that were little more than text editors, with simple features, such as deleting and inserting text, search and replace, and maybe even word wrap.

As competition arose, various word processors had to evolve with new features to stay competitive. At first, the features were honestly useful to the wordsmith: text and paragraph formatting, page numbering, and even spell checking. But as the competition grew fierce, some clunky features were added as each word processing program tried to one-up the other. (This explains why Word has so many commands and options.)

It was in the late 1980s, at the height of the feature wars, that a basic set of word processing duties evolved. Over time, these duties were honed into the core tasks covered by the chapters in this part of the book. These tasks are what I call the word processing basics.

Chapter 4

Moving Around a Document Hither, Thither, and Yon

In This Chapter

▶ Using the scroll bars

▶ Moving the insertion pointer

▶ Getting around with keyboard shortcuts

▶ Navigating with the browse buttons

▶ Getting lost and getting back

▶ Using the Go To command

The beauty of the word processor is that it allows you the freedom to edit your text, and to write and rewrite, without having to start over each time with a new, blank sheet of paper. After the words are on the screen, editing becomes simple: You can delete text, move text, and insert new text, all without starting over. But before you can do that, it's important to know how to move around a document. This chapter covers one of the first things you need to learn in Word: how to move about inside your document.

Scrolling a Document

Word's window can show you only so much of a document at a time. To see more of the document, you can employ the handy scroll bars as well as some nifty mouse tricks.

The vertical scroll bar

On the right side of the document part of the window is the vertical scroll bar (see Figure 4-1). Its operation is similar to the scroll bar in any Windows program:

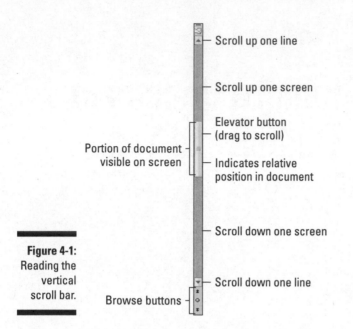

Scroll up one line

Scroll up one screen

Elevator button
(drag to scroll)

Portion of document
visible on screen

Indicates relative
position in document

Scroll down one screen

Figure 4-1:
Reading the
vertical
scroll bar.

Scroll down one line

Browse buttons

✔ Click the up- or down-arrow buttons at the top and bottom of the vertical scroll bar to scroll your document up or down. The document scrolls one line of text for each time you click those up- or down-arrow buttons.

✔ An *elevator button* appears inside the scroll bar. You can drag this button with the mouse, up or down, to scroll the document.

✔ You can click above or below the elevator button to scroll up or down one screen of text at a time.

The elevator button's size reflects how much of your document you can see at a time. When the button doesn't show up, or is dimmed, the whole document appears on-screen. Otherwise, the elevator button gets smaller as your document grows longer.

The elevator button's position also helps show you which part of your document is visible. When the elevator button is at the top of the scroll bar, you're viewing pages near the start of the document. When the elevator button is toward the bottom of the scroll bar, you're seeing pages near the document's end.

Some special bonuses are involved when you drag the elevator button to scroll through your document. As you drag the button up or down, you see a page number displayed, as shown in Figure 4-2. When a document is formatted with heading styles, you also see the heading title below the page number.

Figure 4-2:
Vital page-
numbering
information.

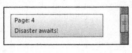

Page: 4
Disaster awaits!

Scrolling through your document doesn't move the insertion pointer. If you start typing, don't be surprised when Word jerks you back to where the insertion pointer lurks. (Refer to the later section "Commanding the insertion pointer with the mouse" for help if such a thing bugs you.)

✔ Scrolling a document doesn't move the insertion pointer!

✔ Also refer to Chapter 26 for information on Word's Reading mode.

✔ Refer to the section "Using Browse Buttons to Navigate," later in this chapter, for information on using the browse buttons, which are located below the vertical scroll bar.

One paragraph on the horizontal scroll bar

The horizontal scroll bar appears just above the status bar at the bottom of Word's window — but only when your document is wider than the window. When that happens, you can use the horizontal scroll bar to shift the page back and forth, left and right.

When the horizontal shifting bugs you, consider using Word's Zoom tool to adjust the size of your document on the screen. See Chapter 30.

Mouse scrolling tricks

Aside from manipulating the scroll bars, you can use your computer mouse to fly and flutter about your document. Sadly, this works only when you have one of those wheel mice. Coincidentally, these tricks are all done by manipulating that unique wheel button:

✔ Roll the wheel up or down to scroll your document up or down. (The Mouse icon in the Windows Control Panel sets the number of lines the document scrolls per wheel click.)

✔ Press and hold the wheel button to activate scrolling mode. With the wheel button down, you can move the mouse up or down to *pan* your document in that direction.

✔ If the mouse's wheel button also tilts from side to side, you can use it to pan left and right.

Moving the Insertion Pointer

The beauty of the word processor is that you can edit any part of your document; you don't always have to work at "the end." The key to pulling off that trick is to know how to move the insertion pointer to the exact spot you want.

Moving the insertion pointer is important! Scientific studies have shown that merely looking at the computer screen does no good. As hard as you wish, new text appears only at the insertion pointer. And, the text you edit or delete? Yup, the insertion pointer's location is important there as well. Obviously, knowing how to move the insertion pointer is a big deal.

Commanding the insertion pointer with the mouse

The easiest way to put the insertion pointer exactly where you want it is to point the mouse at that spot in your text and then click the mouse button. Point, click, move insertion pointer. Simple.

Moving in small increments (basic arrow keys)

Using the mouse is perhaps the easiest way to move the insertion pointer, but most experienced Word users take advantage of the keyboard's cursor keys to quickly move the insertion pointer to any position in their documents.

The four basic arrow keys move the insertion pointer up, down, right, and left:

Key	To Move the Cursor . . .
↑	Up to the preceding line of text
↓	Down to the next line of text
→	Right to the next character
←	Left to the preceding character

Moving the cursor doesn't erase characters. See Chapter 5 for information on deleting stuff.

If you press and hold the Ctrl (Control) key and then press an arrow key, you enter hyper-jump mode. The supercharged insertion pointer leaps desperately in all four directions:

Press These Keys	To Move the Cursor . . .
Ctrl+↑	Up to the start of the previous paragraph
Ctrl+↓	Down to the start of the next paragraph
Ctrl+→	Right to the start (first letter) of the next word
Ctrl+←	Left to the start (first letter) of the previous word

You can use either set of arrow keys on the computer keyboard, but when using the numeric keypad, ensure that the Num Lock light is off. Do this by pressing the Num Lock key. If you don't, you see numbers in your text rather than the insertion pointer dancing all over — like444this.

Moving from beginning to end

The insertion pointer also bows to pressure from those cursor keys without arrows on them. The first couple is End and Home, which move the insertion pointer to the start or end of things, depending on how End and Home are used:

Key or Combination	To Whisk the Insertion Pointer . . .
End	To the end of a line of text
Home	To the start of a line of text
Ctrl+End	To the very end of the document
Ctrl+Home	To the tippy-top of the document

The peculiar cases of PgUp and PgDn

One would think, logically, that the Page Up or PgUp key moves a document up one page and that the Page Down or PgDn key moves a document down. 'Tain't so, though. Rather than slide your document around a page at a time, these keys move things one *screen* at a time:

PgUp	The PgUp key moves the insertion pointer up one screen. Or, if you're looking at the tippy-top of your document, pressing this key moves the insertion pointer to the start of the document.
PgDn	The PgDn key moves the insertion pointer down one screen or to the end of the document, if you happen to be near there.

If the functions of PgUp and PgDn aren't confusing enough, you can absorb these two combinations, which are just this side of pressing all the keys on the keyboard at one time:

Ctrl+Alt+PgUp	Moves the cursor to the top of the current screen.
Ctrl+Alt+PgDn	Moves the cursor to the bottom of the current screen.

Ctrl+PgUp and Ctrl+PgDn? Yup, they're used in Word, but not as you would expect. Refer to the following section for the details.

Using Browse Buttons to Navigate

Lurking at the bottom of the vertical scroll bar are three buttons, as shown in the margin. These *browse* buttons allow you to scroll through your document in leaps and bounds of various sizes.

 The top button is the *Browse Up* button, which is linked to the Ctrl+PgUp key combination.

 The bottom button is the *Browse Down* button, which is linked to the Ctrl+PgDn key combination.

 The center button is the What-the-heck-am-I-browsing-for? button, which is linked to the Alt+Ctrl+Home key combination.

When you click the center button, a pop-up palette of things to browse for appears, as shown in Figure 4-3. Pointing the mouse at any one of the items displays text that explains the item in the bottom part of the palette.

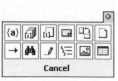

Figure 4-3: Various things to browse for.

Unless you've chosen another item from the browsing palette (refer to Figure 4-3), the browse buttons (and Ctrl+PgUp and Ctrl+PgDn) leap through your document by full pages.

Whenever an option other than Page is chosen from the browsing palette, the browse buttons change color. So, when the buttons are black, you know that you're browsing by page. When the browse buttons turn blue, they're searching for something else. (Alas, the browsing palette doesn't tell you which option is currently chosen.)

Getting Lost and Going Back

With all the various commands for moving the insertion pointer, it's quite possible to make a mistake and not know where you are in a document. Yea, verily, the insertion pointer has gone where no insertion pointer has gone before.

 Rather than click your heels together three times and try to get back the wishful way, just remember this keyboard combination:

Shift+F5

Pressing the Shift+F5 keys forces Word to return you to the last spot you edited. You can do this up to three times before the cycle repeats. But the first time should get you back to where you were before you got lost.

✓ The Shift+F5 command is the same as the Browse by Edits option, found on the Browse palette. Refer to the preceding section.

✓ Sadly, the Shift+F5 keyboard shortcut works only in Word; you can't use this command in real life.

Go to Wherever with the Go To Command

Word's Go To command allows you to send the insertion pointer to a specific page or line or to the location of a number of interesting things Word can potentially cram into your document. The Go To command is your word processing teleporter to anywhere.

 Press the Ctrl+G key combination to see the Go To tab portion of the Find and Replace dialog box, as shown in Figure 4-4.

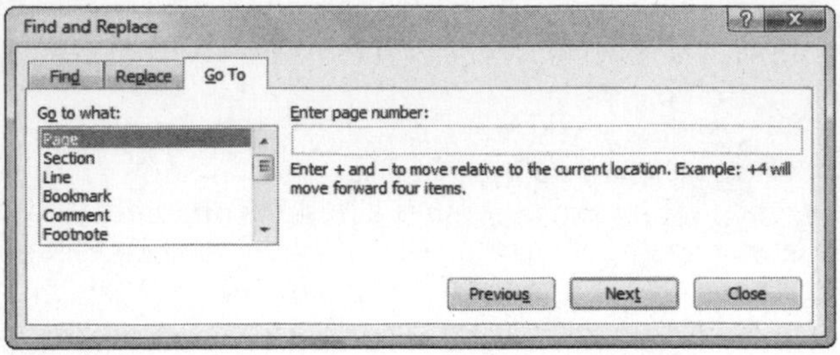

Figure 4-4:
How to tell
Word to
Go To
you-know-
where.

Choose what to go to, such as a page, from the scrolling list on the left side of the dialog box. Then type the relevant information, such as a page number, in the box on the right side of the dialog box. Click the Go To button to go to that location.

For example, type **14** in the box and press Enter, and you go to page 14 — if you have a page 14 to go to.

✔ You can also summon the Go To command by double-clicking the page number on the status bar.

✔ Note that you can go to a page *relative* to the current page. For example, to go three pages forward, choose Page and type **+3**. To go 12 pages backward, type **-12** in the box.

Chapter 5

Editing Text

In This Chapter

▶ Deleting characters with Backspace and Delete

▶ Deleting lines, sentences, paragraphs, and pages

▶ Splitting and joining paragraphs

▶ Undoing your mistakes

▶ Using the Redo (un-undo) command

*W*hat is editing? At its best, *editing* is making the stuff you write read better. A good editor helps a writer perfect his words, guiding him in a way that avoids the ambiguous, keeps the pace tight, completes thoughts, checks this weird thing called "subject-verb agreement," and, above all, ensures that the writer's intention is best understood by the reader.

Okay. I got that off my chest. Now, deep down in that secret place where you hide your desire to jump on the couch and run with scissors, as a writer you resent editing. That's because at its core, editing is about *deleting text*. Despite all good intentions, the editor is at her best when she's slashing, snipping, cutting, gouging, severing, goring, obliterating, and replacing those oh-so-vital words you poured your soul into and struggled over for hours. It's hard to accept (even more so because the editor will say that it's *difficult* to accept), but it's true: Editing text is about deleting stuff, which is also the subject of this chapter. Or this chapter's subject. Whatever.

A good editor also checks your document's spelling and grammar. See Chapter 8 for more information.

Deleting Stuff

Credit the guy who put the eraser on the end of the pencil: It's a given that human beings make mistakes. The round, soft eraser counterbalances the sharp point of the pencil in more ways than one.

When the typewriter was at its peak, the ability to erase or untype text was a popular feature. And, of course, even now — years after the typewriter has been consigned to the curiosity corner of the public library — people still know what WiteOut is and why it was a necessity.

On just about every front, the ability to erase text is just as valuable as the ability to create that text. The same holds true with your word processor. Deleting is part of the creation process, part of thinking and rethinking, and part of self-editing. Writing. Deleting. Rewriting. Redeleting. That's how it goes!

The delete keys: Backspace and Delete

Both creating and destroying text are accomplished by using the computer keyboard. The majority of keys are used to create text. Only two keys delete text: Backspace and Delete. How these keys work, and how much of your text they can delete, depends on how the keys are used.

Deleting single characters

By themselves, the Backspace and Delete keys are used to delete single characters of text:

- ✔ **Backspace key:** Deletes the character to the left of the insertion pointer
- ✔ **Delete key:** Deletes the character to the right of the insertion pointer

In the following example, the insertion pointer is "flashing" (okay, it *would* be flashing on a computer screen) between the *h* and the *a* in *that*. Pressing the Backspace key deletes the *h;* pressing the Delete key deletes the *a.*

```
No one would have suspected th|at you were a robot,
Hubert, until you began to articulate your love for
the waffle iron.
```

- ✔ After you delete a character, any text to the right or below the character shuffles over to fill the void.
- ✔ You can press and hold Backspace or Delete to continuously "machine-gun-delete" characters. Release the key to halt such wanton destruction, although I recommend using other delete commands (covered in this chapter) rather than the machine-gun approach.

- ✔ Special types of text in Word cannot easily be deleted using either the Backspace or Delete key. An example is an updating text *field*, which is special text that always shows, say, today's date. This type of text appears shaded in a light gray color when you try to delete it. That's Word reminding you of the unusualness of the text. Press the Delete or Backspace key again to delete such text.

Deleting a word

To gobble up an entire word, add the Ctrl key to the Backspace or Delete key's destructive power:

- ✔ Ctrl+Backspace deletes the word in front (to the left) of the insertion pointer.
- ✔ Ctrl+Delete deletes the word behind (to the right) of the insertion pointer.

These keyboard shortcuts work best when the insertion pointer is at the start or end of a word. When you're in the middle of the word, the commands delete only from that middle point to the start or end of the word.

After you delete a word, the insertion pointer sits at the end of the preceding word (or paragraph) when you use Ctrl+Backspace. Deleting a word with Ctrl+Delete puts the cursor at the beginning of the next word. This is done to facilitate the rapid deletion of several words in a row.

After deleting the text, Word neatly wraps up the remaining text, snuggling it together in a grammatically proper way.

No mere pencil eraser can match Ctrl+Delete or Ctrl+Backspace for sheer speed and terror!

Deleting more than a word

Beyond deleting a word or character, Word lacks keyboard-specific commands to delete lines or paragraphs of text. There are ways to delete these things — they're just not obvious. Before going into the details, first come some definitions:

- ✔ A **line of text** is merely a line across the page (not really a grammatical thing).
- ✔ A **sentence** is a sentence. You know: Start with a capital letter and end with a period, question mark, or exclamation point. You probably learned this concept in grammar school, which is why they call it *grammar* school anyway.
- ✔ A **paragraph** is one or more sentences, or a heading, ending with a press of the Enter key.
- ✔ A **page** of text is just that — all the text from where the page starts to where the page ends.

Word can also delete odd-size chunks of text by marking that text as a *block*. Refer to Chapter 7 for more information on blocks of text.

Deleting a line of text

The easiest way to delete a line of text is to use the mouse:

1. **Move the mouse into the left margin of your document.**

   You know you've found the sweet spot when the mouse pointer changes into a northeast arrow.

2. **Point the mouse pointer arrow at the line of text you want to obliterate.**

3. **Click the mouse.**

   The line of text is highlighted, or *selected*.

4. **Press the Delete key to send that line into the void.**

Deleting a sentence

Making a sentence go bye-bye is cinchy:

1. **Point the mouse at the offending sentence.**

2. **Press and hold the Ctrl key and click the mouse.**

   The sentence is selected.

3. **Press the Delete key.**

   Oomph! It's gone.

Deleting a paragraph

The fastest way to delete a full paragraph:

1. **Point the mouse at the paragraph.**

2. **Click the mouse button thrice.**

   Thrice means "three times."

3. **Press the Delete key.**

If clicking thrice is befuddling you, move the mouse pointer into the left margin next to the offending paragraph. When the mouse pointer changes to a northeasterly-pointing arrow, click twice. That selects the entire paragraph, which you can now whack by pressing the Delete key.

Deleting a page

Pages aren't something that Word deals with offhand. In fact, pages are really a printer thing. Even so, to delete a page, mind these steps:

1. **Go to the top of the page you want to delete.**

   Refer to Chapter 4 for information on the Go To command. In the Go To dialog box, specify the number of the page to delete. (Remember to click the Close button to banish the Find and Replace dialog box.)

2. **Press the F8 key.**

   The F8 key is used to enter a special selection mode in Word, which I cover in detail in Chapter 7.

3. **Press Ctrl+PgDn.**

   The insertion pointer moves to the bottom of the page.

4. **Press the Delete key.**

   The page is gone.

Refer to Chapter 10 for special information on deleting that annoying extra blank page at the end of your document.

Splitting and Joining

Editing can also involve the basic chores of splitting and joining lines or paragraphs of text. To *split* is to make two paragraphs where once there was one. To *join* is to make one paragraph where once there were two.

Making two paragraphs from one

To split a single paragraph in twain, locate the point where you want them to break — say, between two sentences. Move the insertion pointer to that location, and then press the Enter key. Word splits the paragraph in two; the text above the insertion pointer becomes its own paragraph, and the text following it then becomes the next paragraph.

Depending on where you placed the insertion pointer, you may need to delete an extra space at the beginning of the second paragraph or at the end of the first paragraph.

Making one paragraph from two

To join two paragraphs and turn them into one, you delete the Enter character between the paragraphs. To do that, move the insertion pointer to the start of the second paragraph, and then press the Backspace key. Removing the Enter character joins two paragraphs. (You may need to add a space between the newly joined paragraphs.)

Splitting lines with a soft return

The Enter key inserts a *hard return* into your text to end a paragraph. To end a line of text without ending a paragraph, a *soft return* is used instead. This is done by pressing Shift+Enter.

The *soft return,* or *line break,* is used primarily in titles and headings. For example, when you have a long title and need to split it up between two lines, you press Shift+Enter to insert the soft return. For example, type this line:

```
Filbert & Hazel
```

Press Shift+Enter. A new line starts. Continue typing:

```
A Couple of Nuts
```

The soft return keeps the title text together (in the same paragraph), but on separate lines.

Mistakes? Mistakes? Undo Them with Haste

> *That quaffing and drinking will undo you.*
>
> — Twelfth Night, *William Shakespeare*

There's no need to be afraid of obliterating your text, or of doing anything else in Word. Anything! That's because Word sports a handy Undo command. What you can do, you can also undo.

Now mark me, how 1 will undo myself

The Undo command undoes anything you do in Word, which includes formatting text, moving blocks, typing and deleting text, formatting — the whole lasagna. You have two handy ways to unleash the Undo command:

✔ Press Ctrl+Z.

✔ Click the Undo command button on the Quick Access toolbar.

 I prefer using the Ctrl+Z key combination, but an advantage of the Undo command button is that it sports a drop-down menu that helps you review the past several things you've done, or that can be undone.

✔ Word's Undo command is handy, but don't use it as an excuse to be sloppy!

✔ Regrettably, you cannot pick and choose from the Undo command button's drop-down menu; the menu merely allows you to undo multiple instances of things all at one time.

✔ There are sporadic times when Undo doesn't work. Before this happens, Word warns you. For example, you may see a message such as "There is not enough memory to undo this operation, Continue?" Proceed at your own peril.

✔ The Undo command doesn't work when there's nothing to undo, or if something just cannot be undone. For example, you cannot undo a save-to-disk operation.

✔ To undo an Undo, choose Redo. See the next section.

Redo, the Undo-Undo command

If you undo something and — whoops! — you didn't mean to, you must use the Redo command to set things back. For example, you may type some text and then use Undo to "untype" the text. You can use the Redo command to get the typing back. You have two choices:

✔ Press Ctrl+Y.

✔ Click the Redo command button on the Quick Access toolbar.

For the few who are fond of Overtype mode

The writing you do in Word is in *Insert mode,* which means that any new text you type is inserted just before the blinking insertion pointer. The new stuff pushes any existing text to the right and downward as you type. This is Insert mode. But things don't always have to work that way.

Insert mode's evil twin is Overtype mode. In *Overtype mode,* all the text you type overwrites the existing text and replaces it as you go. The new text you type literally types over *(overtypes)* the existing text, all except for the Enter key; you cannot overtype from one paragraph to the next.

I don't recommend writing in Overtype mode; Insert mode is fine. All the Word documentation, all the Microsoft Office Word Help, and this book assume that Insert mode is what you're using. Still, if you insist, to activate Overtype mode, heed these steps:

1. Choose Word Options from the Office Button menu.

2. Click Advanced from the list on the left side of the Word Options dialog box.

3. Put a check mark by the item on the right labeled Use Overtype Mode.

4. I also recommend putting a check mark by the item above it, Use the Insert key to Control Overtype Mode.

5. Click OK.

No visual clue or message on the screen informs you when Overtype mode is active; you merely know that you're in Overtype mode because any new text you type replaces the existing text. Use the Insert or Ins key to switch between Overtype and Insert modes.

 The Redo command serves two functions. First, it does exactly the opposite of whatever the Undo command does. So, if you type text, Undo untypes the text, and Redo recovers the text. If you use Undo to recover deleted text, Redo deletes the text again. (The second function is covered in the next section.)

Redo, the Repeat Typing command

 When the Redo command has nothing left to redo, it changes functions and becomes the Repeat Typing command. Boy, can the Repeat Typing command be a real timesaver!

For example, type the following lines in Word:

```
Knock, knock.
Who's there?
Knock.
Knock who?
```

Now press Ctrl+Y or choose the Repeat Typing command button from the Quick Access toolbar. Word repeats the last few things you typed. (If you had to press the Backspace key to back up and erase, Ctrl+Y repeats only from that point on.)

✔ The Repeat Typing command can also used to reapply formatting. When you're working through a document and changing styles on various chunks of text, using the Repeat key or Redo command can save oodles of time, especially in applying formatting. (See Part III of this book for information on formatting.)

✔ If you can remember the F4 key, it works the same as Ctrl+Y; both are the Repeat Typing command kcys.

Chapter 6

Find and Replace

● ●

In This Chapter

▶ Finding text in your document

▶ Using various Find command options

▶ Searching for text that cannot be typed at the keyboard

▶ Hunting down formatting codes

▶ Replacing found text with other text

▶ Fixing formatting with the Replace command

● ●

*I*magine being able to combine the power of the computer with the ancient practice of alchemy. Computers are excellent at being obedient; they don't mind doing any task, even the most boring, repetitive things. Alchemy had as its goal the transmutation of lead into gold. Now, combine the two so that the computer, which can easily find the single word *needle* in a haystack of documents, has the ability to change that word *needle* into the word *gold,* and you have a quick and potentially misleading introduction to the powerful yet basic word processing ability of search and replace.

Search and replace is one of the most basic and ancient word processor functions. In Word, it's known as *Find* and Replace (don't ask me why), and it consists of two features: The first feature involves searching up or down through a document for a tidbit of text, and the second adds the ability to change that tidbit of text and replace it with something else.

Text Happily Found

Finding text is the domain of the Editing group, found on the far right end of the Home tab on Word's Ribbon interface. The Editing group may appear in its full glory, as shown in Figure 6-1, or it may simply appear as an Editing button. When it's a button, you must click that button first to see the palette of commands, which (surprisingly) looks like what's shown in Figure 6-1.

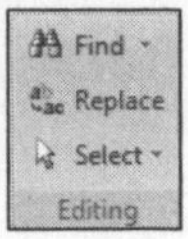

Figure 6-1:
The full
Editing com-
mand button
group.

O villainous text tidbit! Seek it out!

Locating text in your document is a snap, whether it's a protracted diatribe
or the tiniest monosyllabic utterance. Either way, the Find command stands
ready to tackle the task. Abide by these steps:

1. **On the Home tab, click the big Find button in the Editing group.**

   Refer to Figure 6-1; sometimes you may have to click the Editing button
   to get to the Find button. If all else fails, use the keyboard shortcut: Ctrl+F.

   Clicking the Find button summons the Find and Replace dialog box,
   illustrated in Figure 6-2.

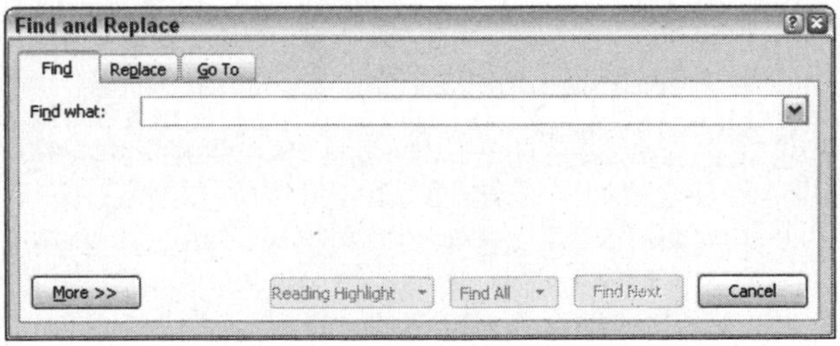

Figure 6-2:
The Find
and Replace
dialog box.

2. **Type the text you want to find into the Find What box.**

   Be exact. For example, if you want to find yourself, type **yourself** — no
   period or spaces or quotes. Type only the text you're looking for.

3. **Click the Find Next button to start the search.**

   Or, you can just press Enter.

Word searches for the text you typed, starting from the insertion pointer's
location to the end of the document. If any text is found, it's highlighted
(or *selected*) onscreen, and the insertion pointer moves to that location in
your document. At that point, you can click the Cancel button to make the
Find and Replace dialog box go away.

✔ The Find and Replace dialog box may already display text in the Find What box. If so, you can delete that text by pressing the Backspace key.

✔ Do not end the text with a period unless you want to find the period too.

✔ The Find command can find things that you can't readily type in, such as the Tab or Enter key. See the section "Finding stuff you can't type in," later in this chapter.

✔ If you're not sure whether the text is typed in uppercase or lowercase letters, use lowercase.

✔ If the text isn't found, you may be asked to search "at the beginning," which means the beginning of the document. Click the Yes button to do so.

✔ If the text isn't found and you're *certain* that it's in there, check your spelling. If that's okay, try searching for a single word rather than two or more words or a sentence.

✔ Word finds text only in the current document (the one you see on the screen). To find text in another document, click that document's button on the taskbar and try searching again.

✔ To find an additional occurrence of the text, click the Find Next button.

✔ You can use the drop-down arrow gizmo (to the right of the Find What text box) to display a scrolling list of text you've previously searched for. To search again for a bit of text you've already searched for, click the drop-down arrow and click the text you want to find again. Click the Find Next button, and Word frantically begins searching.

✔ You can limit the Find command's scope (the range of text it searches through) by marking text as a block. See Chapter 7 for block info.

✔ After using the Find command, you can use the Browse Down button to continue your finding foray. Simply close the Find and Replace dialog box, and then click the Browse Down button (or press Ctrl+PgDn). So, if you've already searched for and found *crap,* clicking the Browse Down button finds even more *crap.*

The Super Find command

On a simple level, the Find command hunts down chunks and chunklettes of text. Yet the Find command is far more powerful than that. You can use the Find command to find text *exactly* as it's typed, text you cannot type, formatting commands, and just about anything in a document. Yes, it's still the same Find command, but it's *more.*

More >>

To unveil the Super Find command, beckon forth the Find and Replace dialog box (press Ctrl+F). Click the More button. The Find and Replace dialog box gets taller, with a bunch of options and doodads at the bottom, as illustrated in Figure 6-3.

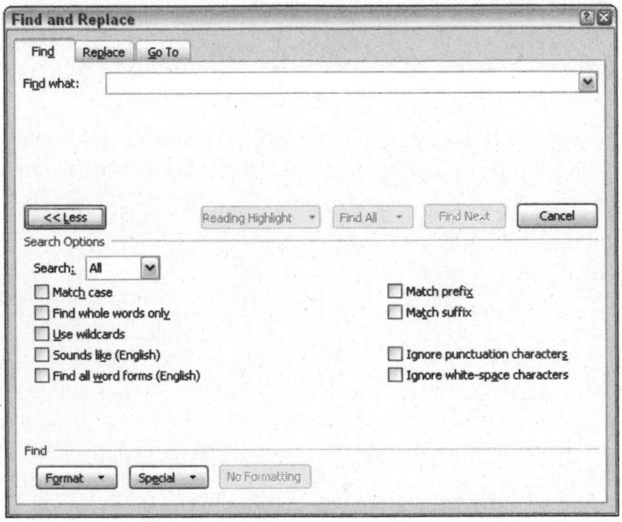

Figure 6-3:
The more
detailed
Find and
Replace
dialog box.

The following sections tell you why you may want to mess with some of the doodads in the Find More dialog box.

Finding an exact bit of text

There's a difference between *Curt* and *curt*. One is a name, and the other is being rude and abrupt. To use the Find command to find one and not the other, select the Match Case option under Search Options. That way, *Curt* matches only words that start with an uppercase *C* and have lowercase *urt* in them.

Finding a whole word

The Find Whole Words Only option allows you to look for words such as *right* and *set* without also finding words like *alright* and *upset*.

Finding text that you know only a small part of (by using wildcards)

Here's a can-o-worms for you. It's possible to use wildcards to find words that you know only a part of, or a group of words with similar letters. This trick is a highly technical operation, so I advise you not to drive or operate heavy machinery when reading the following text.

The two basic wildcard characters are ? and *, where ? represents any single letter and * represents a group of letters. Suppose that you type the following line in the Find What box:

```
?up
```

If you select the Use Wildcards option (in the More part of the Super Find and Replace dialog box), Word searches for any three-letter word that starts with any old letter but must end with "you pee" — *cup, pup,* and *sup,* for example.

The asterisk finds a group of characters, so the following wildcard locates any word starting with *w* and ending with *s* (there are lots of them):

```
w*s
```

Finding text that sounds like something else

The Sounds Like (English) option allows you to search for *homonyms,* or words that sound the same as the search word. You know: *their* and *there* or *deer* and *dear* or *hear* and *here.* How this is useful, I'll never know.

Oh! This isn't a rhyming search command. If you try to use it to find everything that rhymes with *Doris,* for example, it doesn't find *Boris, chorus, pylorus,* or anything of the like.

Finding variations of a word

Thanks to global warming, the protagonist in your novel no longer walks across an isthmus; he *swims.* And that's some journey! To make Word search for every variation of *walk* (*walking, walked,* and so on), type **walk** in the Find What box and select the Find All Word Forms (English) option in the Search Options area.

Searching this way or that

When I'd lose things as a kid, my mom would say "Retrace your steps!" This wisdom can be applied in Word as well, where the Find command can be directed to look not only forward through a document, but backwards as well. The secret is found in the Search drop-down list in the More part of the Find and Replace dialog box:

- ✔ **All:** When this option is chosen, Find searches the entire document, from the insertion pointer's location down to the end of the document, back up to the beginning, and then back to the toothpick cursor's location.

- ✔ **Down:** Find searches from the toothpick cursor's location to the end of your document, and then it stops.

- ✔ **Up:** Find searches from the toothpick cursor's location to the start of your document, backward. Then it stops.

You can also use the Browse buttons to repeat the Find command up or down, depending on which Browse button you press.

Finding stuff you can't type in

There are things you can search for in a document, things that just cannot be typed at the keyboard. No, I'm not talking about nasty things; this isn't a censorship issue. Instead, I'm referring to things like tabs, Enter keys (paragraphs), page breaks, graphics, and other, similar non-typable things.

To find a special, unprintable character, click the More button to see the superdooper Find and Replace dialog box (refer to Figure 6-3), and then click the Special button. Up pops a list of various things Word can search for but that you would have a dickens of a time typing, similar to what's shown in Figure 6-4.

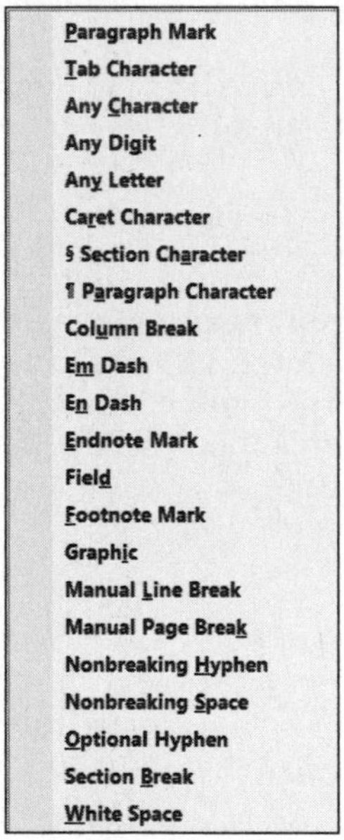

Paragraph Mark
Tab Character
Any Character
Any Digit
Any Letter
Caret Character
§ Section Character
¶ Paragraph Character
Column Break
Em Dash
En Dash
Endnote Mark
Field
Footnote Mark
Graphic
Manual Line Break
Manual Page Break
Nonbreaking Hyphen
Nonbreaking Space
Optional Hyphen
Section Break
White Space

Figure 6-4:
Items to
search for
that you
can't type.

Naturally, the items on the list may not be recognizable to you. That figures. There are 22 things on the list, and I've used maybe 6 of them myself. Here are some of the handier things you can use from the Special pop-up menu:

✔ **Any Character, Any Digit, and Any Letter** are special characters that represent, well, just about anything. These items can be used as wildcards for matching lots of stuff.

- **Caret Character** allows you to search for a caret (^) symbol, which is a special character. If you type just the caret symbol itself (^), Word thinks that you're trying to type something special, as covered later in this section.

- **Paragraph Mark** (¶) is a special character that's the same as the Enter character — what you press to end a paragraph.

- **Tab Character** is the character that moves the cursor to the next tab mark.

- **White Space** is any number of blank characters: one or more spaces, tabs, empty lines, or a combination of each one.

Choose one of the items from the list to search for that special character. When you do, a special, funky shorthand representation for that character (such as ^t for Tab) appears in the Find What box. Click the Find Next button to find that character.

- To search for the Enter key press, which marks the end of a paragraph, choose Paragraph Mark. To search for the paragraph character, ¶, choose Paragraph Character.

- Yes, you can mix special characters with plain text. For example, to find a Tab character followed by *Hunter,* you use the Special button to insert the tab character (^t on the screen), and then type **Hunter**. It looks like this:

```
^tHunter
```

- It's possible, although nerdy, to type the special characters manually. Although this method avoids using the Special menu, which can be big and baffling, it means that you need to memorize the character codes. Each one starts with the caret character, ^, and some of them are logical, such as ^p for Paragraph Mark (Enter) or ^t for Tab. Here are a few other handy shortcuts, for reference:

Paragraph mark	^p
Tab character	^t
Any character	^?
Any digit	^#
Any letter	^$
Caret character	^^
Em dash	^+
En dash	^=
Manual line break	^l
Manual page break	^m
White space	^w

Finding formatting

In its most powerful superhero mode, the Find command can scour your document for formatting information. For example, if you want to find only those instances of the word *lie* in boldface type, you can do that. Before you attempt this task, I recommend that you understand Word's formatting abilities and commands, which are covered in Part III of this book.

The formatting options you can search for are revealed to you with a click of the Format button, which appears in the Find and Replace dialog box when the More button is clicked (refer to Figure 6-3). Clicking the Format button displays a pop-up menu of Word's primary formatting commands, as shown in Figure 6-5. Choosing any item from that list displays a corresponding dialog box, from which you can choose the formatting attributes to search for.

Figure 6-5:
Various
formatting
options to
search.

<u>F</u>ont...
<u>P</u>aragraph...
<u>T</u>abs...
<u>L</u>anguage...
Fra<u>m</u>e...
<u>S</u>tyle...
<u>H</u>ighlight

Suppose that you want to find a large *goose egg* in your document. Follow these steps:

1. **Summon the Find and Replace dialog box.**

   Pressing Ctrl+F is the only sane way to do this step.

2. **Type** goose egg **in the Find What box.**

3. **If needed, click the More button to display the bottom part of the Find and Replace dialog box.**

4. **If the No Formatting button is available, then click it.**

   This button is used to clear any previous formatting attributes you may have searched for. If the button can be clicked, click it to clear out those attributes and start over afresh.

5. **Click the Format button.**

6. Choose Font from the pop-up list.

The Find Font dialog box appears, which is where you set or control various text attributes. Say that the large goose egg you're searching for is 24 points tall.

7. Choose 24 from the Size list.

Look in the upper-right corner of the Find Font dialog box.

8. Click OK.

The Font dialog box goes away, and you return to the Find and Replace dialog box.

Notice the text just beneath the Find What box. It says `Format: Font: 24 pt`. That text is telling you that Word is now geared up to find only text that is 24 points tall — about twice the normal size.

9. Click the Find Next button to find your formatted text.

If you want to search only for a format, leave the Find What text box blank (refer to Step 2). That way, you can search for formatting attributes without caring what the text reads.

✔ To find specific text attributes (bold or underline, for example), use the Find Font dialog box to choose those attributes.

✔ You can use this technique to look for specific occurrences of a font, such as Courier or Times New Roman, by selecting the font from the selection list. Scroll through the font menu to see what you can choose.

✔ You can also search for paragraph formatting, such as an indented paragraph, by choosing Paragraph rather than Font from the Format pop-up list in the Find and Replace dialog box.

✔ Yes, you can search for more than one formatting attribute at a time. Just keep choosing format options from the Format button.

✔ Word remembers your formatting options! The next time you want to search for plain text, you need to click the No Formatting button. Doing so removes the formatting options and allows you to search for text in any format. After you forget to do this a few times, you get really heated up that Word cannot find your text. Do not forget to click the No Formatting button to return Word to normal text-finding mode!

Replacing What's Been Found

The true power behind the Find command is not only its ability to find text but also to replace that text with something else. Call it alchemy, but it works! The key is the Replace command. With it, you can turn lead into gold, change Peoria into Pocatello, or Lance Beauchamp, the multimillionaire playboy and international financier, into Paula Dowd, the renowned psychic and horticulturalist. Here's how you do that, and more:

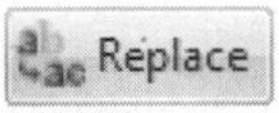

1. **On the Home tab, click the Replace command button, found in the Editing group on the far right side.**

   When the Replace command button isn't visible in the Editing group (refer to Figure 6-1), click the Editing button, and then choose the Replace command button from the pop-up group of command buttons that appears.

   Choosing the Replace command button displays the Find and Replace dialog box, as shown in Figure 6-6. This place should be familiar if you've been using the Find command. After all, finding stuff is the first part of using Find and Replace.

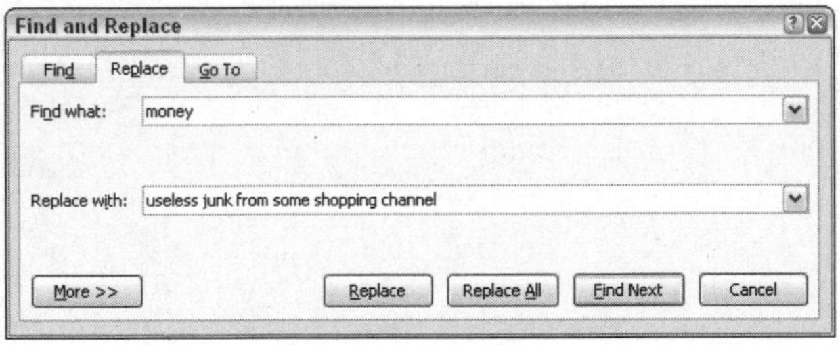

Figure 6-6:
The Replace part of the Find and Replace dialog box.

2. **In the Find What box, type the text you want to find.**

   This is the text you want to replace with something else. So, if you're finding Lance and replacing him with Paula, type **Lance**.

   Press the Tab key when you're done typing.

3. **In the Replace With box, type the text you want to use to replace the original text.**

   To continue from the example in Step 2, you type **Paula** here.

4. **Click the Find Next button.**

At this point, the Replace command works just like the Find command: Word scours your document for the text you typed in the Find What dialog box. When that text is found, you move on to Step 5; otherwise, the Replace command fails because there's nothing to replace.

5. Click the Replace button.

Word replaces the found text, highlighted on-screen, with the text typed in the Replace With box.

6. Keep replacing.

After you click the Replace button, Word immediately searches for the next instance of the text, at which point you keep repeating Step 5 until the entire document has been searched.

7. Read the summary that's displayed.

After the last bit of text is replaced, a dialog box appears and lists a summary for you. For example, it might say "Word has completed its search of the document and has made 9 replacements." Of course, the number of replacements depends on what you were searching for and yadda-yadda.

8. Click the Close button.

You're done!

- ✔ All the restrictions, options, and rules for the Find command also apply to finding and replacing text. Refer to the section "Text Happily Found," at the start of this chapter.

- ✔ The keyboard shortcut for the Replace command is Ctrl+H. Huh? Yeah, Ctrl+H. There's no way to remember it, other than if you look at the computer keyboard, you see that the F, G and H keys appear next to each other, and Ctrl+F, Ctrl+G, and Ctrl+H all summon the same dialog box. Coincidence? Honestly!

- ✔ The Replace command's dialog box also sports a More button, which can be used exactly as the More button for the Find command. See the section "The Super Find command," earlier in this chapter.

- ✔ Word may find your text in the middle of another word, such as *use* in *causes.* Oops! Click the More button and select the Find Whole Words Only option to prevent such a thing from happening.

- ✔ If you don't type anything in the Replace With box, Word replaces your text with *nothing*! It's wanton destruction!

- ✔ Speaking of wanton destruction, the Undo command restores your document to its preceding condition if you foul up the Replace operation. See Chapter 5 for more information.

The miracle of the Replace All button

The steps in the previous section work well to find and replace tidbits of text to and fro in your document. But it can often be tedious to keep pressing that Replace button over and over. That's why the Replace command's dialog box sports a handy Replace All button.

The Replace All button directs the Replace command to find all instances of the Find What text and — without question — replace it with the Replace With text. To use this button, simply click the Replace All button in Step 5 in the previous section. Then skip to Step 8.

Finding and replacing formatting

Just as the Find command can search for text with specific formatting, you can use the Replace command to replace text and apply formatting or to replace one type of formatting with another. Needless to say, this process can be very tricky: Not only do I recommend that you be familiar with Word's formatting commands, but you should also be well-practiced in using the Replace command.

Suppose that you want to replace all instances of underlined text with italic. Underlined text reeks so much of typewriter, and that's just too 20th century for these modern times. By replacing underline with italic, you're searching for one text format and replacing it with another; you're not searching for text at all. So, be careful. Do this:

1. **Press Ctrl+H to summon the Find and Replace dialog box.**

2. **Click the More button, if necessary, to display the full dialog box.**

3. **Click to select any text in the Find What box, and then delete that text by pressing the Backspace key.**

4. **Click the Format button and choose Font from the pop-up menu that appears.**

    The Find Font dialog box appears.

5. **In the Find Font dialog box, choose the single underline graphic from the Underline style drop-down list.**

6. **Click OK.**

    Back in the Find and Replace dialog box, the text Format: Underline should appear before the Find What box.

7. **Click to select any text in the Replace With box and press Backspace to delete that text.**

8. **Choose Font from the Format button's pop-up list.**

9. **In the Find Font dialog box, choose Italic from the Font Style list.**

10. **Click OK to close the Find Font dialog box.**

    Below the Replace With box, it should say `Format: Font: Italic`.

11. **Click the Replace All button.**

    Word scours your document and replaces any underlined text with italic.

12. **Click OK when the find-and-replace is done.**

As long as you set things up carefully, searching and replacing text formatting is a quick and easy way to spiff up a boring document.

✔ To replace one format with another, such as underline with italic, be sure to leave the Find What and Replace With text boxes empty. That way, only the text formatting is replaced.

✔ An easier way to update formatting in a document is to use and apply *styles*. Refer to Chapter 16 for details.

✔ Don't forget about the No Formatting button! You need to click it if you want to change the formats or replace text without paying attention to formats.

Chapter 7

Text Blocks, Stumbling Blocks, Writer's Blocks

In This Chapter

▶ Understanding text blocks

▶ Marking a block with the keyboard

▶ Selecting text with the mouse

▶ Using the F8 key to mark text

▶ Un-blocking text

▶ Copying and moving blocks of text

▶ Pasting text in various ways

▶ Working with collect and paste and the Clipboard

*W*riting involves blocks. This began with the ancient Egyptians, who perfected writing on blocks, quite literally. Entire epochs were presented on a wall of stone. When the ancient Egyptian editor arrived, she would point out problems in the wall, so the writer would have to replace some blocks of text or move other blocks around. And if the writer hesitated, the editor would hit him over the head with what would then become the *writer's block*. It was quite an ingenious system.

As writing moved to paper, working with blocks became obtuse. Thanks to the invention of scissors and rubber cement, it was possible to cut and paste blocks of text, but the result was sloppy. Often the writer would play with the rubber cement, rolling it into tiny balls to flick at the back of the editor's head when she wasn't looking. The system was quite awkward.

Only with the dawn of the word processor has working with blocks returned to its Stone Age glory. Word lets you rope off any random chunk of text — a word, sentence, paragraph, or more — and mark that chunk as a block. You can then do amazing things with that block of text, things that are covered in this chapter. Yes, it's time once again to play with blocks.

What Is a Block of Text?

A *block* of text is simply some portion of text in your document, from a single character to the entire document. The block has a beginning and an end, and the block itself consists of all the text between.

You create a block by selecting text. *Selecting* is done by using the keyboard, the mouse, or various other text-selection techniques covered in this chapter.

On the screen, the block appears highlighted, as shown in Figure 7-1.

By marking off text as a block, you can perform certain actions, or use various Word commands, that affect only the text in that block. Or, you can copy or move the block of text. It's all covered later in this chapter as well as in other places throughout this book. Indeed, blocks are handy things to use in a word processor.

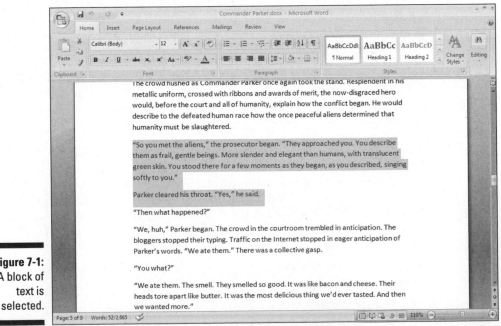

Figure 7-1:
A block of text is selected.

✔ A block of text in Word includes all the letters and characters *and* the text formatting.

✔ Graphics and other nontext elements can also be selected as a block. In fact, you can select graphics along with text in the same block.

✔ When the status bar is displaying a word count, the number of words selected in the block of text is displayed, next to the total number of words in the document. (Refer to Figure 7-1.)

✔ When the Find command locates text, that text is selected as a block. Refer to Chapter 6 for more information on the Find command.

✔ Selecting text also means selecting characters such as tabs and the Enter key press that marks the end of a paragraph. Fortunately, Word shows the Enter "character" as an extra blank space at the end of a paragraph. When you select that blank, you select the whole paragraph as a paragraph. To avoid selecting the Enter character, don't select the blank space at the end of a paragraph.

Marking a Chunk of Text As a Block

Word offers you many ways to *mark* text as a block in your document. This section mulls over the possibilities.

Using the keyboard to select text

The secret to using the keyboard to select text is the Shift key. By holding down the Shift key, you can use the standard keyboard commands that move the insertion pointer to select blocks of text. Table 7-1 has some suggestions for you.

Table 7-1	Shifty Selection Wizardry
To Do This	*Press This*
Select a character at a time to the right of the insertion pointer	Shift+→_
Select a character at a time to the left of the insertion pointer	Shift+←
Select a block of text from the insertion pointer to the end of the line	Shift+End
Select a block of text from the insertion pointer to the beginning of the line	Shift+Home
Select a block of text from the insertion pointer to a line above	Shift+↑
Select a block of text from the insertion pointer to a line below	Shift+↓

Out, damn Mini Toolbar!

When the mouse is used to select text, Word displays the Mini Toolbar, looking like this:

The *Mini Toolbar* is a *palette* of common formatting commands that Word supposes you need for a quick-format on that selected text. After initially disliking the Mini Toolbar, I've grown to enjoy it. But I recognize that you may find the Mini Toolbar more annoying than useful. If so, you can suppress its display. Follow these steps:

1. **Choose the Word Options command from the Office Button menu.**

2. **Choose Popular from the list on the left side of the Word Options window.**

3. **Remove the check mark by the item Show Mini Toolbar on Selection.**

4. **Click OK.**

If you would rather not eternally banish the Mini Toolbar, note that it hides itself whenever you move the mouse beyond the selected chunk of text.

You can use any keyboard cursor-movement command (they're listed in Chapter 4), but I recommend using this Shift key method for selecting only small chunks of text. Otherwise, you may end up tying your fingers into knots!

Either Shift key works, although I prefer to use the left Shift key and then work the arrow keys on the right side of the keyboard.

Marking a block with the mouse

Forget cheese. The computer mouse was born to mark text, by selecting vast swaths of words with a wide sweep of your hand, by clicking a number of times, or by using the old point-and-stretch routine. Mickey may rule a kingdom, but your computer mouse rules over selecting text in your computer.

Dragging over text to select it

The most common way to select text is by using the computer mouse thus:

1. **Point the mouse at the start of the text block.**

2. **Drag the mouse over the text you want to select.**

   As you drag, text becomes highlighted, or selected. (Refer to Figure 7-1.)

3. **Release the mouse — stop the dragging — to mark the end of the block.**

You can use these steps to select any old size of block in your document.

✔ This selection technique works best when you use the mouse to drag over only the text you can actually see on the screen. When you try to select text beyond what you see on the screen, you have to select and scroll — which can be unwieldy; the mouse scrolls the text up and down quickly, and, well, things get out of hand.

✔ When you find yourself becoming frustrated over not selecting all or part of a word, refer to the later sidebar "Would you rather select text by letter or by word?"

Selecting text by clicking the mouse

A speedy way to select specific sizes of chunks of text is to match the power of the mouse with the dexterity of your index finger. Table 7-2 explains some clicking-and-selecting techniques worth noting.

Table 7-2	Mouse Selection Arcana
To Select This Chunk of Text	**Click the Mouse Thus**
A single word	Point at the word with your mouse and double-click.
A line	Move the mouse pointer into the left margin beside the line you want to select. The mouse pointer changes to a northeastward-pointing arrow. Click the mouse to select a line of text, or drag the mouse up or down to select several lines.
A sentence	Point the mouse at the sentence and Ctrl+click. (Press the Ctrl key and click the mouse.)
A paragraph	Point the mouse somewhere in the paragraph's midst and triple-click.

The old poke-and-point method of selecting

Here's the best way to select a chunk of text of any size, especially when that chunk of text is larger than what you can see on the screen at once:

1. **Click the mouse to set the insertion pointer where you want the block to start — the anchor point.**

2. **Scroll through your document using the scroll bar.**

   You must use the scroll bar to scroll through your document. If you use the cursor-movement keys, you reposition the insertion pointer, which isn't what you want.

3. **To mark the end of the block, press and hold the Shift key and click the mouse where you want the block to end.**

   The text from the insertion pointer to wherever you clicked the mouse is selected as a block.

Using the F8 key to mark a block

If you can remember that the F8 key on the computer's keyboard can be used to mark text, you can exploit one of the seldom-used and most powerful text-marking tools that Word has to offer.

Yes, wacky as it sounds, the F8 key is used to mark a block of text. Pressing the F8 key once enters *extended selection* mode. That's where Word drops anchor at the insertion pointer's location and then lets you use either the mouse or the cursor keys to select text. In fact, you cannot do anything but select text in extended selection mode (unless you press the Esc key to exit that mode).

Don't let the F8 key weirdness boggle you. Instead, consider these steps the next time you need to mark a block of text:

1. **Position the insertion pointer at the start of the block of text.**

2. **Press the F8 key.**

   The F8 key drops anchor and marks one end of the block.

3. **Use the keyboard's cursor keys to select the block of text.**

   The cursor-navigation keys are discussed in Chapter 4.

   You can also press a letter key to select text up to and including that letter. If you press N, you select all text up to and including the next *N* in your document. Nice. Nifty. Neat-o.

   Word highlights text from the point where you dropped anchor with F8 to wherever you move the insertion pointer.

4. **Do something with the selected block of text.**

   Word remains in extended selection mode until you actually do something with the block.

Doing something with a block of text is covered in the second half of this chapter.

To cancel the extended selection, press the Esc key. That ends extended selection mode, but still keeps the block of text marked.

✔ You can use the mouse and the F8 key to get really fancy. Position the cursor at either end of the block you want to mark, and press the F8 key. Then position the mouse cursor at the other end of the block and press the left mouse button. Everything from there to there is marked.

- After pressing the F8 key, you can use the Find command to locate a specific bit of text. Word marks all text between the spot where F8 was pressed (the anchor) and the text that the Find command locates.

- Pressing the F8 key twice selects the current word (the one the insertion pointer is blinking inside of).

- Pressing the F8 key thrice (three times) selects the current sentence.

- Pressing the F8 key four times selects the current paragraph as a block of text.

- Pressing the F8 key five times selects the entire document, from top to bottom.

- No matter how many times you press F8, be aware that it always drops anchor. So, pressing F8 once or five times means that you're still in extended selection mode. Do something with the block or press Esc to cancel that mode.

Blocking the whole dang-doodle document

The biggest block you can mark is the entire document. Word has a specific command to do that, to select all the text in a document: From the Home tab, locate the Editing area. (Click the Editing button when the entire Editing area isn't visible.) Then choose Select➪Select All. Instantly, the entire document is marked as a single block-o-text.

From the keyboard, you can use Ctrl+A to select all of a document, or just press the F8 key five times. Or, you can even use the obscure Ctrl+5 (the 5 on the numeric keypad) key combo.

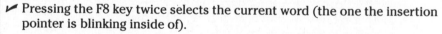

Would you rather select text by letter or by word?

When you're selecting more than a single word, the mouse tends to grab text a full word at a time. If you want Word to select text by characters rather than by words (which is what I prefer), follow these steps:

1. **Choose Word Options from the Office Button menu.**

2. **Choose Advanced from the list on the left side of the Applications Settings window.**

3. **In the Editing Options section (on the right), remove the check mark by the item labeled When Selecting Automatically Select Entire Word.**

4. **Click OK.**

Deselecting a Block

Word treats all text marked in a block the same, by applying the same formatting commands to that text, moving the text, searching within the block, and so on. But when you mark a block of text and change your mind, you must unmark, or deselect, the text. Here are a few handy ways to do that:

✓ **Move the insertion pointer.** It doesn't matter how you move the insertion pointer, with the keyboard or with the mouse — doing so unhighlights the block. Note that this trick does not exit the F8 key's extended selection mode.

✓ **Press the Esc key and then the ← key.** This method works to end extended selection mode.

✓ **Shift+F5.** The Shift+F5 key is the Go Back command (see Chapter 4), but it also deselects a block of text *and* returns you to the text you were editing before making the selection.

You've Marked the Block — Now What?

You can block punches, block hats, block and tackle, play with building blocks and engine blocks, take nerve blocks, suffer from mental blocks, jog for blocks and, naturally, block text. But what can be done with those marked blocks of text?

The primary thing you can do with blocks of text is to copy or move them. Like using search and replace, rearranging your text with blocks is one of the true blessings of a word processor. Call it a typewriter-killing feature.

The subject of copying, moving, and duplicating blocks of text is covered in this section. If you're used to copying, cutting, and pasting in Windows, doing the same with blocks in Word will be easy for you. Beyond that, you can do the following things with a block of text in Word:

✓ Delete the block with the Delete or Backspace keys. (See Chapter 5 for more information on deleting text.)

✓ Use the Search command, or Search and Replace, exclusively within the block of text. See Chapter 6.

✓ Proof the block, by reviewing your spelling and grammar goofs, as covered in Chapter 8.

✓ Print the block. (See Chapter 10.)

✓ Format the block. The various formatting commands are covered in Part III of this book.

The command you use affects only the text within that block.

Copying a block

After a block is marked, you can copy it into another part of your document, to duplicate the text. The original block remains untouched by this operation. Follow these steps to copy a block of text from one place to another:

1. **Mark the block.**

   Detailed instructions about doing this task are offered in the first part of this chapter.

2. **From the Home tab, choose the Copy tool from the Clipboard area.**

   There's no visual clue that the text has been copied; it remains selected.

3. **Move the insertion pointer to the position where you want to copy the block.**

   Don't worry if there's no room there! Word inserts the block into your text.

4. **Choose the Paste tool from the Clipboard area.**

   The block appears. (See the later section "Options for pasting text" to find out what to do about the wee li'l clipboard icon that appears by the pasted text.)

The block of text you copy is inserted into your text just as though you had typed it there by yourself.

- The shortcut key for copying in Word (and Windows) is Ctrl+C.

- The shortcut key for pasting is Ctrl+V.

- After you copy a block, you can paste it into your document a second time. That's because whenever a block of text is cut or copied, Word remembers it. You can yank that block into your document again at any time — sort of like pasting text again after it has already been pasted in. You use Ctrl+V, the Paste shortcut. Pasting text again simply pastes down a second copy of the block, spit-spot (as Mary Poppins would say).

- You can paste the block into another document you're working on, or even into another application. (This is a Windows trick, which most good books on Windows discuss.)

- Refer to the section "The Miracle of Collect-and-Paste," near the end of this chapter, for more copy and paste choices.

Moving a block

To move a block of text, you select the text and then *cut* and paste. This is almost exactly the same as copying a block, described in the previous section, although in Step 2 you choose the Cut tool rather than the Copy tool. Otherwise, all the steps are the same.

Don't be alarmed when the block of text vanishes! That's cutting in action; the block of text is being *moved*, not copied. You see the block of text again when you paste.

✔ The keyboard shortcut for the Cut command is Ctrl+X.

✔ Don't panic! If you screw up, remember that the Ctrl+Z Undo shortcut undoes a block move.

Options for pasting text

When you paste text in Word, the Paste Options icon appears near the end of the pasted block of text, as shown in the margin. Let it not annoy you! That button allows you to select formatting for the pasted block because occasionally the block may contain formatting that, well, looks very ugly after it's pasted in.

Using the Paste Options icon is utterly optional. In fact, you can continue typing or working in Word, and the icon bows out, fading away like some nebbish who boldly asked a power blonde to go out with him and she utterly failed to recognize his existence. Like that. Meanwhile, to use the Paste Options icon to adjust pasted text formatting in Word, comply with these steps:

1. **Point the mouse at the Paste Options icon.**

   The icon turns into a "button," with a downward-pointing triangle on one end. If you've been using Windows for any length of time, you'll recognize this as a drop-down menu gizmo.

2. **Click the downward-pointing triangle.**

   A menu appears, from which you can select various formatting options (see Figure 7-2).

Figure 7-2:
Various
Paste
command
formatting
options.

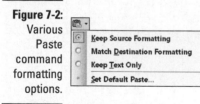

Here's a quick summary of the options available:

- ✔ **Keep Source Formatting:** The formatting is fine; don't do a thing.

- ✔ **Match Destination Formatting:** Reformat the pasted block so that it looks like the text it's being pasted into.

- ✔ **Keep Text Only:** Just paste in the text — no formatting.

- ✔ **Set Default Paste:** Opens the Word Options dialog box where you can, in the Cut, Copy and Paste section, permanently set various pasting options in Word.

Choose an option to match the formatting you want.

Special pasting

Pasting is simple, although trying to figure how the V in Ctrl+V means "paste" can boggle the mind. Regardless, when you know the format of the thing you're pasting or you need to use a specific format, you can employ the Paste Special command: Click the bottom of the Paste button to display a menu, shown in Figure 7-3, and choose Paste Special from the list. The Paste Special dialog box appears.

Figure 7-3:
Using the
Paste
Special
command.

Paste

Paste
Paste Special...
Paste as Hyperlink

The Paste Special dialog box lists options for pasting text, graphics, or whatever was last copied or cut; the number of options depends on what's waiting to be pasted. For example, you can copy a chunk of an Excel spreadsheet and paste it into your Word document as a spreadsheet, table, picture, text, or what-have-you.

I often use Paste Special to paste in text from a Web page but without all the HTML-blah-blah formatting. I choose the Unformatted Text option from the Paste Special dialog box and click OK, and the text is pasted into Word as plain text and not as some Web object doodad.

Copying or moving a block with the mouse

When you have to move a block only a short distance, you can use the mouse to drag-move or drag-copy the block. This feature is handy, but usually works best if you're moving or copying between two locations that you can see right on the screen. Otherwise, you're scrolling your document with the mouse while you're playing with blocks, which is like trying to grab an angry snake.

 To move any selected block of text with the mouse, just drag the block: Point the mouse cursor anywhere in the blocked text, and then drag the block to its new location. Notice how the mouse pointer changes, as shown in the margin. That means you're moving the text.

Copying a block with the mouse works just like moving the block, except that you press the Ctrl key as you drag. When you do that, a plus sign appears in the mouse pointer (see the margin). That's your sign that the block is being copied and not just moved.

✔ The Paste Options icon appears after you've "dropped" the chunk of text. Refer to the preceding section for more information on the Paste Options icon.

✔ When you drag a block of text with the mouse, you're not copying it to the Clipboard. You cannot use the Paste (Ctrl+V) command to paste in the block again.

 ✔ A *linked copy* is created by dragging a selected block of text with the mouse and holding down *both* the Shift and Ctrl keys. When you release the mouse button, the copied block plops down into your document with a dark highlight. That's your clue that the copy is linked to the original; changes in the original are reflected in the copy and vice versa.

Copying and moving with the F2 key

Another way to move or copy a block is to press the F2 key after the block is selected. As long as you can remember the F2 key, moving or copying a block by using this technique can be very handy, as explained here:

1. **Select a block of text.**

2. **Press the F2 key.**

   Notice how the status bar says "Move to where?"

3. **Move the insertion pointer to where you want to paste.**

   Use the cursor keys or scroll with the mouse. Wherever you move the insertion pointer is where the text is pasted.

4. **Press Enter to paste the text.**

   And the block is moved.

To copy rather than move a block, press Shift+F2 in Step 2. The status bar says "Copy to where?"

The Miracle of Collect-and-Paste

When you copy or paste a block of text, that block is placed into a storage place called the *Clipboard*. The block of text remains on the Clipboard until it's replaced by something else — another block of text or a graphic or anything cut or copied in Windows. (The Clipboard is a Windows thing, which is how you can copy and paste between Windows applications.)

In Word, however, the Clipboard can hold more than one thing at time. This allows you to copy, copy, copy, and then use a special Clipboard view pane to selectively paste text back into your document. They call it "collect and paste," and I firmly believe that this is a handy and welcome feature — but one that also takes a bit of explaining.

Looking at the Clipboard

Word lets you see the contents of the Clipboard, to view the last several items that have been cut or copied and, optionally, paste those items back into your document.

To view the Clipboard task pane (its official name), click the *thing* in the lower-right corner of the Clipboard group on the Home tab, right next to the word *Clipboard*. The Clipboard task pane then appears in the writing part of Word's window, perhaps looking similar to what's shown in Figure 7-4.

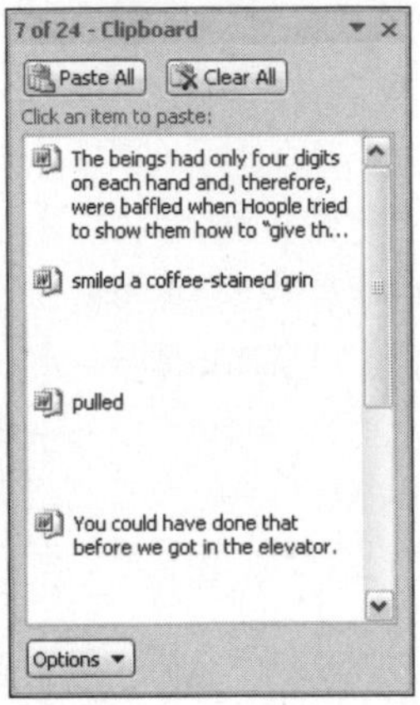

Figure 7-4:
The Clipboard task pane.

The scrolling list contains the last several items you've copied, not only from Word but from other programs as well.

Pasting items from the Clipboard task pane is covered in the next section.

✔ You can use the Copy command multiple times in a row to collect text when the Clipboard task pane is visible.

✔ The Clipboard can hold only 24 items. If any more than that is copied or cut, the older items in the list are "pushed off" to make room for the new ones. The current number of items is shown at the top of the task pane.

✔ Other programs in Microsoft Office (Excel and PowerPoint, for example) also share this collect-and-paste feature.

✔ You can close the task pane when you're done with collect and paste: Click the X in the upper-right corner of the task pane window.

Pasting from the Clipboard task pane

To paste any collected text from the Clipboard view pane into your document, simply click the mouse on that chunk of text. The text is copied from the Clipboard and inserted into your document at the insertion pointer's location, just as though you typed it yourself.

After pasting, the Paste Options icon appears next to the pasted text. Refer to the section "Options for pasting text," earlier in this chapter, to find out what do to with that thing.

✔ You can click the Paste All button to paste each and every item from the Clipboard into your document.

✔ Click only once! When you double-click, you insert *two* copies of the text.

Cleansing the Clipboard task pane

You're free to clean up Word's Clipboard whenever the Clipboard task pane is visible. To remove a single item, point the mouse at that item and click the downward-pointing triangle to the right of the item. Choose Delete from the shortcut menu, and that one item is zapped from the Clipboard.

To whack all the items on the Clipboard, click the Clear All button at the top of the Clipboard task pane. I do this if I plan on collecting several items to be pasted at once elsewhere. For example, I click Clear All and then go out and copy, copy, copy. Then I move the insertion pointer to where I want everything pasted and click the Paste All button — and I'm done.

Note that you cannot undo any clearing or deleting that's done in the Clipboard task pane. Be careful!

Chapter 8

Proofing Your Document (Spelling and Grammar)

In This Chapter

▶ Understanding document proofing

▶ Dealing with typos and spelling errors

▶ Adding or ignoring unknown words

▶ Correcting words automatically

▶ Fixing grammatical boo-boos

▶ Reviewing your document quickly

▶ Finding synonyms with the thesaurus

▶ Using the reference tools

▶ Counting your words

I don't give a damn for a man that can only spell a word one way.

— Mark Twain

I turn to no greater source on the subject of spelling and grammar than my favorite American author, Mark Twain. His thoughts on the topic are abundant.

Twain once described spelling in the English language as "drunken." Specifically, Twain blamed the alphabet. Me? I peg the problem on vowels, but I mostly blame all the foreign words in English. Come to think of it, about 60 percent of English is composed of foreign words. Just pluck them out and the language would be perfect! But I digress.

This chapter covers Word's amazing proofing tools. These include the spell checker, the grammar-checking thing, plus other amazing tools and features to help you get just the right word, use it, and spell it correctly.

Hun Dewing Yore Mist Aches

As the title of this section suggests, it may very well be true that Word's document proofing tools know an impressive number of words and have mastered countless grammatical rules, and they may do their darndest to recognize *context,* but they still often fail. So, just because it appears that your document contains no errors doesn't mean that everything is perfect. There's no better way to proof a document than to read it with human eyes. (My editor enthusiastically agrees!)

Check Your Spelling

Word's built-in spell checker works the second you start typing. Like a hungry leopard, the spell checker is ready to pounce on its unsuspecting prey, the misspelled word or typo!

Spelling is corrected in two ways in Word. The most obvious way is that an unrecognized word is underlined with a red zigzag. More subtly, the offending word is corrected for you automatically. That feature, AutoCorrect, is covered later in this chapter.

The red zigzag of shame

Word has an internal library consisting of tens of thousands of words, all spelled correctly. When you type a word that doesn't exist in the library (yeah, looking up words is one thing the computer can do quickly), the word that's typed is marked as suspect. It appears underlined with a red zigzag, as shown in Figure 8-1. What to do, what to do?

My advice: Keep typing. Don't let the "red zigzag of a failed elementary education" perturb you. It's more important to get your thoughts up on the screen than to stop and fuss over inevitable typos.

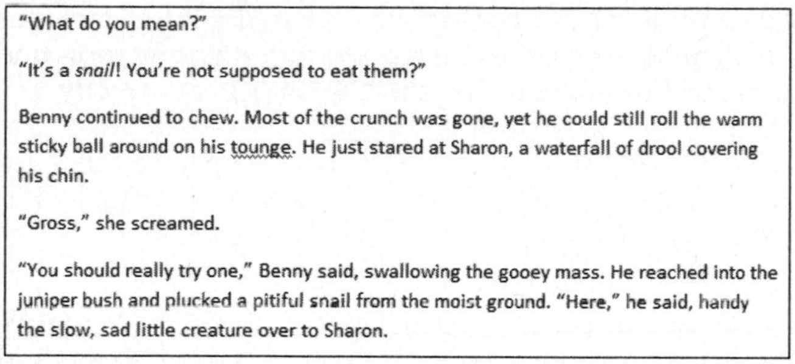

"What do you mean?"

"It's a *snail*! You're not supposed to eat them?"

Benny continued to chew. Most of the crunch was gone, yet he could still roll the warm sticky ball around on his <u>tounge</u>. He just stared at Sharon, a waterfall of drool covering his chin.

"Gross," she screamed.

"You should really try one," Benny said, swallowing the gooey mass. He reached into the juniper bush and plucked a pitiful snail from the moist ground. "Here," he said, handy the slow, sad little creature over to Sharon.

Figure 8-1:
The word *tounge* is flagged as misspelled.

When you're ready, say, during one of those inevitable pauses that takes place as you write, go back and fix your spelling errors. Here's what to do:

1. **Locate the misspelled word.**

   Look for the red zigzag underline.

2. **Right-click the misspelled word.**

   Up pops a shortcut menu and the Mini Toolbar, similar to what's shown in Figure 8-2.

3. **Choose from the list the word you intended to type.**

   In Figure 8-2, the word *tongue* fits the bill. Click that word and it's automatically inserted into your document, to replace the spurious word.

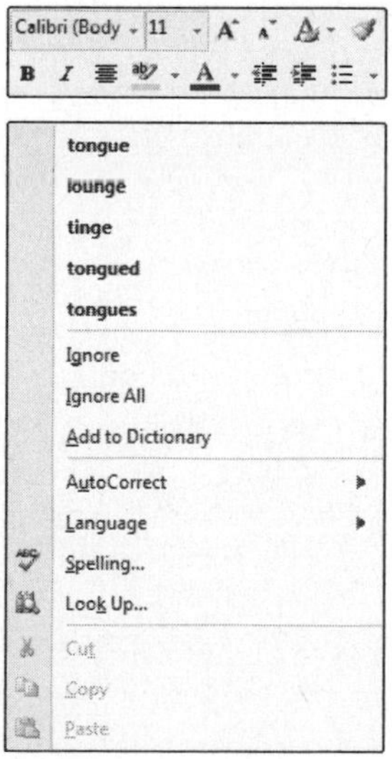

Calibri (Body) · 11 · A˙ A˙ A· ✦

B · I · ☰ · ᵃᵇ✓ · A · ⁼ ⁼ ⁼ ⁚≡ ·

tongue
lounge
tinge
tongued
tongues
Ignore
Ignore All
Add to Dictionary
AutoCorrect ▶
Language ▶
Spelling...
Look Up...
Cut
Copy
Paste

Figure 8-2:
Choose the properly spelled word from the list.

If the word you intended to type isn't on the list, don't fret. Word isn't *that* smart. You may have to use a real dictionary or take another stab at spelling the word phonetically and then correct it again.

✔ The Mini Toolbar, shown at the top of the menu in Figure 8-2, is used for quick formatting. It's the same Mini Toolbar that appears when you select text (see Chapter 7); it also appears whenever you right-click text, as is done with a spell-check correction.

✔ Word turns off automatic proofing when your document grows over a specific size. For example, on my computer, when the document is more than 100 pages long, automatic spell checking is disabled. A warning appears to alert you when this happens. Note that you can still manually spell-check, which is covered in the section "Proofing Your Entire Document at Once," later in this chapter.

What to do when the spell checker stupidly assumes that a word is misspelled but in fact it isn't

Occasionally, Word's spell checker bumps into a word it doesn't recognize, such as your last name or perhaps your city. Word dutifully casts doubt on the word, by underlining it with the notorious red zigzag. Yes, this is one of those cases where the computer is wrong.

When a word is flagged as incorrectly spelled or as a typo, you can use two commands, both of which are found on the pop-up menu when you right-click the word (refer to Figure 8-2). The commands are Ignore All and Add to Dictionary.

Ignore All: Select this command when the word is properly spelled and you don't want Word to keep flagging it as misspelled.

For example, in your science fiction short story, there's a character named Zadlux. Word believes it to be a spelling error, but you (and all the people of the soon-to-be-conquered planet Drebulon) know better. After you choose the Ignore All command, all instances of the suspect word are cheerfully ignored, but only in that one document.

Add to Dictionary: This command adds words to the list that Word refers to so that the word becomes part of the internal Spelled Correctly library.

For example, I once lived on Pilchuck Avenue, which Word thinks is a misspelling of the word *Paycheck*. If only. So, when I right-click the incorrectly flagged word, I choose the Add to Dictionary command. Presto — the word *Pilchuck* is added to Word's internal dictionary. I'll never have to spell-check that work again.

✔ If the word looks correct but is red-wiggly-underlined anyway, it could be a repeated word. Those are flagged as misspelled by Word, so you can either choose to delete the repeated word or just ignore it.

✔ Word ignores certain types of words. For example, words with numbers in them or words written in all capitals, which are usually abbreviations. For example, Pic6 is ignored because it has a 6 in it. The word NYEP is ignored because it's in all caps.

✔ You can adjust how spell-checking works, especially if you feel that it's being too picky. See the section "Customizing Proofing Options," later in this chapter.

Undoing an Ignore All command

Choosing the Ignore All command means that all instances of a given misspelled word or typo are ignored in your document. This holds true even when you save that document and open it again later. So, if you make a mistake and would rather have the ignored word regarded once more, do this:

1. **Click the Word Options button on the Office Button menu.**

   The Word Options window appears.

2. **Choose Proofing on the left side of the window.**

3. **Scroll down the right side of the window (if necessary) until you can see the Recheck Document button; click that button.**

   A warning dialog box appears, reminding you of what you're about to do.

4. **Click the Yes button.**

   Everything you've told Word to ignore while proofing your document is now ignored. It's the ignore-ignore command!

5. **Click the OK button to return to your document.**

The 25 most frequently misspelled words

a lot	atheist	grammar	maneuver	ridiculous
accidentally	collectible	gauge	no one	separate
acquire	consensus	independent	occurrence	supersede
amateur	definite	kernel	realize	their
argument	embarrass	liaison	receive	weird

Note that following these steps causes all ignored words, as well as grammatical errors you've chosen to ignore, to become visible once again. There's no way to undo this command.

These steps affect only the current document. The Ignore All command affects only the current document.

Un-adding words to the dictionary

When you choose the Add to Dictionary command, the given word is placed into something called the Custom dictionary. Recognizing that people may change their minds, Word allows you to edit the Custom dictionary, to remove words you may have added accidentally.

To remove unwanted words from the Custom dictionary, follow these steps:

1. **Click the Word Options button in the Office Button menu.**

   The Word Options window shows up.

2. **From the left side of the window, choose Proofing.**

3. **Click the button labeled Custom Dictionaries.**

   The Custom Dictionaries dialog box appears.

4. **Select the CUSTOM.DIC dictionary file.**

   It's probably the only item in the list.

5. **Click the button labeled Edit Word List.**

   You see a scrolling list of words you've added to the Custom dictionary.

6. **Find and select the word you want to remove from the dictionary.**

   The word is selected by clicking it once.

7. **Click the Delete button.**

8. **Repeat Steps 6 and 7 to, optionally, remove more words.**

9. **Click the OK button when you're done editing the dictionary.**

   Close any other open windows.

Instant Text-Fixin' with AutoCorrect

Some of your typos and spelling errors will never be graced with the red zigzag. That's because Word quickly fixes hundreds of common typos and spelling errors on the fly. It's done by the AutoCorrect feature, and you really have to be quick to see it.

AutoCorrect in action

There's nothing to using AutoCorrect; it happens automatically. In Word, try to type the word *mispell*. You cannot! Word uses AutoCorrect, and suddenly you see *misspell*.

Most of the commonly misspelled words can be found in AutoCorrect's repertoire: *beleive*, *suposed*, *recieve*, and so on. Try a few. See whether you can baffle Word!

In addition to fixing spelling errors, AutoCorrect helps you enter special characters. For example, type **(C)** and AutoCorrect properly inserts the (c) Copyright symbol. Ditto for **(TM)** for Trademark. Typing –> is translated into an arrow, and even **:)** becomes a happy face.

Beyond spelling, AutoCorrect fixes some common punctuation. It automatically capitalizes the first letter of a sentence. AutoCorrect capitalizes *I* when you forget to, it properly capitalizes the names of days, fixes the iNVERSE cAPS lOCK pROBLEM, plus fixes other common typos.

Do your own AutoCorrect entries

One of the joys of AutoCorrect is that you can add your own commonly misspelled words to its list. For example, I'm always goofing up the word *brief*. I before E? E before I? Never mind! I need to fix the spelling error only once by placing my typo and the proper spelling into AutoCorrect's repertoire. This is cinchy:

1. **Right-click the misspelled word.**

   Normally, you choose the proper spelling from the list. But that fixes the word only once. Instead:

2. **Click the AutoCorrect item.**

   Up pops a submenu containing various corrections, as shown in Figure 8-3.

3. **Choose the properly spelled word from the AutoCorrect submenu.**

   The word is added to the AutoCorrect list, and, as a special favor, Word corrects the word in your text as well.

Whenever your typo is encountered, Word automatically corrects it for you. But you must remember to use the AutoCorrect item from the spell-check-thingy pop-up menu on your first sighting of the misspelled word rather than just choose the corrected word from the list.

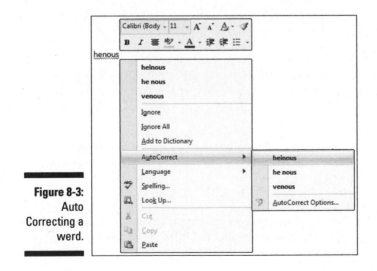

Figure 8-3: Auto Correcting a werd.

If possible, try to add only lowercase words with AutoCorrect. When you add a word with an initial capital letter, such as *Werd*, AutoCorrect replaces only words with an initial capital letter. When you use AutoCorrect on a word that's all lowercase, it's fixed every time.

Undoing an AutoCorrect correction

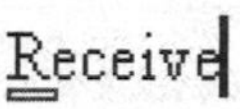

Receive

You can reverse AutoCorrect instant changes, but only when you're quick. The secret is to press Backspace or Ctrl+Z (the Undo command) immediately after AutoCorrect makes its correction. When you do that, you see a blue rectangle under the first letter of the still-corrected word, as shown in the margin.

Point the mouse at the rectangle to see the AutoCorrect Options icon. Clicking the downward-pointing arrow on the icon displays some choices, as shown in Figure 8-4 and explained here:

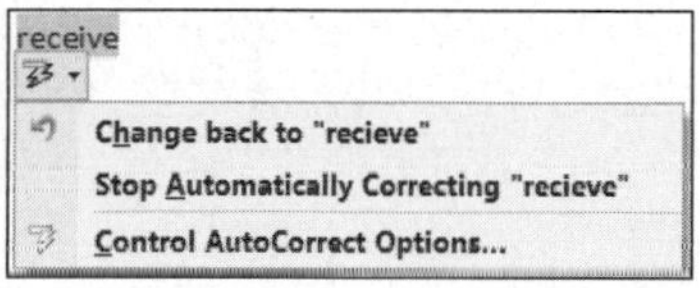

Figure 8-4:
Adjusting
an Auto
Correction.

receive
↺ ▾
↺ Change back to "recieve"
Stop Automatically Correcting "recieve"
⟲ Control AutoCorrect Options...

- ✔ **Change Back to "*whatever*":** Choose this option to undo the AutoCorrection.

- ✔ **Stop Automatically Correcting "*whatever*":** Choose this option to remove the word from the AutoCorrect library so that it's not corrected automatically again. (But it may still be flagged as incorrect by the spell checker.)

- ✔ **Control AutoCorrect Options:** This item displays the AutoCorrect dialog box, which is used to customize various AutoCorrect settings and edit or create new entries in the AutoCorrect library. Refer to the section "Customizing Proofing Options," later in this chapter.

You don't have to go with the AutoCorrection. If you don't like the change, press Ctrl+Z to undo or use Backspace to fix the AutoCorrect option. Clicking the blue rectangle is optional.

Grammar Be Good

If spelling is drunken, grammar is a hallucination. Oh, I could rant on this for hours. Suffice it to say, no matter what the grammarians think, English is not Latin. It can't be. Latin usually has one, very proper way to say something. English has many ways and many words with which to express the same thought. That's why English is so poetic. That's why so-called English grammar has so many exceptions that it's silly to make any rules.

Regardless of what I think, Word does come with a grammar checker, and it does, at times, underline suspicious words or phrases with an angry green zigzag. It's your clue that you've somehow offended Word's sense of grammatical justice.

As with a spelling error, right-click the green-underlined text. The pop-up menu that appears either explains why the sentence is wrong or offers an alternative sentence that you can choose. There's also an option to ignore the error, which I find myself using quite a bit.

- ✔ When you select About This Sentence from the pop-up menu, the Office Help system attempts to explain which part of the *English Language Book of Rules* you offended.

- ✔ Sometimes you may be puzzled about what the grammar checker finds wrong. Don't give up! Always check your entire sentence for a potential error. For example, the grammar checker may suggest *had* in place of *have*. Chances are, *have* is correct but some other word in the sentence has an unwanted *s* attached.

- ✔ It's possible to customize or even turn off grammar checking. Refer to the section "Customizing Proofing Options," later in this document.

Proofing Your Entire Document at Once

Before the days of on-the-fly spell checking, you proofed your document by entering a special spell-check mode. In spell-check mode, the computer would read your document, from top to bottom, and alert you to any goofy words it found. You can still use this type of proofing, which some folks find easier to handle and less disruptive than automatic spell checking. Here's how it's done:

1. **Click the Review tab.**

2. **In the Proofing group, click the Spelling & Grammar button.**

   The Spelling and Grammar dialog box appears, as shown in Figure 8-5. It displays a chunk of your document at a time, with each chunk containing a spelling or grammar error.

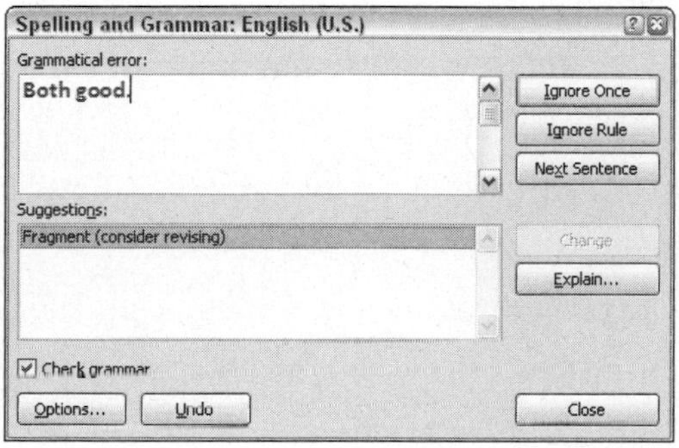

Figure 8-5:
Proofing a
document
one mistake
at a time.

> Spelling and Grammar: English (U.S.)
>
> Grammatical error:
>
> Both good.
>
> Ignore Once
> Ignore Rule
> Next Sentence
>
> Suggestions:
> Fragment (consider revising)
>
> Change
> Explain...
>
> ☑ Check grammar
>
> Options...   Undo   Close

Here's what you can do:

- To fix the error, edit the text in the box.

- Use the Ignore button(s) to skip the error, or click the Next Sentence button to keep moving through the document.

- Choose a proper spelling from the list and then click the Change button.

3. **Continue checking your document until Word says that you're done.**

You may find it even easier to do an all-at-once proof if you turn off automatic spell- and grammar-checking. See the following section to find out how this can be done.

✔ Don't forget that Undo button! Often times, you can enter a trance while you're document proofing. Undo helps you go back and change something you may not have paid attention to.

✔ One of the easiest ways to breeze through a document and check your spelling is to click the Spell icon on the status bar. As you click, you're taken to the next spelling (or grammatical) error, with a handy pop-up window showing up to help you fix your boo-boos.

Customizing Proofing Options

All document proofing options and settings are kept in one place, in the Application Settings window. Here's how to get there:

1. **Click the Word Options button on the Office Button menu.**

   The Word Options dialog box appears.

2. **Choose Proofing on the left side of the window.**

   The right side of the window contains options and settings for document proofing.

Various options are turned on or off by adding or removing check marks; for example:

- ✔ To direct Word not to spell-check a Web page address, put a check mark by the item labeled Ignore Internet and File Addresses.

- ✔ To turn off on-the-fly spell checking, remove the check mark by the item Check Spelling As You Type.

- ✔ To disable the grammar checking, remove the check mark by the item Check Grammar As You Type.

- ✔ Click the Settings button by the Writing Style drop-down list to customize and hone the grammatical transgressions that Word marks. (I typically disable the Fragments warning because Word is often wrong when flagging fragments.)

Here are some other proofing things you can do:

- ✔ You can click the AutoCorrect Options button to display the AutoCorrect dialog box. Use that dialog box to modify AutoCorrect's settings, add new entries, delete bad AutoCorrect decisions, or edit existing entries.

   Click OK to dismiss the Application Settings window.

Improving Your Word Power

Spelling and grammar are important, but beyond the basics, you want to ensure that you use the best word. For example, is it *right,* or is it *correct?* Is something *hard,* or is something *difficult?* It all depends on the context, of course, as well as on your knowledge of the English language, your writing experience, and your ability to cheat by using some handy tools: the Thesaurus, the Translator, and the Research features in Word.

A thesaurus is not a colossal prehistoric beast

When two words share the same meaning, they're said to be *synonyms*; for example, *big* and *large*. Synonyms are helpful in that they allow you to find better, more descriptive words and especially to avoid using the same tired old words over and over. Obviously, knowing synonyms is a handy thing for any writer. When you don't know a lot of them, you can use a handy, nay, practical tool called a thesaurus to help you.

To find the synonym of any word, right-click that word in your document. From the pop-up menu, choose the Synonyms submenu to see a list of words with a similar meaning (see Figure 8-6).

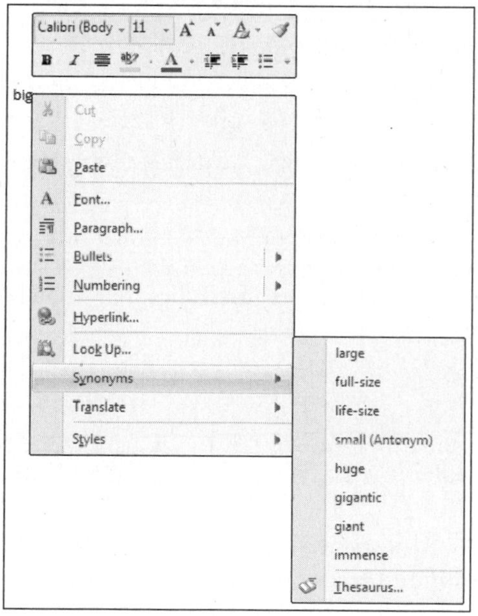

Figure 8-6:
Synonyms
for *big*.

The Synonyms submenu displays a list of a dozen or so synonyms for *big*, plus one antonym (a word with the opposite meaning), as shown in Figure 8-6. To replace the word in the document with a synonym, just choose it from the submenu.

Not all words have synonyms. If so, the Synonyms submenu displays (No Suggestions). Oh, well.

At one time, there were synonyms for all words in the Word thesaurus. Around half a dozen years ago, though, the censorship police took over and hundreds of politically incorrect words were secreted away from Word's Thesaurus list. For example, try looking up the synonyms for *idiot*. Some synonyms list only one aspect of the word, such as the synonyms for *dummy* deal with only mannequins and not "dumb" things. And why are there synonyms for every color except black? Silly Microsoft.

The Research task pane

A better way to play with words, as opposed to just right-clicking and looking up a synonym, is to use the Research view pane in Word. Summon it with these commands:

1. **Click the Review tab.**

2. **In the Proofing group, click the Research button.**

   The Research task pane appears in the document part of the window, as shown in Figure 8-7. The selected word appears at the top.

3. **Click the green Start Searching button — the one with the rightward-pointing arrow.**

   Word uses vast resources to look up oodles of factual tidbits about the word in question. The results are displayed in the list, as shown in Figure 8-7, where Microsoft's online Encarta dictionary has some definitions for the word *blue*.

4. **Narrow the search by selecting Thesaurus English (U.S.) from the drop-down list.**

   The list of synonyms shown in the Research task pane is far more thorough than what you see when you right-click a word and choose the Synonym sub-menu.

5. **To choose a replacement word, point the mouse at the word and choose the Insert command from the menu that appears.**

   Or, if the word intrigues you, choose Look Up from the drop-down menu to see more variations.

6. **Close the Research task pane by clicking the X in its upper-right corner.**

   Or, you can click the Research button again on the Ribbon.

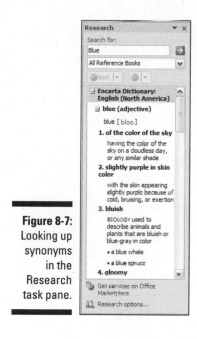

Figure 8-7:
Looking up
synonyms
in the
Research
task pane.

Be sure to check out other options in the drop-down list, such as foreign translations as well as other various and rich sources for finding that right word.

Sadly, this feature is made less handy because it really requires full-time, broadband Internet access to work best. Also, don't be too disappointed with the translation features: My copy of Word came with only French and Spanish translations. Funny, but I can't seem to find the often-ridiculed but necessary Klingon translator.

Making Every Word Count

You pay the butcher by the pound. The dairyman is paid by the gallon. Salesmen are paid by a percentage of the sale. Writers? They're paid by the word.

If you're lucky enough to be paid for your writing, you know the "word count" quite well. Magazine editors demand articles based on word length. "I need 350 hilarious words on Grandma sending her first e-mail," an editor once told me. And, novel writers typically boast of how many words are in their latest efforts. "My next book is 350,000 words," they say in a stuffy, nasal voice. How do they know how many words there are?

The best way to see how many words dwell in your document is to view the status bar. The word count appears after the label Words, and it's updated as you type.

 When the status bar word count isn't enough for you or it isn't visible, you can click the Review tab and then, from the Proofing group, click the Word Count button. A detailed Word Count dialog box, similar to the one shown in Figure 8-8, appears.

Click the Close button to banish the Word Count dialog box.

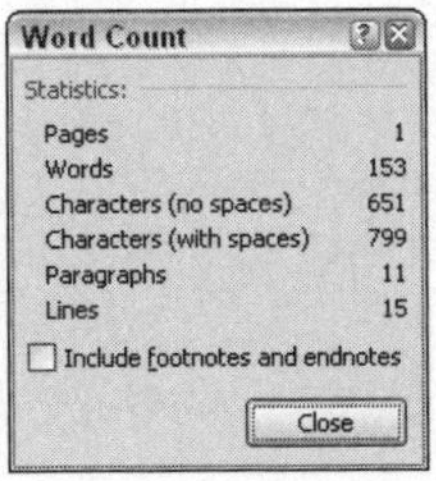

Figure 8-8:
Pulling a
word count.

Word Count	? ☒
Statistics:	
Pages	1
Words	153
Characters (no spaces)	651
Characters (with spaces)	799
Paragraphs	11
Lines	15
☐ Include footnotes and endnotes	
	Close

Chapter 9

Documents and Files

· ·

In This Chapter

▶ Understanding files

▶ Creating a new document

▶ Using templates

▶ Saving your stuff to disk

▶ Using the proper filename

▶ Opening a document already saved to disk

▶ Inserting one document inside another

· ·

Documents created by a word processor are just like documents you create with a typewriter or by scribbling on a piece of paper, although with a word processor your text is better formatted and bolstered by all the fancy things you can do with a computer. Still, the greatest difference between a computer document and a real document is that a computer document is stored inside the computer; it doesn't exist in the real world until it's printed on paper.

This chapter covers how Word deals with documents and how those documents are stored in the computer. Knowing how documents are stored is very important! You want to make Save the command you use most often. Knowing how to save and when to save and how the Open command works are your keys to becoming a happy, productive word processing human.

All About Files

To understand documents, you must first recognize the importance of *files*. This concept is vital to grasp if you ever want your computer experience to be a pleasant one and not a nightmare.

Your computer stores all sorts of information. In addition to word processing documents, the computer can store graphical images, music, and video as well as programs, games, and all sorts of other stuff. Those items are all kept inside the PC and are digitally encoded on the computer's hard drive. The digital information is organized, so unlike you and that drawer in your kitchen filled with all sorts of random items (scissors, candles, plastic spoons, and playing cards), the computer can easily find stuff when you need it.

Information on a computer's hard drive exists as *files*. Each file contains information, just as mason jars may contain fruits and jellies. The information the file contains is electronic, so one file may be an image, another file may contain music, another may be a video, and so on.

 In Windows, a file appears as an icon. Each type of file has its own, unique icon, which is used in Windows to help identify the file's contents. The same holds true with Word, which uses a specific icon to identify its documents, as shown in the margin.

 What's important to remember is that after a Word document is saved to disk, it exists as a file. Documents are their own thing, separate from Word, the program that creates the documents.

Think of the relationship this way: A pianist uses sheet music to play a tune, but the sheet music isn't part of the piano. Just as you can store or mail sheet music, you can store a Word document file (on a CD-R, for example) or send it via e-mail. The Word document that exists on your computer's hard drive as a file is its own, unique thing.

For more information on understanding files as well as hard drives and other basic computer concepts, I highly recommend reading my book *PCs For Dummies*, published by Wiley. The more you know about your computer, the happier you are as a computer user.

Making a New Document

Where did that document come from? I mean, you didn't just pluck it from thin air?

Well, actually, you probably did! The content of a document comes from your brain, transmitted through your neck, shoulders, and arms, and then it appears on the screen, thanks to your fingers fluttering over the computer keyboard. That blank space you write upon? It did come from thin air — or, rather, from thin electrons.

The computer equivalent of a blank sheet of paper comes into being in several ways. That blank sheet of, well, *electrons* is the root of each document you create in Word; all Word documents started out as described in this section. Before pressing on, consider these general Word document tidbits:

✔ Documents in Word aren't limited to any size other than the largest file size allowed by your computer operating system. I believe that's something like 4,096MB under Windows, which may be wrong, but, still, that's a terribly huge file. Put into perspective, all the works of William Shakespeare can fit into a Word document that's only 5MB.

✔ Size-wise, the typical word processing document is maybe 50K. Compare that with 1,000K for the typical digital camera snapshot or 4,000K for a typical MP3 (music) file, and you can see that word processing documents consume relatively little disk space.

✔ K? MB? GB? Bytes? Read my book *PCs For Dummies* (Wiley) for instant computer headache relief.

✔ For speed's sake, I recommend keeping your documents small. If you're writing a proposal, putting the whole thing in one document is fine. If you're writing a novel, make each chapter its own document. If you're writing the U.S. tax code, *please stop!*

✔ Writing long documents — say, over 100 pages — is fine, but when the document size gets that large, Word begins to turn off features. For example, automatic spell checking, image previews, and other "fun" features may be suppressed in longer documents.

Quick! A blank sheet of paper!

Faster than newspaper reporter Clark Kent can whip out a sheet of paper and roll it into his typewriter, you, mild-mannered reader, can summon a new, blank document in Word. It's cinchy, and no amount of kryptonite can thwart you:

1. **Choose the New command from the Office Button menu.**

   The New Document window appears, listing every dang-doodle option known to Word (at least on this planet) for creating a new document.

2. **Ensure that Blank Document is preselected for you in the Blank and Recent area.**

3. **Click the Create button.**

   Instantly, the blank document appears, ready for typing!

Crack your knuckles and get to work!

REMEMBER

✔ A faster way to start a new document? Glad you asked: Press Ctrl+N on the keyboard. That's the shortcut key for New Document. Poof! Instantly, you're off and writing even faster than before.

✔ You don't have to quit Word when you just want to start working on a new document.

Using a template

New, blank documents are fine for creating something from scratch. When you want to save time, though, you can create a new document based on a template rather than start afresh every time.

A *template* is a special type of document that contains preset information and formatting. For example, a template can define a set of styles for use in formatting the text. The template can include the company letterhead and logo. I use a template whenever I write plays or movie scripts, send faxes, or send invoices. A template can even contain *boilerplate* text — a complete document where you merely fill in the blanks.

Using a template is as easy as starting a new document. No matter which template you use, start by choosing the New command from the Office Button menu. The New Document window appears and provides you with access to templates in a variety of ways:

✔ To reuse any template you've recently used, click to select that template from the Recently Used Templates part of the window. Click the Create button to start a new document based on that template.

✔ To see all templates you've created, choose the My Templates item. This action closes the New Document window and opens the New window, which lists all your own templates. Click to select one, and then click the OK button to start a new document based on that template.

✔ You can peruse the vast treasure trove of templates stored online for Microsoft Office. To do so, choose a category from the list under Microsoft Office Online in the New Document window. A list of templates is then fetched from the Internet and displayed in the window. Choose a template that pleases you, and then click the Download button to start a new document based on that template.

As you use Word, you'll doubtless create your own set of templates, especially when you find yourself re-creating the same type of document over and over. Creating your own templates is easy; refer to Chapter 17.

Things to remember:

- ✔ Opening a document with a template doesn't change the template; your new document is merely using the template's styles and any text it already has.

- ✔ Refer to Chapter 17 for more information on templates.

- ✔ Refer to Part III of this book for general information on styles in a document.

- ✔ One option in the New Document dialog box is named New from Existing. Using this option is like using the Open command, although the document you open remains unchanged on disk. The document's contents are placed into a new document for you to edit.

- ✔ Some Word templates can also be used to create a Web page or e-mail message. Honestly, Word makes a lousy Web page editor and an even worse e-mail program. If you want to make Web pages, get a Web page editor. For sending e-mail, use an e-mail program, not a word processor.

Saving a Document

The most important thing you can do to a document is *save it*. Create a permanent copy of what you see on-screen by saving that document as a file on disk. That way, you can use the document again, keep a copy for business reasons, copy the file to a CD-R, e-mail the document, or just keep the thing for sentimental reasons. And all that requires saving!

Saving a new document to disk the first time

Don't think that you have to wait until you finish a document to save it to disk. In fact, saving should be done almost immediately — as soon as you have a few sentences or paragraphs. Save! Save! Save!

To save a document that hasn't already been saved to disk, follow these steps:

1. **Choose the Save As command from the Office Button menu.**

   Just click the Save As item on the menu — not the right-pointing arrow, which lists some interesting but confusing options. Choosing the Save As button displays the Save As dialog box.

   The Save As dialog box appears differently, depending on whether you're using Windows Vista or Windows XP. The Windows XP version is shown in Figure 9-1.

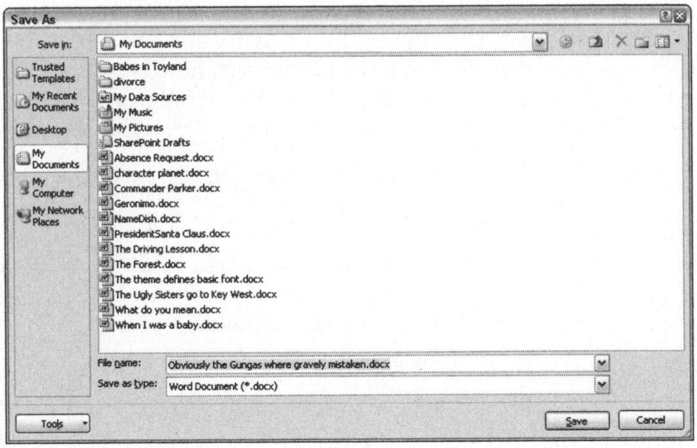

Figure 9-1:
The Save As
dialog box.

2. **Type a name for your document in the File Name box.**

   Word automatically selects the first line or first several words of your document as a filename and puts it in the Save dialog box. If that's okay, you can move on to Step 3. Otherwise, type a name in the File name box. Refer to the later sidebar "Complicated — but important — information about filenames" for file-naming rules.

3. **Optionally, choose a location for your file.**

   Word selects the Documents or My Documents folder as the location for any document you save. This is fine for a while, but eventually you'll want to organize your documents by saving them in their own, unique folders.

You can use the various gizmos in the Save As dialog box to choose another folder for your document. This is really a Windows thing; the Save As dialog box is different between Windows Vista and Windows XP.

4. Click the Save button.

The file is now safely stored on disk.

At this point, you can keep working. As you work, continue to save; refer to the section "Saving or updating a document," later in this chapter.

- There's no need to quit after you save a document. Indeed, the idea is to save as you go.

- The only time you need to use the Save As dialog box is when you first create a document. After that, you can use the Save command merely to update your document, by storing the latest modifications to disk as you write.

- Your clue that the file has been successfully saved is that the filename now appears on the document's title bar, near the top of the screen.

- Always save your document, even after you've typed only a few lines of text.

- The Save As command can also be used to save a document with a new name or to a different location on disk. Refer to Chapter 25 for details.

Problems with saving a document to disk

Saving a document involves working with both Word and Windows. This process doubles the chances for something going wrong, so it's ripe time for an error message. A potential message you may see is

```
The file whatever already exists
```

You have three choices:

- **Replace Existing File:** Nope.
- **Save Change with a Different Name:** Yep.
- **Merge Changes into Existing File:** Nope.

After choosing the middle option, type a different file name in the Save As dialog box.

Complicated — but important — information about filenames

Filenames are a heck of a lot more flexible than they were in the primitive days of computing. Even so, you still have to follow rules about what you can and cannot name a file. Here's the list:

✔ A filename can be longer than 200 ridiculous-something characters; even so, keep your filenames short and descriptive.

✔ A filename can include letters, numbers, and spaces and can start with a letter or number.

✔ A filename can contain periods, commas, hyphens, and even underlines.

✔ A filename cannot contain any of these characters: \ / : * ? " < > |

Word automatically appends a three- or four-character *filename extension* to all your documents — like a last name. You may or may not see this extension, depending on how you've configured Windows. No matter, you don't need to manually type the extension yourself; just worry about giving the document a proper and descriptive filename.

Another common problem is when a message that's displayed reads something like this:

```
The file name, location, or format 'whatever' is not
        valid...
```

That's Word's less-than-cheerful way of telling you that the filename contains a boo-boo character. To be safe, stick to letters, numbers, and spaces when you're naming a file. Check the nearby sidebar, "Complicated — but important — information about filenames." Then click OK and try again.

Saving or updating a document

Every so often as you continue to work on your document, you should save again. That way, any changes you've made since the last time you saved are remembered and recorded on disk permanently. I generally save my documents dozens of times a day, usually when the phone rings or when I get up for a fresh cup of coffee or to use the potty or, often, when I'm just bored.

To resave a document that has already been saved to disk, choose the Save command from the Office Button menu. There's no feedback, and the Save As dialog box doesn't show up. That's because you've already given the file a name; the Save command merely updates the existing file on disk.

✔ The fastest way to save a document is by using the Ctrl+S keyboard shortcut.

✔ You can also click the Save icon on the Quick Access toolbar to save a document to disk.

✔ The most bizarre command for saving a document: Shift+F12.

Saving when you're done

Time to call it quits. The last save you do when you're done with a document happens as you either close the document or quit Word. Either way, when the document hasn't been saved, or was changed since the last save, you're asked to save again, as shown in Figure 9-2.

Figure 9-2:
Your last
chance
to save.

Microsoft Office Word

⚠ Do you want to save the changes to "The Ugly Sisters go to Key West.docx"?

[Yes] [No] [Cancel]

Here are your options:

Yes: The document is saved. If you've been really bad and haven't saved the document at all, the Save As dialog box appears when you choose Yes. See the earlier section "Saving a new document to disk the first time."

No: Don't save the document. Any changes made since the document was last saved are lost, or if the document was never saved, the entire thing is lost forever.

Cancel: Word returns you to your document for more editing and stuff.

Choose, but choose wisely. I recommend the *Yes* option.

✔ To close a document without quitting Word, choose the Close command from the Office Button menu. The keyboard shortcut for the Close command is Ctrl+W.

✔ There's no reason to quit Word and start it again to begin working with a blank slate. Just use the New Document command again: Ctrl+N.

✔ Always quit Word properly. Never turn off your PC or reset it when Word or Windows is still on-screen.

Not saving a document

Yes, it's possible not to save a document. I don't see the reason why: Modern computer hard drives are just brimming with room, and Word documents don't consume much disk space. It doesn't hurt to always save! But, if you want to not save, and remove any possibility of getting your stuff back, either close the document or quit Word.

To close the document, choose the Close command from the Office Button menu or press Ctrl+W.

To quit Word, choose the Exit command from the Office Button menu.

Either way, when you're asked to save the document, choose No.

Opening a Document

Saving a document to disk means nothing unless you have a way of retrieving it. You actually have several ways to *open* a document previously saved as a file on disk. This section mulls the possibilities.

Using the traditional Open command

Open is the standard computer command used to fetch a document from disk. You use Open to hunt down documents that were previously saved and open them like you're unwrapping a present. The document is then displayed in Word's window like it has always been there.

To grab a file from disk — to open it — follow these steps:

1. **Choose the Open command from the Office Button menu.**

   The Open dialog box materializes. It looks different between Windows Vista and Windows XP, although it basically works the same. The Windows XP version of the Open dialog box is shown in Figure 9-3.

2. **Choose the document's name with the mouse.**

   The Open dialog box — vast and wild as it is — contains a list of documents previously saved to disk, as you can see in Figure 9-3. Your job is to find the one you want to open.

   Using the Open dialog box, you can examine various folders on your PC's hard drive, and on any computer network your PC is connected to, to scour for files to open. The way you use the Open dialog box differs between Windows Vista and Windows XP; refer to a Windows reference for specific information.

3. Click the Open button.

Word opens the highlighted file, carefully lifting it from your disk drive and slapping it down on the screen.

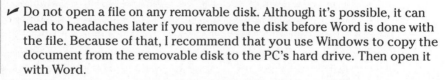

Figure 9-3:
The Open
dialog box.

After the document is open, you can edit it, just look at it, print it, or do whatever you want.

- ✔ Opening a document doesn't erase it from your disk drive. In fact, the original copy of the file stays on the hard drive until you use the Save command to save the document to disk again.

- ✔ When you open a document, there's no need to use the Save As command to save it again. Simply use the Save command (shortcut: Ctrl+S).

- ✔ The shortcut key for the Open command is Ctrl+O.

- ✔ You can also open a document from Windows itself. Merely locate a Word document icon, double-click, and Word starts loading that document for editing.

- ✔ Open is a nifty name for the command, don't you think? If not, consider that the original version of Microsoft Word for the PC used the File⇨ Transfer⇨Load command to open a file on disk.

- ✔ Do not open a file on any removable disk. Although it's possible, it can lead to headaches later if you remove the disk before Word is done with the file. Because of that, I recommend that you use Windows to copy the document from the removable disk to the PC's hard drive. Then open it with Word.

A handy way to open a recent file

Word remembers the last several files you've been working on. It keeps them in a list on the Office Button menu, as shown in Figure 9-4. Chances are good that you probably need to open one of them, so choosing one from the Office Button menu is a handy way to open that document quickly.

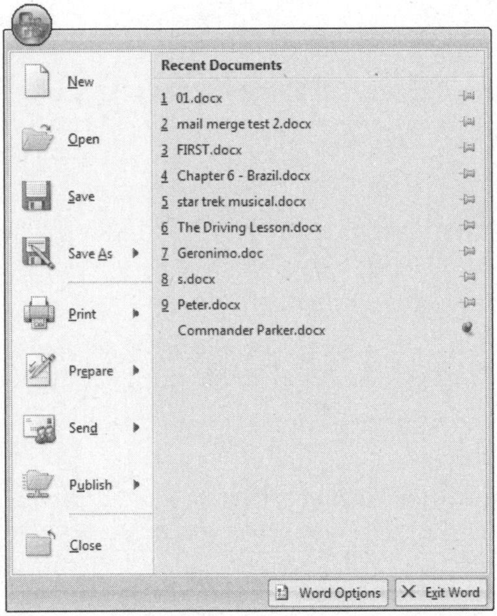

Recent Documents

New	1 01.docx
Open	2 mail merge test 2.docx
Save	3 FIRST.docx
	4 Chapter 6 - Brazil.docx
	5 star trek musical.docx
	6 The Driving Lesson.docx
Save As ▶	7 Geronimo.doc
Print ▶	8 s.docx
Prepare ▶	9 Peter.docx
Send ▶	Commander Parker.docx
Publish ▶	
Close	

Word Options   Exit Word

Figure 9-4:
Recently opened files on the Office Button menu.

Those green pushpins by the document's name allow you to permanently attach a document to the Office Button menu. Click a pushpin to "push it in." That makes the document stick around in the list. Clicking the pushpin again allows the document to fade away after a time.

Opening one document inside another

Sticking one document into the thorax of another document is neither strange, obtuse, nor unnecessary. And, it involves no surgery. For example, you may have your biography, résumé, or curriculum vitae in a file on disk and want to add that information to the end of a letter begging for a job. If so, or in any other circumstances that I can't think of right now, follow these steps:

1. **Position the insertion pointer where you want the other document's text to appear.**

   The text is inserted at that spot.

2. **Click the Insert tab.**

[Object ▾]

3. **From the Text group, choose Object⇨Text from File.**

   A dialog box similar to the Open dialog box appears (refer to Figure 9-3).

4. **Choose the icon representing the document you want to insert.**

   You can also use the gadgets and gizmos in the dialog box to locate a file in another folder or on another disk drive or even on someone else's computer on the network. Such power!

5. **Click the Insert button.**

The document you insert becomes part of the original document, just as though you had typed (and formatted) the whole thing right there with your stubby little fingers.

- The resulting combined document still has the same name as the first document; the document you inserted remains unchanged on disk.

- You can retrieve any number of documents on disk into your document, one at a time. There's no limit.

- The preceding steps allow you to grab a chunk of text saved as a document and stick the text into another document. This process is often called *boilerplating,* where a commonly used piece of text is slapped into several documents. This process is also the way sleazy romance novels are written.

- Biography. Résumé. Curriculum vitae. The more important you think you are, the more alien the language used to describe what you've done.

Chapter 10

The Printer, the Paper, the Document Maker

In This Chapter

▶ Getting the printer ready to print

▶ Previewing your document before printing

▶ Using another printer

▶ Printing a specific part of a document

▶ Printing multiple copies of a document

▶ Canceling the Print command

*W*ord helps you create documents short and small, silly and brilliant. Some documents remain in the digital domain and never hit paper. For example, when I'm done writing this chapter, I'll e-mail this document to my editor. But most documents need to escape from their electronic realm and must manifest themselves in the physical world. For this task, you must employ your computer's printer.

Printing is one of the final steps of your word processing labors, the nirvana to which all documents aspire. Getting it down on paper is historically the way ideas are shared. Indeed, lugging around the computer and showing folks your first novel on the screen just doesn't cut it. No, you need a printer, and you need some paper if you desire to be a document maker.

Preparing the Printer

Printing involves using the computer printer, which really is its own little computer. When you yearn to print a document, the immediate hassle you're presented with is how to use two computers at one time. Coaxing a computer printer into behaving properly is an art form. Therefore, I recommend following these steps to ensure that the printer is ready to actually print something:

1. **Make sure that your printer is plugged in and properly connected to your computer.**

   Refer to my book *PCs For Dummies* (Wiley) for more information on connecting and using a printer as well as various printer tips and stuff like that.

2. **Make sure that your laser printer has enough toner or that your ink printer's cartridges are brimming with ink.**

   Laser printers should have a good toner cartridge installed. If the laser printer's "toner low" indicator is on, replace the toner at once.

   Most ink printers let you know when they're out of ink, or you notice that the image appears streaked or faded or is missing information. Replace the ink cartridge at once.

3. **Check the printer for paper.**

   The paper can feed from the back or top or enter from a paper tray, or it can be manually fed one sheet at a time. However your printer eats paper, make sure that you have it properly stocked before you print.

4. **Your printer must be *online* or *selected* before you can print anything.**

   This is weird: Some printers can be on but not ready to print. The power is on, but unless the printer is online or selected, it ignores the computer. To force those types of printers to listen to the computer, you must press the Online or Select (or similar) button.

When you're certain that the printer is up to the task, you can proceed with the printing operation in Word.

Preview Before You Print

Despite the fact that Word displays your document on the screen so that the document appears pretty much how it will look when printed, I still recommend that you try the Print Preview feature before printing.

Print Preview is a word processing feature from the old days, back when text on the screen looked nothing like what was printed. What Print Preview did was to display an approximation of what a printed page of the document would look like. That way, you could confirm things like margins, fonts, formats, text sizes, headings, footers, and other parts of a document, stuff that didn't show up on the screen but would print on paper.

By taking a sneak peek at what your document looks like before printing, you save yourself the time (and wasted paper) that you otherwise would spend printing, proofing, and then printing again — or so the theory goes.

To sneak a preview of how your printed document will look, choose Print⇨Print Preview from the Office Button menu. Your document then appears in the special Print Preview mode, as shown in Figure 10-1.

Take note of how your text looks on the page. Look at the margins. If you're using footnotes, headers, or footers, look at how they lay out. The idea here is to spot something dreadfully wrong *before* you print.

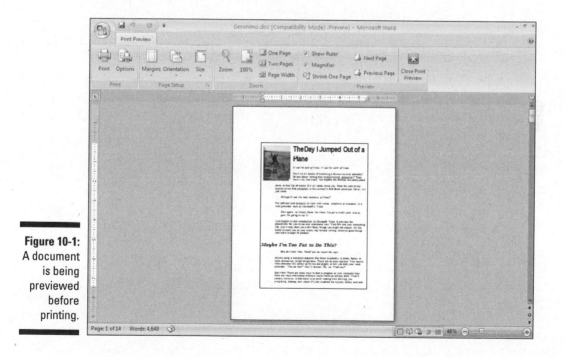

Figure 10-1: A document is being previewed before printing.

When you're done gawking, click the Close Print Preview button to return to your document.

Or, if everything looks hunky and dory, click the Print button to summon the Print dialog box, and refer to the next section.

- ✔ Note how the Page Setup group is visible in Print Preview mode. That gives you fast access to some handy tools for fixing common problems found in Print Preview: margins, paragraph spacing, document orientation, and so on. (Refer to Chapter 14 in this book.)

- ✔ Use the scroll bars to see more of your document.

- ✔ If you have a wheel mouse, like the Microsoft IntelliMouse, you can roll the wheel up or down to scroll one page up or down in your document.

- ✔ If your mouse is wheel-less, you can use the Page Up and Page Down buttons to peruse various pages of your document.

- ✔ Click the mouse on your document to zoom in and get a closer look. Click the mouse again to zoom back out. If this doesn't work, click the Magnifier check box in the Preview group.

- ✔ The Zoom tool on the Status bar can also be used to zoom in or out. In fact, you can zoom out to where you see the entire document displayed as tiny pages on the screen.

 - ✔ Sideways printing, paper sizes, and other document-related items are set when you format your document's pages. These are Word functions, not ones you set when you print. Refer to Chapter 14.

Printing a Whole Document

All documents are printed the same, whether they're absent notes to teachers, heated screeds to editorial pages, company reports, or the next best-selling novels to be turned into Tom Hanks movies. Generally speaking, here's how the printing operation goes:

1. **Make sure that the printer is online and ready to print.**

   See the first section in this chapter, "Preparing the Printer."

2. **Save your document.**

    Ha! Surprised you. Saving before you print is always a good idea. Click the little Save button for a quickie save, and if you need any extra help, refer to Chapter 9, on saving your stuff to disk.

3. Choose the Print command from the Office Button menu to summon the Print dialog box.

The Print dialog box (see Figure 10-2) provides a slew of printing options, the most vital of which are covered elsewhere in this chapter.

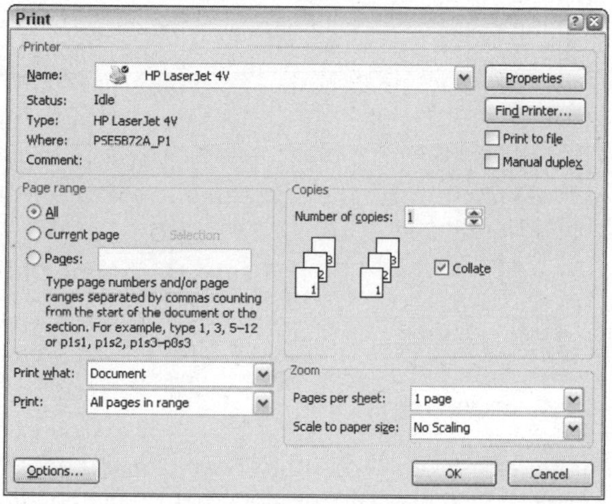

Figure 10-2:
The Print
dialog box.

4. Click the OK button.

The document begins to spew forth from your printer.

Printing may take some time; really, a *long* time. Fortunately, you can continue working while the document prints, falling a page at a time from the printer.

✔ The keyboard shortcut to display the Print dialog box is Ctrl+P. I've made lots of puns about Ctrl+P, which appear in previous editions of this book.

✔ If nothing prints, don't hit the Print command again! There's probably nothing awry; the computer is still thinking or sending text to the printer. If you don't get an error message, everything will probably print, eventually.

✔ The computer prints one copy of your document for every Print command you incant. If the printer is just being slow and you impatiently click the Print button ten times, you get ten copies of your document. See the section "Canceling a Print Job (Omigosh!)," later in this chapter.

✔ To print only a page, block, or other part of a document, refer to the later section in this chapter "Printing Part of a Document."

✔ When your document is formatted using a unique paper size, the printer may prompt you to load that paper size. Printing on paper of different sizes is a printer-specific function, not something that Word does. But you set the paper size in Word as part of the page formatting. Refer to Chapter 14.

✔ Manual-feed printers beg for paper before they can print. The printer may say something like "Feed me paper!" or the ever-popular "PC Load Letter." Like a dutiful mother, you must comply: Stand by the printer, line up the paper, and shove it into the printer's gaping maw until your document is done printing. Fortunately, there's no need to burp the printer after manually feeding it paper.

✔ Aside from saving your document, you may consider proofreading it before you print. See Chapter 8.

Printing backward

.txet drawkcab htiw od ot gnihton sah siht ,oN

Do you have one of those printers where the sheets come out face up? In that case, have you noticed how you must reshuffle your document after it prints because the pages are in order from back to front? Why are you doing that? Don't you have a computer? Aren't computers supposed to make life *easier?* Am I asking too many questions?

To prevent the face-up reshuffle, merely direct Word to print your document *backward*. When you reverse the page order, your document finishes printing face up, saving you time and making you look a lot smarter. Here's how to enact that blessing:

1. **Summon the Print dialog box.**

   Do the Print-command-from-Office-Button jitterbug, the Ctrl+P thing, or however you enjoy bringing forth the Print dialog box.

2. **Click the Properties button in the Print dialog box.**

   The Properties dialog box for the selected printer appears.

3. **On the Layout tab, Page Order area, select the option Back to Front.**

4. **Click OK.**

5. **Click OK to print your document.**

   The document comes out of the printer backward, but because it's face up, the document is in order when printing is complete.

Printing a document quickly

To quickly print your document and avoid the Print dialog box, choose Print⇨Quick Print from the Office Button menu. you get no visual feedback, no chance to change settings; the whole document prints.

Quick, of course, is relative. Just because the command is Quick Print doesn't mean that your printer spews out the pages any faster than it regularly would.

Choosing another printer

Your computer can have more than one printer attached. Even small offices and home offices have computers networked and sharing printers. In any case, you can use the Print dialog box to choose which printer to use to print your document. It's simple.

After bringing forth the Print dialog box, choose a different printer from the Name drop-down list. Click the downward-pointing arrow on the right end of the Name box. A list of available printers appears, as shown in Figure 10-3.

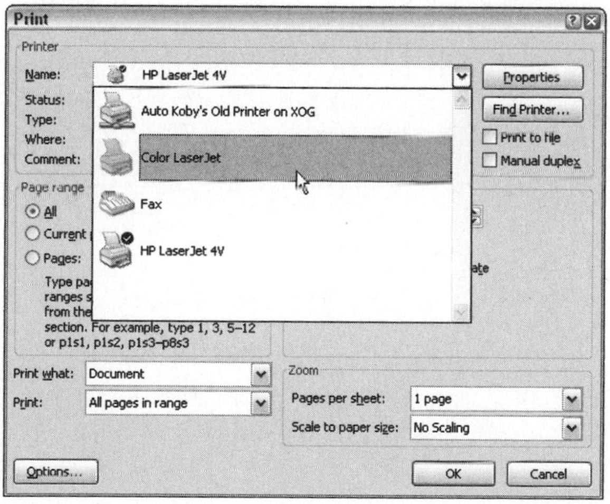

Figure 10-3: Choosing another printer.

Deleting that extra, blank page at the end of a document

Occasionally, you may be surprised when your document prints and there's one, extra page — a blank page. And, it bothers you because you cannot get rid of it! Until now:

To remove that ugly, blank page that often roots at the end of your document, press Ctrl+End.

With the insertion pointer at the end of your document, keep pressing the Backspace key until the extra page is gone. How can you tell? Keep an eye on the total page count on the status bar. When that page count is decremented by one, you know that the extra page is gone.

Simply choose a printer from the list. Click the OK button and your document prints on the printer you've chosen.

- ✔ Yes, you also should check to ensure that the printer you've chosen is on, selected, stocked with paper, and ready to print.

- ✔ Setting up or adding printers is something you do in Windows, not in Word.

- ✔ Faxing works just like printing, although you're printing to a fax machine over a phone line. In Word, simply choose the fax printer from the list of printers. (Installing a fax printer is something you do in Windows, not in Word.)

- ✔ For more information on printing and faxing, I recommend my book *PCs For Dummies* (Wiley).

Printing Part of a Document

Unless you tell Word otherwise, the whole document prints each time you click the OK button in the Print dialog box. For those times when you need only a single page, a range of pages, or a selected block of text, Word lets you print just that part of the document. This section provides the details.

Printing a specific page

Follow these steps to print only one page of your document:

1. **Move the insertion pointer so that it's sitting somewhere on the page you want to print.**

   Check the page number on the status bar to ensure that you're on the right page.

2. **Choose the Print command from the Office Button menu or press Ctrl+P.**

3. **Select the Current Page option in the Print Range part of the Print dialog box.**

4. **Click OK.**

   The dialog box closes, and that one page prints. (It may take some time to print as Word organizes its thoughts.)

The single page prints with all the formatting you applied, including footnotes and page numbers and everything, just as though you plucked that page from a complete printing of the entire document.

Printing a single page in this manner is great for when you goof up (or the printer goofs up) one page in a document and you need to reprint only that page. Printing only a single page doesn't waste paper.

Printing a range of pages

Word enables you to print a single page, a range of pages, or even some hodgepodge combination of random pages from within your document. To print a range or group of pages, follow these steps:

1. **Conjure up the Print dialog box.**

2. **Click the Pages button in the Page Range area of the Print dialog box.**

3. **Type the page numbers or a range of page numbers.**

   To print pages 3 through 5, for example, type **3-5**.

   To print pages 1 through 7, type **1-7**.

   To print pages 2 and 6, type **2,6**.

4. **Click OK.**

   The pages you specify — and only those pages — print.

You can get very specific with the page ranges. For example, to print page 3, pages 5 through 9, pages 15 through 17, and page 19 (boy, that coffee went everywhere, didn't it?), you type **3, 5-9, 15-17, 19**.

To print all the odd pages, or all the even pages, use the Print drop-down list in the lower-left corner of the Print dialog box. Choose either Odd Pages or Even Pages from that list. I've used this option to print on both sides of a sheet of paper: First print all the odd pages. Then flip over the stack of pages, reinsert them into the printer, and print all the even pages.

Printing a block

After you mark a block of text on-screen, you can beg the Print command to print that block. Here's how:

1. **Mark the block of text you want to print.**

   See Chapter 7 for all the block-marking instructions in the world.

2. **Choose the Print command from the Office Button menu.**

3. **Tickle the button by the word *Selection*.**

   The Selection item in the Print dialog box is available only when a block is selected. Selecting it tells Word that you want to print only your high-lighted block.

4. **Click the OK button.**

   In a few moments, you see the hard copy sputtering out of your printer.

The page selection prints in the same position and with the same headers and footers (if any) as it would if you had printed the entire document.

Printing More than One Copy of Something

Imagine how silly it would be to send your résumé to a company but add that you need your résumé back because you have only one copy. No, I'm not trying to convince you that buying a photocopier is necessary. Why do that when Word can easily print multiple copies of any document? Here's how:

1. **Choose the Print command from the Office Button menu.**

2. **Enter the number of copies in the Number of Copies box.**

   For three copies, for example, type **3** into the box.

3. **Click OK to print your copies.**

Under normal circumstances, Word prints each copy of the document one after the other. This process is known as *collating*. However, if you're printing seven copies of something and you want Word to print seven copies of page 1 and then seven copies of page 2 (and so on), click in the Collate check box to *remove* the check mark. (Normally, you leave the check mark there.)

Canceling a Print Job (Omigosh!)

Because you probably need to quickly cancel your printing, here goes:

1. **Double-click the li'l printer dude by the current time on the taskbar.**

   This step opens your printer's window and displays any documents waiting to be printed, as shown in Figure 10-4.

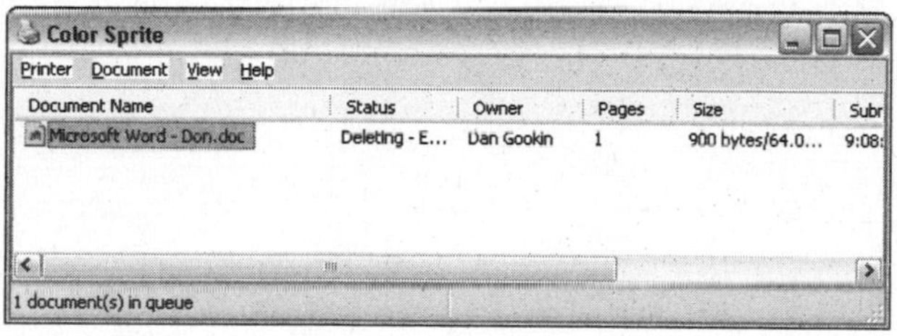

Figure 10-4: The printer queue.

	Color Sprite					_ □ ✕
Printer Document View Help						
Document Name		Status	Owner	Pages	Size	Subr
Microsoft Word - Don.doc		Deleting - E...	Dan Gookin	1	900 bytes/64.0...	9:08:
1 document(s) in queue						

2. **Click the name of your Word document job on the list.**

3. **Choose Document⇨Cancel.**

   The command may be Document⇨Cancel Printing in some versions of Windows.

4. **Click Yes to terminate the job.**

   The command may be OK in some versions of Windows.

5. **Close the printer's window when you're done.**

   Choose Printer⇨Close to make the window run away from the desktop. You're zapped back to Word, ready for more editing action.

Note that it may take a while for the printer to stop printing. That's because the printer has its own memory (RAM), and a few pages of the document may be stored there *and* continue to print even after you've told the printer to stop. (Stupid printer — stupid.)

- ✔ Stopping a print job is a Windows task, not really anything Word has control over.

- ✔ If you're using a network printer, you may not be able to cancel printing. Oh, well.

- ✔ You can use your printer's window (refer to Figure 10-4) to cancel more jobs if you're in an especially vicious mood: Just repeat Steps 2 through 4 for each job you want to sack.

- ✔ To cancel all the documents (the printer *jobs*) waiting to print, choose Printer➪Cancel All Documents.

- ✔ Obviously, canceling a print job is the act of a desperate person. In its efforts to make life easy for computer users, Windows tries hard to help us change our minds. Canceling something that's printing may or may not work as planned. My advice is just to be careful with the Print command in the first place.

Part III
Formatting

The 5th Wave   By Rich Tennant

"I love the way MS Word justifies the text in my resume. Now if I can just get it to justify my asking salary."

In this part . . .

Formatting is the artist's side of word processing. It's what gives your documents a professional, almost typeset look. By properly formatting your text, sentences, paragraphs, and pages, you kick up your document's appeal a notch, by adding to the value of what's written. In fact, forget what you've written — as long as it looks *good,* who cares?

Seriously, formatting is the task of making your document look less ugly. It's something you do after you write, or if you can handle the concept of *styles* and *templates,* you can format while you write. The chapters in this part of the book demonstrate how all that nonsense is done. If you can survive the formatting task, you can truly do anything in Word.

Chapter 11

Formatting Text

- -

In This Chapter

▶ Understanding text formatting

▶ Choosing a font

▶ Applying basic text formats

▶ Changing text size

▶ Adding color to your words

▶ Undoing text formatting

▶ Exploring the Font dialog box

▶ Changing text case

- -

The most basic thing you can format in a document is text — the letters, numbers, and characters you type. Just as your body is composed of millions of cells, documents are composed of thousands of characters. Like a cell, a *character* is the basic building block of the document. Characters include letters, symbols, and Uncle Lloyd, who can play *The Blue Danube* waltz using only his cupped hand and his armpit.

You can format characters to be bold, underlined, italicized, little, or big or in different fonts or colors — all sorts of pretty and distracting attributes. Word gives you a magnificent amount of control over the appearance of your text. This chapter contains the details.

How to Format Text

You can change the format of your text in two ways:

✔ Choose a text-formatting command first, and then type the text. All the text you type is formatted as chosen.

✔ Type the text first, and then select the text as a block and apply the formatting. This technique works best when you're busy with a thought and need to return and format the text later.

You use both methods as you compose text in your document. Sometimes, it's easier to use a formatting command and type the text in that format. For example:

1. **Type the following text:**

   ```
   And we all had a
   ```

2. **Press Ctrl+I to activate *italic text*.**

3. **Type this word:**

   ```
   horribly
   ```

4. **Press Ctrl+I again, which turns off italic.**

5. **Continue typing:**

   ```
   awful time.
   ```

The final sentence looks like this:

```
And we all had a horribly awful time.
```

For more complex formatting, it's better to type the text first, go back, mark the text as a block, and then apply the formatting. Even so, either way works.

See Chapter 7 for more information on marking blocks of text.

Basic Text Formatting

Word stores some of the most common text-formatting commands in one group. On the Home tab, you find the Font group, shown in Figure 11-1. The command buttons in that group carry out most of the basic text formatting you use in Word. This section mulls over the possibilities.

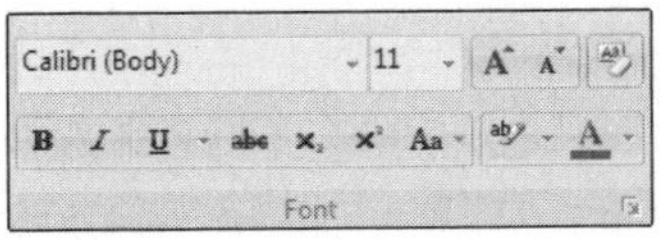

Figure 11-1:
Text-
formatting
attributes in
the Font
group.

✔ Text can also be formatted by using the Mini Toolbar that appears whenever you select text. Refer to Chapter 7.

✔ The Font group can help you quickly determine which formatting is applied to your text. For example, in Figure 11-1, the text where the insertion pointer is blinking is formatted in the Calibri font. The number 12 tells you that the text is 12 points tall. If the B button were highlighted, you would also know that the text was formatted in bold. (These text formats are discussed throughout this section.)

Changing the font

The most basic attribute of text is its *typeface,* often called the *font.* The font sets up how your text looks — its overall text style. Although deciding on a proper font may be agonizing, and indeed many graphic artists are paid well to choose just the right font, the actual task of selecting a font in Word isn't that tough. It generally goes like this:

1. **On the Write tab, in the Font group, click the down arrow to display the Font face list.**

   A menu of font options appears, as shown in Figure 11-2.

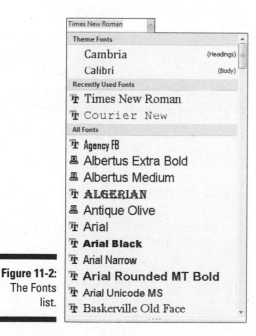

Figure 11-2: The Fonts list.

The top part of the menu shows fonts associated with the document *theme*. The next section contains fonts you've chosen recently, which is handy for reusing fonts. The rest of the list, which can be quite long, shows all the fonts in Windows that are available to Word. It's quite a long list.

2. **Scroll to the font you want.**

   The fonts in the All Fonts part of the list are displayed in context (as they appear when printed) and in alphabetical order.

3. **Click to select a font.**

You can also use the Font menu to preview what fonts look like. Scroll through the list to see which fonts are available and how they may look. As you move the mouse over a font, any selected text in your document is visually updated to show how that text would look in that font. (Note that no changes are made until you select the new font.)

✔ When no font is displayed in the Font group (the listing is blank), it means that more than one font is being used in the selected block of text.

✔ You can quickly scroll to a specific part of the menu by typing the first letter of the font you need, such as T for Times New Roman.

✔ Graphic designers prefer to use two fonts in a document — one for the text and one for headings and titles. Word is configured this way as well. The font you see with `Body` after its name is the current text, or *body*, font. The font marked as `Heading` is used for headings. These two fonts are part of the document theme.

✔ Refer to Chapter 17 for more information on document themes.

✔ Fonts are the responsibility of Windows, not Word. New fonts are installed in the Control Panel's Fonts folder. (The procedure is really no big deal.) Thousands of fonts are available for Windows, and they work in all Windows applications.

Character formats (bold, italic, and so on)

The Font group lists some of the most common character formats. These are applied in addition to the font. In fact, they enhance the font. Use them as you see fit:

To make text bold, press Ctrl+B or click the Bold command button.

Use **bold** to make text stand out on a page — for titles and captions or when you're uncontrollably angry.

To make text italic, press Ctrl+I or click the Italic command button.

Italic is replacing underlining as the preferred text-emphasis format. Italicized text looks so much better than shabby underlined text. It's light and wispy, poetic and free.

 Underline text by pressing Ctrl+U or click the Underline command button. When will this text attribute *die?* I'm baffled. Honestly, I think we're waiting for the last typewriter-clutching librarian from the 1950s to pass on before underlining is officially gone as a text attribute. And please don't fall prey to the old rule about underlining book titles. It's *Crime and Punishment,* not <u>Crime and Punishment</u>.

 Strike through text by clicking the Strikethrough command button. (There's no keyboard shortcut for this one.)

I don't know why strikethrough text made it up on the Font group. If I were King of Microsoft, I would have put Small Caps up there instead. But, who am I? Strikethrough is common in legal stuff, and when you mean to say something but then ~~change your mind~~, think of something better to say.

 Make text subscript by pressing Ctrl+= (equal) or clicking the Subscript command button.

Subscript text appears below the line, such as the 2 in H_2O. Again, it puzzles me why this formatting command ranks up there with bold and italic. I suppose that somewhere there's a lot of subscripting going on.

 Make text superscript by pressing Ctrl+Shift+= (equal sign) or clicking the Superscript command button.

Superscript text appears above the line, such as the 10 in 2^{10}. Note that the command is written as Ctrl++ (plus), but it's really Ctrl+Shift+=. If you can remember that Ctrl+= is subscript, just press the Shift key to get Ctrl+Shift+= for superscript — if you can remember, that is.

More text formats are available in Word, such as small caps, outline, and shadow. These can be accessed through the Font dialog box. Refer to the section "Fun and Formatting in the Font Dialog Box," later in this chapter.

- ✔ To turn off a text attribute, use the command again. For example, press Ctrl+I to type something in *italic.* Then press Ctrl+I again to return to normal text.

- ✔ You can use the down arrow by the Underline command button to display a variety of underline styles and options. When a specific underline style is chosen from the menu, using Ctrl+U or the Underline command button applies that style.

 ✔ Basic character formatting affects only selected text or any new text you type.

✔ You can mix and match character formats. For example, press Ctrl+B and then Ctrl+I to have bold and italic text. You need to use Ctrl+B and Ctrl+I, or the command buttons, to turn those attributes off again.

✔ Obviously, and logically, you cannot apply both superscript and subscript text attributes to the same chunk of text. That's just silly.

✔ The best way to use superscript or subscript is to write your text first. After the text is written, go back, mark as a block the text you want to superscript or subscript, and *then* use these commands. So 42 becomes 4^2, and CnH2n+1OH becomes $C_nH_{2n+1}OH$. The reason is that the text you modify tends to be rather teensy and hard to edit. Better to write it first and then format.

Text Transcending Teeny to Titanic

Big text. Little text. Text! Text! Text!

Text size is considered a text format in Word. You can choose the size of your text, from indecipherably small to monstrously huge. Of course, more common is the subtle text-size adjustment; rare is the student who hasn't fudged the length of a term paper by inching up the text size a notch or two.

To understand how Word (and Windows) deals with text size, you must become one with an official typesetting term: *point*. Text size is measured by the point, where one point is equal to $\frac{1}{72}$ inch.

Here are some point pointers:

✔ The bigger the point size, the larger the text.

✔ Most text is either 10 or 12 points tall.

✔ Headings are typically 14 to 24 points tall.

✔ Most fonts can be sized from 1 point to 1,638 points. Point sizes smaller than 6 are generally too small for a human to read.

✔ Seventy-two points is equal to 1-inch-high letters (roughly).

✔ The point size of text is a measure from the bottom of the descender to the top of the ascender — from the bottom of the lowercase *p* to the top of the capital *E,* for example. So, the typical letter in a font is smaller than the given font size. In fact, depending on the font design, text formatted at the same size but with different fonts *(typefaces)* may not appear to be the same size. That's just one of those typesetting oddities that causes regular computer users to start binge drinking.

Setting the text size

Text size is set in the Font group on the Home tab. Just to the right of the Font box is the Size box (refer to Figure 11-1). Clicking the down arrow displays a list of font sizes for your text, as shown in Figure 11-3.

Figure 11-3:
Select a font size from this list.

You can preview the new text size by pointing the mouse at an item on the Size menu. The word under the insertion pointer, or a selected block of text, is updated on the screen to reflect the new size. Click to choose a size or press Esc to cancel.

The Size menu lists only common text sizes. To set the text size to something not listed or to something specific, type that value into the box. For example, to set the font size to 11.5, click in the Size box and type **11.5**.

Nudging text size

Sometimes, choosing text size is like hanging a picture. To get the picture level, you have to nudge it just a little bit this way and that. Word has similar tools for nudging text size larger or smaller, two of which are found on in the Font group.

 To increase the font size, press Ctrl+Shift+> or click the Grow Font command button.

The Grow Font command nudges the font size up to the next value as listed on the Size menu (refer to Figure 11-3). So, if the text is 12 points, the Grow Font command increases its size to 14 points.

To decrease the font size, press Ctrl+Shift+< or click the Shrink Font command button.

The Shrink Font command works in the opposite direction of the Grow Font command, by reducing the text size to the next-lower value as displayed on the Size menu (refer to Figure 11-3).

I remember the Grow and Shrink keyboard commands easily because > is the greater-than symbol and < is the less-than symbol. Just think, "I'm making my text *greater than* its current size" when you press Ctrl+Shift+> or "I'm making my text *less than* its current size" when you press Ctrl+Shift+<.

 When you want to increase or decrease the font size by smaller increments, use the following shortcut keys:

Ctrl+]	Makes text one point size larger
Ctrl+[	Makes text one point size smaller

More Colorful Text Makes Not for More Colorful Writing

Now that color printers are pretty much standard, you can take advantage of those expensive ink pots by using colored text in Word. Color can add personality to your correspondence, provide punch in a business letter, or make an important document extremely difficult to read. Choose your text color wisely.

 Text color is applied by clicking the Font Color command button. The bar below the A on the Font Color command button indicates which color is applied to text.

A new color can be chosen by clicking the menu arrow just to the right of the Font Color command button. Choose a color from the menu, as shown in Figure 11-4; as you move the mouse pointer over various colors, selected text in your document is updated to reflect that color. When you find the color you like, click it. That color then becomes the new text color associated with the Font Color command button.

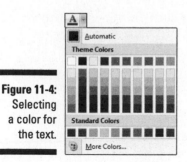

Figure 11-4:
Selecting
a color for
the text.

Of course, colored text prints only when a color printer is available and readily stocked with ink. Refer to Chapter 10 for more information on printing documents.

- ✔ Theme colors are associated with the document theme. Refer to Chapter 17.

- ✔ Select the More Colors item to display a special Colors dialog box. Use that dialog box to craft your own custom colors.

- ✔ The color *Automatic* refers to the color defined for the text style you're using. Refer to Chapter 16 for more information on styles.

- ✔ The Font Color command affects only the text color, not the background. To color the background, you need to use the Shading command, which is covered in Chapter 19.

- ✔ Be careful not to confuse the Font Color command button with the Text Highlight Color command button, to its left. Text highlighting is a text attribute, but it's best used for document markup. See Chapter 27.

Undoing All This Text-Formatting Nonsense

There are so many formatting commands available that it's possible for your text to look more like a pile of formatting remnants than anything readable in any human language. Word understands this problem, so it created the Clear Formatting command to let you peel away all formats from your text, just like you peel the skin from a banana:

To peel away formatting from a block of selected text, or the text the insertion pointer is on, or future text you type, press Ctrl+spacebar or use the Clear Formatting command button in the Font group.

The Clear Formatting command removes any formats you've applied to the text: font, size, text attributes (bold or italic), and color.

✔ Another key combination for Ctrl+spacebar is Ctrl+Shift+Z. Remember that Ctrl+Z is the Undo command. To undo formatting, all you do is add the Shift key, which may make sense — well, heck, if any of this makes sense.

✔ Technically, the Ctrl+spacebar command restores characters to the formatting defined by the *style* you're using. So, if the Body style is 12-point Calibri, pressing Ctrl+spacebar restores that font and size. Don't let this information upset or confuse you! Instead, turn to Chapter 16 for more information on Word's styles.

Fun and Formatting in the Font Dialog Box

There's a place in Word where all your font-formatting delights are kept in a neatly organized fashion. It's the Font dialog box, shown in Figure 11-5.

To summon the Font dialog box, click the Dialog Box Launcher button in the lower-right corner of the Font group or press Ctrl+D.

The Font dialog box contains *all* the commands for formatting text, even quite a few that didn't find their way into the Font group.

Please note the lovely Preview window, at the bottom of the Font dialog box. This window allows you to preview changes to your text. One of my pastimes is to continuously select fonts in the Font dialog box to see what they look like in the Preview window.

When you're done setting up your font stuff, click the OK button. Or, click Cancel if you're just visiting.

✔ The best benefit of the Font dialog box is the Preview window, at the bottom. That window shows you exactly how your choices affect text in your document.

✔ You select the Underline attribute from the Underline Style drop-down list. Word can do several types of underlining.

✔ The Font names *+Body* and *+Heading* refer to the fonts selected by the current document theme. This is done so that you can use Word's theme commands to quickly change body and heading fonts for an entire document all at once.

✔ Save the festive attributes — such as Shadow, Outline, Emboss, or Engrave — for titles and headings.

✔ The Character Spacing tab displays advanced options for changing the size and position of text on a line.

✔ Changes you make in the Font dialog box affect any marked block on the screen or any new text you type after you close the Font dialog box.

✔ The Font dialog box can also be accessed from the Find dialog box or the Find and Replace dialog box. This helps you to search for, or search and replace, specific text formatting in a document.

✔ You can mark all similar text formatting in a document as a block by right-clicking a bit of text and choosing Styles⇨Select Text with Similar Formatting. That way, you can universally change similar text in a document without doing a search-and-replace for text formats. Also see Chapter 7 for more block-marking information.

✔ The Default button in the Font dialog box is used to change the font that Word uses when you're starting up a new document. If you prefer to use a specific font for all your documents, choose the font (plus other text attributes) in the Font dialog box, and then click the Default button. Click the Yes button to answer the question about changing the Normal template. Afterward, all your documents start with the new default font you've selected.

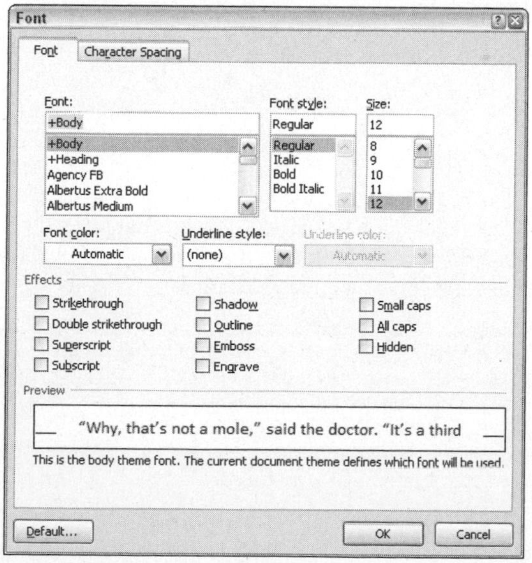

Figure 11-5:
The neatly
organized
Font dialog
box.

Text-attribute effects roundup

Bold and italic are the most common ways to dress up a character. Beyond that, Word has a bucketful of character attributes you can apply to your text. This table shows the lot of them:

Format	Key Combination	Command Button
Clear all formats	Ctrl+spacebar	
ALL CAPS	Ctrl+Shift+A	
Bold	Ctrl+B	**B**
Double underline	Ctrl+Shift+D	
Hidden text	Ctrl+Shift+H	
Italic	Ctrl+I	*I*
SMALL CAPS	Ctrl+Shift+K	
Continuous underline *	Ctrl+U	U
Word underline *	Ctrl+Shift+W	
Strikethrough		abc
$_{sub}$script	Ctrl+=	x_2
^{super}script	Ctrl+Shift+=	x^2

* Note the difference between word underline and continuous underline.

Hidden text is good for what it says — hiding text in a document. Of course, you don't see the text on-screen, either. To show the hidden text, click the Show/Hide command button (in the Paragraph Group on the Write tab) as described in Chapter 2, in the section about spots and clutter in your text. The hidden text shows up in the document with a dotted underline.

Changing the CASE of Text

Believe it or not, upper- and lowercase *do* have something to do with a font. Back in the old mechanical-type days, fonts came in a case, like a briefcase. The top part of the case, the upper case, held the capital letters. The bottom part of the case held the lowercase letters. So, in a way, changing the case of text is kind of a font-formatting trick.

To change the case of text in Word, use the Change Case command button in the Font group. Choosing that button displays a menu of options, shown in Figure 11-6. Select the text you want to change, and then choose the proper item from the Change Case command button. Your text is modified to match the menu item that's selected.

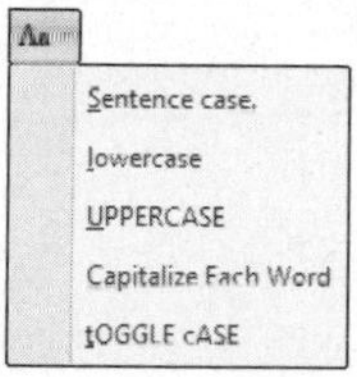

Figure 11-6:
The Change
Case com-
mand button
menu.

Aa

Sentence case.

lowercase

UPPERCASE

Capitalize Each Word

tOGGLE cASE

You can also use the Shift+F3 command to change the case of selected text. But that keyboard shortcut cycles between only three of the menu options shown in Figure 11-6: ALL CAPS, lowercase, and Capitalize Each Word.

Chapter 12

Formatting Paragraphs

In This Chapter

▶ Understanding paragraph formatting

▶ Finding paragraph-formatting commands

▶ Aligning paragraphs left, center, right, and full

▶ Changing line spacing

▶ Adding room between paragraphs

▶ Indenting a paragraph

▶ Making a hanging indent

▶ Double-indenting a paragraph

▶ Using the Ruler

Paragraphs are goodly sized chunks of text. In school, you were probably taught that a paragraph must be one or more sentences expressing a thought. Or something. Anyway, I view a paragraph, formatting-wise, as a veritable text sandwich, bulky enough to qualify for its own round of formatting commands: A paragraph has left and right margins, a top and a bottom, a before and an after, plus space in the middle.

Word provides ample tools for formatting paragraphs of text. There's a simple way, for example, to automatically indent the first line of a paragraph. Imagine! That and other amazing formatting tricks, all designed to impress and inspire, are found in this handy chapter.

How to Format a Paragraph

You can format a paragraph in Word several ways:

- ✔ Use a paragraph-formatting command, and then type a new paragraph in that format.

- ✔ Use the formatting command in a single paragraph to format that paragraph. (Place the insertion pointer in a paragraph, and then use a formatting command.)

- ✔ Use the formatting command on a block of selected paragraphs to format them all together.

Here's an example for you to mess with:

1. **Type the following paragraph:**

   ```
   It was a crushing blow. Francis had practiced her
   lines all week. Her mother had finished the costume.
   Even her brothers were impressed, commenting that she
   really was Chicken Little. But all that meant nothing
   now. While she sat in the bathtub, her father broke
   the terrible news: "I'm sorry, Francis. But you have
   the chicken pox."
   ```

   Did you remember to press Enter to end the paragraph? That's important.

2. **Move the insertion pointer so that it's somewhere amid the paragraph's text.**

3. **Press Ctrl+E.**

   Ctrl+E is the keyboard shortcut for the Center command, which centers the paragraph's text from left to right on the page.

4. **Press Ctrl+L.**

   The paragraph is left justified, undoing the centering.

5. **Press Ctrl+T.**

   The paragraph is now formatted with a *hanging indent*.

6. **Press Shift+Ctrl+T.**

   And the hanging indent is gone.

Hopefully, that little demo gets you in the mood for understanding how paragraph formatting works. The commands used in these steps are explained elsewhere in this chapter.

- ✔ A *paragraph* is a chunk of text that ends when you press the Enter key. Paragraph-formatting commands work only on paragraphs, not on sentences or individual words. Of course, if your paragraph is only a single word or sentence, that's okay.

- ✔ Refer to Chapter 7 for specific and entertaining block-marking instructions.

✔ You can format all the paragraphs in a document by first selecting the entire document. The quick way to do that is to press the Ctrl+A key combination.

✔ To format individual characters or the text inside a paragraph, refer to Chapter 11.

✔ Some folks like to see the Enter key symbol (¶) in their documents, visually marking the end of each paragraph. You can do this in Word by clicking the Word Options button on the Office Button menu. Click Display on the left side of the Word Options dialog box. On the right side, put a check mark by Paragraph Marks. Click OK. Now, every time you press the Enter key, a ¶ symbol appears at the end of the paragraph.

Where the Paragraph Formatting Commands Lurk

Word smuggled some of the most popular paragraph-formatting commands into the Paragraph group, found on the Home tab. Figure 12-1 illustrates the Paragraph group, although you should note that Word may show a different arrangement of the command buttons depending on your computer's screen width.

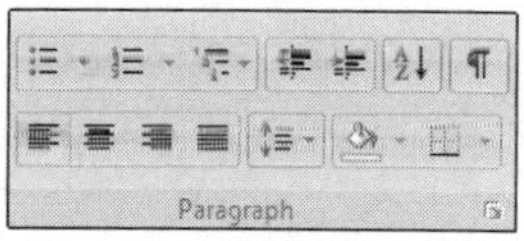

Figure 12-1:
Paragraph-
formatting
commands
on the
Home tab.

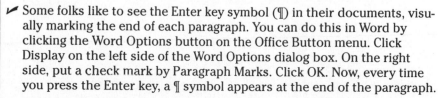

In an odd twist, indenting and paragraph spacing is found in another Paragraph group, this one on the Page Layout tab, shown in Figure 12-2.

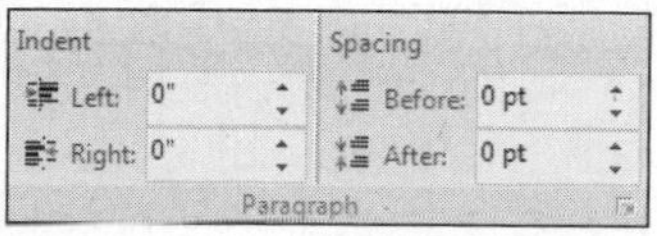

Figure 12-2:
Paragraph-
formatting
commands
on the Page
Layout tab.

Because many of the paragraph-formatting commands require you to enter values, there also exists a Paragraph dialog box, shown in Figure 12-3. There, you find some finer controls that the command buttons just don't offer.

To summon the Paragraph dialog box, click the Dialog Box Launcher button, found in the lower-right corner of the Paragraph group. Or, you can use the forgettable keyboard shortcut Alt+H, P, G.

The commands in the various paragraph-formatting locations are covered throughout the rest of this chapter.

Click the Cancel button or press the Esc key to dismiss the Paragraph dialog box.

The Mini Toolbar, which shows up after you select text, also contains a smattering of paragraph-formatting buttons. Refer to Chapter 7 for more information on the Mini Toolbar.

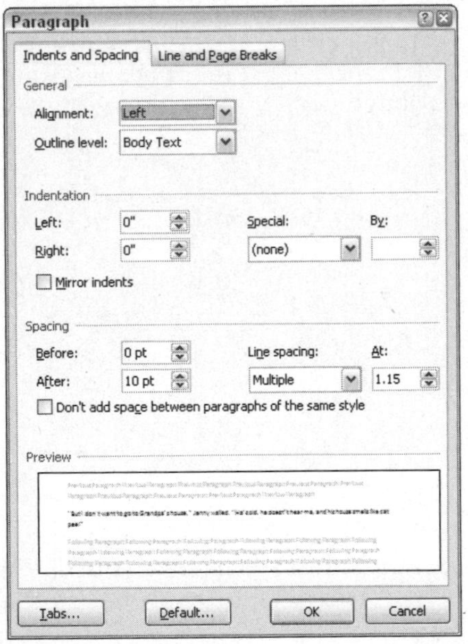

Figure 12-3:
The
Paragraph
dialog box.

Paragraph Justification and Alignment

Paragraph alignment has nothing to do with politics, and justification has nothing to do with the right or wrong of how paragraphs are formatted. Instead, both terms refer to how the left and right edges of the paragraph look on a page. There are four options: Left, Center, Right, and Fully Justified, each covered in this section.

Line up on the left!

Much to the pleasure of southpaws the world over, left-aligning a paragraph is considered normal. That's the way the old typewriter used to do things: The left side of the paragraph is all even and tidy, and the right side is jagged, not lined up.

 To left-align a paragraph, press Ctrl+L or click the Align Left command button.

> ✔ This type of alignment is also known as *ragged right*.
>
> ✔ Left-aligning a paragraph is how you "undo" the other types of alignment.

Everyone center!

Centering a paragraph places each line in that paragraph in the middle of the page, with an equal amount of space to the line's right or left.

 To center a paragraph, press Ctrl+E or use the Center command button.

> ✔ Centering is ideal for titles and single lines of text. It's ugly for paragraphs and makes reading your text more difficult.
>
> ✔ You can center a single word in the middle of a line by using the center tab. Refer to Chapter 13 for the details.

Line up on the right!

A *right-aligned* paragraph has its right margin nice and even. The left margin, however, is jagged. When do you use this type of formatting? I have no idea, but it sure feels funky typing a right-aligned paragraph.

 To flush your text along the right side of the page, press Ctrl+R or click the Align Right command button.

> ✔ This type of alignment is also known as *ragged left* or *flush right*.
>
> ✔ You can right-justify text on a single line by using a right-align tab. Refer to Chapter 13 for more info.

Full justification! (Full justification — aye, sir!)

Full justification occurs when both the left and right sides of a paragraph are lined up neat and tidy, flush with the margins.

 To give your paragraph full justification, press Ctrl+J or click the Justify command button.

✔ Fully justified paragraph formatting is often used in newspapers and magazines, which makes the thin columns of text easier to read.

✔ Word makes each side of the paragraph line up by inserting tiny slivers of extra space between the words in a paragraph.

Making Room Before, After, or Inside Your Paragraphs

Word lets you add air to the space before, after, and in the middle of your paragraphs. Traditionally, the line spacing command lets you add room between the lines of text within a paragraph. From the typesetting planet, your word processor lets you add space before and after each paragraph. Combine these two commands and you have a great deal of control over how tall or tight your paragraph text can be.

Traditional line spacing

Changing the line spacing inserts extra space between *all* lines of text in a paragraph. Word adds the space, or extra blank lines, *below* each line of text in the paragraph. That means that line spacing also affects the space between paragraphs.

 The Line Spacing command button displays a menu listing common line-spacing commands, as shown in Figure 12-4. Choose a new line-spacing value from that list to change the line spacing for the current paragraph or all the paragraphs selected as a block.

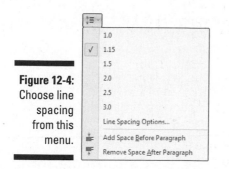

Figure 12-4:
Choose line
spacing
from this
menu.

Before Word 2007, line spacing was preset to 1.0 in Word. Note in Figure 12-4, as well as in your documents, that the setting is now 1.15, which is supposedly more readable and also a blessing to term-paper writers all over.

✔ Double spacing, or the line spacing value 2.0, means that one line of text appears with one blank line below it. Triple spacing, 3.0, means that one line of text appears with two blank lines below.

✔ Ah! The keyboard shortcuts:

- To single-space, press Ctrl+1.

- To double-space, press Ctrl+2.

- To use 1½-spaced lines, press Ctrl+5.

✔ Yes, Ctrl+5 means 1½-line spacing, not 5-line spacing. Use the 5 key on the typewriter part of the computer keyboard. Using the 5 key on the numeric keypad activates the Select All command.

✔ I know some fussy editors, old-school types, who want everything triple-spaced so that they can scribble comments between the lines.

✔ As with justification, there's no such thing as no line spacing. If you want to "remove" fancy line spacing, select the text and press Ctrl+1 for single spacing.

More line spacing options

To set the line spacing to something specific, you need to call on the Paragraph dialog box, as described earlier in this chapter and shown in Figure 12-3.

In the Spacing part of the dialog box, the Line Spacing drop-down list is used to set various line-spacing values: Single, 1.5, and Double, just like the Line Spacing command button's menu.

Additional options in the Line Spacing drop-down list require you to also use the At box. Values you set in the At box indicate line spacing as described here:

✔ **At least:** The line spacing is set to the specified value, which Word treats as a minimum value. Word can disobey that value and add more space whenever necessary to make room for larger type or different fonts on the same line of text.

✔ **Exactly:** Word uses the specified line spacing and doesn't adjust the spacing to accommodate for larger text.

✔ **Multiple:** This option is used to enter line-spacing values other than those specified in the drop-down list. For example, to set the line spacing to 4, choose Multiple from the Line Spacing drop-down list and type **4** in the At box. Word's 1.15 line spacing value is set with the Multiple option.

You can specify values in the At box in increments of 0.1. So, when you want to tighten up text on a page, select all the paragraphs on that page, choose Multiple from the Line Spacing drop-down list, and then type **0.9** in the At box. Or, to add more room subtly, type **1.2**.

Click the OK button to confirm your settings and close the Paragraph dialog box.

That space between paragraphs

It's really a silly thing to do: Press Enter twice to end a paragraph. People say that they need the extra space between the paragraphs, but what they don't realize is that Word can add that space for you, automatically. Here's how:

1. **Position the insertion pointer in the paragraph that you want more air around, or mark a block of paragraphs to affect them all.**

2. **Check the point size of your text.**

   It's listed on the Home tab, in the Font group.

3. **Click the Page Layout tab.**

4. **Use the After button in the Paragraph group to add space after the paragraph.**

   As you adjust the value, the paragraph (or paragraphs) grow extra spacing.

For example, if your text size is 12, click the up arrow by After until the value 12 appears in the box. This adds 12 points, or one blank line, of space after each paragraph you type.

The space you add to the paragraph becomes part of its format, just like line spacing would, although the space afterward appears only *after* the paragraph's text. (You can see this space if you select the paragraph as a block.)

Most of the time, space is added following a paragraph, as just described. Word also lets you add space before a paragraph. For example, you could do this to further separate a paragraph from a heading or graphical image. To add the space before, repeat the preceding steps and put a value into the Before box in Step 4.

✔ You can manually enter values in the After (or Before) box. But remember that the values are *points*, not inches or potrzebies.

✔ This trick is a great way to spread out a list of bullet points or numbered steps without affecting the line spacing within the bullet points or steps.

✔ Refer to Chapter 11 for more information points as they relate to text size.

✔ Adding space before or after a paragraph isn't the same as double-spacing the text inside the paragraph. In fact, adding space around a paragraph doesn't change the paragraph's line spacing.

Paragraph Indentation

Do you suffer from the shame of manual paragraph indenting? It's a hidden secret. Yes, even though computers enjoy doing things automatically, too many Word users still begin a paragraph of text by pressing the Tab key. It's ugly, but it's something that must be discussed.

Word can indent your paragraphs for you just as easily as you can indent your car door in a crowded mall parking lot. This section discusses various paragraph-indenting options.

Indenting the first line of a paragraph

To have Word automatically indent the first line of every paragraph you type, heed these steps:

1. **Conjure up the Paragraph dialog box.**

   Refer to the section "Where the Paragraph Formatting Commands Lurk," earlier in this chapter, for proper conjuring incantations plus a bonus picture of what the Paragraph dialog box looks like (refer to Figure 12-3).

2. **In the Indentation area, locate the Special drop-down list.**

3. **Select First Line from the list.**

4. **Optionally, enter an amount in the By box.**

Unless you've messed with things, the box should automatically say `0.5"`, which means that Word automatically indents the first line of every paragraph a half-inch — a tab stop. Type another value if you want your indents to be more or less outrageous. (Things are measured here in inches, not in points.)

5. **Click OK.**

The selected block, or the current paragraph (and the remaining paragraphs you type), all automatically have an indented first line.

To remove the first-line indent from a paragraph, repeat these steps and select (none) from the drop-down list in Step 3. Then click the OK button.

 Word's AutoCorrect feature can perform these steps for you, but it's tricky. First you must type the paragraph. Then go back to the start of the paragraph and press the Tab key. This instantly fixes the paragraph's indentation (if AutoCorrect is on), and you see the AutoCorrect icon on the screen. Here's the secret: Ignore the AutoCorrect icon and your paragraph indenting is fixed. *Ta-da!*

 There are two ways to separate paragraphs from each other in a document. The first is to add space between each paragraph, which is covered in the earlier section "That space between paragraphs." The second way is to indent each paragraph's first line, as covered in this section. Choose one or the other; you don't need to use both.

Making a hanging indent

A *hanging indent* isn't in imminent peril, nor can it affect the outcome of an election. Instead, it's a paragraph in which the first line sticks out to the left and the rest of the paragraph is indented. It's a preferred way to present paragraph lists — like this:

```
Door-proof. The answer to the question whether the cat
          wants in or out is always yes. The cat merely
          wants to be on the other side of the door. We
          at KittySmart have finally bred that annoyance
          out of our cats.
```

To create such a beast, position the insertion pointer in the paragraph you want to hang and indent. Press Ctrl+T, the Hanging Indent keyboard shortcut.

Because you probably won't remember Ctrl+T all the time (who could?), paragraphs can also be hanged and indented in the Paragraph dialog box. Use the steps from the preceding section, but in Step 3 choose Hanging from the drop-down list.

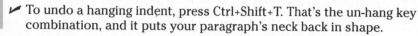

✔ The hanging indent is really an indent-everything-but-the-first-line-of-the-paragraph type of indent.

✔ To undo a hanging indent, press Ctrl+Shift+T. That's the un-hang key combination, and it puts your paragraph's neck back in shape.

Indenting a whole paragraph

Just as you can indent the first line of a paragraph, you can indent every line of a paragraph, by moving the paragraph's left margin over to the right a notch, just like Mr. Bunny: Hop, hop, hop. This technique is popular for typing block quotes or *nested* paragraphs.

 To indent a paragraph one tab stop from the left, press Ctrl+M or click the Increase Indent command button in the Home tab's Paragraph group.

 To unindent an indented paragraph, press Ctrl+Shift+M or click the Decrease Indent command button in the Home tab's Paragraph group.

Each time you use the Increase Indent command, the paragraph's left edge hops over one tab stop (typically, one half-inch). To undo this and shuffle the paragraph back to the left, use the Decrease Indent command.

✔ You cannot decrease the indent beyond the left margin.

✔ The indent isn't affected by the paragraph's alignment. These commands affect only the paragraph's left margin.

✔ To indent both the left and right sides of a paragraph, use the Paragraph dialog box and set both left and right indents to the same value.

✔ Although the Ctrl+M and Ctrl+Shift+M shortcuts aren't mnemonic, their only difference is a Shift key. So, after you get used to using them (hopefully, before the afterlife), they're easy to remember.

Setting the paragraph margins

A paragraph of text in Word sits snugly between the page's left and right margins. Those margins can be broken or extended, allowing you to indent the left and right sides of one or more paragraphs however you want. The secret is found in the Page Layout tab's Paragraph group.

The Left item sets the indentation for the paragraph's left edge.

The Right item sets the indentation for the paragraph's right edge.

Setting positive values moves the edges inward. Setting negative values moves the edges outward. When the values are set to zero, the paragraph's margins match the page's margin.

For example, to double-indent a paragraph as a block quote, you could move both the left and right margins in by 8/10 of an inch. Here's how that happens:

1. **Put the insertion pointer in the paragraph or just select multiple paragraphs as a block.**

2. **Click the Page Layout tab.**

3. **In the Paragraph group, enter .8 in the Left box.**

   You can type .8 in the box or use the spinner gizmo to enter .8. (The spinner increments or decrements in 1/10-inch values.)

4. **Enter .8 in the Right box.**

For a greater indent, enter a larger value in both the Left and Right boxes. Or, to undo an indent, enter **0** in both boxes.

✔ Refer to Chapter 14 for more information on the page margins.

✔ When you're formatting facing pages, with inside and outside margins, it helps to use the Paragraph dialog box. (Refer to Figure 12-3.) Use the Mirror Indents item to set the inside (toward the fold between the pages) and outside (toward the edges) margins so that an indented paragraph on one page mirrors the paragraph on the opposite page.

✔ Do not try to mix left and right indenting with a first-line indent or hanging indent while drowsy or while operating heavy equipment.

Who Died and Made This Thing Ruler?

The Paragraph dialog box can be a daunting place, what with all the numbers and terminology and such. A more graphical, and therefore more fun, way to manipulate a paragraph's indentation and margins is to use the Ruler.

The Ruler may be hidden in your copy of Word. To show it, click the View Ruler button, found atop the vertical (right) scroll bar.

The Ruler appears on the top of the writing part of the Word window, shown in Figure 12-5. In Print Layout view, a vertical ruler also shows up and runs down the left side of the window. (That ruler is just for show.)

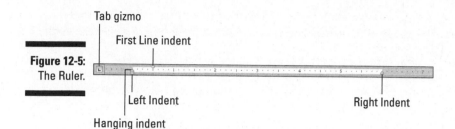

Figure 12-5:
The Ruler.

Tab gizmo

First Line indent

Left Indent

Right Indent

Hanging indent

The dark gray part of the Ruler (outside ends) is beyond the margins that are set for the page. The lighter gray is inside the page margins, and the Ruler measures that space from the left, starting with zero inches.

On the ruler you find four gizmos that control paragraph indenting: one downward-pointing triangle, two upward-pointing triangles, and one block. Those gizmos reflect the current paragraph formatting, and they can be manipulated with the mouse to change the formatting. Here's what they control:

 To adjust a paragraph's right edge, grab the Right Indent guy on the ruler and drag him right or left.

 To adjust the paragraph's left edge, grab the Left Indent thing on the ruler and slide it to the left or right. Note that this gizmo moves both the Hanging Indent and First Line Indent guys together.

 The paragraph's first line can be set independently of the left edge by dragging the First Line Indent doojobbie to the left or right.

 The Hanging Indent thing controls all the paragraph's lines except for the first one. Normally, you don't mess with this gizmo: Use the Left Indent guy to set the paragraph's left margin. The exception is for creating a hanging indent, which is probably why this gizmo has such a clever name.

✔ The Ruler measures from the left margin, not from the left edge of the page.

✔ The left margin is set when you format a page of text. See Chapter 14.

✔ The Tab gizmo is used to set the various tab stops used in Word. This confusing and frustrating subject is covered in Chapter 13.

✔ The Ruler is fine for visually setting indents, but when you need to be precise, use the Paragraph dialog box.

Paragraph-formatting survival guide

This table contains all the paragraph-formatting commands you can summon by holding down the Ctrl key and pressing a letter or number. By no means should you memorize this list.

Format	Key Combination	Command Button
Center	Ctrl+E	
Fully justify	Ctrl+J	
Left-align (flush left)	Ctrl+L	
Right-align (flush right)	Ctrl+R	
Indent	Ctrl+M	
Unindent	Ctrl+Shift+M	
Hanging indent	Ctrl+T	
Unhanging indent	Ctrl+Shift+T	
Line spacing	Alt+H, K	
Single-space lines	Ctrl+1	
1.15 line spacing	Ctrl+0	
Double-space lines	Ctrl+2	
1½-space lines	Ctrl+5	

Chapter 13

Setting Tabs

In This Chapter

▶ Understanding tabs

▶ Setting left tab stops

▶ Using right, center, and decimal tabs

▶ Working in the Tabs dialog box

▶ Setting leader tabs

▶ Fixing the default tab stops

▶ Removing tabs and tab stops

Most people have an issue with tabs in Word. I agree: The topic and the method can be maddening, like seeing Aunt Eunice pour cheap ketchup over her delicious homemade meatloaf. It's really a philosophical thing: When you deal with tabs, you're dealing with the tab character and the tab stop. They go hand in hand. Understand that and you're well on your way to becoming a tenth-level tab master in Word.

Tabs are really part of paragraph formatting, but the topic frustrates so many Word users that I decided to dedicate this entire chapter to the subject of setting tabs.

The Story of Tab

On my ancient Underwood typewriter, the Tab key is on the right side of the keyboard and is named *Tabular Key*. Elsewhere, I've seen it named *Tabulator*. In each case, the root word is *table*. The Tab key is used to help build tables or to organize information in a tabular way.

Pressing the Tab key inserts a tab *character* into your document. That tab character works like a wide space character, but its size is determined by the tab stop. The *tab stop* is a predefined location marked across a page — say, every half-inch — although in Word you can set tab stops at any interval.

It's the tab stop that makes the Tab key work: Press the Tab key, and the insertion pointer hops over to the next tab stop. That way, you can line up text on multiple lines with tabs and tab stops, keeping things nice and even — definitely much nicer than trying to fudge lining up text with the spacebar.

✔ Pressing the Tab key doesn't insert spaces. When you use Backspace or Delete to remove a tab, you delete one character — the tab character.

✔ It's best to format tabs for a single line of text or for only the first line of a paragraph. For anything more complex, use Word's Table command. See Chapter 20.

✔ It helps to have the Ruler visible when you work with tabs. Refer to Chapter 12.

✔ Always use the Tab key when you mean to indent or align text in a document. The worst thing you can do is press the spacebar. That is so wrong! In fact, anytime you press the spacebar more than once, you *need* a tab. Believe me, your documents will look prettier and you'll be happier after you understand and use tabs rather than spaces.

✔ Tab characters can often confuse you because, like spaces, they don't show up on the screen. But you can see them, if you like. To direct Word to display the tab character, which looks like a tiny arrow, as shown in the margin, click the Word Options button on the Office Button menu. Click Display from the left side of the Word Options dialog box. On the right side of the window, put a check mark by Tab Characters. Click OK.

✔ The diet beverage Tab was named for people who like to keep a tab on what they consume.

The Tab Stops Here

The Tab key works because of tab stops. So, using the Tab key really means setting a tab stop at a certain position in a line of text. That seems simple enough, if it weren't for two problems: Setting tab stops isn't the most logical thing in Word, and there are five different types of tab stops.

The handiest way to set tab stops in Word is to use the Ruler, shown in Figure 13-1. The tab stops appear as tiny black symbols clinging to the bottom of the Ruler, shown in the figure. As you may guess, these tab stops are easily set and manipulated by moving the mouse.

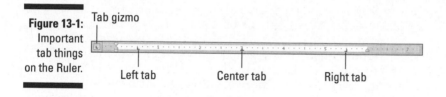

Figure 13-1:
Important
tab things
on the Ruler.

Tab gizmo

Left tab   Center tab   Right tab

Here are the five types of tab stops available on the Ruler:

The left tab is the traditional type of tab stop.

The center tab centers text, mostly for titles or headers.

The right tab right-justifies text.

The decimal tab aligns numbers by their decimal parts.

The bar tab isn't a tab stop at all, but, rather, a decorative ornament.

Setting a tab involves two steps. First, you select one of these tabs from the Tab gizmo on the left end of the Ruler. Clicking the Tab gizmo displays a different tab type. (The Tab gizmo also displays some of the paragraph-indent symbols, covered in Chapter 12.) The second step is to click the mouse on the Ruler at the exact spot where you want the tab stop set. To set a left tab stop, you choose the left tab from the Tab gizmo and then click the ruler where you want that tab stop positioned. Click the 3-inch mark, and the plump L of the left tab stop settles down at that position nicely.

✔ Using and setting each of these tab stops listed in this section is covered elsewhere in this chapter.

✔ Tabs are paragraph-level things. Setting tabs affects only the paragraph that the toothpick cursor is blinking in. To set the tabs for several paragraphs, you must first select them as a block. Refer to Chapter 7 for more blocky stuff.

✔ Figure 13-1 shows three tab stops set: A left tab stop at the half-inch mark, a center tab stop at the 3-inch mark, and a right tab stop at the 5½-inch mark.

✔ When you're selecting several paragraphs, you may spot a light gray or phantom tab stop on the ruler. That indicates a tab stop set in one paragraph, but not all. To apply the tab stop to all selected paragraphs, click the phantom tab stop once. Otherwise, you can remove the tab stop per the instructions found in this chapter's later section "Unsetting a Tab Stop."

The Standard Left Tab Stop

The left tab stop is the traditional type of tab stop. When you press the Tab key, the insertion pointer advances to the left tab stop, where you can continue to type text. This works best for typing lists, for organizing information on a single line paragraph, or when you want to indent the first line of a multi-line paragraph. This section provides some examples.

The tabbed list

A common use for the tab stop is to create a simple two-column list, as shown in Figure 13-2.

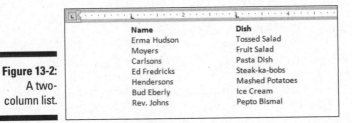

Figure 13-2:
A two-column list.

The following steps describe how to easily set up such a list:

1. **On a new line, press Tab.**

2. **Type the item for the first column.**

   It works best when this is a short item, two or three words max.

3. **Press Tab.**

4. **Type the item for the second column.**

   Again, this should be something short.

5. **Press Enter to end that line and start a new line.**

   Yes, your list looks horrible! Don't worry. It's more important to get the data typed first and then format it second.

6. **Repeat Steps 1 through 5 for each item in the list.**

   After the list is finished, setting the tab stops is done visually by using the ruler.

7. **Summon the ruler, if necessary.**

Click the View Ruler button to display the ruler if it's hidden.

8. **Select all the lines of text that you want to organize into a two-column tabbed list.**

Refer to Chapter 7 for more information on marking blocks of text.

9. **Click the Tab gizmo until the Left Tab icon appears.**

If it already shows up in the Tab gizmo, you're set to go.

You can see what a Left Tab icon looks like right here in the margin.

10. **Click the mouse on the Ruler at the number 1, the 1-inch position.**

This step sets a left tab stop at one inch. You see how the text you selected immediately falls into place.

11. **Click the mouse to set a second tab stop at the 3-inch mark.**

The list looks nice and even, in two columns (refer to Figure 13-2).

12. **Adjust the tab stops if necessary.**

Slide the tab stops left or right on the ruler as needed to help clean up your list. As you slide the tab stops, do you notice how a dashed vertical line extends through your text? That shows you where text lines up.

These steps can also be used to create a three- or even a four-column list. The idea is to keep the text brief, on one line, and separated by single tabs. Then use the tab stops on the ruler to line things up and make them pretty.

Here are the key points to remember here:

✔ You need only one tab between items in a column list. That's because:

It's the *tab stop*, not the tab character, that lines up your text. As with using two spaces in a row, you never really need two tabs in a row.

✔ You type the text first and then select the text and set the tab stops last.

✔ The tab stops can be adjusted for the entire block of text by using the mouse and the ruler.

✔ For a tabbed list to work, each paragraph must be a line by itself, and the items in each column should be only a word or two long. Any longer, and you need to use Word's Table command, as covered in Chapter 20.

The tab-tab-paragraph thing

Tabs can also be used to form an item list where the paragraph text is kept in the rightmost column. Figure 13-3 shows how the tab-tab-paragraph thing works. It combines both paragraph- and tab-formatting skills.

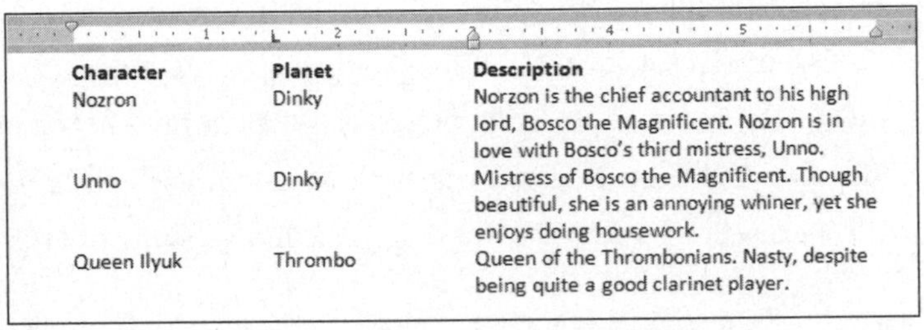

Figure 13-3:
A tab-tab-
paragraph
format
for text.

Character	Planet	Description
Nozron	Dinky	Norzon is the chief accountant to his high lord, Bosco the Magnificent. Nozron is in love with Bosco's third mistress, Unno.
Unno	Dinky	Mistress of Bosco the Magnificent. Though beautiful, she is an annoying whiner, yet she enjoys doing housework.
Queen Ilyuk	Thrombo	Queen of the Thrombonians. Nasty, despite being quite a good clarinet player.

Follow these steps to create something similar:

1. **On a new line, type the item for the first column.**

   The shorter, the better.

2. **Press Tab.**

3. **Type the second column's text and press Tab.**

   This step is optional; it's possible to create a simpler tab-paragraph list, which looks just like Figure 13-3, but without the *Planet* column (and spaced accordingly).

4. **Type the paragraph text.**

   Unlike with the first two items, you're free to type more text here. That's because this final paragraph column will wrap, as shown in Figure 13-3.

5. **Press Enter to end the line and start a new line.**

   Don't let the ugly text format fool you at this point. The text beautifies itself when you add the tab stops.

6. **Repeat Steps 1 through 5 for all the items in the tab-paragraph list.**

   When you're done, you can set the tab stops. You need the ruler for this next step:

7. **Bid the Ruler appear, if need be.**

   Click the View Ruler button to show a hidden ruler.

8. **Select all the lines of text you want to organize into a tab-tab-paragraph list.**

   Chapter 7 discusses block-selection techniques.

9. **Slide the Hanging Indent triangle to the 3-inch position on the ruler.**

   The paragraph appears.

10. **Ensure that the left tab is chosen on the Tab gizmo.**

    The margin shows the Left Tab symbol.

11. **Click the mouse to set a tab stop at 1.5 inches.**

    The second column snaps into place.

12. **Adjust the tab stop and hanging indent triangle as necessary.**

    With the text still selected, you can slide the tab stop and the Hanging Indent things on the Ruler to the left or right to adjust the look of your tab-tab-paragraph. Whatever looks best works best.

You can vary these rules to have a tab-paragraph or even a tab-tab-tab-paragraph. The more tabs you have, the tighter the paragraph gets, so be careful. (The notes from the preceding section also apply to this technique.)

The Center Tab Stop

The center tab is a unique critter, and it has a special purpose: Text placed at a center tab is centered on a line. Unlike centering a paragraph, only text placed at the center tab stop is centered. This is ideal for centering something in a header or footer, which is about the only time you use this type of tab stop.

Figure 13-4 shows an example of a center tab. The text on the left is at the start of the paragraph, which is left-justified. But the text typed after the tab is centered on the line.

Figure 13-4:
A center tab
in action.

D. Gookin   Chapter 12: The Missing Toe

Here's how to make that happen:

1. **Start a new paragraph, one containing text that you want to center.**

   Center tabs are found in one-line paragraphs.

2. **Set a center tab.**

    If necessary, show the ruler: Click the View Ruler button. Click the Tab gizmo until a center tab appears, as shown in Figure 13-4. Click the mouse on the light gray part of the Ruler to set the tab. In Figure 13-4, the center tab is set at the center of the page, at the 3-inch position.

3. **Optionally, type some text to start the line.**

   The text you type should be short; it appears only at the start of the line.

4. **Press the Tab key.**

   The insertion pointer hops over to the center tab stop.

5. **Type the text to center.**

   As you type, the text is centered on the line. Don't type too much; remember that the center tab is a single-line thing.

6. **Press Enter to end the line of text.**

Obviously, if you just want to center text on a line, centering the entire paragraph is a better choice; see Chapter 12. Otherwise, this technique finds itself used mostly in page headers and footers, which are covered in Chapter 15. Look there for an additional example.

✔ The center tab stop allows you to center text in a line without having to center the entire line.

✔ Center tabs are best used on a single line of text, usually by themselves. There's no reason to do them any other way.

The Right Tab Stop

Right tabs are possibly the most confusing tab stop, until you've seen one in action. What they do is to allow you to right-justify text at a tab stop, allowing a single line of text to contain both right- and left-justified text. You've probably seen examples of this all over, but not recognized what it was, so here are Figures 13-5 and 13-6 for you to gawk at.

 As with the other tabs, right tab stops work best on a single line of text. The following two sections describe how to set up right tab stops as shown in Figures 13-5 and 13-6. In both cases, note that it's assumed that the Ruler is visible on the screen. Click the View Ruler button to show the Ruler in Word.

Right stop, left stop list

To create a centered, two-column list with a right tab stop and a left tab stop, as shown in Figure 13-5, obey these steps:

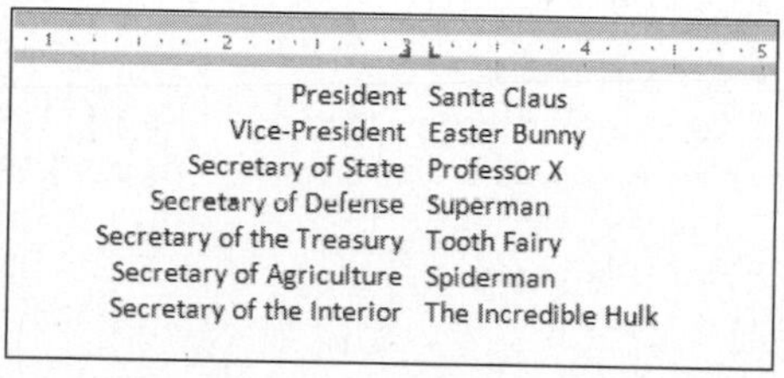

Figure 13-5:
Right tab
stops are
used to
center-align
this list.

President	Santa Claus
Vice-President	Easter Bunny
Secretary of State	Professor X
Secretary of Defense	Superman
Secretary of the Treasury	Tooth Fairy
Secretary of Agriculture	Spiderman
Secretary of the Interior	The Incredible Hulk

1. **Start out on a blank line, the line you want to format.**

2. **Choose the right tab stop from the Tab gizmo.**

   Keep clicking the Tab gizmo with the mouse until the right tab stop appears.

3. **Click the mouse at the 3-inch position on the Ruler.**

4. **Choose the left tab stop from the Tab gizmo.**

   Click, click, click until you see the left tab stop.

5. **Click the mouse at the 3⅛-inch position on the Ruler.**

   Use Figure 13-5 as your guide. Don't fret; you can change the tab stop positions when you're just about done.

6. **Press the Tab key.**

   The insertion pointer hops over to the 3-inch stop, the right tab stop.

7. **Type your text.**

   The text is right-justified at the right tab stop.

8. **Press the Tab key.**

9. **Type your text.**

   The text is left-justified (normal).

10. **Press Enter to end the line of text.**

11. **Repeat Steps 6 through 10 for each line in the list.**

As long as you keep the text to one line, the list should look great, just like in Figure 13-5.

To make adjustments, select the list as a block (see Chapter 7) and use the mouse to adjust the tab stops on the ruler. As you move the tab stops, a dashed line extends down through your text, showing you where the text lines up.

Tab, right stop list

The right tab stop can also be used in a list, as shown in Figure 13-6, commonly found in dramatic programs but just as good for a variety of purposes.

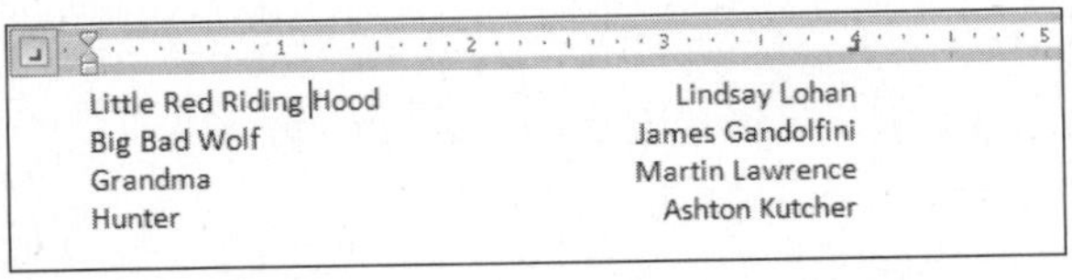

Figure 13-6:
Right tab
stops right-
align the
second
column of
this list.

Little Red Riding Hood	Lindsay Lohan
Big Bad Wolf	James Gandolfini
Grandma	Martin Lawrence
Hunter	Ashton Kutcher

Here's how to concoct such a thing:

1. **Start out with a blank line of text.**

2. **Ensure that the Tab gizmo on the Ruler shows the right tab stop.**

   Refer to Figure 13-6.

3. **Click the mouse at the 4-inch position on the Ruler.**

   The position is just a guess at this point. Later, you can adjust the right tab stop setting to whatever is more visually appealing.

4. **Type the left column text.**

   The text is left-justified, like normal.

5. **Press the Tab key.**

   The insertion pointer hops to the right tab stop.

6. **Type the right column text.**

   The text you type is right-justified, pushing to the left as you type.

7. **Press Enter to end the line of text.**

8. **Repeat Steps 4 through 7 for each line in the list.**

Afterward, you can mark the text as a block and then use the mouse to drag the right tab stop back and forth to whatever looks more visually appealing.

✔ You can drag the left indent toward the center of the page to offset the list from the left margin.

✔ Also refer to the section "Setting leader tabs," later in this chapter, for adding a dotted leader to the right tab stop.

The Decimal Tab

The decimal tab lives to line up columns of numbers. Although you could use a right tab to do this, the decimal tab is a better choice. Rather than right-align text, as the right tab does (see the previous sections), the decimal tab aligns numbers by their decimal portion — that period in the number, as shown in Figure 13-7.

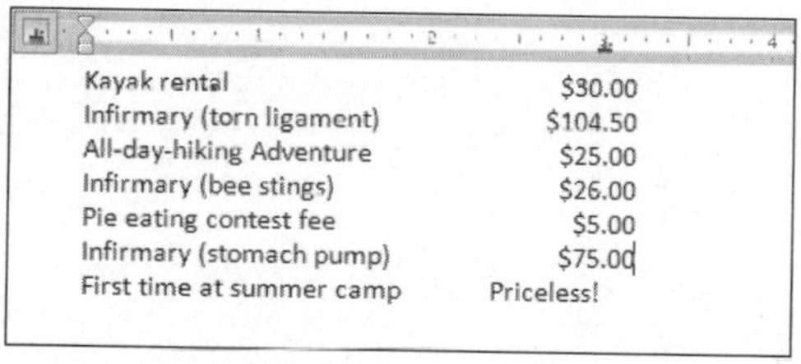

Figure 13-7:
Lining up
numbers
with the
decimal tab.

Kayak rental	$30.00
Infirmary (torn ligament)	$104.50
All-day-hiking Adventure	$25.00
Infirmary (bee stings)	$26.00
Pie eating contest fee	$5.00
Infirmary (stomach pump)	$75.00
First time at summer camp	Priceless!

Here's how to work with such a beast:

1. **Start a blank line of text.**

2. **Choose the Decimal tab stop from the Tab gizmo on the Ruler.**

   Refer to Figure 13-7.

3. **Set the tab stop on the ruler by clicking the mouse at the 3-inch position.**

4. **Type the left column text.**

5. **Press the Tab key.**

6. **Type the numerical amount.**

   The number is right-justified until you press the period key. After that, the rest of the number is left-justified. The effect is that the amount is lined up at the decimal tab stop by the period in the number.

7. **End that line of text by pressing Enter.**

8. **Repeat Steps 4 through 7 for each line in the list.**

When you type something without a period in it (refer to Figure 13-7), it's shown right-justified.

You can adjust your text by selecting all the lines as a block and then moving the decimal tab stop on the Ruler with the mouse.

The Bar Tab

Aside from being a most excellent pun, the bar tab isn't a true tab stop in Word. Instead, consider it as a text decoration. Setting a bar tab merely inserts a vertical line into a line of text, as shown in Figure 13-8. It's much better than using the | (pipe) character on the keyboard for drawing a vertical line in your document.

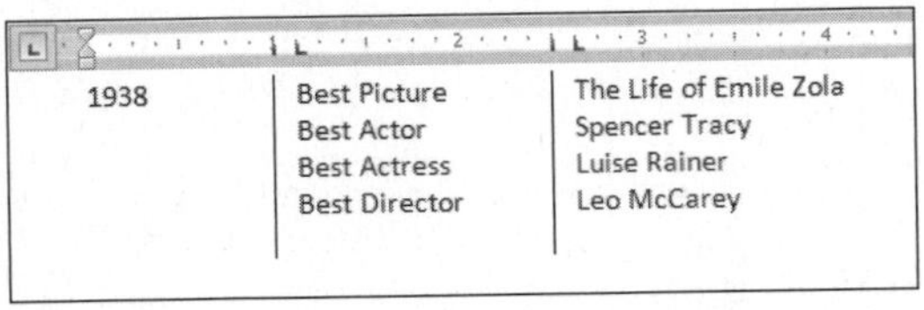

Figure 13-8:
The mysterious bar tab.

1938	Best Picture	The Life of Emile Zola
	Best Actor	Spencer Tracy
	Best Actress	Luise Rainer
	Best Director	Leo McCarey

The setup to create the three-column text shown in Figure 13-8 is similar to what's presented earlier in this chapter for a two-column list (see the earlier section "The tabbed list"), although Figure 13-8 shows a three-column list with the first column at the start of a line.

A bar tab is set like any other tab. But, rather than insert a tab, it inserts a black vertical line in the text. The line appears always, even when no text or tabs are used on a line, as you can see in the last row of text (empty) in Figure 13-8.

In Figure 13-8, observe that a left tab stop is set immediately after the bar tab to help organize text on a line. This is normally how bar tabs are used, although for all practical purposes it's just easier in Word to surrender here and use the Table function instead; see Chapter 20.

The Tabs Dialog Box

If setting tabs on the Ruler is the left-brain approach, using the Tabs dialog box is the right-brain method of setting tab stops in Word. The Tabs dialog box, shown in Figure 13-9, allows you more precision over using the Ruler by itself.

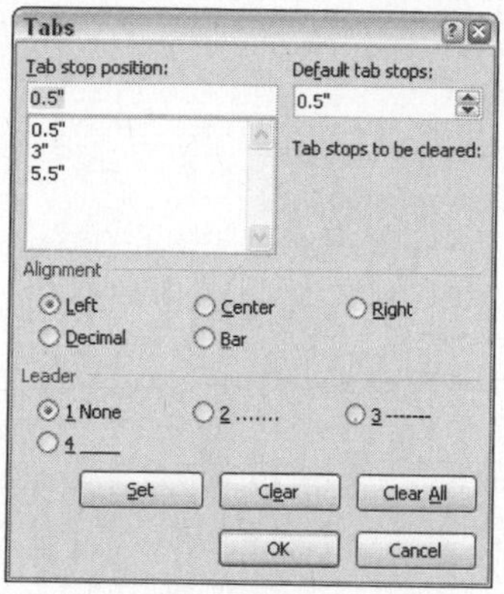

Figure 13-9:
The Tabs
dialog box.

Getting to the Tabs dialog box is a journey, the type of journey that ends with an "All I got was this stupid Tabs dialog box t-shirt." The simplest way to beckon forth the Tabs dialog box is to double-click the mouse in the middle of the Ruler (on the light gray part). Of course, that also *sets* a tab stop, which can be frustrating.

The other way to get to the Tabs dialog box is to summon the Paragraph dialog box: do so by clicking the Dialog Box Launcher button in the lower-right corner of the Paragraph group, on the Home tab. When the Paragraph dialog box is visible, click the Tabs button in the lower-left corner to bring forth the Tabs dialog box.

Setting a tab in the Tabs dialog box

When you need to be precise with your tab stops and the Ruler is proving unruly, follow these steps to set your tabs in the Tab dialog box:

1. **Enter the exact tab stop position in the Tab Stop Position box.**

   For example, type **1.1875** to set a tab at exactly that spot.

2. **Choose the type of tab stop from the Alignment area.**

   The standard tab stop is Left. Other tab stops are covered elsewhere in this chapter.

3. **Click the Set button.**

   The Set button — not the OK button — is what creates the tab stop. After you click Set, your tab stop is placed on the list below the Tab Stop Position dialog box. (You may notice that numbers are rounded to the nearest tenth; Word interprets 1.1875 as 1.9, for example.)

4. **Continue setting tabs.**

   Repeat Steps 1 through 3 for as many tabs as you need to set.

5. **Click OK.**

The tabs you set affect the current paragraph or a selected group of paragraphs. If the Ruler is visible, you can see the tabs and adjust them by using the mouse.

✔ You must click the Set button to set a tab! I don't know how many times I click OK, thinking that the tab stop is set, and it's not.

✔ For most of your tab-setting exercises, I recommend using the Ruler. The Tab dialog box is only necessary when you need to be precise, when you're setting multiple tabs close to each other, or when you're defining leader tabs, as described next.

Setting leader tabs

There's only one task that must be done in the Tabs dialog box that you cannot do with the Ruler: Set a leader tab.

What is a leader tab?

A *leader tab* produces a row of dots, underlining (in a fashion) the tab character. Three styles are available:

Fearless dot leader tabs 180

Zipper line leader tabs _180

U-boat underline leader tabs _____180

You can apply a leader tab to any tab stop in Word other than the bar tab. To do so, refer to other sections in this chapter on how to set the various tab stops — specifically, the right tab stops. To add the dot leader to the tabbed list you've created, follow these steps:

1. **Select the text as a block.**

   Refer to Chapter 7 for block-marking directions.

2. **Bring forth the Tabs dialog box.**

3. **Select the tab stop from the Tab Stop Position list.**

For example, in Figure 13-6, the right tab stop shows up in the Tab Stop Position list as 4". Click to select that item in the list.

4. **In the Leader area, choose the leader style.**

None means "no leader," and it's selected already. Choose one of the three other options.

5. **Click the Set button.**

Don't click OK before you set the tab stop to add the leader. This step is the one you'll screw up most often.

6. **Click OK.**

After clicking the Set button, you can click OK to close the Tabs dialog box and gawk at your text.

Leader tabs with the underline character are also the best way to create fill-in-the-blanks forms. Use the Tabs dialog box to set a left tab stop at the far left margin (usually, 6.0 inches). Choose an underline leader for that tab. Click Set and then OK. Back in your document, type the prompt for the fill-in-the-blanks line, such as

```
Your name:
```

Rather than press a brazillian underlines, just press the Tab key. Instantly, a line extends from the colon to the right margin.

Default tab stops

Word automatically sets tab stops for you in each new document you create. These *default tab stops* are set at half-inch intervals. That's fine for most people, but you can change those defaults, if you like.

New default tab stops are set in the upper-right corner of the Tab dialog box (refer to Figure 13-9), where a new interval for the default tab stops is entered. For example, to set the default tab stops three-quarters of an inch apart, type **0.75"** in the Default Tab Stops box. Click the OK button to confirm and close the Tabs dialog box. The default tab stops appear as dark brown ticks (they're very hard to see) on the gray line below the ruler.

When you set your own tab stops, Word removes the default tab stops between the left margin and wherever any tab stop is set. For example, in Figure 13-8, you can see the default half-inch tab stops starting at the 3-inch position.

Unsetting a Tab Stop

Removing a tab stop is as easy as dragging the Tab Stop icon from the Ruler: Point and click at the tab stop and drag the mouse downward, and the tab stop is gone.

The Tabs dialog box can also be used to remove tab stops. It's especially good for those times when you may have several tab stops close together and plucking one out with the mouse would be tiresome. In the Tabs dialog box, choose the tab stop position in the Tab Stop Position list, and then click the Clear button. Poof! It's gone!

Clicking the Clear All button in the Tabs dialog box removes all tabs from the ruler in one drastic sweep.

To delete a Tab character, of course, simply back up over it with the Backspace key.

Chapter 14

Formatting Pages

In This Chapter

▶ Setting the page and paper size

▶ Choosing landscape or portrait layout

▶ Setting margins for your document

▶ Automatically numbering your pages

▶ Changing page numbers

▶ Creating a new page

▶ Coloring a page

▶ Adding a watermark

Normally, Word doesn't ask questions about the paper you're using. Nope. It's not that Word doesn't care. It cares! But rather than ask questions, Word just guesses that you're using a typical, boring sheet of paper. That's fine, until you need something more interesting or set up a page differently than Word normally guesses. For that, you need to properly describe the sheet of paper to Word. Thus, you have the dawn of *page formatting*.

Page formatting starts with a piece of paper, the final destination of your word processing journey. It covers the margins, or air around the text you write. And, just to be different, in this chapter at least, page formatting also covers page numbering.

Describe That Sheet o' Paper

No matter what size paper you're printing on, Word refers to it as a *page*. As you can possibly guess, not all pages are alike; even within a single document, page size or orientation can change, so pages must be flexible in order for them to be useful.

This section discusses the various ways Word deals with paper and pages.

A page is a sheet of paper about "this" big

Word can print on any size sheet of paper, from a wee postage stamp to the same broadsheet a newspaper is printed on, or even larger. There are only three things to keep in mind here:

✔ You must find that specific paper size, possibly at an office supply store.

✔ You must have a printer that can swallow that specific paper size.

✔ You must tell Word that you're using that specific paper size.

The paper-size-setting stuff is done in the Page Setup group on the Page Layout tab. Choosing a specific size of paper is done by clicking the Size button in that group, which displays a menu, as shown in Figure 14-1. Choose your paper size from that list.

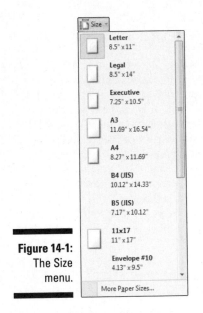

Figure 14-1:
The Size
menu.

For example, if you want to print on that tall, legal-size paper, choose Legal 8.5" x 14" from the list. Your entire document is then updated to reflect the new page size.

✔ To select a size not shown on the menu, choose the More Paper Sizes command to summon the Paper tab of the Page Setup dialog box. Refer to the section "Behold the Page Setup dialog box," elsewhere in this chapter, for more information.

✔ Page-size changes are reflected in the entire document, from first page to last. That is, unless you divide your documents into sections. Then you can use different page sizes within each section. Refer to Chapter 15 for information on sections.

✔ Most PC printers can print on several sizes of paper. Weird sizes, although available on the list, may not be compatible with your printer.

✔ A typical sheet of paper, at least in the United States, measures 8½ inches across by 11 inches tall. Most of the rest of the world uses the A4 paper-size standard, which is slightly longer and a tad narrower.

✔ If you're printing on an odd-size piece of paper, remember to load that special paper into your printer before you start printing. Some smarter printers even tell you which paper size they want to print on. Mine nags at me all the time for the proper paper size. It's like a second mother.

Page orientation (landscape or portrait)

Word normally prints on a sheet of paper from top to bottom with the narrow edge on top. This is called *portrait* mode because its orientation is vertical, like a portrait.

Word can also be told to print longways, or in *landscape* mode. This trick is done by choosing Landscape from the Orientation command in the Page Layout tab's Page Setup group, as shown in Figure 14-2.

Figure 14-2: Setting a page's orientation.

Choosing Orientation⇨Landscape directs Word to shift the paper orientation for every page in your document. This doesn't mean that the text is sideways more than it means that the text prints wide on a page (though I suppose that it could be looked at as printing sideways).

To change the pages back, choose Orientation➪Portrait.

✔ Changing between portrait and landscape modes may require you to adjust the document's margins; see the next section.

✔ Make the decision to have your document in landscape mode before you do any extensive formatting. That mode affects your paragraphs and other "lower-level" formatting, so you should have it done first, before you start composing your text.

✔ Scientists and other people in white lab coats who study such things have determined that human reading speed slows drastically when people must scan a long line of text, which happens when you use landscape mode. Reserve landscape mode for printing lists, tables, and items for which normal paper is too narrow.

✔ Consider using multiple columns in landscape mode. See Chapter 21.

✔ Also see the section "Behold the Page Setup dialog box," later in this chapter, for more page-orientation settings and options.

Marginal information

Every page has *margins*. They provide the air around your document — that inch or so of breathing space that sets off the text from the rest of the page. As with other things in Word, these margins can be adjusted, fooled, cajoled, or otherwise obsessed with.

Word automatically sets your margins at 1 inch from the top and bottom of the page and 1.25 inches from the left and right sides of the page. Most English teachers and book editors want margins of this size because these people love to scribble in margins. (They even write that way on blank paper.) In Word, you can adjust the margins to suit any fussy professional.

To change the margins, use the Page Setup group on the Page Layout tab. Clicking the Margins button in that group displays a menu full of common margin options, as shown in Figure 14-3.

Specific margins can be set by clicking the Custom Margins button at the bottom of the Margins menu. Doing so displays the Margins tab in the Page Setup dialog box, where specific margin information can be entered, including information on printing more than one page on a sheet of paper. Refer to the next section for more information.

✔ Margins on a page are covered in this chapter. To set the indents for a single paragraph, you need to use a paragraph-formatting command. See Chapter 12.

✔ The stars on the Margin menu's icons represent popular or recent margin choices you've made.

✔ Keep in mind that most laser printers cannot print on the outside half-inch of a piece of paper — top, bottom, left, and right. This space is an absolute margin; although you can tell Word to set a margin of 0 inches right and 0 inches left, text still does not print there. Instead, choose a minimum of 0.5 inches for the left and right margins.

✔ Likewise, many ink printers have a taller top or bottom margin requirement. If you attempt to print outside that area, a dialog box appears, informing you of your offense.

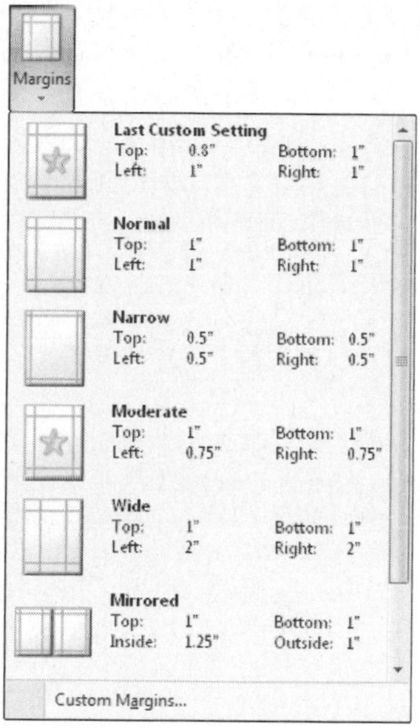

Figure 14-3:
Stuff on the Margins menu.

Behold the Page Setup dialog box

As with many things in Word, when you want more control over page formatting, you must surrender from the Ribbon interface and use an old-fashioned dialog box. In this case, it's the Page Setup dialog box, shown in Figure 14-4.

Dangerous treading in the Multiple Pages area of the Page Setup dialog box

Nestled on the Margins tab of the Page Setup dialog box is the Pages area (refer to Figure 14-4). The Multiple Pages drop-down list tells Word how to use the paper on which your document is printed. Surprisingly, there's more than one way to print a document on a page. The following definitions help, as does the little preview page at the bottom of the Page Setup dialog box:

Normal means one page per sheet of paper. You can't get more normal than that.

Mirror Margins is used when your printer is smart enough to print on both sides of a sheet of paper. That way, every other page is flip-flopped so that your margins always line up. For example, the "gutter" may be on the left of one page, but on the right for the page's back side.

2 Pages per Sheet splits the paper right down the center and forces Word to print two "pages" per sheet of paper. Note that this option works best when used in landscape mode.

Book Fold is Word's attempt to create a multiple-page booklet by printing the proper pages on both sides of a sheet of paper. This option works best if you have a printer capable of printing on both sides of a sheet of paper. The Sheets Per Booklet option that appears helps tell Word how long your booklet is.

Despite these options, Word is a poor bookbinding program. If you're into any type of publishing, consider getting a desktop publishing program, such as Adobe InDesign or Microsoft Publisher, which are far better equipped to deal with such things.

To summon the Page Setup dialog box, click the Dialog Box Launcher in the lower-right corner of the Page Setup group on the Page Layout tab. Or, you can use the keyboard shortcut: Alt+P, P, S.

The Page Setup dialog box sports three tabs: Margins for setting margins, Paper for selecting the paper size, and Layout for dealing with other page-formatting issues.

Click the OK button to confirm your changes and close the Page Setup dialog box.

✔ To print on three-hole paper, use the Margins tab in the Page Setup dialog box to set the gutter margin to about half an inch. That moves the entire margin "frame" over one half-inch from where the three holes are punched. You can set the Gutter Position to Left option, unless the holes are punched on the top of the page, in which case you set the Gutter Position to Top option.

✔ Changes made to a page's format — paper size, orientation, and margins — normally affect an entire document. By using the Apply To drop-down list in the Page Setup dialog box, however, you can determine which portion of a document will be affected by the margin change. You have three options:

- **Whole Document** changes the margins for your whole document, from bonnet to boot.

- **This Point Forward** means that the new margins take place from the toothpick cursor's position onward.

- **This Section** means that the margins apply to only the current section. (See Chapter 15 for more information on sections.)

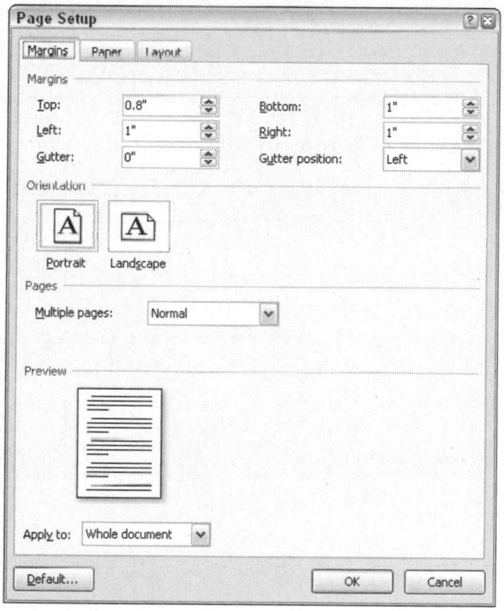

Figure 14-4:
The Page
Setup
dialog box;
Margins tab.

Page Numbering

Woe to the human who manually numbers pages in a word processor! Yea, ye shall be smote upon with fire, brimstone, and blistering typos!

Your word processor will number your pages for you!

Memorize it. Live it. Be it.

Where to stick the page number?

Word not only can automatically number your pages, but it also lets you place the page number just about anywhere on the page and in a variety of fun and interesting formats.

Start your page numbering odyssey thus:

1. **In the Insert tab's Header & Footer area, click the Page Number command button.**

   A menu drops down, listing various page-numbering options. The first three are locations: Top of Page, Bottom of Page, and Page Margins or the sides of the page.

2. **Choose where to place the page numbers.**

   I want my page numbers on the bottom of the page, so I regularly choose the Bottom of Page option.

3. **Pluck a page-numbering style from the scrolling list.**

   There are oodles of samples, so don't cut yourself short by not scrolling through the menu. You can even choose those famous *page X of Y* formats.

In Print Layout view, you can see the page numbers. In Draft view, they remain hidden. (Use Print Layout or Print Preview to see them.) Dutifully, Word numbers each page in your document, starting with 1 for the first page, up to however many pages long the thing grows.

Delete a page? Word renumbers for you.

Insert a page? Word renumbers for you.

As long as you insert the page number per the preceding steps, Word handles everything.

> ✔ Headers and footers are parts of a page that you can format with all sorts of interesting things, including your own page number style or even page numbers on both the top *and* bottom of the page. Refer to Chapter 15 for details.

> ✔ To change the page number format, simply choose a new one from the Page Number menu.

Starting off with a different page number

You and I know that the first page of a document is really page 1, but Word doesn't care. It lets you start numbering your document at whatever page number you want. If you want to start numbering Chapter 2 at page 47, you can do so, if you follow these instructions:

1. **Click the Insert tab.**

2. **In the Header & Footer area, choose Page Number⇨Format Page Numbers.**

    The Page Number Format dialog box materializes, as shown in Figure 14-5.

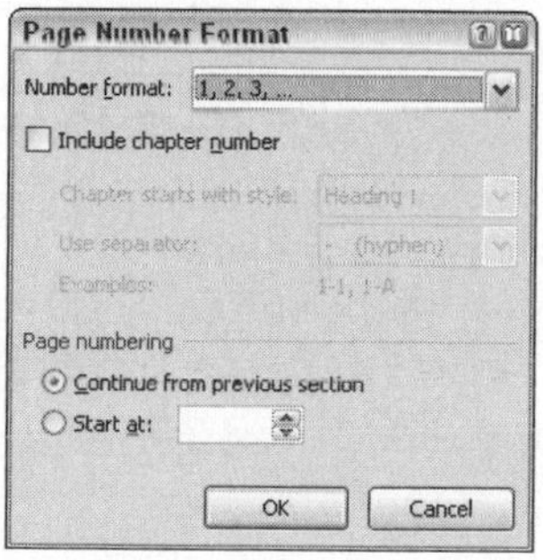

Figure 14-5:
More control over page numbers is given here.

3. **Click the Start At radio button and type the beginning page number in the box.**

4. **Click OK to close the Page Number Format dialog box.**

Word starts numbering your document at the specified page number. So, if you enter 47 in Step 3, the first page of your document is now page 47, the next page is 48, and so on.

When you want the page number to jump in the middle of your document, say, from page 5 to page 16 or (more likely) from page *iv* to page 1, you need to use sections to divide the document. You can start page numbering over again, and at any number or in a new section. See Chapter 15 for more information on sections.

Numbering with Roman numerals

When the urge hits you to regress a few centuries and use Roman numerals to tally a document's pages, Word is happy to oblige. Summon the Page Number Format dialog box (refer to Figure 14-5) per Steps 1 and 2 in the preceding section. Simply choose the style you want from the Number Format drop-down list.

Removing page numbers

To strip out page numbers you've inserted into your document, choose the Remove Page Numbers command from the Page Number menu (in the Header & Footer group on the Insert tab).

The Remove Page Numbers command rids your document of only those page numbers you've inserted by using the Page Number menu. If you've manually added a page number in a header or footer, you must manually delete it. See Chapter 15.

New Pages from Nowhere

As you type your document, Word keeps adding new, blank pages for you to write on. These pages are appended to the end of the document, so even if you're typing in the midst of some chapter, the extra pages keep appearing so that no text is lost and nothing falls off the edge. That's all normal and good.

For those times when you need to stick a blank page in the middle of a document, Word provides two interesting commands. This section explains things.

Starting afresh on a new, blank page

To start typing on a new page in your document, you need to insert a manual page break, also called a *hard page break*. The simplest way to do this is to press the Ctrl+Enter key combination. Word then begins a new page On That Very Spot. All text before the insertion pointer is on the previous page, and all text afterward is on a new page.

 You can also insert a hard page break by choosing the Page Break command from the Pages group on the Insert tab.

In Print Layout view, a hard page break looks like any other page break. The only way to know the difference is to switch to Draft view and use the Show/Hide command. In Draft view, the words *Page Break* appear before the break in your document. That's your clue that you have a hard page break.

Keep these points in mind when you're dealing with hard page breaks:

✔ Never, never, never start a new page by pressing the Enter key over and over until a new page pops up. That's just leads to trouble later as you edit your document.

✔ Pressing Ctrl+Enter inserts a hard page-break *character* in your document. That character stays there, always creating a hard page break no matter how much you edit the text on previous pages.

✔ You can delete a hard page break by pressing the Backspace or Delete key. If you do this accidentally, just press Ctrl+Enter again or press Ctrl+Z to undelete.

✔ If you set hard page breaks, remember to use Print Preview to look at your document before you print it. Sometimes, the process of editing moves text around, making the hard page breaks unnecessary and awkward. Refer to Chapter 10 for more information on the Print Preview command.

✔ The keyboard shortcut for the Show/Hide command is Ctrl+Shift+8. You can also use the Show/Hide command button in the Home tab's Paragraph group.

✔ You can also insert a hard page break by choosing Breaks⇨Page from the Page Setup group. Remember that this command is on the Page Layout tab, not on the Insert tab.

✔ Don't fall into the trap of using hard page breaks to adjust your page numbering. You can use the power of the computer to alter your page numbers without having to mess with page formatting. See the section "Where to stick the page number?" earlier in this chapter.

Inserting a whole, blank page

To shove a fresh, blank sheet of paper into the middle of a document, you can use the Blank Page command button, found in the Insert tab's Pages group. What that command does is to insert *two* hard page breaks into a document, which creates a blank sheet of paper.

Protecting the widows and orphans

Occasionally, a paragraph of text may be split between two pages in an awkward way. A single line from a paragraph on the bottom of one page is an *orphan*. A single line from a paragraph ending at the top of a page is a *widow*. Word offers orphan and widow protection, which you can apply to paragraphs of text to prevent that lone line from appearing at the top or bottom of a page. The feature is Widow/Orphan control.

Normally, Widow/Orphan control is turned on. But you can disable it and set other options for keeping paragraphs of text on one page or another. This magic is done in the Paragraph dialog box, on the Line and Page Breaks tab: Press Alt+H, P, G to summon the Paragraph dialog box, and then click the Page Breaks tab. The options you set there are applied to the current paragraph, or to any selected paragraph. Click OK when you finish making your settings.

I don't recommend using this command unless you really need a blank page in the midst of a document. That is, you never plan on writing on that page. Putting graphics on the page is fine. Adding a table, or any other one-page element to the blank page is also fine. But because the blank page is inserted by using two hard page breaks, writing on the page leads to formatting woes down the line.

Remember that Word automatically adds new pages as you write. So don't use the Blank Page command unless you truly want a *blank* page in your document.

Page Froufrou

Page formatting happens above your text, below your text, to the sides of your text, and even *behind* your text. This section demonstrates the things you can format on a page that appear behind your words.

Color your page

To color your document's pages, use the Page Color command button from the Page Layout tab's Page Background group. Clicking that button displays a menu full of colors, some based on the document theme and some based on standard colors, or you can choose your own color by choosing the More Colors menu command. *Gradients,* or multiple colors, can be chosen by using the Fill Effects menu command.

As you move the mouse over the various colors on the Page Color menu, your document's page color is updated to reflect that new color. The text color may change as well (for example, from black to white) to remain visible.

The color you choose is produced by your printer, but you must direct the printer to print the page color by following these steps:

1. **Press Ctrl+P to summon the Print dialog box.**

2. **Click the Options button in the lower-left corner of the Print dialog box.**

   The Word Options window appears, with the Display item chosen on the left.

3. **In the Printing Options area, put a check mark by the item labeled Print Background Colors and Images.**

4. **Click OK.**

   You can now print the background color.

Note that the color doesn't cover the entire printed page. That's because your printer cannot mechanically access the outside edge of a page, so a white (or whatever color the paper is) border appears around your colored page. At this point, you need to ask yourself whether it's just easier to use colored paper rather than expensive printer ink or toner.

- ✔ To remove page coloring, choose the No Color command from the Page Color menu.

- ✔ See Chapter 11 for information on coloring text.

The distinguished watermark

When finer papers are held up to the light, they show a *watermark,* an image embedded into the paper. The image is impressive but faint. Word lets you fake a watermark by inserting faint text or graphics behind every page in your document. Here's how:

1. **Click the Page Layout tab.**

2. **In the Page Background group, click the Watermark button.**

   A menu plops down with a host of predefined watermarks that you can safely duck behind the text on your document's pages.

3. **Choose a watermark from the long, long list.**

   The watermark is applied to every page in your document.

Sadly, there are few options for customizing the watermark. You can choose the More Watermarks command from the Watermark menu, which displays the Printed Watermark dialog box. In there, you can choose between a picture or text watermark. The picture item is handy because you can choose any graphical image available on your PC (such as a company logo) to use as a watermark. The text item, however, lets you only choose only predefined bits of text.

To rid your document's pages of the watermark, choose the Remove Watermark command from the Watermark menu.

If the watermark doesn't show up in the printed document, you may need to enable the Print Background Text and Images setting. Refer to the steps in the preceding section.

Chapter 15

Formatting Documents

In This Chapter

▶ Breaking your document into chunks

▶ Getting the most from sections

▶ Placing a cover page on your document

▶ Adding a header or footer

▶ Creating unique headers

▶ Suppressing the header on the first page

▶ Working with headers and sections

▶ Deleting a header

*D*ocument is an impressive, important-sounding word. It's also easier than saying "that thing I made in my word processor." In a way, *document* is almost too serious to use for describing everything you write. It just seems pretentious to say that this week's kids' chore chart, a grocery list, or the random bawdy limerick ranks up there with documents like the Declaration of Independence or Martin Luther's *95 Theses*.

As far as formatting is concerned, formatting a document is something you'll probably do only for those few big or formal documents you create. *Real* documents. This includes the concept of sections, which are very useful yet confusing to many beginners, as well as the more rational topic of headers and footers.

The Oft Misunderstood Yet Useful Concept of Sections

Most of the Word page-formatting commands affect every page in a document: The settings for margins, page orientation, paper size, and other types of formatting apply themselves not to a single page but rather to every dang doodle page, from 1 to N, where N is the mathematical value best expressed as "I don't know how huge this value could be."

But sometimes you need a document that isn't formatted the same way page after page. For example, you may want to number Pages 1 through 4 in Roman numerals and then start over on Page 5 with Page 1 in human numerals. Or, you may want the first page of a document to be blank. Or, you may need to display a table on Page 14 in landscape orientation. All those tricks are possible if you understand the concept of *sections*.

Understanding sections

A *section* is a part of a document that contains its own page formatting. You can direct page-formatting commands to affect only a section rather than span an entire document. With each section separate from the others, a document can have multiple page formats.

For example, in Figure 15-1, the document that's illustrated contains two sections. The first is four pages long and uses Roman numeral page numbers. The second section starts on Page 5, where the page number format is restored to normal but starting at page number 1.

Figure 15-1:
A document
with two
sections.

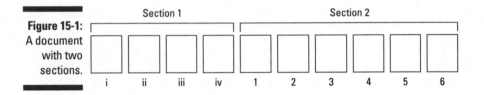

The document illustrated in Figure 15-2 has four sections. The first is the cover page, followed by a regular document format. Section 3, however, contains one page in landscape format. That's followed by Section 4, which is back to normal.

Figure 15-2:
A document
with four
sections.

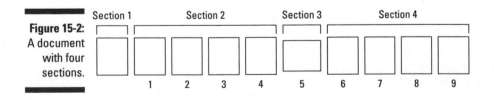

Obviously, when your document's page formatting is the same from head to tail, there's no need to fuss with sections. For anything else, sections are truly a blessing.

- ✔ A *section* is basically an area in your document whose page formatting is different from or unique to the rest of your document.

- ✔ Text and paragraph formatting, as well as any styles you may create, don't give a hoot about sections.

Creating a section

Breaking up your document isn't hard to do. Word has wisely placed all its breaking commands on the Breaks menu: Click the Page Layout tab, and then click the Breaks command button, found in the Page Setup group. The menu is shown in Figure 15-3. Page-breaking commands are at the top of the menu; section breaks are at the bottom.

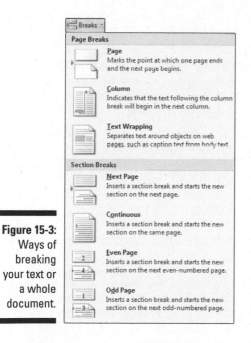

Figure 15-3:
Ways of
breaking
your text or
a whole
document.

The simplest way to create a new section is to choose Next Page from the Breaks menu. This creates a page break, by starting a new page as a new section in your document.

 In Print Layout view, the section break appears just like any other page break. To determine whether a page break is a real page break or something else, you must switch to Draft view and use the Show/Hide command: click the Show/Hide command button on the Home tab or press Ctrl+Shift+8.

In Draft view, the section break appears with the text `Section Break (Next Page)` in the middle of a double row of dots.

After the section is created, you can then modify the page layout and format for each of the sections, as covered next.

- ✔ Use the Continuous section break to mix formatting styles within a page. For example, if you have columns of text sharing a page with regular text, the Continuous section break is the ideal way to separate the individual formats. See Chapter 21 for more information on columns.

- ✔ You can use the Even Page and Odd Page options to start the next section on the next even or odd page — ideal for those futile times when you try to use Word to bind a book or pamphlet.

 ✔ Column and Text Wrapping breaks have nothing to do with sections. Text Wrapping breaks work like soft returns (see Chapter 2), except that they're designed to be used on text that wraps around a figure or table. See Chapter 21 for information on a Column break.

Using a section

To apply a specific page format to one section only, use the dialog box associated with the format, such as the Page Setup dialog box. In the dialog box, look for the Apply To drop-down list. To apply the format to the current section, choose This Section. That way, the format controls only the pages in the current section.

 To determine which section you're in, right-click the status bar (at the bottom of Word's window). A pop-up Status Bar Configuration menu appears. Near the top, you see the item named Section, and on the right, you see the current section number. To see that information always displayed on the status bar, choose Section from the menu; otherwise, press the Esc key to make the pop-up menu go away.

Deleting a section break

You can delete a section break with the Delete key: Position the insertion pointer just before the section break, and then press the Delete key. This technique works best in Draft view with the Show/Hide command working to display the section breaks.

✔ The Show/Hide command's keyboard shortcut is Ctrl+Shift+8.

✔ Deleting a section removes any formatting, including headers and footers, that were unique to that section.

✔ If you accidentally delete a section break, you lose any special formatting you applied to the section. In this case, press the Undo shortcut, Ctrl+Z, before you do anything else.

Adding a Cover Page (Sneaky and Quick)

I'd guess that the most popular use of section breaks is to thwack down a title or cover page to a document. Typically, you don't want page numbers or header or footer information on the title page, so making that page its own section is ideal. But conniving Word to create a single page section and then fussing with headers and footers isn't anyone's idea of a fun time. Therefore, Word 2007 has introduced the Cover Page menu. Here's how it works:

1. **Click the Insert tab.**

2. **In the Pages group, click the Cover Page button.**

   A fat, fun menu full of various cover-page layouts appears.

3. **Choose a cover-page layout that titillates you.**

   That cover page is immediately inserted as the first page in your document. Then Word displays it on the screen for further editing.

4. **Select the bracketed text on the cover page.**

5. **Type the required replacement text.**

   For example, click [Enter Document Title]. Then type your document's real title. The text you type replaces the bracketed text.

6. **Repeat Steps 4 and 5 until the cover page looks the way you like it.**

You can change a cover page at any time by choosing a new one from the Cover Page menu, although I recommend removing the old one first: To remove a cover page you've inserted, choose the Remove Current Cover Page command from the Cover Page menu. It helps to have the insertion pointer on the cover page to delete it.

✔ The Cover Page menu doesn't create a new section in your document. If you're using headers and footers, they appear on the inserted cover page. To avoid this, position the insertion pointer at the top of Page 2 (after the cover page), and from the Page Layout tab, choose Break➪ Continuous. You can then modify the header and footer as described elsewhere in this chapter.

✔ As you learn more about Word, you can even modify or add elements to the cover page after it's inserted. Refer to Chapter 23 for more information about Word's drawing commands.

✔ Leaving the bracketed text on your title page is tacky. Your boss doesn't want to see a report that has [Company Name] on it rather than your company's real name.

Hats and Shoes for Your Pages (Headers and Footers)

Documents can have headers and headings, footers and footnotes. It's easy to confuse things — until you read these handy bullets and peruse this section.

✔ A *header* is text that appears at the top of every page. It's contained in a special, roped-off part of the page where you can place special text.

✔ A *heading* is a text style used to break up a long document, to introduce new concepts and help keep the text organized. See Chapter 16 for more information on headings.

✔ A *footer* is text that appears at the bottom of every page. Like the header, it has its own special area and contains special text.

✔ A *footnote* is a tiny bit of text that appears at the bottom of a page, usually a reference for some bit of text on that page. See Chapter 22.

✔ Headers and footers contain elements such as your name, the document name, date, page number, title, and phone numbers. ("Hurry! Buy now! Operators are standing by!")

✔ Headers can also be called *eyebrows*. Weird, huh?

✔ Footers can include page numbers, a chapter or document title, and soft, cushiony insoles.

The following sections refer to headers, but the information applies to footers as well. (It's just that I get tired of typing "header or footer" over and over). Generally speaking, replace "header" with "footer" and it all works the same.

Adding a header

You can use a header. You can use a footer. You can use them both. You can use neither. Either way, the technique is the same:

1. **Click the Insert tab.**

2. **From the Header & Footer group, choose the Header button.**

   A list of preformatted headers is displayed.

3. **Choose the format you want from the list.**

   The header is added to your document, saved as part of the page format.

   If you were in Draft view, you're immediately switched to Print Layout view so that you can edit the header. (Headers and footers do not appear in Draft view.)

   Notice the new tab on the screen? When you're editing a header, the Design tab appears. Refer to the following section for details.

4. **Select any bracketed text.**

   Select the brackets too!

5. **Type the required replacement text.**

   For example, replace [Enter Document Title] with the real title of your document.

6. **Repeat Steps 4 and 5 for all bracketed text in the header.**

7. **When you're done, click the Close Header and Footer command button in the Close group on the far right side of the Ribbon.**

In Print Layout view, you can see the header or footer displayed in ghostly gray text. In Draft view, you can't see any header or footer, even though it's still there. (You can also use the Print Preview command, as covered in Chapter 10, to see the header or footer.)

✔ You can also exit from editing a header by double-clicking the mouse in the main part of your document

✔ You don't have to go to Page 1 to insert a page number in the header. Word is smart enough to put the proper number on the proper page no matter where you're editing the header in your document.

REMEMBER

✔ Headers and footers are geared to sections in your document. Therefore, as long as you're in the same (or only) section, you can edit the header or footer for that section.

✔ The Header and Footer command buttons are found on the Insert tab, not on the Page Layout tab.

Editing a header

Face it: Word's preset designs for the header are dull. Splashy, but dull. And, chances are that they don't contain all the information you want or need. That's no problem. You can edit the header using what Word created as a starting point, or you can just quickly whip up your own header. It's easy. Here's how:

1. **Click the Insert tab.**

2. **In the Header & Footer group, choose Header⇨Edit Header.**

   When you edit the header, Word tosses you into a special mode of operation. The header appears on the screen as part of the page in Print Layout view. Plus, a new tab appears with groups customized for creating and editing headers, as shown in Figure 15-4.

Figure 15-4:
Tools for editing a header or footer.

3. **Use the Go to Header or Go to Footer command button to switch between the header and footer for editing.**

4. **Edit or modify the header.**

   Items in the header are edited just like anything else in Word. You can add or edit text and format that text by using any of Word's text- and paragraph-formatting commands, including tabs. (See Chapters 11, 12, and 13.)

   You can modify any graphics in the header, although I recommend that you review Chapter 23 before doing so.

Word preformats headers with center and right tabs at the center and far right side of the page. This allows you to press the Tab key and type some text to have the text automatically centered at the bottom (or top) of the header or footer.

5. **Use the command buttons on the Design tab's Insert group for special items.**

Here are some of the more useful special items you can insert into a header. The inserted items appear wherever the insertion pointer is located:

- **Page number:** Choose Quick Parts⇨Page Numbers and choose a page number format from the list. The page number text then appears in the header. If you want to center the page number, press the Tab key and then insert the page number.

- **Date & Time:** Clicking the Date & Time button displays a Date and Time dialog box, which lists various date, time, and combination formats. Choose one, and then click the OK button to insert that date or time text into the header.

- **Graphics:** Use the Picture button to browse for graphics images on your PC's hard drive, which you can insert into the header. The Clip Art button can also be used. Be sure to brush up on graphics in Word by reading Chapter 23 before you try this.

- **Fields:** The most versatile thing you can insert into a header or footer is a field; choose Quick Parts⇨Field from the Insert group. Fields, however, require extra explanation. Refer to Chapter 18 for the details.

6. **Click the Close Header and Footer command button when you're done.**

You're back in your document.

The header is the same for every page in your document. Word is happy to oblige, however, whenever you want a different header, such as for the first page or alternating pages or for different sections in a document. The last few sections in this chapter explain the details.

- ✔ The Design tab (refer to Figure 15-4) may look subtly different on your computer monitor, depending on the screen's resolution.

- ✔ In Print Layout view, you can quickly edit any header or footer by double-clicking its ghostly gray image.

- ✔ If all you need a header for is just a page number, I highly recommend using the page-numbering tricks covered in Chapter 14 as an easier alternative to working with headers directly.

Making odd and even headers

This book is formatted with odd and even headers: The header on the odd (left) pages contains the page number and then the part number and title. On the (right) even pages, the header shows the chapter number, title, and then the page number. You can pull off such a trick in your document as well.

To force Word to accept odd and even headers, obey these steps:

1. **Click the Insert tab.**

2. **From the Header & Footer group, choose Header⇨Edit Header.**

   The Header & Footer Tools Design tab is displayed on the screen (refer to Figure 15-4).

3. **Click to put a check in the box by Different Odd & Even Pages, found in the Options group.**

   This step tells Word that you want two sets of headers: one for odd pages and one for even pages. Notice how the tag identifying the header changes:

   | Odd Page Header |

   The tag tells you which header you're editing; in this case, it's the Odd Page header.

4. **Create the header for the odd pages.**

   Refer to the preceding section for notes on making a header or footer. Remember that the footer can contain any formatted text you would otherwise stick into a Word document.

5. **Click the Next Section button.**

   Word displays the even page's header, allowing you to create or edit its contents. The Header tag changes to reflect which header you're editing:

   | Even Page Header |

   By the way, you click the Next Section button to go from the odd header to the even header. You must click the Previous Section button to return to the odd header from the even header.

6. **Click the Go To Footer button to edit the footer's odd and even pages.**

   Edit the footer's contents and click the Next Section button to ensure that you work on both the odd and even footers (as you do in Steps 4 and 5 for the header).

7. **Click the Close Header and Footer button when you're done.**

Removing the odd/even header option is as simple as unchecking the Different Odd & Even Pages option in the Options group (the opposite of Step 3). When you do that, the even page header and footer are deleted, leaving only the odd header and footer.

"But I don't want a header on my first page!"

Most people don't want the header or footer on the first page, which is usually the title page or a cover page. Suppressing the header for that page is easy. Just follow these steps:

1. **Click the Insert tab.**

2. **From the Header & Footer group, choose Header⇨Edit Header.**

3. **In the Options group, select Different First Page.**

   You see the Header tag change to First Page header, and the Footer tag change likewise. That's your visual clue that the first page of the document sports a different header from the one in the rest of the document.

You can still edit the First Page header, if you like. It's merely different, not necessarily empty.

Headers and document sections

Just as Superman is limited in his powers by the crippling force of kryptonite, the mighty header is limited in its scope and power by the limiting force of the document section. A header, or footer, can exist within only one section. Creating a new section creates a new set of headers and footers.

Word flags each set of headers and footers in the tag just below or above the header or footer area, such as:

    Footer -Section 2-

That helps you determine which section's header or footer you're editing.

 To switch to the next section's header, click the Next Section button.

To switch to the previous section's header, click the Previous Section button.

A source of frustration with multiple sections exists when you use the Link to Previous option. What this option does is set one section's header to match the previous section. That way, you can keep the same header in multiple sections. For example, sometimes you merely want to change page orientation in the middle of a document, but you don't need to change the header. At other times, the Link to Previous button may be source of frustration because it causes any changes made in one section to be either replaced in another section or ignored.

As a hint, when you have the Link to Previous option enabled, the header is tagged on the left with the following:

Same as Previous

That's a big clue to why you may be unable to edit a header, when such a thing causes you frustration.

- ✔ A header is a section-long thing. By placing multiple sections in your document, you can have multiple headers. Refer to the first part of this chapter for information on sections.

- ✔ Multiple sections allow you to change headers throughout a document or to suppress the header on a single page and then pick it up again after that page.

- ✔ To suppress the header on the first page of a document, follow the instructions in this chapter's earlier section "But I don't want a header on my first page!"

- ✔ Changing a header in one section doesn't affect any other section in the document — unless you're using the Link to Previous option.

- ✔ When you have the Different First Page option checked (as you do in the earlier section "But I don't want a header on my first page!"), note that each section has its own first-page header and footer, which are different from (and separate to) the other headers in that section.

- ✔ The Different Odd & Even Pages option affects all sections of a document.

Removing a header

The simplest way to remove a document header is to use the Header⇨ Remove Header command. Here's how it's done:

1. **Go to the page where the header exists.**

   Use Print Layout view for this step so that you can see the ghostly image of the header at the top of the page.

2. **Click the Insert tab.**

3. **From the Header & Footer group, choose Header⇨Remove Header.**

   The header is gone.

This trick removes only the header for the current section. To remove headers in other sections, you must repeat these steps.

To remove a footer, choose Footer⇨Remove Footer in Step 3.

Another way to remove a header is to delete all the text in a header: Press Ctrl+A to select all the text in the header, and then press the Delete key. *Poof!* The header is gone.

I recommend removing the header on any pages in your document that change orientation. That's because the header prints on the "wrong" edge of the page, which is inconsistent with the rest of the document. Because the page (or pages) with a different orientation is in its own section anyway, simply delete the header for that section. Then the reoriented pages can continue with headers and footers for the rest of the document.

Chapter 16

The Styles of Word

In This Chapter

▶ Understanding styles

▶ Using Quick Styles

▶ Finding where Word hides styles

▶ Switching between style sets

▶ Removing styles

▶ Creating your own styles

▶ Modifying styles

▶ Assigning a style shortcut key

▶ Organizing styles between documents

Document formatting can be a snack or a banquet. You can choose not to format anything, or you can format your document to distraction. Formatting can become an obsession, often more important than what the document has to say in the first place!

Microsoft has seen the light, and the happy minions who design Word have created a formatting gift for you: styles. A *style* is a preset format, something you can quickly slap down on your text to present your words in the best way possible. This chapter discusses the details and timesaving abilities of Word's styles.

The Big Style Overview

Styles are a traditional ingredient of the word processing stew, designed to save you formatting toil. As word processors grew in power and computer printers were capable of fancier fonts, it grew tedious to continue applying the same formats to text over and over.

For example, every time your document needed a heading, you had to apply the same font, size, bold, paragraph-spacing, and other attributes again and again. That was a pain — especially given how computers are supposed to excel at doing repetitive things.

By combining various text and paragraph formats into a *style*, Word saves you time and effort. To format your text, simply apply the style. And, if you change your mind, you can instantly update all the text formatted with the same style. Such is the beauty — and power — of the style.

✔ A style is nothing more than a collection of Word's formatting commands all stuffed into a single container.

✔ All text in Word has a style. As configured, Word uses the Normal style to format your text. Unless you specify otherwise, Word uses the Normal style — typically, the Calibri font, 11 points, left-aligned paragraphs, line spacing at 1.15, and no indenting.

✔ Word doesn't demand that you use styles. They do, however, make formatting your documents easier.

Types of styles

Word sports five different types of styles:

✔ **Paragraph:** The paragraph style contains any formatting: paragraphs, indents, tabs, font, text size, attributes — you name it. The paragraph style can format all the standard paragraph or character formats, part of both, or just one aspect of either.

✔ **Character:** The character style formats only characters, not paragraphs. Anything mentioned in Chapter 11 can be stuffed into a character style.

✔ **Linked:** The linked style is a combination style that can be applied to both paragraphs and individual characters. The difference depends on which text is selected when you apply the style.

✔ **Table:** The table style is applied to tables, to add lines and shading to the table cells' contents. Refer to Chapter 20 for more information on tables in Word.

✔ **List:** The list style is customized for presenting lists of information. The styles can include bullets, numbers, indentation, and other formats typical for the parts of a document that present lists of information.

Character styles allow you to uniformly apply attributes to your text. The Emphasis Quick Style, for example, typically formats characters in italic. The Strong Quick Style formats text in bold. By using these styles, you can universally change all text formatting in that style within your document. So, if you decide that Emphasis isn't only bold but also red-colored text, you can make the change once and it's reflected throughout your document.

Styles quick and custom

Word comes with a slew of styles created by professional designers, styles that are ready to use in any document. These are known as the *Quick Styles*.

When you tire of the Quick Styles, or when you need more than what they offer, you can create your own styles. That way, you can go beyond what's offered with the Quick Styles or simply do your own designing.

Making your own style isn't that tough; later sections in this chapter show you the ropes.

Using a style

Applying a style to your text works just like formatting. The major difference is that rather than a single format being applied, the style slaps down multiple formats on your text.

The most popular way to apply a style is to select the text you want to change. Choose the style (as explained in the next section) after selecting the text, and that style is applied to the selected text.

You can also choose a new style and then just start typing; the new style affects the new text you type.

Paragraph styles can be applied by either selecting the entire paragraph (or more than one paragraph) or simply putting the insertion pointer into a paragraph and then applying the style.

- ✔ The current style is highlighted in the Home tab's Styles group, although that group doesn't list all styles. The Styles task pane and the Apply Styles task pane do a better job of describing the style that's in use. See the sections "Employing the Styles task pane" and "Discovering which style you're using," later in this chapter, for more information.

- ✔ When you select part of a paragraph, a character or combination style is applied to only the selected text. A paragraph style, however, is applied to the entire paragraph — never mind that only part of the paragraph is selected.

Effortless Formatting Fun with Quick Styles

Using Quick Styles helps you avoid the sitting, stewing, and fussing that are required when you must create your own styles. Word blesses you with a vast assortment of Quick Styles to use and choose for formatting your text. This section mulls over the possibilities and potentials.

When you use Quick Styles, you don't have to bother yourself with any text or paragraph formatting. Simply choose the Quick Style, and the text size, font, attributes, and paragraph formatting are chosen for you automatically.

Applying a Quick Style to your text

You can apply a Quick Style to your text before or after you write, although I recommend writing first and applying style later.

The easiest way to apply a Quick Styles style is to use the Quick Styles gallery, found in the Home tab's Styles group (see Figure 16-1). Use the arrows to scroll through the gallery's styles, or use the More button to display the menu detailing each option.

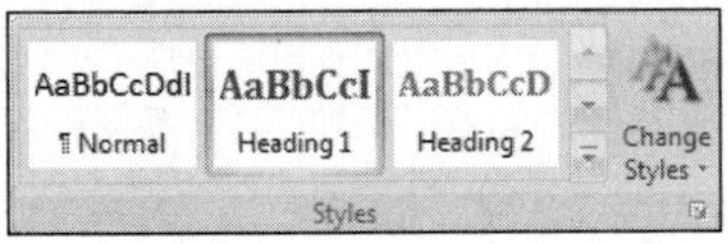

Figure 16-1: The Home tab's Styles group.

The following steps demonstrate how to apply a style to text you've already written:

1. **Select the text you want to format.**

2. **Choose a style from the Quick Styles gallery.**

   You can scroll through the list to find the style you want, or drop down the menu to see a smattering of styles.

   As you hover the mouse over each Quick Style, text in your document is updated to reflect the style's appearance — a boon to help you make that difficult choice.

Each style has a name that helps describe how best to use it, and those names are important! Table 16-1 lists some common Quick Styles names and how best to put them to use. (Many more styles are available than can fit in the table; only some of the more common or useful styles are listed as examples.)

Table 16-1		Quick Styles Format Roundup
Quick Style Name	**Paragraph or Character Style**	**Best Used for This Task**
Block Text	Paragraph	Set aside one or two paragraphs separately from the rest of the text, as in a quotation or reference.
Book Title	Character	Format the title of a book in the body text, such as *War and Peace*.
Caption	Paragraph	Describe an image or table.
Emphasis	Character	Add weight to a word or two in a paragraph, similar to formatting the characters in bold or italic.
Heading 1	Paragraph	Apply main section titles in a document.
Heading 2	Both	Apply secondary section titles in a document.
Intense Emphasis	Character	Apply a higher degree of emphasis than the Emphasis style offers.
Intense Quote	Both	Add weight to a quote that's in a paragraph or that make up an entire paragraph of text.
Intense Reference	Character	Add a higher degree of emphasis to a reference in a paragraph.
List Paragraph	Paragraph	Set off a series of paragraphs as a list of items.
No Spacing	Paragraph	Refer to paragraphs with no space between them.
Normal	Paragraph	Refer to text that otherwise needs no special format.
Plain Text	Both	Refer to boring text; plain text is the format that most closely resembles what a typewriter once produced.
Quote	Both	Format quotations that are in a paragraph or that make up an entire paragraph.
Strong	Character	Format text in bold.
Subtitle	Both	Create a line of text beneath a title.
Title	Both	Make big, bright, attractive document titles or any time humongous text is required.

✔ The heading styles are special. Your document can be organized with Heading 1 main headings, Heading 2 subheadings under Heading 1 styles, and down the line through Heading 3 and Heading 4, and so on. When you use the heading styles this way, you not only help keep your document organized, but also take advantage of other Word features as noted throughout this book.

✔ Heading 1 is similar to the A-level heading found in other word processors and desktop publishing programs. Heading 2 is the B-level heading, and so on.

✔ Headings should be only one line long.

✔ You can break up headings: Press Shift+Enter to create a soft return in the middle of a long heading.

✔ When you're done typing a heading formatted with Heading 1 or Heading 2 or some other heading level, press the Enter key. Automatically, the following paragraph is formatted using the Normal style. Normal is the "follow me" style used for all the heading styles. Refer to the sidebar "The follow-me style," later in this chapter, to find out how that works.

✔ The Title style isn't a heading style.

✔ Normal is the name of the style that Word applies to all text unless another style is chosen.

✔ There's an advantage to using character styles such as Emphasis and Strong instead of formatting your text as italic or bold. Refer to the section "Switching to another style set," later in this chapter, for one reason why you might want to use those Quick Styles rather than manually format your text.

✔ Quick Styles work with only Word 2007 documents. To use Quick Styles with an older Word document, you must convert the document's format. Refer to Chapter 25 for information on how to do that.

Employing the Styles task pane

The Quick Styles gallery, shown on the Ribbon, shows only the last several styles you've used. Often, that's not enough! Like wee little Oliver, you want some more! Happily, more styles — lots more — can be found in the Styles task pane, shown in Figure 16-2.

To display the Styles task pane, click the Dialog Box Launcher in the lower-right corner of the Styles group on the Home tab. The keyboard shortcut is Alt+Ctrl+Shift+S.

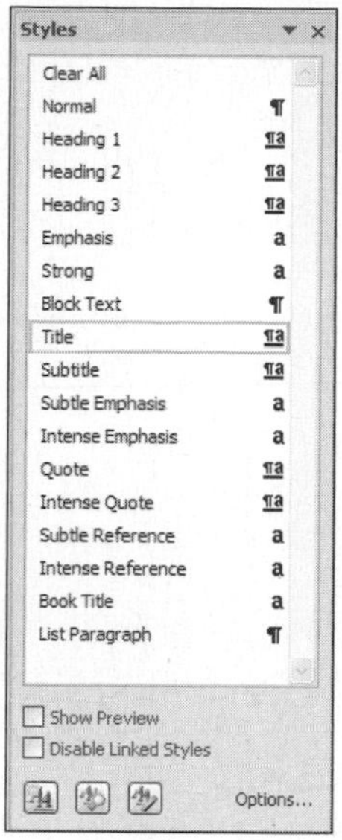

Figure 16-2:
The Styles
task pane.

The Styles task pain, er, pane works just like the Styles group on the Ribbon: To select a style, choose it from the list. Unlike with the Ribbon, however, text in your document doesn't change as you point your mouse at the various styles; you must click the mouse on a style to see it applied to your text.

Dismiss the Styles task pane by clicking the X (close) button in the upper-right corner of its window.

Here are some other things to note about the Styles task pane:

✔ Choosing the Show Preview option displays the styles in their given formats.

✔ The Styles task pane lists only "recommended" styles. To see the whole slew of styles available in Word, click the Options link in the lower-right corner. In the Styles Gallery Options dialog box, use the Select Styles to Show drop-down list to choose the item labeled All Styles. Click OK, and the Styles task pane is updated to list every dang doodle style available in Word.

✔ When you idle the mouse pointer over a style, a technical description appears in a pop-up bubble. Gross!

✔ Pointing the mouse at a style reveals its menu button to the right of the style's name. Options on that menu help you control the style. The last option on the menu lets you add or remove the style from the Quick Style gallery on the Ribbon.

The Styles task pane lite

If the Styles task pane seems a bit unwieldy, especially on a small monitor, you can use the Apply Styles task pane as an alternative, as shown in Figure 16-3. Regardless of whatever text is selected, or whichever text the insertion pointer is blinking inside, that format is reflected inside the Apply Styles task pane, on the Style Name list. You can also reformat text by choosing a new style from that list.

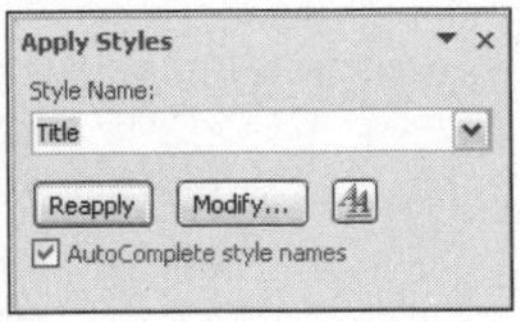

Figure 16-3:
The Apply
Styles
task pane.

To conjure up the Apply Styles task pane, click the More arrow in the Quick Style gallery and choose the Apply Styles command. The keyboard shortcut is Ctrl+Shift+S.

Discovering which style you're using

It's often difficult to discover which style is applied to your text. Sometimes, the style is highlighted in the Quick Styles gallery. The Home tab's Font group displays the text (Heading) or (Body) when you've selected Heading- or Normal-formatted text. But that's just not good enough.

 To determine which styles you're using, summon the Style Inspector by clicking the Style Inspector button at the bottom of the Styles task pane (shown in the margin). The Style Inspector dialog box appears, shown in Figure 16-4. It's quite the informative thing.

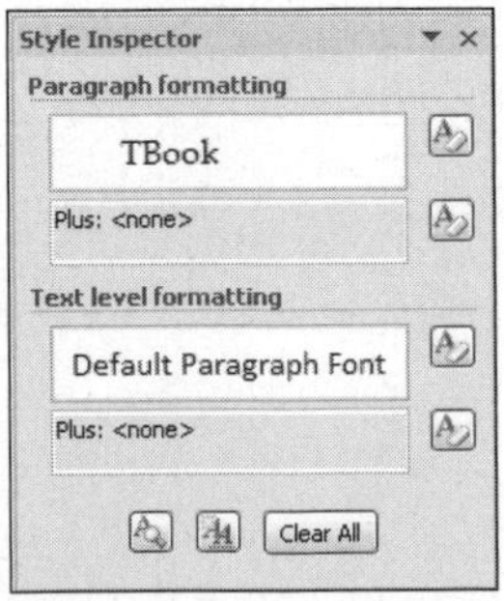

Figure 16-4:
The Style
Inspector.

Close the Style Inspector task pane by clicking the X in its upper-right corner.

 To *really* see the details of how your text is formatted, click the Reveal Formatting button in the Style Inspector. Clicking that button summons the gruesome Reveal Formatting task pane, which shows the specifics of which formats are applied to any text. It's quite the display! Click the X button in the task pane's upper-right corner to hide the thing at once!

The keyboard shortcut for the Reveal Formatting command is Shift+F1.

Switching to another style set

One of the reasons you would want to use the Emphasis style rather than apply italics directly to your text is that Word comes with a bunch of style sets. You can universally change the look of your document by simply choosing a new style set.

To select a new style set, from the Home tab's Styles group, click the Change Styles button. From the menu that's displayed, choose Style Set, and then move the mouse over the various menu items. As each menu item is highlighted, your document's formatting is updated with new styles (if you used Quick Styles to format your document). Choose a style you find pleasing.

- The Default style set is the one you probably used originally, unless you specifically chose a style set to use.
- Also refer to the topic of document themes, which is covered in Chapter 17.

Unapplying a style

Choosing a new style for your text replaces the old style. Changing paragraph styles doesn't change any character styles. All that makes sense as you play with it, but sometimes what you really want to do is rid yourself of styles entirely. To do that, you need a style scrubber, strong as any household bathroom cleanser. In Word, that's the Clear Formatting command.

 To peel away stubborn style stains, select the text you want to cleanse and choose the Clear Formatting command button from the Font group on the Home tab. Whatever text you have selected is stripped of formatting by that command.

- The keyboard shortcut for the Clear Formatting command is Ctrl+ spacebar. When you think about it, the spacebar produces the "clear" character, so that makes sense — at least more sense than the alternative keyboard shortcut, Alt+H, E.

✔ The Style Inspector is a great place to remove specific formatting from text without affecting other formatting. Refer to the earlier section "Discovering which style you're using" for information; use the Clear Formatting buttons in the Style Inspector to selectively peel off formatting.

✔ The Clear Formatting command removes all text formatting, whether it was applied with a Quick Style or a style you created yourself or was manually applied.

✔ Because formatting cannot be utterly removed, what the Clear Formatting command really does is to reapply the Normal style to the selected text.

Do-It-Yourself Styles

Despite the fact that the good folks at Swanson Foods offer a variety of interesting and delicious frozen dinner selections, some people are still foolish enough to cook their own meals. That's because no matter the variety, no matter the brilliance, some people know what they want and prefer to do things themselves. The same holds true with styles in Word, although without any nutritional value whatsoever.

You can use your formatting prowess in Word to create your own custom styles, which you can then apply to your text as you see fit, saving you valuable formatting time. This section describes how it's all done.

Creating a style based on text you've already formatted

The easiest way to make up a new style is to use all your formatting skills and power to format a single paragraph just the way you like. Then create the style based on that formatted paragraph. Here's how:

1. **Type and format a paragraph of text.**

   Keep all text formats (font, size, attributes) the same inside the block. Paragraph formatting uses only one text format for the whole paragraph.

2. **Mark your paragraph as a block.**

   See Chapter 7 to find out how to mark a block of text.

3. **Press Alt+Ctrl+Shift+S to summon the Styles task pane.**

   The task pane may already show your paragraph style, but not as a named style; the highlighted item in the Styles dialog box reflects the formatting you've directly applied to your text. Your next job is to give that formatting a style name.

4. **Click the New Style button.**

   Look in the lower-left corner for this button.

   The Create New Style from Formatting dialog box appears, as shown in Figure 16-5. It's the place where new styles are born.

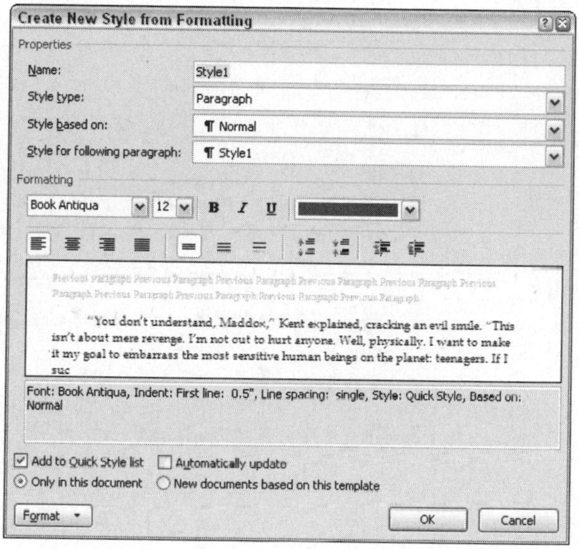

Figure 16-5:
The Create
New Style
from
Formatting
dialog box.

5. **In the Name box, type a name for your style.**

   As usual, short and descriptive names work best. Also, try not to use the name of an existing style or else you replace that style with the new one.

6. **Ensure that Paragraph is chosen from the Style Type drop-down list.**

   The drop-down list is where you change the style type, as described elsewhere in this chapter.

7. **Make any further adjustments to the style as necessary.**

   The whole dialog box is geared toward creating styles. There are some command buttons for quick changes, but note the Format button in the lower-left corner of the dialog box. Clicking that button displays a pop-up list of formatting dialog boxes. Select one to further customize aspects of your style.

8. **Put a check mark by the item labeled Add to Quick Style List if you want your style to appear in that list.**

9. **Click the OK button to create your style.**

   The style is added to Word's repertoire of styles for your document.

The follow-me style

When I write a new chapter in a book, I start off with my own Chapter Title style. The next style I use is my Intro Paragraph style. Intro Paragraph is followed by TextBody, which is followed by TextBody, TextBody, TextBody, and on and on. There's no point in my having to apply those styles because I can tell Word to switch styles automatically.

In the Create New Style from Formatting dialog box (refer to Figure 16-5), locate the Style for Following Paragraph drop-down list. The style shown on that list tells Word which style to switch to when you press the Enter key to end a paragraph. Normally, it's the same style, which makes sense for most of your work. But in situations where you *know* that the style will switch, you can demand that Word do the switching for you. You can edit the Chapter Title style so that the Intro Paragraph style is selected from the Style for Following Paragraph drop-down list. That way, pressing the Enter key after typing the chapter title switches the style to Intro Paragraph. Very nice.

The style you created now applies to the paragraph you typed (on which the style is based), and you can apply the style to other paragraphs.

And now, the shortcut!

The fastest way to create a new paragraph style based on text you've typed and formatted is to follow Steps 1 and 2 in the preceding steps and then, from the Quick Styles gallery menu, choose the command Save Selection As New Quick Style. Doing so displays a tiny dialog box in which you merely have to type the name of your style. Click the OK button and you're done. Cinchy.

Now, even though there's a quick way to create a style, you may still find yourself using the Create New Style from Formatting dialog box (refer to Figure 16-5), so don't go around telling people that you were ripped off by marching through all those steps.

✔ The styles you create are available only to the document in which they're created.

✔ If you create scads of styles that you love and you want to use them for several documents, you need to create a *template*. Chapter 17 covers this procedure, in the section about making a new template from scratch.

✔ You may have to tweak some things in your style. If so, you need to use the Style and Formatting task pane. See the section "Modifying a style," later in this chapter.

TIP

- A quick way to create a style is to base it on another, existing style. Choose that existing style from the Style Based On drop-down list in the Create New Style from Formatting dialog box (refer to Figure 16-5). Use the dialog box to subtly modify the style, but be sure to give the style a new name.

- When you create one style based on another, any changes to the first style are reflected in all styles based on that style.

- You can use the Create New Style from Formatting dialog box to whip up a style from scratch: Just summon the dialog box and use its controls to whip out a new style based on the formatting options you choose.

Creating character, list, and other types of styles

The Create New Style from Formatting dialog box (refer to Figure 16-5) allows you to create any one of Word's five style types. The key is to choose the type from the Style Type drop-down list. When you do, the contents of the dialog box change to reflect whatever options are available for that style type.

For example, when you choose Character from the Style Type drop-down list, only character-formatting commands and settings are available in the Create New Style from Formatting dialog box.

- See the "Types of styles" section, earlier in this chapter, for more information on Word's five different style types.

- Character styles don't affect paragraph formatting. Selecting a character style changes only the font, style, size, underlining, bold, and so on.

- Also refer to the section in Chapter 18 about stealing this format, for a quick method of applying font formats.

Modifying a style

Styles change. Those wedgie shoes that were sworn off in the early 1980s seem to have made a surprising comeback. Maybe there's hope for bell-bottoms again?

Just as fashion styles change, you may need to change styles in your document. There's nothing wrong with that. In fact, by changing a style, you demonstrate the power of Word: Changing a style once causes all text formatted with that style to be updated with the change in your document. That beats the (bell-bottom) pants off making that change manually.

To modify a style, heed these steps:

1. **Summon the Styles task pane.**

   Click the Dialog Box Launcher in the lower-right corner of the Styles group (on the Home tab), or press Ctrl+Shift+Alt+S.

2. **Point the mouse at the style you want to change.**

   A menu button appears on the right end of the style's entry.

3. **Click the menu button to display the style's menu.**

4. **Choose Modify.**

   A Modify Style dialog box appears, although it's really the same Create New Style from Formatting dialog box (refer to Figure 16-5) you've used before. This time, however, the settings you make now *change* the style rather than create a new style.

5. **Change the formatting for your style.**

   You're free to use any of the formatting options to change your style. You can even add new formatting options or a shortcut key (which is covered in the next section).

6. **Click OK when you're done.**

Close the task pane if you're done with it.

Giving your style a shortcut key

Style shortcut keys make formatting even better because pressing Alt+Shift+T to get at the TextBody style is often faster than messing with the Quick Styles gallery or the various task panes.

To give your style a shortcut key, follow these steps:

1. **Work through Steps 1 through 4 from the previous section.**

   Your goal is to display the Modify Style dialog box for your soon-to-be shortcut-key-blessed style.

2. **Display the style's menu thing (refer to Figure 16-3).**

3. **Click the Format button.**

   It dwells in the lower-left corner of the dialog box.

4. **Choose Shortcut Key from the menu.**

   A cryptic Customize Keyboard dialog box appears.

5. **Press your shortcut key combination.**

Notice that the key combination you press appears as text in the Press New Shortcut Key box. (See the middle right side of the dialog box.) If you make a mistake, press the Backspace key to erase it and choose another key combination.

6. **Check to see whether the combination is already in use.**

For example, Word uses Ctrl+B as the Bold character-formatting shortcut key. This key combination appears under the heading Currently Assigned To, which shows up under the Current Keys box. Keep an eye on that box! If something else in Word uses the shortcut key, press the Backspace key and go back to Step 5.

When the key combination you press isn't used by anything, you see [unassigned] displayed under the Currently Assigned To heading. That's your signal that it's okay to use that keystroke.

7. **Click the Assign button.**

8. **Click the Close button.**

The Customize Keyboard dialog box skulks away.

9. **Click the OK button.**

You can also close the Style task pane, if you're done with it.

Congratulations; you now have a usable shortcut key for your style. Try it out: Position the toothpick cursor in a block of text and press the key. Ta-da! It should apply the formatting without messing with any of the other formatting or task pane widgets discussed elsewhere in this chapter.

Deleting a style

You can delete any style you create. It's easy: Display the Styles task pane (press Ctrl+Shift+Alt+S), select the style, and choose Delete from its menu. You're asked whether you're sure that you want to delete the style. Choose Yes to delete it for real.

You cannot delete the Normal, Heading, or any other standard Word style.

Managing All Your Various Styles

Styles can be like trading cards. And they should be! If you create a great style, it's nice to use it in several documents. You can do this without re-creating the style (and even without using a document template, which is covered in Chapter 17).

To trade or manage all the styles you have in Word, you need to use the Style Organizer. It's not the easiest thing to find:

1. **Summon the Styles task pane.**

2. **Click the Manage Styles button at the bottom of the task pane.**

   The Manage Styles dialog box appears, but it's not your final destination.

3. **Click the Import/Export button.**

   Finally. The Organizer dialog box appears, with the Styles tab forward, as shown in Figure 16-6.

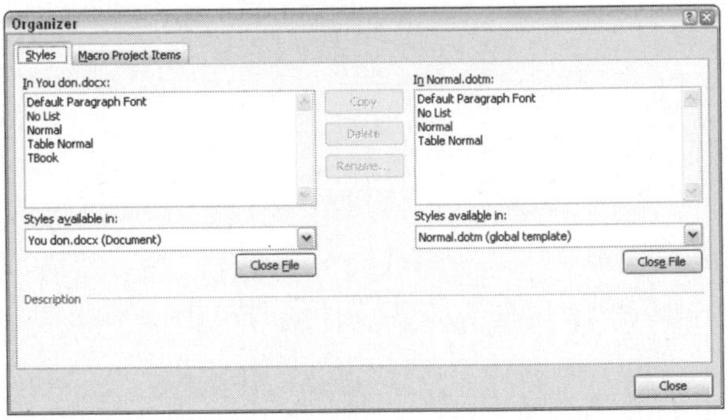

Figure 16-6:
The Organizer dialog box is buried deep within Word's guts.

The purpose of the Organizer is to manage styles (and other things, but this chapter talks about styles). You can do that by moving styles between various documents and document templates in Word.

For example, on the left side of Figure 16-6, you see the styles available in the document: YOU DON.DOCX. On the right are the styles that appear in the NORMAL.DOTM document template. (NORMAL.DOTM is a file that contains all the standard Word settings.)

Choose from either side of the dialog box the style you want to copy. After selecting the style, click the Copy button to copy it to the other side. That's how you swap and share styles between documents and templates.

To choose another document or template, click the Close File button. That button changes to the Open File button, which you can then use to open any Word document or template stored on disk. After the document is open, a list of styles in that document is displayed in the window.

Click the Close button when you're done managing the styles.

Chapter 17

Themes and Templates

In This Chapter

- ▶ Understanding themes
- ▶ Formatting a document with a theme
- ▶ Creating your own themes
- ▶ Understanding templates
- ▶ Creating a document template
- ▶ Modifying a document template
- ▶ Attaching a template to a document
- ▶ Understanding NORMAL.DOTM

*W*ord sports some formatting commands and techniques that allow you to craft or build an entire document in one swift stroke, like a magician making an elephant appear, but without all that money spent on Purina Elephant Chow. The tools that make such magic possible are themes and templates.

With a mere click of the mouse, you can employ the power of themes to quickly format your document in a most professional manner. With a few skillful keystrokes, you can turn a template into a formatted, finished masterpiece. This chapter shows you how you can use these simple tools to fool everyone into thinking that you're a Word processing genius.

Formatting Fast and Fancy with a Theme

Themes are used to apply certain decorative styles to your document, giving it a professionally formatted look and appeal. It's like hiring an interior decorator named Fránž but not having to struggle with his heavily accented English.

A theme consists of three elements:

Colors: A set of colors is chosen to format the text foreground and background, any graphics or design elements in the theme, plus hyperlinks.

Fonts: Two fonts are chosen as part of the theme — one for the heading styles and a second for the body text.

Graphical effects: These effects are applied to any graphics or design elements in your document. The effects can include 3D, shading, gradation, drop-shadows, and other design subtleties.

Each of these elements is organized into a theme, given a name, and placed on the Themes menu for easy application in your document.

Refer to the next section for information on applying a theme.

- A theme's fonts, colors, and design effects are created by a professionally licensed graphics designer so that they look good and work well together.

- The graphical effects of a theme are only applied to any graphics in your document; the theme doesn't insert graphics into your text. See Chapter 23 for information on graphics in Word.

- You can use the various Themes menu commands to search for even more themes.

- Choosing a theme affects your entire document all at once. To affect individual paragraphs or bits of text, apply a style or format manually. Refer to Chapter 16.

- A theme doesn't overrule styles chosen for a document. Instead, it accents those styles. The theme may add color information, choose different fonts, or present various graphical elements. Beyond that, it doesn't change any styles applied to the text.

- Themes work only with Word 2007 documents. To apply a theme to an older Word document, you must *convert* the document's format. Refer to Chapter 25 for more on converting old Word documents.

Applying a document theme

Choosing a theme is done from the Page Layout tab, in the Themes group. Built-in themes are listed on the Themes button's menu along with any custom themes you've created yourself. Figure 17-1 illustrates the Themes menu.

- Each of the built-in themes controls all three of the major theme elements, changing your document's contents accordingly.

- Pointing the mouse at a theme previews your document, by showing how it would look if you went ahead and applied that theme.

  ✔ Click to select a theme.

  ✔ Because a document can use only one theme at a time, choosing a new theme replaces the current theme.

  ✔ To remove a theme from your document, choose the Office theme or the menu command Reset to Theme from Template (refer to Figure 17-1).

  ✔ If you would rather change only one part of a theme, such as a document's fonts, use the Theme Colors, Theme Fonts, or Theme Effects command button in the Themes group.

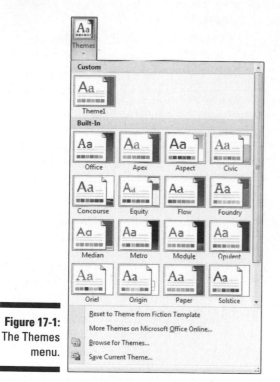

Figure 17-1: The Themes menu.

Modifying or creating a theme

You can't really create your own themes from scratch, but you can modify existing themes to make your own, custom theme. To do so, use the Theme Colors, Theme Fonts, or Theme Effects button to select the fonts, colors, or effects you want for your theme. Mix and match. Pick and choose.

When you have things the way you like, click the Themes button and choose the Save Current Theme command. Use the Save Current Theme dialog box to give your theme a proper descriptive name and save it to disk. That theme you create then appears in the Custom area of the Themes menu (refer to Figure 17-1).

The selections offered in Word's themes are fairly rich. Still, it's possible to create custom colors or fonts for use in themes. To do so, use the Theme Colors or Theme Fonts button:

> **To create a custom color theme,** choose Theme Colors⇨Create New Theme Colors. Use the Create New Theme Colors dialog box to pick and choose which colors apply to text or various graphical elements in your document.

> **To create a custom font theme,** choose Theme Fonts⇨Create New Theme Fonts. Use the Create New Theme Fonts dialog box to select your fonts — one for the headings and another for the body text.

In each case, give the new theme a name and save it to disk. You can then choose that theme from the Custom area of either the Theme Colors or Theme Fonts menu.

> ✔ To remove a custom theme, right-click it on the Themes menu and choose the Delete command.

> ✔ You can remove a custom theme color or theme font by right-clicking the Theme Color or Theme Font in the Custom area of the menu. Choose Edit from the pop-up menu. In the editing dialog box that appears, click the Delete button. Click the Yes button when you're prompted to remove your custom efforts.

Whipping Out Similar Documents Based on a Template

A *template* is a pattern you follow to create something. Had you asked a computer user from the 1980s about templates, he would have thought about something that was placed over a computer keyboard, a stiff piece of cardboard to help locate keyboard shortcuts used in various programs. Even early *For Dummies* books back in the 1990s came with such keyboard templates as a "free" bonus (a $2.99 "value").

In Word, *template* refers to a skeleton document you can build upon to create a final document. Templates are really quite handy to have and use, as this section demonstrates.

What is a template?

Templates are special types of Word documents. They can contain styles, formatting, perhaps a header or footer, plus even some text. They're created just like documents but are saved to disk in a unique way. That's because you never really use the template itself, but rather a copy. By using that copy, you can create an entirely new document; the template merely helps you get started by doing some of the routine things for you.

Document templates help to save time and prevent you from having to repeat your efforts. I use one template for sending faxes, one for writing letters, one for writing plays, and so on. This book has its own _Dummies_ template that contains all the text styles the publisher's production department uses to produce the book. Whenever I need to start a new chapter, I use the _Dummies_ template so that the paragraph, heading, caption, and other styles match what my publisher uses, which keeps them happy. I hope.

It's worth your time to create a template for all the common document types you use regularly. The following sections describe how.

- Just as all text in Word sports a specific style (see Chapter 16), all documents in Word are based upon a template, whether you choose a template to start with or not.

- In Word, all documents are based on the Normal document template, NORMAL.DOTM. Refer to the section "Understanding NORMAL.DOTM," at the end of this chapter, for more information.

- Information on using templates is in Chapter 9.

- There are three filename extensions for document templates in Word: DOT was the template filename extension used for older versions of Word. With Word 2007, DOTX and DOTM are used. DOTX refers to a template that doesn't employ macros; the DOTM indicates a template that uses macros. (This book does not cover macros.)

Creating a template based on a document you already have

Building the pyramids was hard. Building your own document template is comparatively easy. In fact, it's probably easier than what you're doing already, which is most likely re-creating the same document and the same formats over and over and over again. That's tedious, even without 100,000 slaves. And, if there's one thing computers are good at, it's reducing tedium.

To create a template, follow these steps:

1. **Find a common document, one that has styles or formats or text you plan on using again and again.**

   When you're using an existing document, save it to disk one last time, just to be sure. Next, strip out all the text that you don't want in the template; keep the text that you plan on using over and over. Delete all the graphics that you don't want in the template; keep the graphics that you need to use again and again. Edit the header and footer so that they contain only the items you repeatedly need every time you create a similar document.

   Figure 17-2 shows a sample template I created, complete with some text and graphics. Remember that the template needs to contain only the styles you need for that document, plus any text that is common to all documents. In Figure 17-2, only the text that stays the same is included; other text is added when the user opens the template, to help him create a new document.

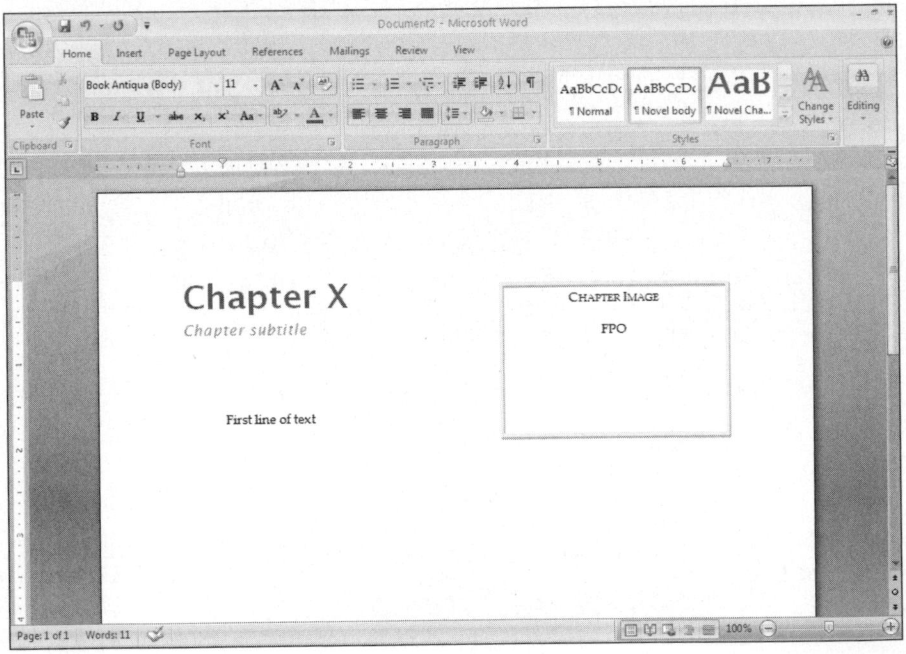

Figure 17-2:
A sample template, created with love.

2. **Choose the Save As command from the Office Button menu.**

   The Save As dialog box appears. It's the same Save As dialog box that Word uses for saving anything. Refer to Chapter 9 if you need a refresher.

3. **Type a name for the template.**

   The name goes into the File Name box. Be descriptive.

   You don't need to name the template using the word *template*.

4. **From the Save As Type drop-down list, choose** `Word Template` **(*.dotx).**

   Ah-ha! This is the secret. The document must be saved as a document template. Choosing that item directs Word to save the document as a template in Word's special Templates folder. Word does all that work for you, but you must choose Word Template as the file type.

5. **Click the Save button.**

   Your efforts are saved to disk as a document template, nestled in the proper place where Word keeps all its document templates.

6. **Close the template.**

   Choose the Close command from the Office Button menu, just as you would close any other document in Word.

   The reason for closing it is that any changes you make from now on are made to the template. If you want to use the template to start a new document, you need to choose that template from the New Document window as described in Chapter 9.

Refer to the later section "Modifying a template you created" for information on updating or changing a template.

- ✔ Yes, it helps to be well-versed with Word's formatting and style commands if you attempt to create a template from scratch. Even then, you most likely have to go back and "fix" things.

- ✔ Remember the purpose of a template: to store styles and often-used information in a single place.

- ✔ You can give a template any name, although if you choose the name of a template that already exists, Word warns you. This is standard file-saving stuff; just choose another name and be on your merry way.

Making a new template from scratch

The first thing I do before I begin some projects is to start a new template for the project. It's only a guess, of course, but it's enough to get me started and save me time for each new document I create. Here's what to do:

1. **From the Office Button menu, choose the New command.**

   The New Document window appears.

2. **Double-click the item labeled Blank Template.**

   A fresh, new document appears on the screen, although it's not a document! Check the title bar. It's a *template!*

3. **Build the template by adding needed text, formatting, and other stuff.**

   When you're creating a new template, simply put into the document all the styles you plan on using, plus common text. For example, my Book template (for when I stop writing computer books and start writing "real" books) contains all the styles I need for writing books plus the word *Chapter* at the start of each page. That's because each document is a chapter, and starting it with the text *Chapter* already in the template saves me valuable typing energy molecules.

4. **Save the template by choosing the Save As command from the Office Button menu.**

5. **Use the Save As dialog box to give the template a proper, descriptive name.**

   Note that the Save As dialog box chooses a special Templates folder in which to place your document templates. Use that folder!

6. **Click the Save button.**

   And the template is saved.

Refer to Chapter 9 for information on using the new template.

Modifying a template you created

Changing or editing a document template is identical to changing or editing any document. You simply create a new document by using the existing template. Make your changes, and then use the Save As command to either overwrite the existing template or save the document as a new template, per Steps 4 through 6 in the preceding section.

Yes, there are other ways to edit a document template. You can actually open the template itself in Word, but the steps involved are rather convoluted.

It's just much better to start off with the template like you're creating a new document and then simply save that document back to disk as a template.

You're updating a template, not just a single document on disk. Any style changes you make to a document template affect all the documents already created with that template.

Attaching a template to a document

Documents have templates like people have last names. Mostly, the documents are born with their templates. You either choose the template when the document is first created (see Chapter 9) or just create a new document, in which case the NORMAL.DOTM template is used. You can change that by assigning or attaching a new template to a document. Here's how:

1. **Open the document that needs a new template attached.**

2. **From the Office Button menu, choose the Word Options command.**

3. **Choose Add-Ins from the left side of the Word Options dialog box.**

4. **On the right side of the window, near the bottom, choose Templates from the Manage drop-down list.**

5. **Click the Go button.**

   The Templates and Add-ins dialog box appears, as shown in Figure 17-3. You should see which template is currently attached to the document, such as Normal, as shown in the figure. Whatever template name appears there is whichever template is attached to the document.

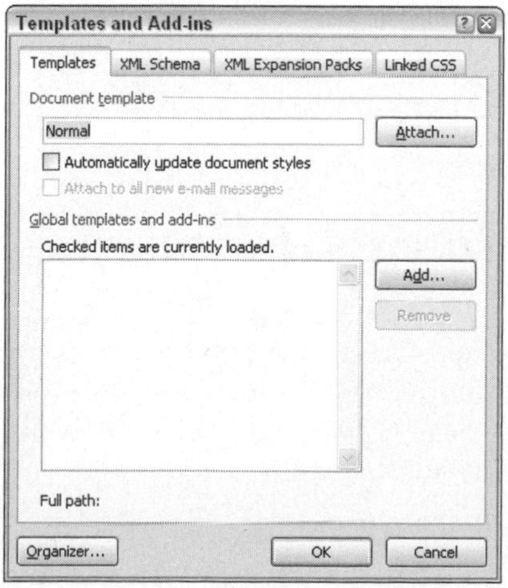

Figure 17-3:
The Templates and Add-ins dialog box.

6. **Click the Attach button.**

   Word displays the Attach Template dialog box, which looks and works like the Open dialog box. Normally, this dialog box opens in the Templates folder, where you've probably stored a host of templates available for the plucking.

7. **Select the template you want to attach.**

8. **Click the Open button.**

   The template is now attached, but you may need to do one more thing back in the Templates and Add-ins dialog box (refer to Figure 17-3).

9. **Optionally, select Automatically Update Document Styles.**

   Updating the styles means that your document's current styles are changed to reflect those of the new template, which is probably what you want. If not, skip this step.

10. **Click OK.**

    The styles (and toolbars and macros) stored in that template are now available to your document, and the document is now attached to the template.

Note that attaching a template doesn't merge any text or graphics stored in that template. Only the styles (and toolbar and macros) are merged into your document.

You can also use these steps to unattach a template. Do that by selecting NORMAL.DOTM as the template to attach.

✔ The template that's attached to a document may be just a name (refer to Figure 17-3) or a *pathname* indicating the location and name of a template document on disk.

✔ Any time you change or update a template, the changes are reflected in any document created by or attached to that template.

Understanding NORMAL.DOTM

The Normal template is a special beast. Referred to by its filename, NORMAL.DOTM, the Normal template is where Word stores all the settings made for any new document you create with the Ctrl+N shortcut or by choosing Blank Document from the New Document window (see Chapter 9).

Knowing about NORMAL.DOTM is important because you can change the Normal template, if you want.

For example, if you want to change the standard font and size (and whatever other formatting) Word uses when it opens a new document, simply make those changes to NORMAL.DOTM. Change the font and margins for the Normal style. Then save NORMAL.DOTM back to disk.

Now, just after saying that, let me warn against modifying NORMAL.DOTM too much. It's a good idea to keep NORMAL.DOTM as a baseline standard, so rather than modify it too much, consider creating another template instead.

✔ Refer to the section "Modifying a template you created," earlier in this chapter, for more information on how to find and change NORMAL.DOTM.

✔ Another reason to change NORMAL.DOTM may be if someone else got there first and made a modification you don't like. In that case, you need to edit NORMAL.DOTM to remove the change.

✔ If you just want to change the default font, refer to Chapter 11, the section about fun and formatting in the Font dialog box. Use the Font dialog box to Set Text options as you want them in the Normal template, and then click the Default button to make the change. The same can be done with the Paragraph dialog box (refer to Chapter 12) and its Default button.

Chapter 18

Misc. Formatting Stuff

. . . .

In This Chapter

▶ Formatting magic

▶ Creating automatic lists and borders

▶ Understanding fields

▶ Inserting document information

▶ Centering a title page

▶ Swiping text formats

. . . .

The stuff in the previous several chapters describes specific things you can do to inject some life into a dreary, unformatted document. Before leaving this formatting part of the book, however, I'd like to toss in an et cetera chapter. You'll find the information on the following pages chockfull of formatting goodness, including a plethora of formatting tricks and tidbits that just quite couldn't fit elsewhere in this part of the book. Welcome to the Word formatting buffet dessert bar!

Automatic Formatting

Word sports a feature called AutoFormat that does for formatting what AutoCorrect does for typing. Where AutoCorrect instantly retypes your spelling boo-boos (see Chapter 8), AutoFormat instantly fixes common formatting faux pas. This section demonstrates AutoFormat's prowess.

✔ AutoFormat must be activated for it to work. Refer to the inaptly named section "Disabling the @#$%&! AutoFormat," later in this chapter, if you're having trouble working with any of the AutoFormat features.

✔ Likewise, AutoFormat tends to annoy people. Refer to the aptly named section "Disabling the @#$%&! AutoFormat" for directions on turning the booger off.

Enjoying automagical text

AutoFormat controls some of the minor text formatting you type. The best way to demonstrate this concept is to have a Word document up on the screen and then type the examples in the following sections. Note that these are only a few of the things AutoFormat can do.

Smart quotes

The quote characters on the keyboard are tick marks: " and '. AutoFormat converts them into more stylish open and closed curly quotes. Type hither:

```
She said, "Take off my dress! And don't you ever let
me catch you wearing my clothes again!"
```

Both the single and double quotes are properly used and converted.

Real fractions

You can format a fraction by typing the first value in superscript, and then the slash, and then the second value in subscript. Or, you can let AutoFormat do it for you. Here's an example:

I spend twice the time doing ½ the work.

The 1/2 is converted into the single character ½. This trick works for some, but not all, common fractions. When it doesn't work, use the superscript/subscript trick described in Chapter 32, in the section about building your own fractions.

Hyperlinks

Word can underline *and* activate hyperlinks typed in your document, such as

```
I've been to www.hell.com and back.
```

Now, I don't like this trick and prefer *not* to have hyperlinks in a document. Visit the section "Disabling the @#$%&! AutoFormat," later in this chapter, if you agree.

Ordinals

You're guessing wrong if you think that ordinals are a baseball team or a group of religious leaders. They're numbers with *st*, *nd*, or *rd* after them, as this line demonstrates:

```
I came in 1st and Blake came in 3rd.
```

Word automatically superscripts the ordinals, making them look oh-so-spiffy.

Em dashes

An _em dash_ is the official typesetting term for a long dash, longer than the hyphen (or its evil twin, the en dash). Most people type two hyphens to emulate the _em dash_. Word fixes that:

```
Bart's first stage appearance was a triumph --
except for the zipper incident.
```

As you type the – (dash-dash), AutoFormat replaces it with the official em dash character.

- ✔ The keyboard shortcut for typing an em dash is Ctrl+Alt+minus, where minus is the minus key on the numeric keypad.

- ✔ The keyboard shortcut for typing an en dash is Ctrl+minus.

- ✔ Don't type Ctrl+Alt+hyphen, where the hyphen key is on the typewriter keyboard. That changes the mouse pointer to a heavy black bar and activates a secret destructive mode in Word. Quickly press the Esc key to cancel.

Paragraph formatting tricks

At the paragraph level, AutoFormat helps you quickly handle some otherwise troublesome formatting issues. Some folks like this, some don't. The following sections provide a few examples of what AutoFormat is capable of.

If you find any of these AutoFormat tricks annoying, refer to the later section "Disabling the @#$%&! AutoFormat" for information on shutting the dumb thing off!

Numbered lists

Any time you start a paragraph with a number, Word assumes (through AutoFormat) that you need all your paragraphs numbered. Here's the proof:

```
Things to do today:
1. Buy new freezer for the cat.
```

Immediately after typing the **1.**, you probably saw the infamous AutoFormat lightning bolt icon and noticed your text being reformatted. Darn, this thing is quick! That's AutoFormat guessing that you're about to type a list. Go ahead and finish typing the line; after you press Enter, you see the next line begin with **2**.

Keep typing until your list ends or you get angry, whichever comes first. To end the list, press the Enter key again. That erases the final number and restores the paragraph formatting to Normal.

- ✓ This trick also works for letters (and Roman numerals). Just start something with a letter and a period, and Word picks up at the next line with the next letter in the alphabet and another period.

- ✓ Bulleted lists can also be created this way: Start a line by typing * and a space to see what happens.

- ✓ See Chapter 22 for more information on creating numbered or bulleted lists.

- ✓ I know that I say earlier in this book not to press the Enter key twice to end a paragraph. That still holds true: When you press Enter twice to end an AutoFormat list, Word sticks only one Enter "character" into the text.

Borders (lines)

A line above or below a paragraph in Word is a *border*. Most folks call them lines, but they're borders. Here's how to whip out a few borders by using AutoFormat:

Typing three hyphens and pressing the Enter key causes Word to instantly transmute the three little hyphens into a solid line that touches the left and right paragraph margins.

- ✓ To create a double line, type three equal signs and press Enter.

- ✓ To create a bold line, type three underlines and press Enter.

- ✓ Refer to Chapter 19 for more information on borders and boxes around your text.

Undoing an AutoFormat

There are two quick ways to undo AutoFormatting. The first, obviously, is to press Ctrl+Z on the keyboard, to give the Undo command. That's easy.

You can also use the lightning bolt icon to undo an AutoFormat. Clicking the icon displays a drop-down menu, as shown in Figure 18-1. Three options are usually available: Undo what's been done, disable what's been done so that it doesn't happen again, and, the final option, display the AutoFormat dialog box, which is covered in the next section. Choose wisely.

Figure 18-1:
Controlling
the
AutoFormat
options as
you type.

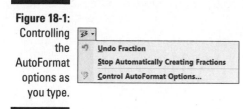

Disabling the @#$%&! AutoFormat

Formatting is subjective. Sometimes you want AutoFormat to help you out, and sometimes it makes you angry enough to hurl the computer into a lake. Either way, AutoFormat is controlled by a special dialog box buried deep within Word's bosom. Here's the treacherous trail that leads to that location:

1. **Choose the Word Options command from the Office Button menu.**

   The Word Options window steps front and center.

2. **Select Proofing from the left side of the window.**

3. **Click the button labeled AutoCorrect Options.**

4. **Click the AutoFormat As You Type tab in the AutoCorrect dialog box.**

   This part of the dialog box, shown in Figure 18-2, is where all the AutoFormat options dwell. Turning an option off or on is as easy as removing or adding a check mark.

5. **Set the options as you like.**

   I don't mind some of the options, but I detest the Apply As You Type options, so I unchecked them all.

6. **Click the AutoFormat tab.**

   Gadzooks! More options.

7. **Set the options on the AutoFormat tab.**

   Repeat your choices here; I don't know why some of the things are listed twice in the dialog box. Silly Microsoft.

8. **Click OK to confirm your choices, and close the Word Options window.**

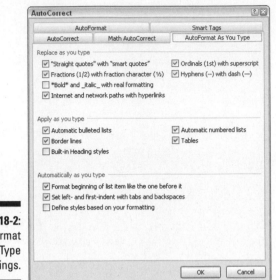

Figure 18-2:
AutoFormat
As You Type
settings.

Become an Expert in Your Fields

The text you write in Word is as everlasting as text forged by electrons can be. You're the only one who can change your text by editing it. Or, I should say, only humans can change the text because on the 19th day, when God was angry over just having created lawyers and mortgage brokers, God created copy editors. But I digress. . . .

There's such a thing as changing text in Word. By using a nifty device called a *field,* you can insert a special chunk of text into your document, text that changes to reflect information about your document: the current page, today's date, your name, and other changing stuff.

Inserting a field into your document

To take advantage of fields, you use the Field dialog box, shown in Figure 18-3. To display this dialog box, click the Insert tab and then choose Quick Parts⇨ Field from the Text group.

The left side of the Field dialog box contains scrolling lists of categories and then field names. The right side of the dialog box changes to let you further select options, based on what type of field you're messing with.

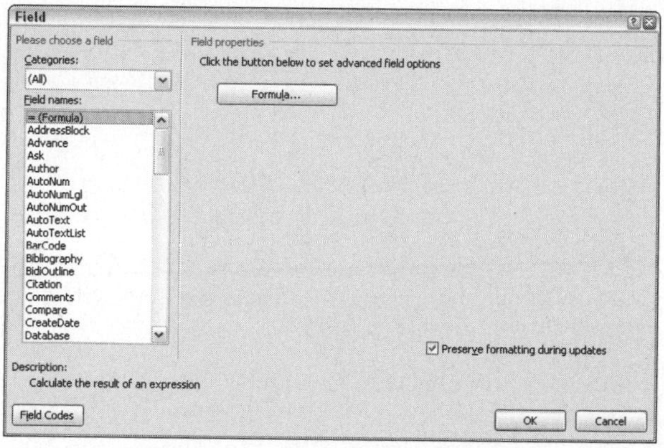

Figure 18-3:
The Field
dialog box.

As an example, choose Author from the list of field names. In the Field
Properties part of the dialog box, select how you want the author's name formatted, such as Title case. Click the OK button to insert the field into your
document. Lo and behold, that should stick *your* name into the document.
Hello, author!

Those mystery tag-like things

When Word creates a header or footer for you
or you insert a page number, you see that special content formatted differently from a field. It
looks something like this:

8/6/2008

That's a *content control,* a special type of field
that contains dynamic information pertaining to
a document. The content controls are usually
inserted by Word commands, such as those that
automatically create headers or footers or insert
page numbers. You can also use the Quick Parts⇨
Properties command (found in the Insert tab's
Text group) to insert a property control.

You can edit a content control's contents if you
like, and some controls are designed that way.
But editing the text in other controls changes
the thing to plain text, so be careful.

Time-sensitive content controls can be updated
by pressing the F9 key.

Some Date content controls have a pick-the-
date button, displaying a tiny calendar from
which you can set the property's date.

To automatically insert a Date content control
into your document, press Alt+Shift+D. To insert
a Time content control, press Alt+Shift+T.

Though fields look like regular text, they're not. For example, when you press Backspace to erase a field, the entire field becomes highlighted. That's your clue that you're about to erase a field, not regular text. Press Backspace again to erase the field (and its text).

✔ You cannot edit text in a field. You can only delete it: Do so by selecting the entire field as a block and then pressing the Delete key.

✔ To adjust a field, right-click the field and choose Edit Field from the pop-up menu. The Field dialog box is redisplayed, allowing you to make modifications to the field.

✔ Some field's contents can change. To ensure that the field is up-to-date, right-click it and choose the Update Field command. For example, a date field is updated to the current date when you choose the Update Field command.

✔ You can display the field's true, ugly self. Just as those mutants at the end of *Beneath the Planet of the Apes* removed their human masks, you can remove a field's mask by right-clicking it and choosing the Toggle Field Codes command. Repeat those steps to put the mask back on. Whew!

Playing with fields

You can insert a variety of interesting, dynamic information into a document by using fields. The following sections go over some of my favorite fields. In each case, I assume that the Field dialog box (refer to Figure 18-3) is visible so that you can make your selections.

Page numbers

My favorite fields are the page number fields. For example, I may write in a document "Here you are on page 246, and you still have to refer to Chapter 12 to find out about hanging indents!" To ensure that the document accurately reflects the current page number, insert a current page number field:

1. **In the Field dialog box, select Numbering from the Categories drop-down list.**

2. **Select Page from the Field Names list.**

3. **In the Field Properties section of the Field dialog box, select a format for the page number.**

4. **Click OK.**

The current page's number is plopped into your document. Of course, it could also land in a header or footer or anywhere else.

Total number of pages

To insert the total number of pages in your document, heed these directions:

1. **Select Document Information from the Categories drop-down list.**

2. **Select NumPages from the Field names list.**

3. **Select a format.**

4. **Click OK.**

Word count

Getting paid by the word? Be sure to stick an automatic word count at the end of your document:

1. **From the Categories list, select Document Information.**

2. **Select NumWords from the Field Names list.**

3. **In the Field Properties section of the Field dialog box, select a format.**

4. **Click OK.**

The print date

I like to stick the current date in my document's header so that I know on which day it was printed. Here's how:

1. **Select Date and Time from the Categories drop-down list.**

2. **Select PrintDate from the Field Names list.**

3. **In the Field Properties section of the Field dialog box, select a format.**

4. **Click OK.**

Other date formats can be selected from the Date and Time category, but only the PrintDate is updated each time you print the document.

Inserting the current-date-and-time trick

![Date & Time]

If you just want the date or time inserted into your document, use the Text group on the Insert tab. Clicking the Date and Time button in that group displays a dialog box from which you can choose how to insert the current date or time into your document. You can even click the Update Automatically option so that the date and time text are always current.

Center a Page, Top to Bottom

Nothing makes a document title nice and crisp like having it sit squat in the center of a page. The title is centered left to right, which you can do by selecting Center alignment for the title's paragraph. But how about centering the title top to bottom? Word can do that too:

1. **Move the insertion pointer to the start of your document.**

   The Ctrl+Home key combination moves you there instantly.

2. **Type and format your document's title.**

   It can be on a single line or on several lines.

   To center the title, select it and press Ctrl+E, the Center keyboard short-cut. Apply any additional font or paragraph formatting as necessary.

   Avoid the temptation to press the Enter key to add space above or below your title. Right now, the title sits by itself at the top of the page. That will be fixed in a jiffy.

3. **Insert a section break after the title's last line: On the Page Layout tab, choose Breaks⇨Next Page from the Page Setup area.**

   The section break ensures that only the first page of your document is centered top to bottom. Refer to Chapter 16 for more information on document sections.

4. **Ensure that the insertion pointer is once again on the document's first page.**

   You need to be on the page you want to format.

5. **Summon the Page Setup dialog box: Click the Page Layout tab and choose the Dialog Box Launcher from the lower-right corner of the Page Setup area.**

   The Page Setup dialog box appears.

6. **Click the Layout tab.**

7. **Select Center from the Vertical Alignment drop-down list.**

   You can find this item in the bottom half of the dialog box.

8. **Confirm that the Apply To drop-down list shows This Section.**

9. **Click OK.**

In Print Layout view, it's easier to see the change than when you're in Draft view. Of course, you can use Print Preview (refer to Chapter 10) to confirm that, indeed, the first page — and only the first page — of the document is centered top to bottom.

Steal This Format!

Speaking of mad artists, the Paintbrush tool in the Clipboard group, on the Home tab, can be used to *paint* character styles, by copying them from one bit of text to another in your document. Here's how:

1. **Force the insertion pointer into the middle of the text that has the formatting you want to copy.**

   The insertion pointer must be in the midst of the word, not to the left or right of it. (The pointer doesn't have to be exactly in the middle — just "in the word"). If it's not, this trick doesn't work.

2. **On the Home tab, click the Format Painter command button in the Clipboard group.**

   The cursor changes to a paintbrush/I-beam pointer, as depicted in the margin. This special cursor is used to highlight and then reformat text in your document.

3. **Hunt for the text you want to change.**

4. **Highlight the text.**

   Drag the mouse over the text you want to change — to "paint" it. (You must use the mouse here.)

   Voilà! The text is changed.

Mad modern artists can also make use of the following tips and tidbits:

- The Format Painter works with only character and paragraph formatting, not with page formatting.

- To change the formatting of multiple bits of text, double-click the Format Painter. That way, the Format Painter cursor stays active, ready to paint lots of text. Press the Esc key to cancel your Dutch Boy frenzy.

- If you tire of the mouse, you can use the Ctrl+Shift+C key command to copy the character format from a highlighted block to another location in your document. Use the Ctrl+Shift+V key combination to paste the character format elsewhere. Just highlight the text in your document and press Ctrl+Shift+V to paste in the font formatting.

- You can sorta kinda remember Ctrl+Shift+C to copy character formatting and Ctrl+Shift+V to paste because Ctrl+C and Ctrl+V are the copy-and-paste shortcut keys. Sorta kinda.

- Don't confuse the Format Painter with the highlighting tool, found in the Font group. See Chapter 27.

Part IV
Making Your Document All Fancy-Schmancy

The 5th Wave — By Rich Tennant

AIRPORT SECURITY

"They won't let me through security until I remove the bullets from my Word document."

In this part . . .

The notion of a word processor goes well beyond simply creating and formatting documents. During the Great Word Processor Feature Wars of the 1980s and 1990s, the duties and tasks assumed by the lowly word processor grew to include complex drawing, graphics, and desktop publishing abilities. Concerned that this would drive away consumers, limited ("lite") versions of word processors were offered. No one bought them. So, obviously, there's a need in word processing for more than just writing and formatting. Yea, verily, there's a need to make your documents all fancy-schmancy. In this part of the book, you're introduced to some tools that help make that happen.

Chapter 19

Borders, Boxes, and Background Color

In This Chapter

▶ Understanding lines and borders

▶ Using the Border menu and the Borders and Shading dialog box

▶ Drawing lines around your text

▶ Putting a border around a page

▶ Coloring the background

The days of whacking the hyphen, equal sign, or underline keys to decorate your text are long over. It's sad, too, because I knew quite a few people who were adept at using the computer keyboard's more interesting symbol keys to draw boxes and lines and even graphics within their text. I can understand the need, but what I don't understand is why people don't simply use the borders, lines, and shading commands in Word, which are so cleverly discussed in this very chapter.

This Border Situation

To fully understand how Word draws lines, you need to accept a few things. First, they're *borders*, not *lines*. I have this chapter indexed under both items because too many people get frustrated with random lines in their text, yet cannot find a solution because they think "line" and not "border."

No, that's not your fault.

The second thing to know about borders in Word is that they're primarily paragraph things. Borders are added above, below, or to either side of a paragraph. You cannot add individual borders around single words, although you can box words on all four sides.

- ✔ The border is applied to the paragraph that the insertion pointer is blinking in.

- ✔ To apply the border to multiple paragraphs, select them with the mouse.

- ✔ Borders can also be applied to a page. Refer to the section "Putting a border around a page of text," later in this chapter.

- ✔ Not all lines in Word are borders. A thin border on the left margin of a line of text can be a sign that something was changed on that line. Refer to Chapter 27 for more information on revision marking.

The Border command button

Quick application of a border is possible, thanks to the Border command button, found in the Home tab's Paragraph group. Clicking that button immediately applies a border to your text, or removes the borders, as is the case with the No Border button shown in the margin.

When you click the menu part of the Border command button, a menu full of border choices is made available, as shown in Figure 19-1. Choosing a border from the menu not only applies that border to your text, but also changes the Border command button to reflect that new border style.

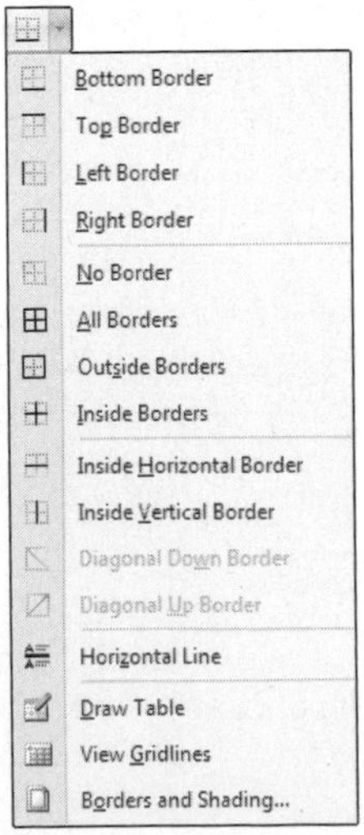

	Bottom Border
	Top Border
	Left Border
	Right Border
	No Border
	All Borders
	Outside Borders
	Inside Borders
	Inside Horizontal Border
	Inside Vertical Border
	Diagonal Down Border
	Diagonal Up Border
	Horizontal Line
	Draw Table
	View Gridlines
	Borders and Shading...

Figure 19-1:
The Border
menu.

You can use only one border style from the Border menu at a time. Choosing another style replaces the first style. If you want some combination of borders, you must use the Borders and Shading dialog box, as described in the next section. That dialog box also allows you to change the line style, color, and thickness of your border.

The Borders and Shading dialog box

For real control over borders, you summon the Borders and Shading dialog box, shown in Figure 19-2. Choosing the Borders and Shading command from the bottom of the Border menu (refer to Figure 19-1) does the job.

Unlike on the Border menu, several options are available in the Borders and Shading dialog box for setting borders. Most notably, you can set the border line style, thickness, and color.

Click the OK button to apply your border settings and close the dialog box, or press Cancel to give up and quit.

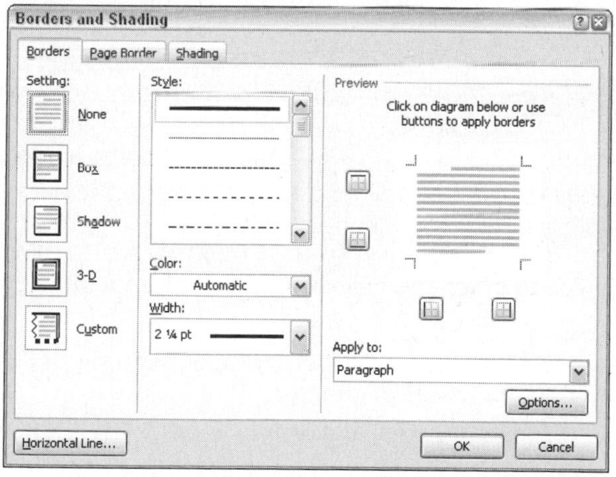

Figure 19-2:
The Borders
and Shading
dialog box.

Lines and Boxes Around Your Text

Here a line. There a line. Everywhere a line-line. This section describes various ways to apply borders to your text. This section refers to the Border menu and Borders and Shading dialog box, as described earlier in this chapter.

Drawing a fat, thick line

Sometimes you need one of those fat, thick lines to break up your text. I dunno *why*, but the *how* is to choose the Horizontal Line command from the Border menu. Word inserts a thin, inky stroke running from the left to right margins on a line all by itself.

- Unlike a border, the Horizontal Line isn't attached to a paragraph, so it doesn't repeat for every new paragraph you type.

- To adjust the Horizontal Line, click to select it with the mouse. Six "handles" appear (top, bottom, and the four corners) around the selected image. You can drag those handles with the mouse to set the line's width or thickness.

- Double-clicking the Horizontal Line displays a Format Horizontal Line dialog box, where further adjustments can be made and color added.

- To remove the Horizontal Line, click once to select it and then press either the Delete or Backspace key.

- Word's Horizontal Line is essentially the same thing as the `<HL>` tag in HTML Web page formatting.

Making rules

A common trick in page design is to apply a line above or below text. The line is a *rule,* and it helps to break up the text, highlight a specific paragraph, or create a *block quote,* *callout,* or *pull quote.* Here's how:

1. **Click the mouse to place the insertion pointer into a given paragraph of text.**

   Yes, it works best if you've already written that paragraph. Remember my admonition: Write first, format later.

2. **Summon the Borders and Shading dialog box.**

3. **Choose a line style, thickness, and color, if needed.**

4. **Click the Top button.**

5. **Click the Bottom button.**

6. **Click OK.**

You may also want to adjust the paragraph margins inward so that your text further stands out on the page. Refer to Chapter 12 for more information.

If you press Enter to end the paragraph, you carry the border formatting with the insertion pointer to the following paragraph. See the section "Removing borders," later in this chapter, to find out how to prevent that.

Boxing text or paragraphs

To stick a box around any spate of words or paragraphs, summon the Borders and Shading dialog box and choose a Box style from the Setting column: Box, Shadow, or 3-D. Click OK.

To ensure that the border is applied to text (words) and not to the entire paragraph, choose Text from the Apply To drop-down list in the Borders and Shading dialog box.

Word lets you create graphical pull quotes by putting text in graphical boxes. Refer to Chapter 24 for more information on text boxes and pull quotes.

Boxing a title

Someday when you're tasked with creating the organizational newsletter, you can surprise all your coworkers by coming up with a fancy title, similar to what's shown in Figure 19-3. It looks all complex and such, but it's really nothing more than the careful application of borders plus some deft text, paragraph, and tab stop skills.

Figure 19-3:
Top and bottom borders in a newsletter heading.

> *We couldn't print it if it weren't true!*
>
> **☢ Conspiracy Theorist ☠**
>
> Aliens! JFK! The Gold Standard! 9-11! International Bankers! UFOs! The Holy Grail! Pearl Harbor! Free Masons! New World Order!
>
> Vol. XXII, Issue 13   August, 2008

The key to creating such a heading is to type the text first and then use the Borders and Shading dialog box to add different border styles above and below the paragraphs.

Use the Preview window to help determine the line style. You can click the mouse on the lines in the Preview window to add or remove lines above or below or to either side of the text.

Putting a border around a page of text

Borders are popular for pages as well as for paragraphs, although this can often be a frustrating thing because the border may not print completely. I've studied the issue and found the problem. My solution to the putting-a-border-around-a-page-of-text puzzle is presented in these steps:

1. **Put the insertion pointer on the page you want to border.**

   For example, on the first page in your document.

2. **Summon the Borders and Shading dialog box.**

3. **Click the Page Border tab.**

   Whoa! The Page Border tab looks *exactly* like the Borders tab (refer to Figure 19-2). Incredible.

4. **Choose the border you want: Use a preset box or pick a line style, color, and width.**

   Optionally, you can select a funky art pattern from the Art drop-down list.

5. **Choose which pages you want bordered from the Apply To drop-down list.**

   You can select Whole Document to put borders on every page. To select the first page, choose the This Section - First Page Only item. Other options let you choose other pages and groups, as shown in the drop-down list.

   And now, the secret:

6. **Click the Options button.**

   The Border and Shading Options dialog box appears.

7. **From the Measure From drop-down list choose the option labeled Text.**

   The Edge of Page option just doesn't work with most printers. Text does.

8. **Click OK.**

9. **Click OK to close the Borders and Shading dialog box.**

In Print Layout view, you can see the border applied. Yep, that's how it's gonna look.

To add more "air" between your text and the border, use the Border Shading Options dialog box (from Step 6) and *increase* the values in the Margin area.

Refer to Chapter 15 for more information on creating a section break in your document. By using sections, you can greatly control which pages in a document have borders and which do not.

To remove the page border, choose None under Setting and then click OK.

Removing borders

When you don't listen to my advice and you format a paragraph before you type its contents, notice that the borders stick with the paragraph like discarded gum under your shoe. To peel the annoying borders from a paragraph, you need to choose the No Border style.

From the Border menu, choose No Border.

In the Borders and Shading dialog box, double-click the None button and then click OK.

You can also use the Borders and Shading dialog box to selectively remove borders from text. Use the Preview window and click a specific border to remove it.

Background Colors

The Borders and Shading dialog box is also the place where you apply a background color, or *shade,* to your text. The background color can go under individual words, sentences, or paragraphs — any block of text — and weird parts of your document, like a title, as shown in Figure 19-4. You can shade in gray, color, and patterns with or without a border around it. It's a veritable smorgasbord of scribbles to junk up your text.

Figure 19-4:
A sample bit o' text with a border and shading.

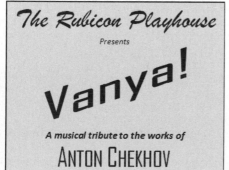

Heed these steps:

1. **Mark your text or title as a block.**

   Refer to Chapter 7 for efficient block-marking instructions.

   If you want the shaded area to cover more than the title line, highlight the lines before and after the title. That creates a "buffer" of shading around the text.

2. **Conjure up the Borders and Shading dialog box.**

3. **Make sure that the Shading panel is up front.**

4. **Select a shade from the Fill palette.**

   You have a choice of theme colors or standard colors, or you can whip up your own color by choosing the More Colors command.

5. **Click OK.**

The text is shaded.

- ✔ You can apply shading to a single word by choosing Text from the Apply To drop-down list.

- ✔ Applying background color to a page is best done by using the Page Color command, as described in Chapter 14.

- ✔ To create white text on a black background, select the text and apply white as the text foreground color (refer to Chapter 11). Then, from the Shading tab in the Borders and Shading dialog box, apply black as the background color.

- ✔ The best values to select for shading your text are gray. I'm fond of the `Text/Background 1, Shade 85%` setting because it prints nicely without wiping out the text.

- ✔ Try to avoid using the patterns. Although some of them may look like gray-fills, they're really ugly. I suppose that someone somewhere may find them useful, but for shading text, they're probably not what you need.

Chapter 20

Turning the Tables

· ·

In This Chapter

▶ Understanding tables in Word

▶ Creating a table of any size

▶ Drawing a table in your document

▶ Converting between text and a table

▶ Working a table with the mouse

▶ Adding text into the table

▶ Formatting the table

▶ Adding or inserting rows and columns

▶ Aligning and orienting text in cells

▶ Deleting rows and columns and the table itself

· ·

I don't mean to dash your dreams here, but set aside those thoughts of buying power tools and visiting the lumber store. Take off the silly-looking safety goggles. When you build a table in Word, you're not working with something that has four legs or a flat top or that anyone could consider as furniture. A *table* in Word is a grid. It has rows and columns, into which you can place text or graphics or — if you want to be eccentric — mathematical formulas. All that is explained in this chapter, which touches upon tables, from the teensy to the spectabular.

Furnish Forth the Tables

It can be argued that tables belong on the slate of things that a word processor can do. A table is merely information organized in a grid. The Tab key can accomplish the same thing as a table, but the table just does it so much more elegantly.

This section explores the various ways to create a table in Word. Before reading it, I recommend mulling over the following points:

- ✔ Any time you need information in a grid, or in columns and rows, you're better off creating a table in Word than fussing with tabs and tab stops.

- ✔ Rows in a table go left and right across the screen.

- ✔ Columns in a table go up and down.

- ✔ Each cubbyhole in a table is a *cell*.

- ✔ Cells can have their own margins, text, and paragraph formats. You can even stick graphics into cells.

- ✔ Unlike working with tabs, Word tables can be resized and rearranged to fit your data. Try doing that with tabs!

- ✔ It helps to be in Print Layout view to best work with tables. The sections in this chapter assume that you're using Print Layout view, not Draft view.

Starting your table-creation fun

You can build a table from scratch, or you can convert text that's already in your document into a table. My advice is to start from scratch: Create the table first and then fill it with information. Word allows you to add or remove rows or columns, so there's no need to be precise when you first start out.

Table creation happens on Word's Insert tab, in the Tables group. Clicking the Table button displays a menu of table-creation options, as shown in Figure 20-1. The following sections discuss using the various items on the menu.

When you enter Table view in Word, two new tabs appear on the Ribbon: Design and Layout, both of which appear beneath the label Table Tools. Using these tabs is covered in the section "Table Craftsmanship," later in this chapter.

After filling the table, you can format it using the various table-formatting tricks and techniques covered in the latter half of this chapter.

- ✔ Go ahead and be lazy! Use the Quick Tables submenu from the Table menu (refer to Figure 20-1) to select a predesigned table and slap it down into your document. Unless the table you need is on that submenu, though, you're better off manually creating a table, as described in this chapter.

✔ If you've already typed the table's data, or maybe the data you want to put into a table is now formatted with tabs, refer to the section "Transmuting tabbed text into a table," later in this chapter.

✔ I recommend starting the table on a blank line by itself. Furthermore, type a second blank line *after* the line you put the table on. That makes it easier to continue typing text after the table is created.

✔ Consider placing large tables on a page by themselves. You can even reorient the page horizontally in the middle of your document. Refer to Chapter 14 for hints and tips.

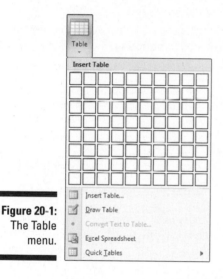

Figure 20-1:
The Table
menu.

Creating a table yay-by-yay big

The quickest way to instantly slap down a table in your document is to use the grid thing at the top of the Table menu. (Refer to Figure 20-1.) Drag the mouse through the grid to create a table in your document with the same number of rows and columns as you select in the grid.

Figure 20-2 shows a 4-column-by-3-row table being created by dragging the mouse. As you drag the mouse on the menu, the table's grid appears in your document.

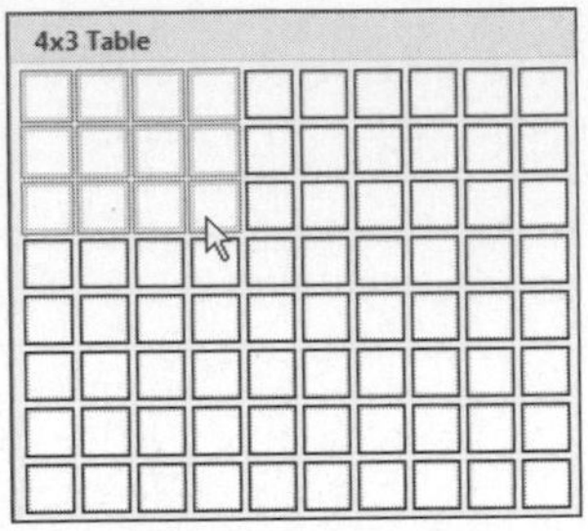

4x3 Table

Figure 20-2:
The "I want
a table *this*
big" table-
creation
technique.

- ✔ Just guess! You can add or remove rows or columns at any time in Word.

- ✔ The table is created with the same width as your document's paragraph margins. When you add more columns, each column gets smaller.

- ✔ Column width can be adjusted, as described elsewhere in this chapter.

- ✔ If you prefer a more right-brain approach to creating a table, choose the Insert Table command from the Table menu. Use the Insert Table dialog box to manually enter the number of rows and columns you need. Click the OK button to plop down your table.

Drawing a table

Feeling artistic? Especially when your table may not be a pure grid or need even columns and text, you can use a special drawing mode to splash down a unique table in your document. Here's how:

1. **From the Table menu, choose Draw Table.**

   The insertion pointer changes to a pencil, which I call the *pencil pointer*.

2. **Drag the mouse to "draw" the table's outline in your document.**

   Start in the upper-left corner of where you envision your table and drag to the lower-right corner, which tells Word where to put your table. You see an outline of the table as you drag down and to the right, as shown in Figure 20-3.

   As you begin drawing, you see the Design tab appear and come forward. The Draw Borders group contains tools to help you draw tables.

   Don't worry about making the table the right size; you can resize it later.

   Notice that any text you already have in your document moves aside to make room for the new table.

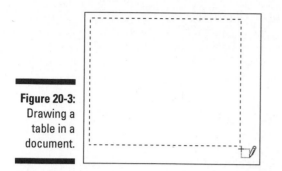

Figure 20-3:
Drawing a
table in a
document.

3. **Use the pencil pointer to draw rows and columns.**

As long as the mouse pointer looks like a pencil, you can use it to draw the rows and columns in your table.

To draw a row, drag the pencil pointer from the left side to the right side of the table.

To draw a column, drag the pencil pointer from the top to the bottom of the table, as shown in Figure 20-4.

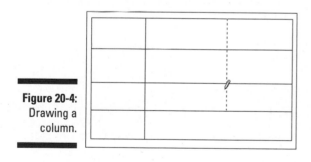

Figure 20-4:
Drawing a
column.

As you drag the pencil pointer, a dashed line appears, showing you where the new row or column will be split. Figure 20-4 shows a table shaping up. Also notice that you can split columns or rows into more cells by simply dragging the pencil pointer inside a cell and not across the entire table.

Again, don't worry if you have too many or too few rows or columns. You can add or delete them later, as you see fit. And, don't worry about things being uneven; you can rearrange your rows and columns later.

4. **Click the Draw Table button when you're done creating the table's columns and rows.**

The mouse pointer returns to normal. You can begin putting text in the table.

You can draw more lines in a table by simply clicking the Draw Table button in the Design tab's Draw Border's group. The table you modify need not be created by the Draw Table command, either; any table can be modified by using that tool.

Transmuting tabbed text into a table

Tables make organizing data so easy that at some point you may be eager to convert one of your crafty tabbed lists into a true table. This is cinchy in theory, but in practice requires some tidying up. Still, it's easier than turning lead into gold. The basic steps to take are these:

1. **Select the text you want to convert into a table.**

   It helps if the text is arranged into columns, with each column separated by a tab character. If not, things get screwy, but still workable.

2. **Choose Table⇨Convert Text to Table.**

   The Convert Text to Table dialog box, which assists in the conversion.

   As long as the text you selected is formatted into columns with tabs, there's no need to modify the settings in the dialog box. Otherwise, the settings assist in converting your text.

3. **Click OK.**

   A table is born.

You probably need to adjust things, reset column widths, and so on and so forth. It may be a pain, but it's better than retyping all that text.

✔ Sections elsewhere in this chapter explain how to adjust the text in your table.

✔ The Convert Text to Table item is available only when text is selected, and you'll notice that the Table menu appears shorter than normal. (Refer to Figure 20-1.)

Turning a table back into plain text

Word lets you easily help your text escape from the prison of a table's cells. It's as easy as turning a beautiful princess into a toad, although unless you have a magic wand handy, you probably want to follow these steps:

1. **Click the mouse inside the table you want to convert.**

2. **Click the Layout tab.**

   The commands you need in order to perform the conversion are found on the Table Tools Layout tab.

3. **From the Table group, choose Select⇨Select Table.**

4. **From the Data group, choose Convert to Text.**

   The Convert to Text dialog box appears.

5. **Ensure that Tabs is chosen in the Convert Table to Text dialog box.**

6. **Click OK.**

   Bye-bye, table. Hello, ugly text.

As with converting text to a table, some cleanup is involved. Mostly, it's resetting the tabs (or removing them) — nothing complex or bothersome.

When a table's cells contain longer expanses of text, consider choosing Paragraph Marks in Step 5. That makes the text look less ugly after the conversion.

It's Your Turn to Set the Table

Text pours into a table on a cell-by-cell basis. Each cell can have its own paragraph format and its own set of tabs. Groups of cells, rows, columns, and the entire table can be selected and formatted at one time, if you like. All the standard text and paragraph formats apply to cells in a table just as they do to regular text.

✔ You should take care to avoid paragraph indents and first-line indents for text in a cell. It just works *funky*.

✔ It's a boon to show the Ruler when you work with formatting a table. Use the View Ruler button, as explained in Chapter 2.

Using the mouse with a table

A typical table skeleton is shown in Figure 20-5. You can use the mouse to manipulate the table, whether it's empty (as in the figure) or populated with text. Here's what you can do:

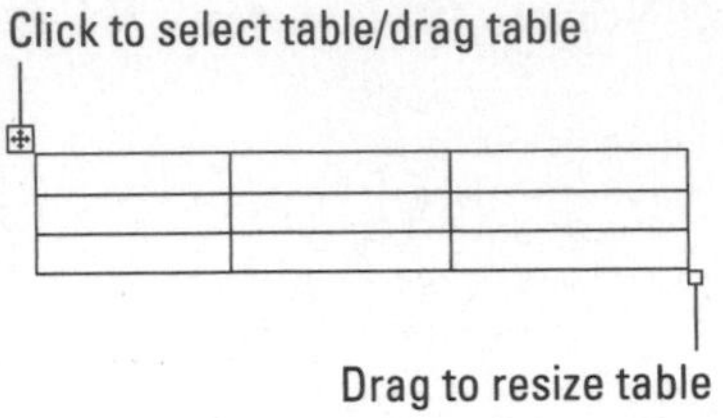

Click to select table/drag table

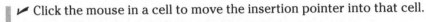

Figure 20-5:
Parts of the
basic table.

Drag to resize table

- Click the mouse in a cell to move the insertion pointer into that cell.

- Triple-click the mouse in a cell to select all text in that cell.

- You can select a single cell by positioning the mouse in the cell's lower-left corner. The mouse pointer changes to a northeastward-pointing arrow, as shown in the margin. Click to select the cell.

- Move the mouse into the left margin and click to select a row of cells.

- Move the mouse above a column and click to select that column. When the mouse is in the "sweet spot," the pointer changes to a downward-pointing arrow (shown in the margin).

- Selecting stuff in a table can also be accomplished from the Table group on the Layout tab. Use the Select menu to select the entire table, a row, a column, or a single cell.

-  Positioning the mouse on a vertical line in the table's grid changes the mouse pointer to the thing shown in the margin. That allows you to adjust the line left or right and resize the surrounding cells.

- You can also adjust cell width by using the ruler, by pointing the mouse at the Move Table Column button that appears above each table cell gridline.

- Pointing the mouse at a horizontal line changes the mouse pointer to what's shown in the margin. At that time, you can use the mouse to adjust the line up or down and change the row height of surrounding cells.

- Although you can use the Move Thing in the upper-left corner of the table to move the table around your document, it's often easier to select the entire table and then copy and paste it elsewhere. The standard Cut and Copy commands, described in Chapter 7, also work with tables in Word.

Putting text into a table

To populate your table with text, simply type. All the text you type fits into a single cell. Cells grow taller to accommodate long bits of text. Certain keys perform special functions within the table:

- ✔ **Tab:** To move to the next cell, press the Tab key. This moves you from cell to cell, from left to right. Pressing Tab in the last column moves you down to the next row.

- ✔ **Shift+Tab:** To move backward to the previous cell, press Shift+Tab.

- ✔ **Arrow keys:** The up, down, left, and right keys also move you around within the table, but they still move within any text in a cell. Therefore, using the arrow keys to move from cell to cell is rather inefficient.

- ✔ **Enter:** The Enter key adds a new paragraph to a cell.

- ✔ **Shift+Enter:** The Shift+Enter key combination can break up long lines of text in a cell with a soft return.

- ✔ **Ctrl+Tab:** To use any tabs or indentation within a cell, press Ctrl+Tab rather than Tab.

By the way, pressing the Tab key in the table's last, lower-right cell automatically adds another row to the table.

Table Craftsmanship

There's no point in making ugly tables. Word gives you the basic table layout, which you fill with text. The next thing you can do, after filling the tables with text, is to give them *style*. To help you do so, two Table Tools tabs appear whenever you work with a table: Design and Layout. This section describes various things you can do with the commands found on those two tabs.

The Table Tools tabs show up only when a table is being edited or selected.

Designing a table

Use the Table Tools Design tab, shown in Figure 20-6, to quickly or slowly format your table.

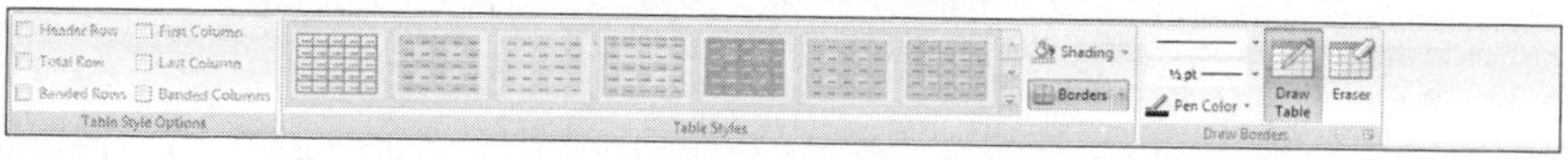

Figure 20-6:
The Design tab.

The Table Styles group can quickly apply formatting to any table. Choose a style or click the menu button to see a whole smattering of styles. As with Quick Styles (refer to Chapter 16), as you point the mouse at a table style, your table is updated to reflect the new style.

Settings chosen in the Table Style Options group determine how the table styles shape up. Choose an option to apply that type of formatting to the table styles, such as Header Row to format a separate header row for the table.

The following sections discuss various things you can play with to design a table.

Setting table line styles

The lines you see in a table's grid are the same borders you can apply to text with the Border command button, discussed in Chapter 19. The Border command button chooses where the lines go; items on the left side of the Draw Borders group set the border line style, width, and color.

The border changes you make apply to whichever part of the table is selected. Refer to the section "Using the mouse with a table," earlier in this chapter, for tips on selecting parts of a table.

Removing a table's lines

Occasionally, you may want a table without any lines. For example, I typically use a one-column, two-row table to put a picture and its caption in my text. To remove the table's grid in that and other situations, select the table and choose No Border from the Borders menu.

Having no lines (borders) in a table makes working with the table more difficult. The solution is to show the table *gridlines,* which aren't printed. To do that, select the table and choose the Show Gridlines command from the Border menu.

Merging cells

 You can combine two or more cells in a table by simply erasing the line that separates them. To do so, click the Eraser command button found in the Draw Borders group. The mouse pointer changes to a bar of soap, but it's really supposed to be an eraser (shown in the margin). Use that tool to erase lines in the table: Click a line and it's gone.

Erasing the line between cells merges the cells' contents, by combining the text.

You cannot remove the outside lines of the table. (To convert the table to text, see the section "Turning a table back into plain text," earlier in this chapter. To delete a table, see the section "Deleting a table," at the end of this chapter.

Click the Eraser button again when you're done merging.

Splitting cells

To turn one cell into two, you simply draw a line, horizontally or vertically, through the cell. Do so by clicking the Draw Table command button in the Draw Borders group. The mouse pointer changes to the pencil pointer, which you can use to draw new lines in the table.

Click the Draw Table button again to turn off this feature.

Adjusting the table

After the table is splashed down into your document, you can mess with it in uncountable ways. The messing is made possible by the Table Tools Layout tab, shown in Figure 20-7. Various commands in the Layout tab's groups help you customize and adjust your table. The sections that follow highlight some popular tricks.

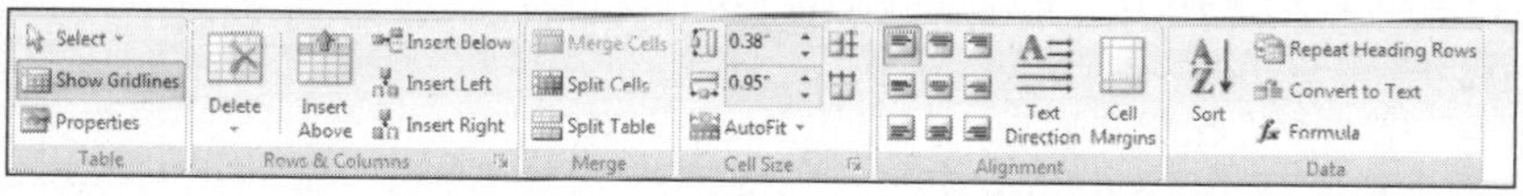

Figure 20-7: The Layout tab.

Deleting cells, columns, or rows

The key to deleting all or part of a table is to first position the insertion pointer in the part of the table you want to remove. Then choose the table element to remove from the Delete button's menu.

- ✔ The table's contents are also deleted when you delete parts of a table.
- ✔ The Delete Cells command displays a dialog box asking what to do with the other cells in the row or column: move them up or to the left. Yes, deleting a cell may make your table asymmetrical.

Inserting columns or rows

You can expand a table by adding rows or columns, and the rows or columns can be added inside the table or appended to any of the table's four sides. Four commands in the Rows & Columns group make this possible: Insert Above, Insert Below, Insert Left, and Insert Right. The row or column that's added is relative to where the insertion pointer is within the table.

Adjusting row and column size

Gizmos in the Cell Size group let you fine-tune the table's row height or column width. Adjustments that are made affect the row or column containing the insertion pointer.

 The Distribute Rows and Distribute Columns command buttons help clean up uneven column or row spacing in a table. With the insertion pointer anywhere in the table, click either or both buttons to even things out.

Aligning text

Text within a cell can be aligned just like a paragraph: left, center, or right. Additionally, the text can be aligned vertically: top, middle, or bottom. Combine these options and you have an explanation for the nine orientation buttons in the Alignment group.

 For example, to make the title row align at the bottom center of each cell, first select the top row in your table and then click the Align Top Center button.

Reorienting text

The Text Direction button in the Alignment group changes the way text reads in a cell or group of selected cells. Normally, text is oriented from left to right. By clicking the Text Direction button once, you change the text direction to top-to-bottom. Click the button again and direction is changed to bottom-to-top. Clicking a third time restores the text to normal.

Sadly, you cannot do upside-down text with the Text Direction button.

Deleting a table

To utterly remove the table from your document, click the mouse inside the table and then choose Delete⇨Table from the Rows & Columns group on the Layout tab.. The table is blown to smithereens.

 ✔ Yes, deleting the table deletes its contents as well.

 ✔ If you'd rather merely convert the table's contents into plain text, refer to the section "Turning a table back into plain text," earlier in this chapter.

Chapter 21

Carousing with Columns

- -

In This Chapter

▶ Understanding columns

▶ Breaking up your text into columns

▶ Using the Columns dialog box

▶ Formatting columns

▶ Inserting column breaks

▶ Restoring "normal" text from columnar text

▶ Undoing columns

- -

*I*f someone asks about columns and you immediately think of Doric, Ionic, and Corinthian, then know that somewhere your ninth-grade history teacher is smiling proudly. That's because few people outside the publishing industry relate columns to text. The fact that Word bothers to place text into multiple columns on a page is merely fallout from the word processor feature wars of decades past. Yet columns remain something that Word lets you do with your document. Whether you find columns a useful feature or not, you can better decide after wading through this chapter.

All About Columns

All text you write in Word is already formatted in a column, one column per page. Most folks don't think of things that way — that is, until you start talking about two or three columns of text per page. Such a feat is entirely possible, thanks to the Columns command button, found in the Page Setup group on the Page Layout tab.

For advanced formatting, nothing beats DTP

I'll be honest up front: When you desire columns for whatever you're writing, what you really need is *desktop publishing*, or DTP, software. Desktop publishing isn't about writing; it's about assembling already written text with graphics and other design elements and then laying things out as a professional would. DTP is built for such a thing. It can handle it.

Word's ability to march text into columns isn't its best feature. Columns work for smaller documents — say, one-sheet newsletters or fliers. Beyond that, I highly recommend using DTP software for your demanding documents. Both Adobe InDesign and Microsoft Publisher are good places to start, if you're interested in DTP software.

Clicking the Columns button displays a menu of handy column-formatting options, as shown in Figure 21-1. Splitting your text into columns is as easy as choosing a column format from that list. Or, you can choose the More Columns command, which displays the enticing Columns dialog box. By using that dialog box, you can create and design your own set of multiple columns.

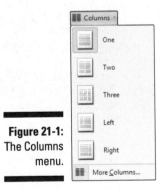

Figure 21-1:
The Columns
menu.

Consider the following advice when you're creating or working with columns:

✔ Word's paragraph formatting also applies to columns. The column's left and right sides are equivalent to the paragraph margins.

✔ Rather than use the cursor-movement keys to move the insertion pointer between columns, use the mouse. It's much easier to point and click in a column than to watch the insertion pointer fly all over the page.

✔ Columns are a section thing. You can break up your document between pages formatted normally and pages with columns by using sections. Refer to Chapter 15 for the details.

- When you're working with columns and notice that Word starts acting slow and fussy, *save your work!*

- Although using columns for a short document seems to work well in Word, putting text into columns in a document of ten pages or more is better done in a desktop publishing program (DTP). See the nearby sidebar "For advanced formatting, nothing beats DTP."

Here Come the Columns!

To convert your standard single- (or no-) column document into one with multiple columns, simply choose the column format you want from the Columns menu. (Refer to Figure 21-1.) Instantly, your document is transformed into a multicolumn wonder!

- To best see columns in action, use Print Layout view.

- Two columns are sufficient to impress anyone. More columns make your text skinnier and more difficult to read.

- To have only a portion of your document use columns, refer to the section "Mixing column formats," a little later in this chapter.

Making more than three columns

The Columns menu lists only two-column formats, plus one three-column format. For anything different, such as more than three columns, choose Columns⇨More Columns and use the Number of Columns box, shown in Figure 21-2.

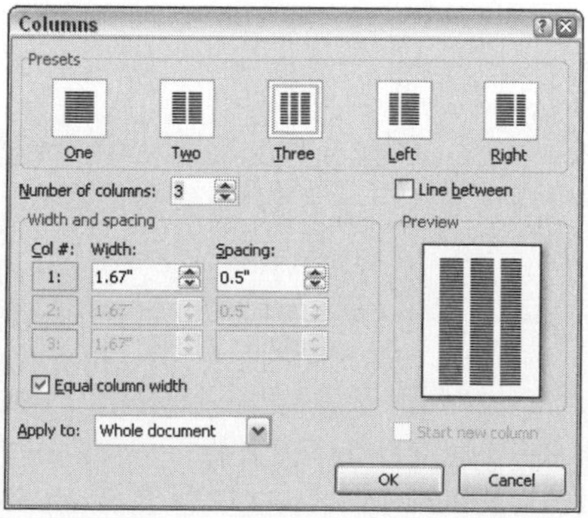

Figure 21-2: The Columns dialog box.

Set the number of columns you want by using the Number of Columns box. Use the Preview window to help determine how your page is formatted. Click the OK button to apply the column format to your document.

✔ The three-column text format works nicely on paper in Landscape mode. This method is how most trifold brochures are created. Refer to Chapter 14 for information on Landscape mode.

✔ Maximum number of columns per page? That depends on the size of the page. Word's minimum column width is half an inch, so a typical sheet of paper can have up to 12 columns on it — not that such a layout would be appealing or anything.

Mixing column formats

Your whole document doesn't have to sport just one column format. You can split things up so that part of the document is one column, and another part is two columns, and then maybe another part goes back to one column. The secret is to use the Columns dialog box. (Refer to Figure 21-2.)

When you're choosing a new column format, be sure to check the Apply To drop-down list. When you choose Whole Document, the format applies to the entire document. If you choose This Point Forward, the new columns start at the insertion pointer's location.

Choosing This Point Forward inserts a continuous section break into your document. So the real solution to mixing column formats is to read about sections in Chapter 15 and then divide your document into sections and apply the column formats accordingly.

Adjusting the columns in the Columns dialog box

There isn't much to formatting columns, other than setting their width and the space between them. This is done in the Columns dialog box. (Refer to Figure 21-2.) Here are some points to ponder:

✔ You can make specific column adjustments in the Width and Spacing area of the dialog box.

✔ If you want an attractive line between the columns of text, put a check in the Line Between box. (*Note:* There's no attractiveness guarantee for the line.)

✔ Use the Preview window to get an idea of what the heck you're doing.

✔ The space between columns is the *gutter*. Word sets the width of the gutter at 0.5" — half an inch. This amount of white space is pleasing to the eye without being too much of a good thing.

The End of the Column

There are several ways to end a column of text. Here are three of them:

✔ **Create a column break.** When you want to keep on using columns but want the text you're writing to start at the top of the next column, you need a *column break*. Heed these steps:

  1. **Place the insertion pointer where you want your text to start at the top of the next column.**

  2. **Click the Page Layout tab.**

  3. **From the Page Setup group, choose Breaks➪Column.**

     The text hops up to the top of the next column.

✔ **Return to Single Column mode.** To stop the page format from including columns and return to standard one-column text, follow these steps:

  1. **Place the insertion pointer where you want your columns to stop.**

  2. **Click the Page Layout tab.**

  3. **From the Page Setup area, choose Columns➪More Columns.**

  4. **In the Columns dialog box, choose One from the Presets area.**

  5. **From the Apply To drop-down list, select This Point Forward.**

  6. **Click OK.**

     The columns stop, and regular, one-column text is restored.

✔ **Remove columns from a document.** To remove all signs of columns from your document, repeat the previous set of steps, but in Step 5, select Whole Document. All text is then restored to Single-Column mode.

Removing columns from a document doesn't remove any section breaks. You must manually delete them. See Chapter 15.

Chapter 22

I Love Lists

In This Chapter

▶ Automatically bulleting or numbering text

▶ Numbering lines on a page

▶ Adding a TOC to your document

▶ Creating an index

▶ Using footnotes and endnotes

*W*ord deals with lists in several ways. Allow me to list them: First, it can help you organize and spiff up lists you may have in your document by applying bullets or numbers. Second, Word lets you create specialized lists based on your document's contents, such as a table of contents, a list of figures, or an index. Finally, Word lets you "go academic" by providing easy ways to create footnotes or endnotes, which aren't lists but are handy to have when fussy professors demand such things. This chapter lists all that stuff.

Basic Bullets and Numbers

There are many ways to punctuate a list. You can try hanging indents, make the first few words **bold**, or take advantage of Word's list-enhancing features, as covered in this section.

✔ Bullets and numbers are handled in the Home tab's Paragraph group.

✔ The Multilevel List command is best applied when you have a list that's indented. Pressing the Tab key to indent a line uses the next level's format.

Making a bulleted list

In typesetting, a *bullet* is merely a graphic, such as a ball or dot, used to high-light items in a list. The word *bullet* comes from the French word *boulette* and has nothing to do with those things that come flinging from a firearm, like this:

- ✔ Bang!
- ✔ Bang!
- ✔ Bang!

 To apply bullets to your text, highlight the paragraphs you want to shoot and choose the Bullets command button, from either the Home tab's Paragraph group or the Mini Toolbar. Instantly, your text is not only formatted with bul-lets but is also indented and made all tidy.

- ✔ You can choose a different bullet by clicking the menu button by the Bullets command. Choose your new bullet graphic from the list that appears, or use the Define New Bullet command to dream up your own bullet style.
- ✔ Bullets are a paragraph format. As such, they *stick* to the paragraphs you type. To halt the bullets, click the Bullet command button again, and they're removed from the paragraph format.

Numbering a list

One good way to punctuate a list is to number it. The numbers make it easy to refer to items within the list as well as to prioritize items in the list.

 To number a list, select the paragraphs with the mouse and click the Numbering command button. Each paragraph is numbered starting with 1 and continuing through however many paragraphs are in the list. The para-graphs are also formatted so that the number appears as a hanging indent.

- ✔ Choose a different number style or format, including Roman numerals or ABCs, by clicking the menu button next to the Numbering command. Choose the numbering style you want from the menu, or click the Define New Number Format command to create your own numbering style.
- ✔ To remove numbers, simply click the Numbering button again. This removes numbering from the paragraph format.

Numbering lines of text

Word lets you slap down numbers for every line on a page, which is a feature that's popular with those in the legal profession as well as with folks who write radio scripts. It was also a feature that many former WordPerfect users demanded from Word. Here's how it goes:

1. **Click the Page Layout tab.**

2. **In the Page Setup group, click the Line Numbers command button to display its menu.**

   The menu is shown in Figure 22-1.

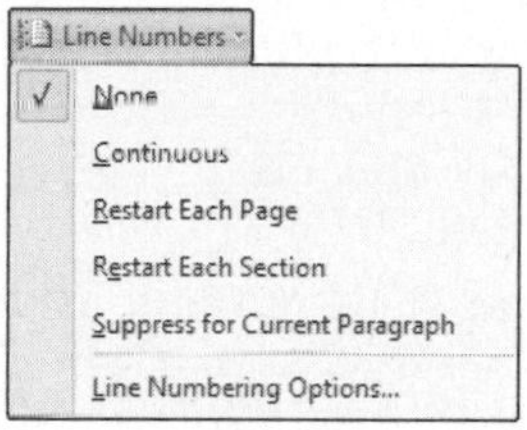

Figure 22-1:
Page line-
numbering
options.

⌐ Line Numbers ·
✓   None
Continuous
Restart Each Page
Restart Each Section
Suppress for Current Paragraph
Line Numbering Options...

3. **Choose a numbering format from the menu.**

   Now each line in your document is numbered.

Choosing the Line Numbering Options command from the menu displays the Page Setup dialog box. From there, click the Line Numbers button to summon the Line Numbers dialog box. Use that dialog box to create custom numbers and formatting for your document.

For example, use the Line Numbers dialog box to start each page with a number other than 1 or to number lines by twos or threes.

Lists of Things in Your Document

Word sports a References tab that contains groups of commands you can use to build custom lists in your documents. For example, Word can automatically build a table of contents. Or, you can quickly create a list of figure captions. Word can also whip together an index, complete with the real page numbers. This section covers the two most common list-making tricks: the table of contents and the index.

Creating a table of contents

One great example of how computers can save you time — and I'm not kidding — is to let Word create a table of contents (TOC) for your document. No, there's no need to manually type in a TOC. As long as you use the built-in heading styles, Word can slap down a custom TOC in your document as easy as following these steps:

1. **Create a separate page for the TOC.**

   Word slaps down the table of contents wherever you put the insertion pointer, but I prefer to have the thing on its own page. Refer to Chapter 14 for information on creating new pages; a new, blank page near the start of your document is ideal for a TOC.

2. **Click the mouse to place the insertion pointer on the new, blank page.**

   The TOC will be inserted at that point.

3. **Click the References tab.**

4. **In the Table of Contents group, click the Table of Contents button.**

   The Table of Contents menu appears.

5. **Choose an item from the menu based on what you want the table of contents to look like.**

   And, there's your TOC.

You may have to scroll up to see the Table of Contents. You may also want to add a title above the TOC, something clever like, "Table of Contents."

✔ Cool people in publishing refer to a table of contents as a TOC, pronounced either "tee-o-see" or "tock."

✔ You can update a TOC if your document's contents change: Click the mouse in the TOC and choose the Update Field command from the pop-up menu.

✔ Use the Table of Contents dialog box (refer to Step 5) to modify the way your TOC looks, set various options, and apply interesting styles.

✔ When the steps in this section don't seem to produce anything, it usually means that your document headings aren't formatted with the Heading styles.

✔ Word bases the TOC on text formatted with the Heading styles in your document. As long as you use Heading 1 for main heads, Heading 2 for subheads, and Heading 3 (and so on) for lower-level heads and titles, the TOC will be spot-on.

✔ Word's Table of Contents command also picks up your own styles formatting with a specific *outline level*. Suppose that you create a style named Ahead. Because that style is formatted as Outline Level 1, it's treated the same as the Heading 1 style when Word creates a TOC. To set the outline level for a paragraph style, use the Outline Level drop-down list in the Paragraph dialog box. (See Chapter 12 for paragraph-formatting information.)

Building an index

An *index* does the same thing as a table of contents, but with more detail and at the opposite end of the document. Also, the index is organized by topic or keyword as opposed to the organizational description a TOC offers.

Creating an index in Word is a two-part process. The first step is to identify the words or phrases in a document that need to be referenced in the index. The second part involves Word taking those references and automatically building the index for you. The following sections explain the details.

All indexing actions and commands take place under the realm of the References tab, in the Index group.

✔ Yes, it's a really good thing to have written your document before you create the index.

✔ Word allows you to change your document after the index is created. Note that you first have to rebuild the index as well as mark any new text for inclusion in the index.

✔ Studies done by people wearing white lab coats have shown that more readers refer to an index than to a table of contents. Therefore, make sure that your index is good and thorough.

Selecting text for the index

To flag a bit of text for inclusion in the index, follow these steps:

1. **Select the text you want to reference in the index.**

   The text can be a word or phrase or any old bit of text. Mark that text as a block.

2. **Click the Mark Entry button (in the Index group on the References tab).**

   The Mark Index Entry dialog box appears, as shown in Figure 22-2. Notice that the text you selected in your document appears in the Main Entry box. (You can edit that text, if you want.)

   You can optionally type a subentry, which further clarifies the main entry. This is especially useful when the main entry is a broad topic.

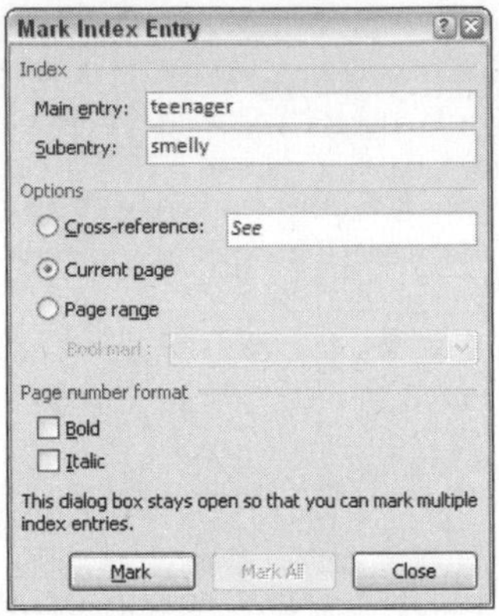

Figure 22-2:
The Mark
Index Entry
dialog box.

3. Click *either* the Mark button or the Mark All button.

The Mark button marks only this particular instance of the word for inclusion in the index. Use this button when you want to mark only instances that you think will benefit the reader the most.

The Mark All button directs Word to seek out and flag all instances of the text in your document, to create an index entry for each and every one. Use this option when you would rather leave it to your reader to decide what's relevant.

When you mark an index entry, Word activates the Show/Hide command, where characters such as spaces, paragraph marks, and tabs appear in your document. Don't let it freak you out. Step 6 tells you how to turn that thing off.

The Index code appears in the document something like this: `{·XE·"spanking"·}`. The code is hidden when you turn off Show/Hide mode.

4. Continue scrolling through your document and looking for stuff to put into the index.

The Mark Index Entry dialog box stays open, allowing you to continue to create your index: Just select text in the document, and then click the Mark Index Entry dialog box. The selected text appears in the Main Entry box. Click the Mark or Mark All button to continue building the index.

5. Click the Close button when you're done.

The Mark Index Entry dialog box goes away.

6. Press Ctrl+Shift+8 to cancel the Show/Hide command.

Use the 8 key on the keyboard, not on the numeric keypad.

Creating the index

After selecting, collecting, and marking all bits and pieces of text from your document for inclusion in the index, the next step is to create the index. Do this:

1. **Position the insertion pointer where you want the index to appear.**

   The Index is inserted at that point in your document. If you want the index to start on a new page, create a new page in Word (see Chapter 14). I also recommend putting the index at the *end* of your document, which is what the reader expects.

2. **Choose the Insert Index button from the Index group on the References tab.**

   The Index dialog box appears, as shown in Figure 22-3.

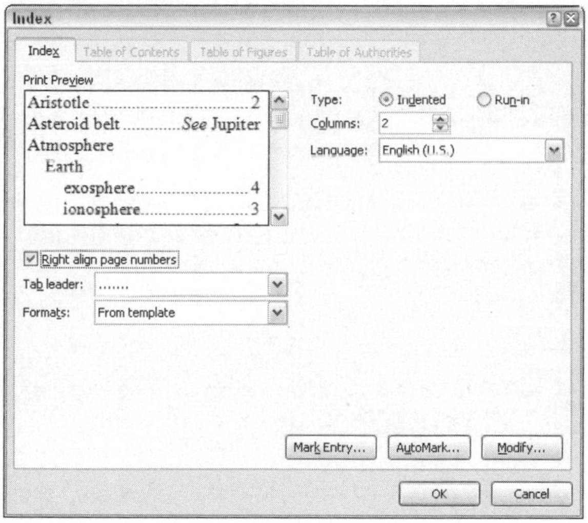

Insert Index

Figure 22-3:
The Index
and
Tables/Index
dialog box.

Here are some recommendations I have for this dialog box:

- The Print Preview window is misleading. It shows how your index will look but doesn't use your actual index contents.

- Use the Formats drop-down list to select a style for your index. Just about any choice in that list is better than the From Template example.

- The Columns list tells Word how many columns wide to make the index. Note that two columns are standard, although I usually switch to one column, which looks better on the page, especially for shorter documents.

- I prefer to use the Right Align Page Numbers option.

3. **Click the OK button to insert the index into your document.**

4. **Review the index.**

   Do this now, and do not edit any text. Just look.

5. **Press Ctrl+Z if you dislike the index layout, and start these steps over again.**

   If you think that the index is okay, you're done.

As with other magical lists in Word, the index can be updated when you go back and change your document. Refer to the next section.

✔ Feel free to add a heading for the index because Word doesn't do this for you.

✔ Word places the index into its own document section by using continuous section breaks. Refer to Chapter 15 for more information on sections.

Updating the index

Word has made it easy for you to update a document's index in case you go back and meddle with things or decide to mark more entries for inclusion in the index.

To update a document's index, click the mouse on the index. Then choose the Update Index command button from the Index group. Instantly, Word updates the index to reference any new page numbers and include new marked index entries.

Footnotes and Endnotes

The difference between a footnote and an endnote is that one appears on the same page as the reference and the other appears at the end of the document. A footnote contains bonus information, a clarification, or an aside, and an endnote is a reference or citation. But I'm only guessing.

In both cases, the footnote or endnote is flagged by a superscripted number or letter in the text, like this[1]. And, both are created in the same manner, like this:

1. **Click the mouse so that the insertion pointer is immediately to the right of the text that you want the footnote or endnote to reference.**

2. **Click the References tab.**

[1]Made you look!

3. **From the Footnotes group, choose either the Insert Footnote or Insert Endnote command button.**

   A number is superscripted to the text.

   In Print Layout view, you're instantly whisked to the bottom of the page (footnote) or the end of the document (endnote), where you type the footnote or endnote.

   In Draft view, a special window near the bottom of the document opens, displaying footnotes or endnotes.

4. **Type the footnote or endnote.**

   There's no need to type the note's number; that's done for you automatically.

   Footnotes are automatically numbered starting with 1.

   Endnotes are automatically numbered starting with Roman numeral *i*.

5. **Click the Show Notes button to exit the footnote or endnote.**

   You return to the spot in your document where the insertion pointer blinks (from Step 1).

Here are some non-footnote endnote notes:

- The keyboard shortcut for inserting a footnote is Alt+Ctrl+F.
- The keyboard shortcut for inserting an endnote is Atl+Ctrl+D.
- The footnote and endnote numbers are updated automatically so that all footnotes and endnotes are sequential in your document.
- Use the Next Footnote button's menu to browse between footnote and endnote references in your document.
- You can see a footnote or endnote's contents by pointing the mouse at the superscripted number in the document's text.
- Use the Show Notes button to help you examine footnotes or endnotes themselves.
- To quick-edit a footnote or endnote, double-click the footnote number on the page. Use the Show Notes button to return to your document.
- To delete a footnote, highlight the footnote's number in your document and press the Delete key. Word magically renumbers any remaining footnotes for you.

Chapter 23

Going Graphical

In This Chapter

▶ Inserting a picture or clip art

▶ Building line art with AutoShapes

▶ Framing a picture

▶ Wrapping text around an image

▶ Arranging images on a page

▶ Resizing an image

▶ Cropping an image

▶ Arranging multiple images

▶ Adding a caption

▶ Undoing graphical boo-boos

A picture is worth a thousand words.

It doesn't matter that this so-called ancient Chinese proverb was coined by an American in the 20th century. The essence of the saying is true: It's much easier to just paste in a picture of your time machine plans than it is to describe everything with words. Word understands this truth, and therefore it's more than accommodating when you want to mix words and pictures. This chapter provides the details.

✔ Word prefers that you view your document in Print Layout mode when you're working with graphics.

✔ The more images you add in Word, the more sluggish it becomes. My advice: Write first. Add the graphics last. Save often.

✔ Word lets you use graphics from any other graphics program you have in Windows. Often times, it works better to use those other programs to create and refine an image, save the image to disk, and then put it into Word.

Here Come the Graphics!

Watch out, text! You're no longer alone in the document, naked to fend for yourself. Behold the graphic image! It's nothing to fear. In fact, well-placed, a graphic can enhance a document's value.

Inserting a picture from a file on disk

The most common type of image you stick into your documents is a graphical file stored on your PC's hard drive. No matter how the image got on the hard drive, you can stick a copy of that image into your document by heeding these steps:

1. **Click the Insert tab.**

2. **From the Illustrations group, click the Picture button.**

   The Insert Picture dialog box appears.

   It looks similar to the Open dialog box, and it works exactly the same. (Refer to Chapter 9 for details.) The difference is that you use the Insert Picture dialog box to hunt down graphical images.

   Use the Insert Picture's dialog box Views command button menu (in the far upper-right corner) to help you visually browse for images. In Windows Vista, choose the Extra Large Icons command; in Windows XP, choose Preview.

3. **Use the dialog box controls to browse for the image you want.**

4. **Click to select the image file.**

5. **Click the Insert button.**

   The image is plopped down into your document.

The image is placed *in-line* with your text, meaning that it appears wherever the insertion pointer is blinking. You may also notice that the image is *huge*. Don't fret! Working with graphics in Word involves more than just inserting images into a document. Here are some things to consider:

- ✔ You can move the image around in your document; refer to the directions starting with the section "Images and Text Can Mix," later in this chapter.

- ✔ After inserting images, most folks do some image editing, or at least some resizing. See the section "Image Editing," later in this chapter.

✔ Word recognizes and understands just about all popular graphics file formats.

✔ A cool thing to stick at the end of a letter is your signature. Use a desktop scanner to scan your John Hancock. Save it as a file on disk, and then follow the preceding steps to insert the signature in the proper place in your document.

Inserting a clip art image

Clip art is a collection of images, both line art and pictures, that you're free to use in your documents. In most cases, the result is the same as inserting a picture, although you're using images from a clip art library rather than graphics files on your PC's hard drive. Here's how it goes:

1. **Click the Insert tab.**

2. **From the Illustrations group, click the Clip Art button.**

   The Clip Art task pane appears, as shown in Figure 23-1.

   Just as you would search your hard drive for a picture, you search the Clip Art library for artwork. The difference is that, unlike your digital life on the computer's hard drive, the Clip Art library is *organized*.

Figure 23-1: The Clip Art task pane.

3. **In the Search For box, type a description of what you want.**

   For example, a picture of Napoleon may go well with your report on the War of 1812. Type **Napoleon** in the box.

4. **Click the Go button.**

   The results are displayed in the task pane (refer to Figure 23-1). Peruse the results and note that you may have to scroll a bit to see all of them.

   If you don't find what you want, go back to Step 3 and refine your search.

5. **Point the mouse at the image you want.**

   A menu button appears. (Look to the right of the heart in Figure 23-1).

6. **Click the menu button and choose Insert.**

   The image is plopped down into your document.

7. **Close the Clip Art task pane by clicking the X in its upper-right corner.**

Word sticks the clip art graphic right into your text, just like it's a big character, right where the insertion pointer is blinking. At this point, you probably want to move the image, resize it, or do other things. Later sections in this chapter explain the details.

✔ Apparently, the clips are free to use; I don't see anything saying otherwise. But, then again . . .

✔ The problem with clip art is that it's inanely common. For example, only four images of Napoleon are available (as this book goes to press). That means the image you choose will doubtless be used by someone else. This gives clip art an air of unoriginality.

✔ Clip art libraries exist that you can buy at the software store, such as those One Zillion Clip Art Pix things that also come with fonts and other interesting toys. Because those images are stored on CDs or DVDs, you need to use the Picture command button to insert them into your documents. Refer to the preceding section.

Slapping down an AutoShape

Rather than have you fuss over creating basic shapes with various line-drawing tools, Word comes with a library of common line art shapes ready to insert into your document. These can be used decoratively or to create illustrations. Here's how to stick some AutoShapes into your document:

To stick an AutoShape line art image into your document, follow these whimsical steps:

1. **Click the Insert tab.**

2. **On the Insert tab, click the Shapes button to display a menu full of AutoShapes.**

   The Shapes button is found in the Illustrations group.

3. **Click to select the shape you desire.**

   And . . . nothing happens! Actually, the mouse pointer changes to a large plus sign. Unlike with pictures and clip art, you must draw the shape in your document:

4. **Drag the mouse down and to the right to create the AutoShape.**

   The AutoShape artwork appears.

AutoShapes float over your text, so you probably want to use some type of text wrapping to ensure that your artwork doesn't hide your writing. (I explain how to do that later in this chapter, starting with the section "Images and Text Can Mix.") Other sections in this chapter tell you how to modify the AutoShape, by giving it color, effects, and a whole lotta *flair*.

> ✔ All shapes are drawn with black lines, although some shapes are solid and some are see-through. (Actually, the solid images merely have a white fill color.)

> ✔ Some shapes require you to click the mouse two or three times to draw a line or create a curve.

Inserting a picture or text into an AutoShape

Certain AutoShapes can be used as frames, to enclose a picture or even some text. Simply follow the directions in the preceding section, but choose instead an AutoShape that can be used as a frame, like a polygon. With that shape selected, follow the steps in the following section as appropriate.

Making an AutoShape framed picture

Stick a picture in your AutoShape by obeying these steps:

1. **From the Format tab's Shape Styles group, choose Shape Fill⇨Picture.**

   A Select Picture dialog box appears. It works just like any Open dialog box, but it's geared toward finding pictures.

2. **Use the Select Picture dialog box to hunt down and choose an image.**

3. **Click the Insert button.**

   The picture is placed in the frame.

Making an AutoShape text box

Turn your AutoShape into a text box this way:

1. **From the Format tab's Insert Shapes group, click the Edit Text button.**

   The AutoShape is changed into a text box, and the Text Box Tools Format tab appears.

2. **Type and format the text you want in the box.**

   Be careful! Only the text you see appears in the box. Any excess text doesn't show up.

Refer to Chapter 24 for more information on text boxes.

Deleting an image or artwork

Getting rid of artwork in a document isn't the same as removing text. Graphics are special. The proper way to delete them is to click the image once to select it. Then press the Delete key.

Images and Text Can Mix

There are three different ways you can place graphics into your document:

- ✔ **In-line:** The graphic works like a large, single character sitting in the middle of your text. The graphic stays with the text, so you can press Enter to put it on a line by itself, press Tab to indent the image, and so on.

- ✔ **Wrapped:** Text flows around the graphic, avoiding the image like everyone at the casino buffet avoids the healthy fruit bar.

- ✔ **Floating:** The image appears behind your text like it's part of the paper, or it slaps down on top of your text like some bureaucratic tax stamp.

You're not stuck with these choices. You can modify any graphic in Word to be in-line, wrapped, or floating. The next section tells you how.

- ✔ The Picture and Clip Art commands insert art as in-line graphics.

- ✔ AutoShapes are inserted floating in front of your text.

Wrapping text around the image

I use the terms *in-line, wrapped,* and *floating* to describe how Word places text into a document. Word uses seven different terms to control how graphics and text mix. But as long as you think *in-line, wrapped,* and *floating,* you'll keep your sanity.

To control how an image and text interact, click the image to select it. When the image is selected, the Format tab appears, from which you can choose the Text Wrapping menu, found in the Arrange group and shown in Figure 23-2. Here are my general thoughts on the wrapping options available on that menu:

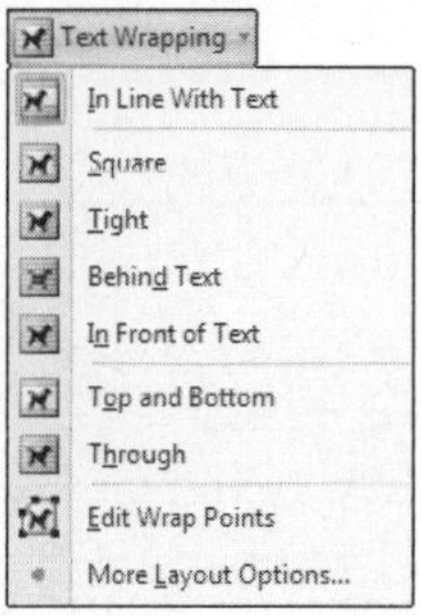

Figure 23-2:
The Text
Wrapping
menu.

- Text Wrapping
- In Line With Text
- Square
- Tight
- Behind Text
- In Front of Text
- Top and Bottom
- Through
- Edit Wrap Points
- More Layout Options...

✔ **In Line With Text:** The image is treated like text — specifically, like a large, single character. The image can have text before it or behind it, be in the middle of a paragraph of text, or be on a line by itself. But the image stays with the text as you edit, and the line that the image is on grows extra vertical space to accommodate the image.

✔ **Square:** The image sits on the same plane as the text, but the text flows around the image in a square pattern, regardless of the image's shape.

✔ **Tight:** Text flows around the image and hugs its shape.

✔ **Behind Text:** The image floats behind the text, looking almost like the image is part of the paper.

✔ **In Front of Text:** The image floats on top of your text, like a photograph dropped on the paper.

✔ **Top and Bottom:** Text stops at the top of the image and continues below the image.

✔ **Through:** Text flows around the image as best it can, similar to the Tight option.

✔ **Edit Wrap Points:** This command allows you to specifically control how text wraps around an image. By adjusting tiny handles and dashed red lines, you can really make text wrapping as tight or creative as you like. Of course, selecting the Tight option pretty much does the same thing.

✔ **More Layout Options:** This option summons the Advanced Layout dialog box, which provides custom controls for image position as well as wrapping options.

Should you make the gutsy choice to edit the wrap points, here's a quick summary of the mouse commands used to manipulate the dashed red lines and handles that separate the image from the text:

✔ Use the mouse to move a handle.

✔ Ctrl+click a handle to delete it.

✔ Ctrl+click a red line to add a handle.

Moving an image hither and thither

You can lug around graphics in a document as easily as you move text. Consider the graphic as a *block,* and simply drag it by using the mouse. Of course, how the graphic sits with your text, as covered in the preceding section, determines where and how you can move it. Basically, it works like this:

✔ Point the mouse in the center of the image to drag it around.

✔ Try not to point at one of the image's handles and drag. (Look ahead to Figure 23-3.) When you do, you end up resizing the image rather than moving it.

Choosing a specific position for the image

A handy way to place any graphic at a specific spot on the page is to use the Position command button, found in the Drawing Tools Format tab's Arrange group. Clicking that button displays a menu full of options for locating an image to the left, right, center, top, or bottom, or a combination of these.

✔ Before using the Position command button, zoom out so that your document's page fills the screen. Then you can see how choosing different options from the Position menu affects the page as you point the mouse at each one. See Chapter 30 for more information on zooming.

✔ To center an in-line image, put the image on a line by itself (a paragraph) and then center that line by pressing Ctrl+E, the Center command keyboard shortcut.

Unlinking the image from the surrounding text

Most images stay with the text that they're near. When you edit text, the image shuffles up or down on the page to be near the original text it was placed in. When you want an image *not* to move with the text, you need to follow these steps:

1. **Click to select the image.**

2. **From the Format tab, in the Arrange group, choose Text Wrapping⇨ More Layout Options.**

    The Advanced Layout dialog box appears.

3. **Choose the Picture Position tab.**

4. **From the Horizontal area, choose Absolute Position.**

5. **Choose Page from the To the Right Of drop-down list.**

6. **From the Vertical area, choose Absolute Position.**

7. **Select Page from the Below drop-down list.**

8. **Click OK.**

This trick works best (but not exclusively) with objects placed behind your text. It makes the graphic or image appear to be part of the paper. (To further the effect, I recommend using very light colors or "washing out" any picture framed in an AutoShape.)

Image Editing

Just as people edit their text, you'll wind up editing images you put into your documents. Word comes with a host of tools for manipulating images, organizing drawings, adding special effects, and performing other fancy stunts for working with graphics. Indeed, a whole book could be written on the possibilities alone. But this is primarily a word processing book, so this section explores only some of the more common things you can do with graphics in Word.

When you're using a Document Theme, theme effects are automatically applied to any graphic inserted into your document. Refer to Chapter 17 for more information on themes.

Changing an image's size

Resizing an image is cinchy:

1. **Click to select the image.**

   The image grows handles, as shown in Figure 23-3.

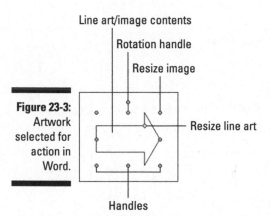

Line art/image contents

Rotation handle

Resize image

Resize line art

Figure 23-3:
Artwork
selected for
action in
Word.

Handles

2. **Press and hold the Shift key.**

3. **Use the mouse to drag one of the image's four corner handles inward or outward to make the image proportionally smaller or larger.**

4. **Release the Shift key.**

Holding down the Shift key keeps the image proportional. Otherwise, you're changing the image's dimensions when you resize, which distorts the image.

- You can use either Shift key on the keyboard.

- When you would rather not keep the image proportional, you can grab any handle to resize the image in that direction. For example, grab the top handle and drag up or down to make the image taller or shorter.

Cropping an image

In graphics lingo, *cropping* works like taking a pair of scissors to the image: You make the image smaller, but by doing so, you eliminate some of the content, just as some angry, sullen teen would use shears to remove his cheating-scumbag former girlfriend from a prom picture. Figure 23-4 shows an example.

Figure 23-4:
Cropping an
image.

To crop, click the image once to select it, and then click the Crop command button in the Size group. You're now in cropping mode, which works much like resizing an image. Drag one of the image's handles inward to crop, which slices off a side or two from the image.

I usually use the outside (left, right, top, or bottom) handles to crop. The corner handles never crop quite the way I want them to.

After you're done cropping, click the Crop command button again to turn off that mode.

Rotating the image

There are two handy ways to rotate an image, or twist it 'round like it's Dorothy stuck in the cyclone on her way to Oz.

The easy way to rotate an image is to use the Rotate menu in the Arrange group. From the menu, you can choose to rotate the image 90 degrees to the left or right or to flip the image horizontally or vertically.

To freely rotate an image, use the mouse to grab the rotation handle at the top of the image. (Refer to Figure 23-3). Drag the mouse to twist the image to any angle.

Arranging multiple images

New images that you plunk down on a page appear one atop the other. You don't notice this unless two images overlap. When you're displeased with the overlapping, you can change the order of an image by using the Bring to Front and Send to Back buttons in the Arrange group.

To help you keep multiple images lined up, use the Align button's menu. First select several images by holding down the Shift key as you click each one. Then choose an alignment option, such as Align Middle, from the Align button's menu to properly arrange images in a horizontal line.

To help you organize multiple images on a page, show the grid: Click the View tab; and then, from the Show/Hide group, select Gridlines. Instantly, the page turns into graph paper, to assist you in positioning your graphics and text.

Chapter 24

Stick *This* in Your Document

In This Chapter

▶ Typing nonbreaking spaces and hyphens

▶ Inserting characters that you cannot type

▶ Playing with WordArt

▶ Breaking up text with a text box

▶ Looking good with SmartArt

Some people say that you just can't stick a round peg into a square hole. I'd like to inform those people that they're just not trying hard enough. With a large-enough hammer, industrial lubricant, and perhaps some explosives, it's possible to not only stick a round peg into a square hole, but to also insert a round peg into just about anything — even a Word document.

Word has a slew of items clustered on the Insert tab that just don't fit in anywhere else in the word processing spectrum. Those items have ended up here, in this chapter, which tells you how to stick all sorts of things wonderful and strange, odd and useful, into your document. Industrial lubricant optional.

Characters Fun and Funky

You use your computer's keyboard to type all sorts of wonderful things in your document. The 26 alphabet keys plus the numbers, symbols, and punctuation allow you to craft any story you like using any of the several thousand words available in English. But not everything you type is in English. For those desperate times when you need more than the characters on your keyboard can produce, refer to this section.

Nonbreaking spaces and hyphens

Two unique characters in a document are the space and the dash, or hyphen. These characters are special because Word uses either of them to wrap a line of text: The space splits a line between two words, and the hyphen (using hyphenation) splits a line between two word chunks.

There are times, however, when you don't want a line to be split by a space or a hyphen. For example, splitting a phone number is bad — you want the phone number to stay intact. There are also times when you need two words separated by a space to stick like glue. For those times, you need *unbreakable* characters.

✔ To prevent the hyphen character from breaking a line, press Ctrl+Shift+- (hyphen).

✔ To prevent the space character from breaking a line, press Ctrl+Shift+spacebar.

In either case, a nonbreaking character is inserted into the text. Word doesn't break a line of text when you use these special characters.

Typing characters such as Ü, ç, and Ñ

You can be boring and type *deja vu* or be all fancy and type *déjà vu* or *café* or *résumé*. Your readers will think that you really know your stuff, but what you really know is how to use Word's diacritical prefix keys.

Diacritical symbols appear over certain letters in foreign languages and in foreign words borrowed (*stolen,* really) into English. To create a diacritical when you're typing in Word, you press a special Control-key combination. The key combination you press somewhat represents the diacritical you need, such as Ctrl+' to produce a ' diacritical. The Ctrl-key combination is followed by the character that needs the new "hat," as shown in Table 24-1.

Table 24-1	Typing Those Pesky Foreign-Language Characters
Prefix Key	*Characters Rendered*
Ctrl+'	á é í ó ú ð
Ctrl+`	à è ì ò ù
Ctrl+,	ç
Ctrl+@	å
Ctrl+:	ä ë ï ö ü
Ctrl+^	â ê î ô û
Ctrl+~	ã õ ñ
Ctrl+/	ø

For example, to get an é into your document, type Ctrl+' and then the letter *E*. Uppercase *E* gives you É, and lowercase *e* gives you é. That makes sense because the ' (apostrophe) is essentially the character you're adding to the vowel.

Ctrl+' followed by a D equals Đ (or ð).

Be sure to note the difference between the apostrophe (or *tick*) and back tick, or *accent grave*. The apostrophe (') is next to your keyboard's Enter key. The back tick (`) is below the Esc key.

For the Ctrl+@, Ctrl+:, Ctrl+^, and Ctrl+~ key combinations, you also need to press the Shift key, which is required anyway to get the @, :, ^, or ~ symbols on your keyboard. Therefore, Ctrl+~ is really Ctrl+Shift+`. Keep that in mind.

Word's AutoCorrect feature has been trained to know some of the special characters. For example, when you're typing *café,* Word automatically sticks that whoopty-doop over the E.

Adding a dash of en or em

Advanced word processing humans don't type the hyphen. They don't mess with the minus sign. No, they prefer to use the typesetter's *en dash* or the longer *em dash*.

- ✔ To produce an en dash, press Ctrl+minus.
- ✔ To produce an em dash, press Ctrl+Alt+minus.
- ✔ Minus is the - (hyphen) key on the numeric keypad.

The en dash is approximately the width of the N character. Likewise, the em dash is the width of the M character.

Inserting special characters and symbols

Ω Symbol ▾

The Symbol menu is nestled in the Symbol group on the Insert tab. Clicking the Symbol command button lists some popular or recently used symbols that you can insert into your document. Choosing a symbol from the menu inserts that special symbol right into your text, just like you insert any other character.

Choosing More Symbols from the Symbol menu displays the Symbol dialog box, shown in Figure 24-1. Choose a decorative font, such as Wingdings, from the Font menu to see strange and unusual characters. To see the gamut of what's possible with normal text, choose (normal text) from the Font drop-down list. Use the Subset drop-down list to see even more symbols and such.

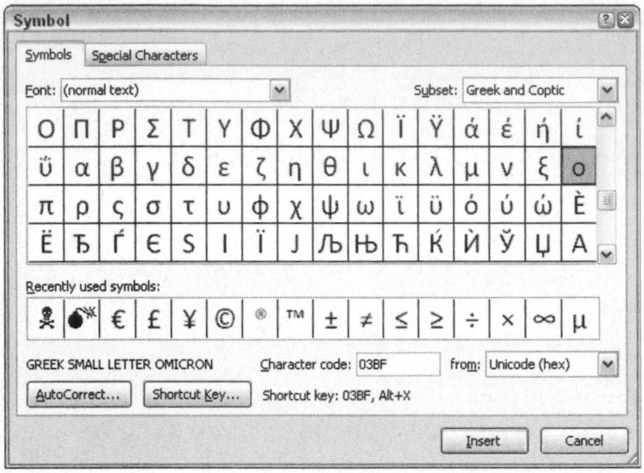

Figure 24-1:
The Symbol
dialog box.

To stick a character into your document from the Symbol dialog box, select the symbol and click the Insert button.

You need to click the Cancel button when you're done using the Symbol dialog box.

✔ Click the Insert button once for each symbol you want inserted. When you're putting three Σ (sigma) symbols into your document, you must locate that symbol on the grid and then click the Insert button three times.

✔ Some symbols have shortcut keys. These appear at the bottom of the Symbol dialog box. For example, the shortcut for the degree symbol (°) is Ctrl+@, Space, which means to type Ctrl+@ (actually, Ctrl+Shift+2) and then type a space. Doing so gives you the degree symbol.

✔ You can insert symbols by typing the symbol's code and then pressing the Alt+X key combination. For example, the code for Σ (sigma) is 2211: Type **2211** in your document and then press Alt+X. The 2211 is magically transformed into the Σ character.

Say It in WordArt

I probably don't need to write a lot about WordArt because too many Word users find it fun and enjoyable and they overuse the feature to death. In fact, the only burning question you may have is "Where the heck is WordArt?"

WordArt's command button is in the Text group, on the Insert tab. Here's how you work it:

1. **Click the WordArt button to display the WordArt menu.**

   It looks like a wall of movie posters down at the cinema, as shown in Figure 24-2.

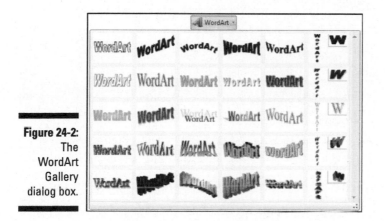

Figure 24-2: The WordArt Gallery dialog box.

2. **Choose a style from the gallery for your WordArt.**

   The Edit WordArt Text dialog box appears.

3. **Type the (short and sweet) text you want WordArt-ified.**

4. **Optionally, choose a font, a font size, and maybe bold or italics — you know the drill.**

5. **Click OK when you're done.**

Your bit of text appears as an image in your document.

To modify or adjust the WordArt, click it once with the mouse to select it. The Word Art Formatting tab appears, along with a ribbon full o' command buttons for editing and formatting your graphical masterpiece. Rather than explain what to do here, I refer you to Chapter 23 because the same information for editing, moving, and refining graphics in your document also applies to WordArt.

Spice Up Your Document with a Text Box

A *text box* is a graphical element that contains — hold your breath, wait for it, wait — *text*. It can be used as a decorative element (called a *pull quote*) to highlight a passage of text on the page, or it can be just an information box or an aside, such as those that litter the pages of the *USA Today* newspaper. Overall, the purpose of the text box is to prevent your document from becoming what layout artists refer to as the dreaded Great Wall of Text.

Text boxes are easily shoved into a document by following these steps:

1. **Click the Insert tab.**

2. **In the Text group, choose Text Box⇨Draw Text Box.**

   The mouse pointer changes to a large plus sign.

3. **Draw the mouse pointer in your document to create the text box.**

   Drag from the upper-left down and to the right to create the box, similar to the way AutoShapes are drawn in a document, as discussed in Chapter 23.

4. **Type the text you need into the box.**

   Click anywhere outside of the box when you're done typing.

After a text box is on the screen, or whenever you click the mouse to select a text box, the Text Box Tools Format tab appears. It contains a lot of formatting and style commands for the text box. Most of them are similar, if not identical to, the formatting commands used on images and graphics in Word. Refer to Chapter 23 for details, hints and tips.

- ✔ As with most graphical things, Print Layout view is the preferred way to deal with text boxes. In fact, they don't even show up when you use Draft view.

- ✔ Of course, you can always choose a pre-designed text box from the Text Box menu. In that case Word does the formatting for you.

- ✔ You can use all your basic text-writing and -formatting skills inside the box, just as you would type text outside the box. You can, for example, apply a bold font and center the text, which is common for creating text box *callouts*.

- ✔ You can turn text sideways inside the text box by using the Text Direction button. Look in the Text group on the Text Box Tools Format tab.

- ✔ To delete a text box, click it with the mouse and press the Delete button on the keyboard.

Instant Graphical Goodness with SmartArt

Word's SmartArt feature lets you quickly create complex graphics, charts, and designs by selecting them from a gallery. The result is an informative illustration for your document, something that looks like it took you hours to craft in some other program. Yes, SmartArt is another way you can cheat inside Word, to make your stuff look better than it should.

The SmartArt journey works like this:

1. **Click the Insert tab.**

2. **In the Illustrations group, click the SmartArt button.**

   The Choose A SmartArt Graphic dialog box appears, listing a bunch of designs for presenting information in its center. The left side of the dialog box categorizes things; the right side gives you a preview.

3. **Choose the type of artwork you want from the center part of the dialog box.**

4. **Click OK.**

   Immediately, an image is inserted into your document, as shown in Figure 24-3.

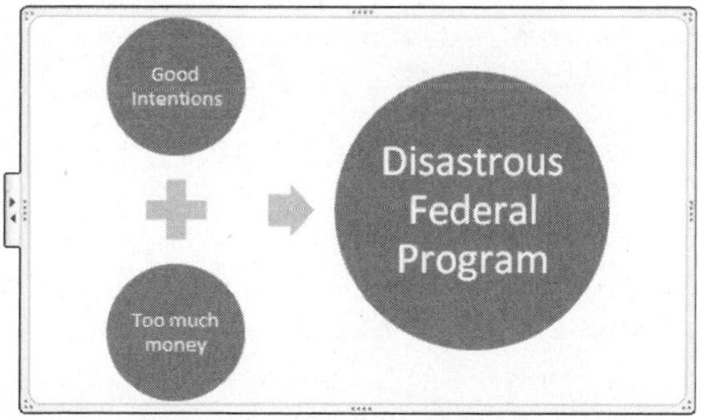

Figure 24-3:
Creating
SmartArt
in your
document.

5. **Type to replace the [Text] .**

6. **Click to select the next bit of text.**

   You can click the mouse to select a bit of text or use the down-arrow key.

7. **Repeat Steps 5 and 6 for each text item.**

8. **Click outside the SmartArt graphic to resume editing your document.**

Use the SmartArt Tools Design and Format tabs to help spiff up your document's SmartArt. Refer to Chapter 23 for some tips and hints because many of the commands I describe in that chapter are similar to commands for formatting and designing SmartArt.

✔ Use the Change Colors button to apply some life to the otherwise dreary SmartArt. The command button is in the Quick Styles group on the SmartArt Tools Design tab.

✔ Use the Text Pane command button on the SmartArt Tools Design tab to summon a text pane for help in editing the artwork's text.

Part V
What Else Is Left?

The 5th Wave   By Rich Tennant

"Sure, at first it sounded great — an intuitive network adapter that helps people write memos by finishing their thoughts for them."

In this part . . .

*W*ord's main job is to process words, but that's too fancy a description. If Word were merely a word processor, this book would be a heck of a lot thinner! Then again, were I to write about *everything* Word is capable of, this book would be (seriously) six times thicker. And, even if you could find a book that documents everything Word can do, few people would bother to read the entire thing.

The depths of Word may never truly be explored. Then again, why bother? My preference is really to get as much from Word as anyone can. When you need those extra, fancy-schmancy features, they're available. And, when you desire even more from Word, there's the stuff I explore in this part of the book. It's not everything, but the chapters that follow do cover some important things you may yet find useful, all without wasting your time or boring you to death.

Chapter 25

Multiple Documents, Multiple Windows, Multiple Formats, Multiple Madness

In This Chapter

▶ Using more than one document at a time

▶ Comparing documents side by side

▶ Seeing one document in two windows

▶ Splitting the screen

▶ Opening a non-Word document

▶ Saving a document in another format

▶ Updating older Word documents

Most people I know use Word to edit one document at a time. That's okay. The program can do more than that, of course. You can have, and work with, multiple documents at one time. You can view the same document in multiple windows or on a split screen. You can edit documents created by other word processors (if there are any others left). It's multiple document madness time!

Multiple Document Mania

It frustrates me to see people open and close documents in Word, bouncing back and forth between two documents when they can just keep both document windows open at the same time. Yea verily, in Word you can have multiple documents open at once. While writing this book, I often had six different documents open, to edit here and there, copy back and forth, and refer to specific bits of text. It's a highly productive way to get work done.

Don't let Word's multidocument mania intimidate you. Instead, use it to your advantage. Word comes with an abundance of tools to make it easy to manage the multiple documents and their many windows. This section describes the details.

Managing multiple documents

Word keeps each document you create or open in its own, separate window. The documents are all independent of each other, so what you do in one document doesn't affect another (unless you want it to). Rather than let this feature make you go crazy, consider taking advantage of it. The following sections provide suggestions and tips for getting the most from multiple document mania.

Switching between documents

Each document dwells in its own Word program window. The sanest way to switch between them is to use the Switch Windows menu on the View tab. The menu lists up to nine open documents in Word, as shown in Figure 25-1. To switch to another document, choose it from the menu.

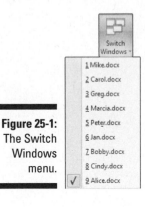

Figure 25-1:
The Switch
Windows
menu.

When more than nine documents are open at a time, the last item on the Switch Windows menu is the More Windows command. Choosing that item displays the Activate dialog box, which lists *all* open document windows. Select a document from the window and click OK to switch to it.

✔ A quick way to switch from one document window to another is to press the Alt+Tab key combination.

✔ Each window also has its own button on the Windows taskbar. To switch between windows in Word, choose the document name from a button on the taskbar.

✔ Pointing the mouse at a taskbar button in Windows Vista displays a tiny preview window detailing the document's contents.

✔ The names on the taskbar buttons are the names you gave your documents after saving them to disk for the first time. When you see *Document* displayed, that means you haven't yet saved your stuff to disk. *Do so now!* Refer to Chapter 9.

Viewing more than one document at a time

To see two or more documents displayed on the screen at the same time, click the View tab and choose the Arrange All button. Immediately, Word organizes all its windows, by placing them on the screen like a jigsaw puzzle. This arrangement is fine for a few documents, but for too many, you end up with a mess, as shown in Figure 25-2.

✔ Because Word doesn't arrange minimized windows, one way to keep multiple windows open yet arrange only two is to minimize the windows you don't want arranged. Then click the Arrange All button.

✔ Yes, the Ribbon disappears when the document window gets too small.

✔ Although you can see more than one document at a time, you can *work* on only one at a time. The document with the highlighted title bar is the one "on top."

✔ After the windows are arranged, you can manipulate their size and change their positions with the mouse. This is a Windows thing, not a Word thing.

✔ Clicking a window's Maximize button restores the document to its normal, full-screen view.

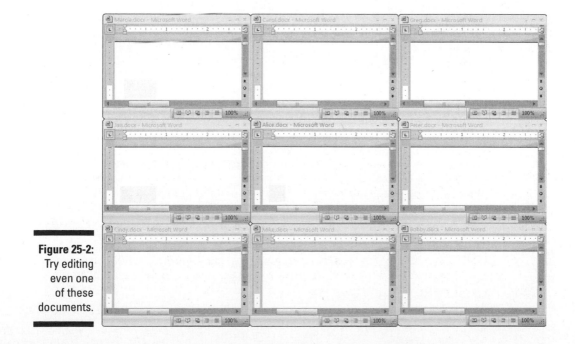

Figure 25-2:
Try editing
even one
of these
documents.

Comparing two documents side-by-side

A quick and handy way to review two separate documents is to arrange them side by side in two separate windows and lock their scrolling so that you can peruse both at one time. Here's how such a trick is accomplished:

1. **Have both documents open.**

2. **Click the View tab.**

3. **Choose View Side by Side.**

   Word instantly arranges both documents in vertical windows, with the current document on the left and the other on the right.

   When more than one document is open, you have to choose the second one from a list.

4. **Scroll either document.**

   Scrolling one document also scrolls the other. In this mode, you can compare two different or similar documents.

5. **When you're done, choose View Side by Side again.**

✔ You can disable the synchronous scrolling by clicking the Synchronous Scrolling button.

✔ Also refer to Chapter 27, which discusses how to detect changes made to a document.

Viewing the same document in multiple windows

It's possible in Word to show one document in two windows. I do this trick all the time, especially with longer documents. It's easier to have two windows into the same document than to hop back and forth and potentially lose your place.

To open another window displaying your document, click the View tab and click the New Window button. No, this doesn't create a new document; instead, it opens a second view into the current document. You can confirm this by noting that both windows have the same document name in their titles — the first window suffixed with :1 and the second with :2.

Even though two windows are open, you're still working on only one document. The changes you make in one window are updated in the second. Consider this trick like watching the same television show, but with two different cameras and TV sets.

When you don't need the second window any more, simply close it. Actually, you can close either window :1 or :2; it doesn't matter. Closing the second window merely removes that view. The document is still open and available for editing in the other window.

- ✔ This feature is useful for cutting and pasting text or graphics between sections of the same document, especially when you have a very long document.

- ✔ You can even open a third window by choosing the New Window command a second time.

- ✔ Another way to view two parts of the same document is by using the old split-screen trick. This feature is discussed . . . why, it's right here, in the next section.

Using the old split-screen trick

Splitting the screen allows you to view two parts of your document in the same window. No need to bother with extra windows here: The top part of the window shows one part of the document, and the bottom part another, as shown in Figure 25-3. Each half of the screen scrolls individually, so you can peruse different parts of the same document without switching windows.

To split a window, heed these steps:

1. **Click the View tab.**

2. **Click the Split button.**

   A gray bar slashes the document window from left to right. That's where the window splits, eventually.

3. **Use the mouse to move the gray bar up or down.**

4. **Click the mouse to split the window.**

   The split falls into place.

Both document views, above or below the split, can be scrolled individually. To edit in one half or the other, click the mouse.

To undo the split, double-click it with the mouse. Poof! It's gone.

- ✔ When the ruler is visible, a second ruler appears just below the split.

- ✔ Just above the Show/Hide Ruler button is a tiny, black bar. Double-clicking that bar, or dragging it downward with the mouse, is the fastest way to split a window.

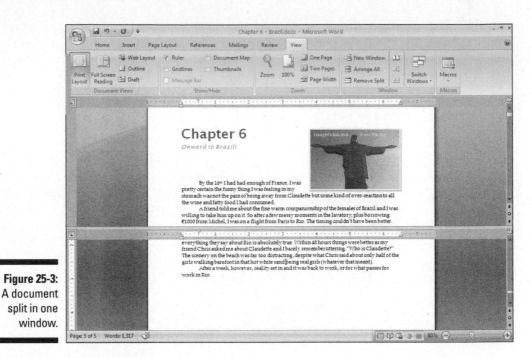

Figure 25-3:
A document
split in one
window.

Working with Non-Word Document Formats

When you save a document to disk, Word not only places the document's text into a file but also stores other information: formatting, graphics, page layout — everything. To keep all that stuff organized, Word uses a specific *file format* for your document. It's the Word file format that makes a Word document unique and different from other types of files you may store on the computer's hard drive.

Word's document format is popular, but it's not the only word processing document format available. Other word processors (believe it or not) use their own formats. Plus, some popular common file formats are designed to make sharing documents between incompatible computers easier. Yes, Word accepts these formats and allows you to save your stuff in those formats if you desire to do so. This section explains everything.

Using the Files Type drop-down list

The key to opening or saving a document in one file format or another is to use the file type drop-down list. That list sets the file format Word uses, for either opening a file or saving a file under a format other than Word's standard .*doc* format. A version of the file type drop-down list is found in both the Open dialog box and the Save As dialog box.

In the Open dialog box, the drop-down list is named Files of Type, although in Windows Vista it has no name. Choosing a file type from that list directs the Open dialog box to not only display those specific file types, but also open them properly for editing in Word.

In the Save As dialog box, the drop-down list is named Save As Type. It lists file formats you can use to save your document in addition to Word's own Word Document file type.

Loading an alien document

Choose your alien: homely ol' E.T. or the slithery alien from *Aliens?* Meh — it doesn't really matter because Word is prepared to welcome any intruder. You name the funky file format, and Word can most likely take its magic can opener to the thing and see what's inside. Here's how:

1. **Do the Open command.**

2. **From the Files of Type drop-down list, select the file format.**

   If you're using Windows Vista, the drop-down list lacks a name; it just says All Word Documents. Click that button to choose a format.

   By choosing a specific file format, you make Word narrow the files displayed in the Open dialog box. Only files matching the specific file format are shown.

   If you don't know the format, choose All Files from the drop-down list. Word then makes its best guess.

3. **Choose the file from the list.**

   Or, work the controls in the dialog box to find another disk drive or folder that contains the file. Chapter 9 explains how this works in detail.

4. **Click Open.**

   The alien file appears on-screen, ready for editing, just like any Word document.

Well, the file may not be perfect. It may not even open. But be prepared to fix some things or do some tidying up. Word tries its best.

- ✔ Word may display a File Conversion dialog box, allowing you to preview how the document appears. Generally speaking, clicking the OK button in this step is your best bet.

- ✔ The Recover Text from Any File option is great for peering into unknown file formats, especially from antique and obscure word processing file formats.

- ✔ Word *remembers* the file type! When you go to use the Open dialog box again, it has the same file type chosen from the Files of Type drop-down list.

- ✔ Accordingly, when you want to open a Word document after opening an HTML document, or especially by using the Recover Text from Any File option, you *must* choose Word Documents from the list. Otherwise, Word may open documents in a manner that seems strange to you.

Saving a PDF
(oh, and XPS as well)

The PDF, or Portable Document Format, pioneered by Adobe and used with its common Acrobat Reader program, is perhaps the most common complex file format around. PDF documents are everywhere, and the Acrobat Reader is free, which makes for a killer combination. By saving your document as a PDF file, you ensure that folks all over the world can read it — complete with any formatting and graphics — just the way you want it to look.

Microsoft has also developed a file-sharing format that it calls XPS, for XML Paper Specification. Like PDF, it's a file format that anyone can read, although it's rather new and most likely will never be as popular as PDF.

The best way to save a document in the PDF format is to plunk down your hard-earned cash and buy the Adobe Acrobat Writer program. The Writer, unlike the Reader, is used to create PDF files. You simply print the document to the Acrobat Writer program: Press Ctrl+P and choose Acrobat Writer from the list of printers. That's the best way.

Your version of Word may sport PDF and XPS as file formats on the Save As dialog box's Save As Type drop-down list. If so, great. If not, you can contact Microsoft to obtain an add-on package for Word 2007, one that includes the ability to save documents in the PDF and XPS file formats. The Web page link to use can be found in the Word help system: Search for **PDF** or **XPS** and choose the search result titled Enable Support for Other File Formats or something similar.

Saving a file in a horridly strange and unnatural format

Word is quite smart when it comes to saving files to disk. For example, when you open a WordPerfect document, Word automatically saves it back to disk in the WordPerfect format. Ditto for any other alien file format: Whichever format was used to open the document, Word chooses the same format for writing the document back to disk.

The secret, as with opening files of another type, is to check the Save As Type drop-down list in the Save As dialog box. In fact, choosing a new item from that drop-down list is the only way to save a document in another format.

For example, if you need to save a document as a text file, choose Text Only from the Save As Type drop-down list. Click the Save button, and your document is saved. Ditto for the HTML or RTF format or for any other alien document format.

Word may explain that saving the document in an alien format is, well, bad. Whatever. Click Yes to save the document.

✔ You can save a document to disk by using both the Word format and another format. First, save the file to disk as a Word document by selecting Word Document from the Save As Type list. Then save the file to disk by using another format, such as Plain Text.

✔ Word remembers the format! If you notice that your documents aren't being saved to disk the way you want, the Save As Type drop-down list is to blame! Always double-check it to ensure that you're saving documents to disk in the proper format.

Updating older Word documents

Word 2007 easily opens documents created by older versions of Word. It even saves them in those older Word formats, so normally nothing goes wrong. Well, except that certain features available to Word 2007 documents, such as Quick Styles and themes, aren't available to files saved in older Word formats. To fix that, you must update the older Word documents. Here's how:

1. **Use the Open dialog box to locate an older Word document.**

    Word is smart and displays older Word documents with special icons representing their versions, such as the icon shown in the margin.

2. **Choose the older word document.**

3. **Click the Open button.**

   The Word document opens and is displayed on the screen. And now, the secret:

4. **From the Office button, choose Convert.**

   The Convert command appears only when you open an older Word document, one that can be converted into the Word 2007 document format.

   A boring dialog box appears.

5. **Click the OK button.**

   The document is updated — but you're not done yet.

6. **Save the document.**

   Now you're done.

Chapter 26

Other Ways of Viewing a Document

***

In This Chapter

▶ Creating an outline in Word

▶ Adding topics, subtopics, and text topics

▶ Promoting and demoting topics

▶ Rearranging topics in an outline

▶ Printing an outline

▶ Using Reading Layout mode

***

*I*n the beginning . . . Word was a DOS program. It showed ugly text on the screen and looked nothing like what actually got printed. Then came Windows, and Word users beheld *Normal* view, which actually had no name because it was the only way you could look at your document. Then came *Print Preview* view, which changed into *Print Layout* view. Meanwhile, Normal view became *Draft* view — probably because someone left a window open.

Today, Word offers five different ways of viewing a document. Print Layout and Draft are covered throughout this book. Web Layout, well, that's a wacky view that I don't even bother to cover in this book. That leaves Outline and Full Screen Reading views, which are covered in this chapter.

✔ The views can be changed by using the command buttons in the Document Views group on the View tab.

✔ Views are also controlled by the five wee little View buttons near the right end of the status bar. Refer to Figure 1-2, over in Chapter 1.

Organize Your Thoughts

Word offers Outline view, which isn't really used for writing as much as it's used for organizing things. Outline view can help you create a simple list of items — if that's really all you need to keep your thoughts lined up correctly — or it can hunker down and create a fancy *hierarchical* list with topics and subtopics and even pesky little sub-subtopics. This section explains the details, which are well organized because I used Outline view to help create them.

Entering Outline view

An outline in Word is just like any other document. The only difference is in how Word displays the text on the screen.

To create a new outline, follow these steps:

1. **Start a new, blank document.**

   Ctrl+N is my favorite new-blank-document keyboard shortcut.

2. **Click the View tab.**

3. **Choose Outline from the Document Views group.**

   The screen changes, as shown in Figure 26-1, although the outline in the figure is more extensive than what you probably see on your screen now. Note the appearance of the Outlining tab, along with its various groups and buttons.

4. **You're ready to start your outline.**

Any typing you do now is really list making, or organizing information in major topics, and then subtopics, and so on.

You can keep a document in Outline mode, if you like. I do; I keep all my book outlines as documents in Word's Outline view. Remember that it's simply a way of looking at a document.

To see the outline in Print Layout view, close the outline by clicking the Close Outline View button.

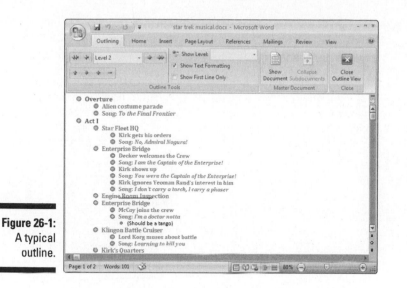

Figure 26-1:
A typical
outline.

All the outlining details are covered in the next few sections. In the meantime, I offer some general tidbits:

- ✔ That thick, short, horizontal line marks the end of your outline. It also appears in Draft view for the same reason.

- ✔ All Word's basic commands work in Outline view. You can use the cursor keys, delete text, check spelling, save, insert oddball characters, print, and so on. Don't worry about paragraph formatting.

- ✔ Word uses the Heading 1 through Heading 9 styles for your outline. Main topics are formatted in Heading 1, subtopics in Heading 2, and so on.

- ✔ The Body style can also be used in an outline, mostly for making notes and such. See the section "Adding a text topic," later in this chapter.

Adding topics to your outline

An outline is composed of topics and subtopics. The topics are your main ideas, with the subtopics describing the details. You should start your outline by adding the main topics. To do so, just type them out.

In Figure 26-2, you see several topics typed out, each on a line by itself. Pressing Enter after typing a topic produces a new gray circle, at which you can type your next topic. This is basically using outline mode as a list processor.

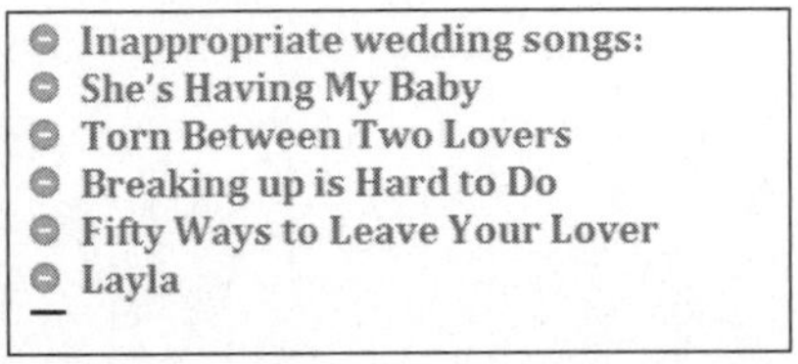

Figure 26-2:
Level 1
topics.

> ⊙ **Inappropriate wedding songs:**
> ⊙ **She's Having My Baby**
> ⊙ **Torn Between Two Lovers**
> ⊙ **Breaking up is Hard to Do**
> ⊙ **Fifty Ways to Leave Your Lover**
> ⊙ **Layla**

By the way, that black bar below your list simply shows you where the end of the document is located. The bar doesn't go away in Outline mode, so don't try to delete it.

✔ Press Enter at the end of each topic. This creates another topic at the same *level* as the first topic.

✔ See the next section for information on creating a subtopic.

✔ Main topics should be short and descriptive, like in a book's table of contents.

✔ Use the Enter key to split a topic. For example, to split the topic Pins and Needles, first delete the word *and,* and then with the insertion pointer placed between the two words, press the Enter key.

✔ To join two topics, put the insertion pointer at the end of the first topic and press the Delete key. (This method works just like joining two paragraphs in a regular document.)

✔ It doesn't matter whether you get the order right at first. The beauty of creating your outline with a word processor is that you can rearrange your topics as your ideas solidify. My advice is just to start writing things down now and concentrate on organization later.

Demoting a topic (creating subtopics)

Outlines have several levels. Beneath topics are subtopics, and those subtopics can have sub-subtopics. For example, your main topic may be Food I'd Rather Not Eat, and the subtopics would be what those things actually are.

To create a subtopic, simply type your subtopic at the main topic level, but don't press Enter when you're done. Instead, click the Demote command button or press Alt+Shift+→.

Demoting a topic has these effects in Outline mode:

- ✔ The topic is shifted over one notch to the right in the outline.

- ✔ The text style changes from one heading style to the next-highest-numbered, such as from Heading 1 to Heading 2.

- ✔ The Level item in the Outline Tools group changes to reflect the new topic level.

- ✔ The parent topic (the one the subtopic lives in) grows a + symbol. That's the sign that subtopics exist.

You can continue creating subtopics by typing them and then pressing the Enter key at the end of each subtopic. Word keeps giving you subtopics, one for each press of the Enter key.

- ✔ You don't really *create* subtopics in Word as much as you *demote* main topics.

- ✔ Not only does the Level drop-down list tell you a topic's level, but you can also use the list to instantly promote or demote the topic to any specific level in the outline.

- ✔ Unlike when you're creating main topics, you can get a little wordy with your subtopics. After all, the idea here is to expand on the main topic.

- ✔ You can demote a topic several levels down without having any parent topics. Although Word lets you do this, it's not really best for an outline.

- ✔ According to Those Who Know Such Things, each topic must have at least two subtopics. A single subtopic isn't a subtopic at all. I tend to agree with this line of thinking.

Promoting a topic

Moving a topic to the right demotes it. Likewise, you can move a topic to the left to promote it. For example, as you work on one of your subtopics, it grows powerful enough to be its own main-level topic. If so, promote it:

- ✔ To promote a subtopic, put the insertion pointer in the topic's text and click the Promote command button. You can also press Alt+Shift+← on the keyboard.

- ✔ To instantly make any topic a main-level topic, click the Promote to Heading 1 button.

Adding a text topic

When you feel the need to break out and actually write a paragraph in your outline, you can do so. Although it's perfectly legit to write the paragraph on the topic level, what you should really do is stick in a text topic by using the Demote to Body Text button. Here's how:

1. **Press the Enter key to start a new topic.**

2. **Click the Demote to Body Text button.**

   Or, you can press Ctrl+Shift+N, the keyboard shortcut for the Normal style.

What these steps do is change the text style to Body text, which is the Normal style. In your outline, however, that style change allows you to write an actual bit of text for your speech, instructions in a list, or dialogue from your novel.

Rearranging topics

The beauty of creating an outline on a computer is that you can not only pro- mote and demote topics, but also shuffle them around and reorganize them as your thought process becomes more organized. To move a topic, click the mouse so that the insertion pointer is blinking inside that topic. Then choose one of these techniques to rearrange that topic:

✔ Click the Move Up button (or press Alt+Shift+↑) to move a topic up a line.

✔ Click the Move Down button (or press Alt+Shift+↓) to move a topic down a line.

The mouse can also lug topics around. The secret is to drag the topic by its circle. When the mouse is positioned just right, the mouse pointer changes to a four-way arrow (see the margin). I recommend using this trick only when you're moving topics around a short distance; dragging with the mouse beyond the current screen can prove unwieldy.

Expanding and contracting topics

Unless you tell Word otherwise, it displays all the topics in your outline, from top to bottom — everything. That's fine for the details, but as your outline grows, you may want to see just part of the picture — perhaps a grand overview of only the main topics or just Level 2 topics. That's done by expanding and contracting portions of the outline.

The outline shortcut-key summary box

I'm a keyboard freak, and I like using shortcut keys whenever possible. You may be the same way, in which case you'll enjoy using the following keyboard shortcuts when you're dealing with an outline:

Key Combo	What It Does
Alt+Shift+→	Demotes a topic
Alt+Shift+←	Promotes a topic
Alt+Shift+↑	Shifts a topic up one line
Alt+Shift+↓	Shifts a topic down one line
Ctrl+Shift+N	Inserts or demotes to body text
Alt+Shift+1	Displays only top topics
Alt+Shift+2	Displays first- and second-level topics
Alt+Shift+#	Displays all topics up to number #
Alt+Shift+A	Displays all topics
Alt+Shift+plus (+)	Displays all subtopics in the current topic
Alt+Shift+minus (–)	Hides all subtopics in the current topic

A topic with subtopics has a plus sign in its circle. To collapse that topic and temporarily hide the subtopics, choose the Collapse button or press Alt+Shift+_ (underline). You can also double-click the plus sign with the mouse to collapse a topic.

To expand a collapsed topic, choose the Expand button or press Alt+Shift++ (plus). Again, you can also click the plus sign with the mouse to expand a collapsed topic.

Rather than expand and collapse topics all over, you can view your outline at any level by choosing that level from the Show Level drop-down list. For example, choose Level 2 from list so that only Level 1 and Level 2 topics are displayed; Levels 3 and higher are hidden.

✔ When a topic is collapsed, you see a fuzzy line extending over the last part of the topic text. That's a second hint (along with the plus sign) that the topic has subtopics and is collapsed.

- ✔ To see the entire outline, choose Show All Levels from the Show Level drop-down list.

- ✔ If you have wordy topic levels, you can direct Word to display only the first topic line by clicking to put a check mark by the Show First Line Only option.

- ✔ As your outline nears perfection, you can copy parts of it and paste them into other, new documents. This method is the way some writers create their books and novels; the document is merely a longer, more complete version of what starts as an outline.

Printing an outline

Printing your outline works just like printing any other document in Word. But because it's an outline, there's one difference: Only those topics visible in your outline are printed.

For example, if you want to print only the first two levels of your outline, choose Level 2 from the Show Level drop-down list. To print the entire outline, choose All Levels from the Show Level drop-down list. Whatever option is chosen determines what is printed.

The outline isn't printed with any indents, although it's printed using the heading styles of each topic level.

Sit Back and Read

As a popular and common file format, Word documents crop up all over. Just the other day, I downloaded a program from the Internet, and its instructions were contained in a Word document. Or, maybe you receive Word documents as e-mail attachments. Either way, Word provides a special mode for reading documents (not editing — *reading*): It's Full Screen Reading view (*duh*).

 To switch to Full Screen Reading view, click the View tab and then the Full Screen Reading command button. Your document then appears in a special side-by-side page format, as shown in Figure 26-3.

Only a thin toolbar remains in Full Screen Reading mode. You can do some things in this mode, but mostly you read.

To exit Full Screen Reading mode, choose the Close button in the upper-right corner of the window.

- ✔ Use the gizmo in the top-center area of the screen to go from page to page, or use the arrows that appear in the lower-right and -left corners.

- ✔ Use the PgUp or ↑ key to see the previous page(s); use PgDn or ↓ to see the next page.

- ✔ By the way, Full Screen Reading mode shows your document on special pages, customized for reading on-screen. These pages aren't the same ones you would see when your document is printed or when you're using Print Preview.

- ✔ The Home and End keys move you to the start and end of your document, respectively.

- ✔ The View Options menu contains commands to help enlarge or reduce text size.

- ✔ You can also use the View Options menu to view a document one page at a time or read the document as it will be printed on the page (which is harder to see).

- ✔ Reading Layout mode *is* ideal for reviewing and collaborating on documents with others. This topic is covered in Chapter 27.

1. Poker Night

We are men and we are afraid. Not yet fully emasculated, but getting there. Like the defeated dog, we approach the enemy. Our only defense is the lowered head. Which will it be? A pat this time? Or yet another swat? Oh, bother; either way, we are afraid. And defeated.

Take this bathroom for example. It's poker night. It's guy's night. But you could never tell by looking at the bathroom. It's a girl's bathroom. A chick's bathroom. It has all the signs of feminine, from the bowl of potpourri to the angel statue. The wall is trimmed in dainty wallpaper, pastel blue. There is a candle. A basket of women's magazines sits by the head. The towels match everything

else and have never been used -- the final and most tell-tale sign that this is a women's restroom. I mean, would a guy have matching, never-used towels in his garage bathroom? Nope!

Because it's poker night, I'm not going to lower the seat. The seat goes both up and down, thank you. Women complain about us leaving it up, but men should also complain about women leaving it down. The thing is hinged both ways. And besides, if it were important enough to leave the seat down all the time, then some man would have designed a toilet with a seat that operates that way. Give me a cocktail napkin, my friend Tom, and two Bud Lites and we could figure it out in half an hour. Patent it. Make a million.

Figure 26-3:
Reading Layout view.

Chapter 27

Working This Out Together

In This Chapter

▶ Sticking comments in a document

▶ Highlighting text

▶ Finding changes in a document

▶ Reviewing document changes

▶ Tracking changes in any document you edit

*W*riting is but a lonely art. For those raw times when writing becomes a team sport, however, Word is happy to oblige with tools both offensive and defensive. On the offense are commands that let others litter your text with comments and suggestions, which may or may not be offensive. On the defensive, Word has modes of operation that disclose any altered jot or title in your text. Amazing tools these, and covered well in this chapter.

Here Are My Thoughts

Word has devised a clever way to let you insert comments or notes into a document. The Comment command works like a combination of the old blue pencil from copy editing days of yore and the modern sticky note. This command allows you to insert notes, suggestions, ideas, or advice into a document without botching up the whole thing. This section explains.

✔ It's best to use Print Layout view when you're making comments.

✔ Folks reviewing your document can use your computer to do so, but most likely they'll read your document using Word on another computer.

✔ This section refers to commands found on the Review tab.

Adding a comment

To shove a comment into your document, follow these steps:

1. **Select the chunk of text you want to comment on.**

   Be specific; although you may be tempted to select the entire document, just the first few words of a longer chunk are all that's necessary.

2. **Click the Review tab.**

3. **Click the New Comment button from the Comments group.**

   Immediately, the document shrinks a tad to make room for the *markup area,* on the right. Your selected text is hugged by red parentheses and highlighted in pink. Off to the right, in the markup area, appears a comment *bubble,* inside of which is the comment number and your initials.

4. **Type your comment.**

   The bubble expands to contain all your comment text. Comments can be endless, although short and to the point is best. Figure 27-1 illustrates several comments in a document.

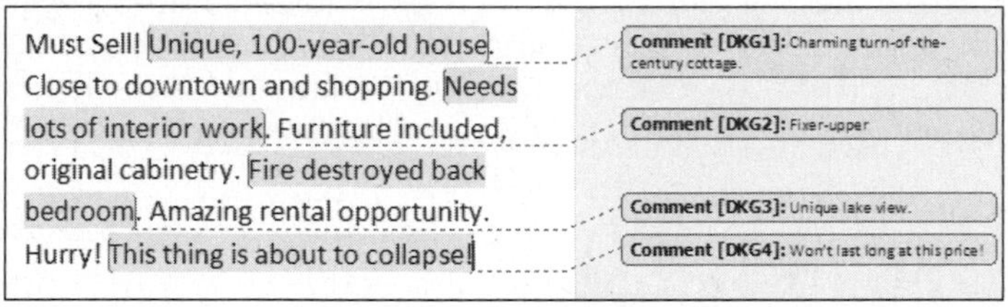

Figure 27-1:
Several
comments
are noted in
this text
passage.

Must Sell! Unique, 100-year-old house. Close to downtown and shopping. Needs lots of interior work. Furniture included, original cabinetry. Fire destroyed back bedroom. Amazing rental opportunity. Hurry! This thing is about to collapse!	**Comment [DKG1]:** Charming turn-of-the-century cottage. **Comment [DKG2]:** Fixer-upper **Comment [DKG3]:** Unique lake view. **Comment [DKG4]:** Won't last long at this price!

5. **Continue reading or reviewing the document.**

   The comments and the markup area stay visible until you hide them, which is covered in the next section.

Comments are best made in Print Layout view, as just described, but it's possible to add comments in Full Screen Reading view by using the Insert Comment button on the wee toolbar (refer to Figure 26-3).

In Draft view, comments appear highlighted and numbered in the text; to see the actual comments, however, you must show the Reviewing pane. Click the Reviewing Pane button to see the comments; click the button again to hide them.

- ✔ Comments are labeled with your initials and a number.
- ✔ Comment numbers are sequential, starting with 1 for the first comment in a document.

✔ When new comments are inserted, the numbering changes so that the comments are always sequential.

✔ When someone else reviews your document and makes comments, their initials are used. Furthermore, their comments appear in a different color.

✔ You can edit the comments the same as you edit any text in Word.

✔ Comment text has its own style: *Comment Text.* Refer to Chapter 16 for more information on styles.

✔ The initials you see next to the comment are supposed to be your initials, which you entered when Word was first configured. To change the initials, choose Word Options from the Office Button menu to display the Word Options dialog box. Choose the Personalize category on the left side of the window. On the right side, near the bottom, enter your user name and initials. Click OK.

Hiding comments

There are various ways to hide comments that are made in your document. These tricks don't delete the comments; for that topic, refer to the section "Deleting comments," later in this chapter. Instead, just like a good wrinkle cream, you can cover up the comments temporarily.

To get rid of the markup area (to the right of your document, where the comments dwell), choose Balloons⇨Show All Revisions Inline. Highlighted text still appears in the document; you can point at the text with the mouse to see a pop-up bubble with the comment. But at least the markup area is gone.

To restore the markup area, choose Balloons⇨Show Revisions in Balloons.

When you want to hide the markup area as well as all the comments, choose Show Markup⇨Comments to remove the check mark next to the Comments option.

To restore the markup area and comments in your text, choose Show Markup⇨Comments to restore the check mark.

Reviewing comments

Perusing comments is done by using two commands in the Comments group:

Choosing Next jumps to the next comment in your document.

Choosing Previous jumps to the previous comment in your document.

 To see all of a document's comments at one time, click the Reviewing Pane button. A special frame opens to the left of or beneath the document window, listing all the comments in sequence for easy review. (To locate a comment from the Reviewing pane in the document text, just click the comment with the mouse.)

Close the Reviewing pane by clicking the Reviewing Pane button again.

Printing comments (or not)

Putting comments into your text means that Word prints them when you print your document. Yes, this has shocked many a Word user. The key to preventing it from happening is to direct Word *not* to print the comments. Here's how:

1. **Summon the Print dialog box.**

   Press Ctrl+P or choose Print from the Office Button menu.

2. **From the Print What drop-down list, choose Document.**

   Do not choose Document Showing Markup, which is what Word has pre-selected for you.

3. **Click the OK button to print the document.**

   And the document prints without comments.

 The change made by these steps isn't permanent. You must follow these steps every time you print the document or else the comments print as well.

Deleting comments

To delete a comment, point at it and click the right mouse button. Choose Delete Comment from the pop-up menu.

 To delete all comments from your document at one time, use the Delete button's menu; choose Delete➪Delete All Comments in Document.

Whip Out the Yellow Highlighter

Word comes with a digital highlighter pen that lets you mark up and colorize the text in your document without damaging your computer monitor. To highlight your text, obey these steps:

1. **Click the Home tab.**

2. **Click the Text Highlight button in the Font group.**

   The mouse pointer changes to a, well, I don't know what it is, but the point is that you're now in Highlighting mode.

3. **Drag the mouse over the text you want highlighted.**

   The text becomes highlighted — just like you can do with a highlighter on regular paper.

4. **Click the Text Highlight button again to return the mouse to normal operation.**

   Or, you can press the Esc key to exit Highlighting mode.

The highlight doesn't necessarily need to be yellow. Clicking the menu button to the right of the Text Highlight button displays a palette of highlighter colors for you to choose from.

To remove the highlighting from your text, you can highlight it again with the same color, which erases it. Or, you can choose None as the highlight color and then drag the mouse over any color of highlighted text to unhighlight.

- ✔ Highlighting is a text format. It's not the background color, but rather its own text format.

- ✔ You can also highlight a block of text by first marking the block and then clicking the Highlight button that appears on the Mini Toolbar.

- ✔ The highlighted text prints, so be careful with it. If you don't have a color printer, highlighted text prints black on gray on your hard copy.

Look What They've Done to My Text, Ma

Be elated when all your critics do is stick comments in your text or use the Highlight tool. More likely, what your enemies, uh, I mean editors will do is to rewrite your text. Unless you're a total brainiac or you have a very bad editor, there's really no way to determine which was your original text and which was modified. That is, unless you use Word's revision-tracking tools, as discussed in this section.

Comparing two versions of the same document

You have two copies of the same document: the original you created and a duplicate that someone has modified, edited, changed, mutilated, folded, or spindled. Assuming that both documents have different names (which is a must under Windows), here are the steps you take to determine what has been changed:

1. **Click the Review tab.**

2. **From the Compare group, choose Compare⇨Compare.**

   The Compare Documents dialog box shows up.

3. **Choose your original document from the Original Document drop-down list.**

4. **Choose the edited document from the Revised Document drop-down list.**

   In either case, when you cannot find the original or revised document, choose Browse to use an Open dialog box to help you hunt down the documents.

5. **Click OK.**

   Word compares the two documents and notes all the changes. Then it displays a list of the changes, the compared document with changes marked, plus the original and revised documents, laid out as shown in Figure 27-2.

   If your screen doesn't look like Figure 27-2, choose Show Both from the Show Source Documents menu.

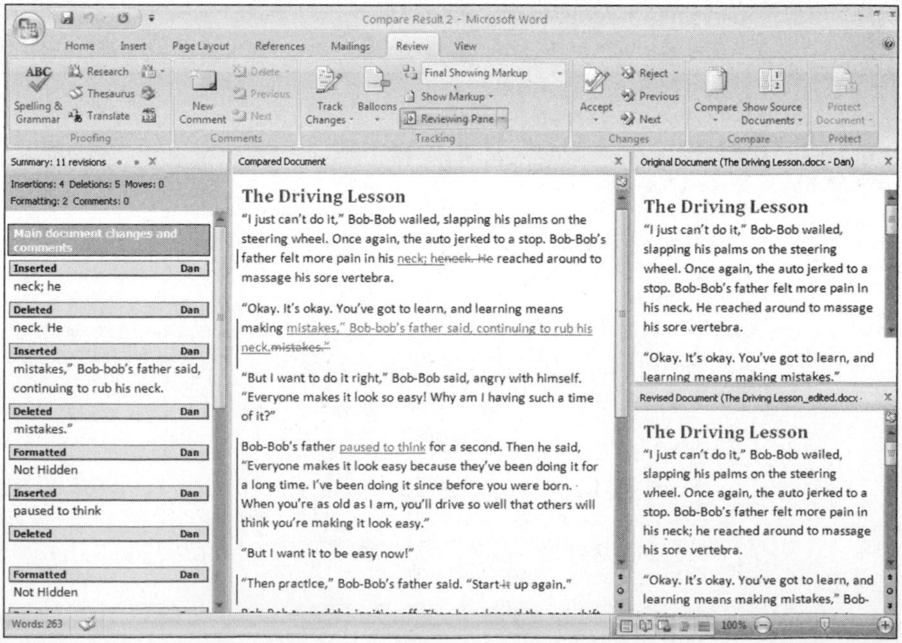

Figure 27-2:
The shameful changes show up here.

Look things over! Peruse the changes made to your pristine prose by the barbarian interlopers. Continue with the next section for reviewing, accepting, and rejecting tips. Here are some additional suggestions:

- ✔ The full list of changes is shown in the Summary panel to the left. Click a change to go to that spot in the document.

- ✔ The Compared Document (middle pane) is the same as the revised (edited) document, but with the changes noted. New text is red-underlined. Removed text is in red strikethrough. Any text that has been modified has a vertical line appearing to its left.

- ✔ Your original document and the edited version appear on the right.

- ✔ Scrolling is synchronized between all three documents: original, edited, and compared.

- ✔ Each "reviewer" is given his own color on your screen. For example, on my screen, I see the revision marks in red. Had a second reviewer gone over the text, those comments would appear in a second color, and so on for other reviewers.

Reviewing the changes

It's understood that you want to scrutinize every change made to your document. Word makes the task easy, thanks to commands in the Changes group, found on the Review tab. Here's how things go:

1. **Press Ctrl+Home to start at the top of the document.**

   Ensure that you're looking at the compared document, not the original or edited version (refer to the preceding section).

2. **Click the Next button to locate the next change in your document.**

3a. **To accept the change, click the Accept button.**

   The change is approved, and you're taken to the next bit of modified text. Or:

3b. **To reject the change, click the Reject button.**

   The change is removed from your document, and you're taken to the next location where text has been modified.

4. **Save the final document.**

   When you've found the last change and fixed it (or not), a dialog box explains that your quest is over. The document has been reviewed. You should now save it to disk, by giving it a new name so that you know it's the result of combined efforts.

Going through this process removes all the revision marks from your document. If you want to re-review the revisions, you have to repeat the steps in the preceding section for comparing two documents.

✔ Use the X buttons to close various task panes that are open for the reviewing process.

✔ When you're in a real hurry, you can use the drop-down menus beneath either the Accept or Reject command button to choose either the Accept All Changes in Document or Reject All Changes in Document commands, respectively.

✔ When you goof, you can choose Edit⇨Undo, just as you can undo any other boo-boo.

✔ You can also right-click any revision mark to accept or reject it.

Tracking changes as you make them

Comparing documents after they've been edited is the defensive way to locate changed text. A more friendly way to do things is simply to direct your editor to activate Word's revision-tracking feature. That way, changes are noted on the screen as they're made.

Turn on revision tracking by clicking the Review tab and then clicking the Track Changes button. The keyboard shortcut is Ctrl+Shift+E.

With revision tracking turned on, simply start editing the document. Any new text you add appears in red underlining. Text you delete is colored red with strikethrough. (Those aren't really text attributes, but rather are Word showing you which text has been messed with.

To turn off revision tracking, click the Track Changes button again.

✔ The only clue that you've properly activated revision tracking is that the Track Changes button appears highlighted.

✔ It's common for Word users not familiar with revision tracking to be frustrated with unexpected red-underlined text. This is simply revision tracking, which someone has enabled. To disable it, click the Track Changes button in the Review tab's Tracking group.

Chapter 28

Merrily We Mail Merge

- -

In This Chapter

▶ Understanding Mail Merge

▶ Building the main document

▶ Conjuring up an address list

▶ Making records

▶ Inserting fields into the main document

▶ Merging (the final act)

- -

Despite being back here in this book's darker chapters, Mail Merge is perhaps one of the oldest and truest word processing abilities. The *mail* comes from the ancient concept of form letters. The *merge* comes from combining a list of names and other informative tidbits and mixing them into a fill-in-the-blanks form letter. The result is a series of documents, each of which appears to be painstakingly customized to a specific individual, but which in fact were quickly created with scant effort, thanks to the power of Mail Merge.

All About Mail Merge

Mail merge is the process of taking a single letter, stirring in a list of names and data, and combining *(merging)* everything into a final set of documents, each of which is customized and nearly personal. Obviously, Mail Merge is a useful thing, but before immersing yourself in the process, I believe that you'll find it useful to become familiar with the following terms:

✔ **Main document:** This is the form letter, the document that contains the various fill-in-the-blanks places. But it starts just like any other document in Word, complete with formatting, page numbers, or anything else you want to add, fancy or schmancy.

✔ **Address list:** The information you use to create customized letters is held in a type of *database file* — basically, a list of names and other data. It's those names and such that are merged with the main document to form individual customized letters.

✔ **Fields:** These are the fill-in-the-blanks items inside the main document. Each field represents an item from the address list, a data tidbit. The field's contents flow from the address list and into the main document, where the field's data appears (after merging). Fields are what make the mail merge possible.

Getting these three things to work together is the essence of Mail Merge. In Word 2007, the tools to make that happen are found on the Mailings tab. This section explains the details.

✔ In Word, you can also mail-merge e-mail messages, envelopes, labels, and lists of information — all of which are a little eccentric but still capitalize on the basic mail-merge formula. Whether this book covers any of that stuff depends on my mood.

✔ In Word, the key to mail merging is the address list. If you plan on doing a mail merge as part of your regular routine, you want to build an address list that you can use over and over.

✔ Word can also pull in addresses and other information from lists created in the Outlook program. This trick seems to work best when you use special server software to help Word and Outlook sort things out. When you cannot get Outlook and Word to share information, it's probably because you're missing some other piece of software.

✔ Please note that Outlook isn't the same thing as Outlook Express. Outlook is the "Professional" e-mail and contact management program that comes with Microsoft Office. Outlook Express is a stupid version of Outlook that comes with every copy of Windows XP.

✔ The address list is actually a Microsoft Access database file. It's possible to use Access to create or manipulate the address list files, though I have no idea how that would work.

Mail Merge Ho!

Doing a mail merge isn't the easiest thing, but it's not impossible — not like weaving a basket out of ramen noodles. The way I see it, there are five separate tasks you must complete:

1. Build the main document.

2. Decide which fields are needed for the main document.

3. Create the address list, or the data for the mail merge. This step involves combining the fields into records and filling in the data.

4. Place the fields into the main document.

5. Merge the records and their fields from the address list into the main document to create the merged documents.

This section covers each of these tasks with sequentially numbered steps — 36 of them altogether.

 It's also possible to use a Mail Merge Wizard in Word. From the Start Mail Merge menu, choose Step By Step Mail Merge Wizard. Then use the Mail Merge task pane to proceed through six complex and terrifying steps. Or, just chuck that and keep reading in the next section.

Creating the main document (Task 1 of 5)

Mail Merge begins with a document, what I call the *main document*. Eventually, it will have those fill-in-the-blanks elements, but don't get ahead of me!

The mail-merge journey begins with a single step:

1. **Create the main document.**

   Write all the text. Add necessary formatting and other fancy elements. Basically, you're just making the unchanging parts of the document now.

2. **Type the fill-in-the-blanks parts in ALL CAPS.**

   The text you type in ALL CAPS is the text that will be replaced during the mail merge. Try to use descriptive terms in ALL CAPS. What you type can be replaced with any length of text, but short and vivid terms work best. Figure 28-1 shows an example.

3. **Save the main document to disk.**

   Continue with steps in the next section.

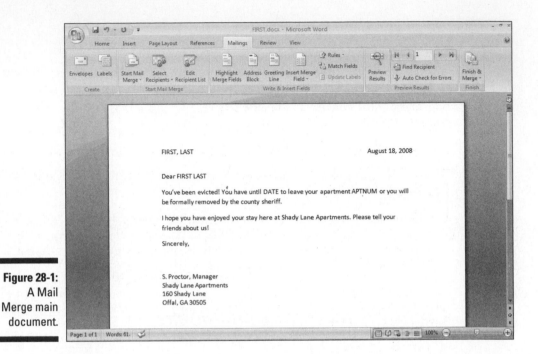

Figure 28-1:
A Mail
Merge main
document.

The ALL CAPS thing is my idea, not Word's. I use them as placeholders for the fields to come, and also to determine which and how many fields I'll need in a document.

- ✔ The main document can be created from a new, blank document, a template, or an existing document.

- ✔ The fill-in-the-blanks items are officially known as *fields*.

- ✔ The document can have as many fields as it needs. In fact, any item that you want to change from letter to letter can be a field: the greeting, a banal pleasantry, gossip, whatever. Anything can be changed from document to document, but you need to specify it now.

- ✔ In addition to mail-merging fields, I inserted a PrintDate field in the document shown in Figure 28-1. See the section "Inserting a field into your document" in Chapter 18 for more information.

- ✔ Don't let the simplicity of this first task lead you down the merry path; this is the easiest step there is.

Assigning fields (Task 2 of 5)

By building the main document first, you get a good idea of what type and how many fields you need. The next step is to create the address list, which contains the data that eventually is merged into the main document.

From Figure 28-1, the example shows the following as needed fields for the main document:

- ✔ FIRST
- ✔ LAST
- ✔ DATE
- ✔ APTNUM

Each one of these fields will be collected into a group called a *record*. Each record, representing a different document to be produced by the mail merge, is what comprises the address list. But at the heart of the game, it's the fields that make the mail-merged document appear customized.

Here's how to create the fields and build the structure of each record in the address list:

4. **Jot down the fields you need.**

   Yes, this is a non-computer step, but believe me, you need it. Make a list of the fields you need on paper with the old-fashioned pen or pencil.

5. **Click the Select Recipients button (on the Mailings tab, in the Start Mail Merge group).**

   A menu drops down with several options:

   - **Type New List:** Unless you already have a list created for mail merging, you have to build a new one. You start with Step 6, next.

   - **Use Existing List:** When you've been through this before or you have handy a database list you want to use, this option makes the most sense. After choosing the list from the Select Data Source dialog box, skip cheerfully over to Step 23 in the section "Inserting fields into the main document (Task 4 of 5)."

   - **Select from Outlook Contacts:** Unless your PC is on a network with the proper kind of Microsoft Server software installed, you can forget this option.

   For this example, I'm assuming that you need to make up a new list.

6. Choose Type New List.

The new Address List dialog box appears, but it's empty. Don't start typing the list yet! First, you need to customize the fields shown in the Address List dialog box, by eliminating what you don't need and adding what you do need.

7. Click the Customize Columns button.

A Customize Address List dialog box appears, as shown in Figure 28-2. The dialog box is populated with a standard set of fields that Word assumes you need in each document. When this is enough, you're done; skip over to Step 15. But often it's not, so:

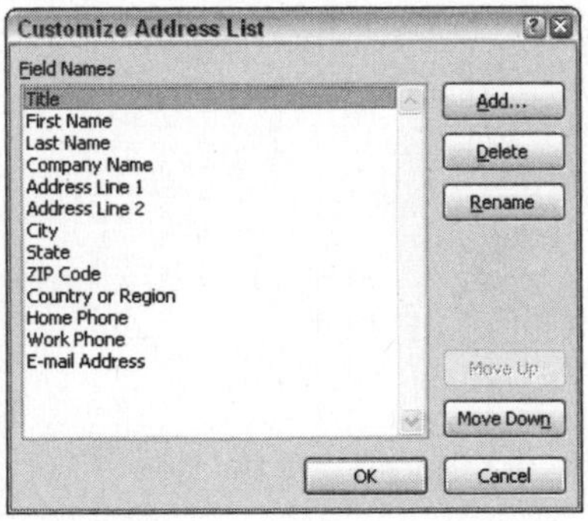

Figure 28-2:
Adding and
deleting
fields are
done here.

8. Select a field that you *do not* need.

Click it with your mouse.

9. Click the Delete button.

10. Click Yes in the confirmation dialog box.

The field you don't need is gone.

11. Repeat Steps 8 through 10 for each field you don't need.

After removing the excess fields you don't need, the next step is to add those fields you do need — if any.

You can also rename fields to match what you want in your document. To do so, select the field and click the Rename button. For example, I renamed First Name to just First; Last Name to Last; and Address Line 1 to simply Address.

12. To add a field, click the Add button.

The teeny Add Field dialog box pops into view.

13. Type the field name and click the OK button.

14. **Repeat Steps 12 and 13 for each new field you need in your main document.**

    When you're done, review the list. You can change the order of items by selecting a field name and using the Move Up and Move Down buttons to change its order — though that isn't really vital.

15. **Click OK.**

    You now see the customized fields appear as column headings in the New Address List dialog box. The next step is to create the records for the mail merge, as continued in the next section.

Here are some suggestions for field names:

- Name the field to reflect the kind of information in it; for example, `Shark Bite Location`.
- No two fields can have the same name.
- Field names can contain spaces, but cannot start with a space.
- Field names can be quite long, though shorter is best.
- The following characters are forbidden in a field name: `. ! ` [ ]`

Building records (Task 3 of 5)

Continuing from the preceding section. . . .

After defining the fields you need, the next step is to complete the address list. To do that, you create a list of records, by entering the data for each field in each record. This happens in the New Address List dialog box, shown partially filled-in in Figure 28-3. Yeah, this is all just basic data entry.

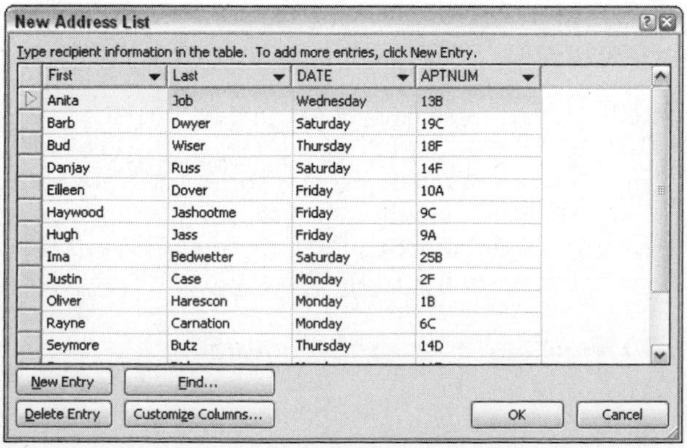
New Address List
Type recipient information in the table. To add more entries, click New Entry.
First
Last
DATE
APTNUM
Anita Job Wednesday 13B
Barb Dwyer Saturday 19C
Bud Wiser Thursday 18F
Danjay Russ Saturday 14F
Eilleen Dover Friday 10A
Haywood Jashootme Friday 9C
Hugh Jass Friday 9A
Ima Bedwetter Saturday 25B
Justin Case Monday 2F
Oliver Harescon Monday 1B
Rayne Carnation Monday 6C
Seymore Butz Thursday 14D
New Entry
Find...
Delete Entry
Customize Columns...
OK
Cancel

Figure 28-3: We will come rejoicing, filling in the fields.

Fields are columns; records are rows.

16. **Type in the first field's data.**

    Type the information appropriate to the field: a name, title, hair style, favorite way to eat pork, and so on.

17. **Press Tab to enter the next field.**

    Keep filling in the data and pressing Tab to move between fields.

18. **Press Tab to start a new record.**

    When you press the Tab key on the last field in a record, a new record is automatically created and added on the next line. Keep filling in data!

19. **Review your work when you're done.**

    You can edit any field in any record by selecting it with the mouse.

    If you accidentally added a blank field at the end, click to select it and then click the Delete Entry button. (Blank records are still processed in a mail merge, which results in wasted paper.)

20. **Click OK.**

    A special Save As dialog box pops up, allowing you to save your address list to disk.

21. **Type a name for the address list.**

    Short and descriptive names are best.

    I recommend not choosing another location for the address list; use the folder chosen for you by Word.

22. **Click the Save button.**

    The address list is now saved to disk.

By saving the address list to disk, you can use it again, which comes in handy for future mail-merge operations.

The next step in the mail-merge process is to stir the fields from the address list into the main document. That's covered in the next section.

You can return to edit the address list at any time by clicking the Edit Recipient List button, located in the Start Mail Merge group on the Mailings tab. In the Mail Merge Recipients dialog box, choose the Data Source file in the lower-left corner and then click the Edit button. (If there's an error, you may need to close the main document.) Clicking the Edit button displays the Edit Data Source dialog box, similar to the New Address List dialog box (refer to Figure 28-3).

Inserting fields into the main document (Task 4 of 5)

The final step before actual merging is to place the fields into the main document, by replacing the ALL CAPS placeholders you inserted earlier. Continue from the preceding section:

23. Return to the main document (if necessary).

24. Select an ALL CAPS text of a field placeholder in the main document.

Or, you can simply stick the insertion pointer where you want a field to appear.

25. Use the Insert Merge Field menu to stick the proper field in the document.

Clicking the Insert Merge Field command button displays a menu of fields according to the address list associated with the main document. Choose the proper field to insert into your text.

For example, if you're replacing the text FIRST in your document with a First field, choose it from the list. The field is inserted into your document and replaces the ALL CAPS text.

26. Continue adding fields until the document is complete.

Repeat Steps 24 and 25 as necessary to stick all the fields in your document.

When you're done, you have a standard Word document, but one that's also associated with an address list from which certain fields are used to help fill in and complete the document. Actual merging happens with the next step, as continued in the following section.

✔ Fields appear with double angle brackets around their names, such as <<Name>>.

✔ To delete an unwanted field, select it with the mouse and press the Delete key.

✔ A tad bit of editing may be required after inserting the field. I typically have to add a space, comma, colon, or whatever after fields as Word inserts them.

✔ If the Insert Merge field button isn't available, you've lost the association between your main document and the address list. To reattach the address list, choose Select Recipients⇨Use Existing List. Use the Select Data Source dialog box to choose your address list. Then you can start inserting fields.

Merging it all together (Last task)

With the merge fields inserted into the main document and the address list standing by, you're ready to merge away! Next to creating the main document, this is the simplest part of all this mail-merging nonsense:

27. Save the main document.

Clicking the Save button on the Quick Access toolbar does this step best.

28. Click the Preview Results command button (on the Mailings tab, in the Preview Results group).

The fields in the main document vanish! They're replaced by information from the first record in the address list. What you see on the screen is how the first customized mail-merge letter appears. Hopefully, everything looks spiffy.

29. Peruse the records.

Review each of the merged documents to ensure that everything looks right. Use the record-browsing buttons in the Preview Results group to move forward or backward through the records. You want to look for the following things:

- Formatting mistakes, such as text that obviously looks pasted in or not part of the surrounding text

- Punctuation errors and missing commas and periods

- Missing spaces between and around fields

- Double fields or unwanted fields, which happen when you believe that you've deleted a field but didn't

- Awkward text layout, strange line breaks, or margins caused by missing or long fields

To fix any boo-boos, you must leave Preview mode and then go back and reedit the main document.

30. Click the Preview Results command button again to exit Preview mode.

You're now ready to perform the actual merge.

31. **Click the Finish & Merge button to display its menu.**

    The Finish & Merge button's menu lists three options for completing the mail merge:

    - **Print Documents:** This is the obvious choice in most cases: The documents have been previewed, and they're ready to go. If the printer is all set up, choosing this option prints your documents and completes the process.

    - **Edit Individual Documents:** This choice creates a new Word document, one containing all the merged documents one after the other. This option is ideal for long mail merges that may screw up when printing; it's easier to print from the merged documents than to repeat the steps in this section.

    - **Send E-mail Messages:** This option frightens me, so I've never chosen it.

32. **Choose an option from the Finish & Merge button's menu.**

    A dialog box appears from which you can choose which records to save or print (or e-mail).

33. **Click the All button to print or save everything.**

    Or, make whichever choice you feel is best for your needs.

34. **Click OK.**

35a. **If you've chosen to print your documents, click OK in the Print dialog box to print them.**

    Or, make whatever settings you need in the Print dialog box, and then click OK to print your merged documents.

35b. **If you've chosen to save your documents, choose Save As from the Office Button's menu.**

    The merged documents appear all together in a single document created by the mail merge. (This isn't the same as the main document — it's a new document.) You can also edit the document, print it, or do what-have-you, but it's more important to save it in this step.

35c. **If you've chosen to e-mail the documents, hey, Bud — you're on your own. Good luck.**

    And don't forget about your ISP's anti-spamming rules.

36. **Tidy up.**

    Save and close the main document plus any other open documents or windows lurking about. You're done.

Now you know how to get those custom, uniquely crafted documents out to the jokers who actually think that you took the time to compose a personal letter. Ha! Mail Merge fools them all!

✔ When you choose to merge to individual documents, each is contained within a section break inside a larger document.

✔ Always examine the results of the merge. Some things may not fit properly, and some editing will no doubt be required.

Chapter 29

Labels of Love

· ·

In This Chapter

▶ Understanding labels

▶ Printing a sheet of identical labels

▶ Merging an address list onto mail labels

▶ Adding graphics to your labels

· ·

*W*ord has the interesting ability to print out sheets of labels. They can be all the same label or be labels produced as the result of a mail-merge operation. This works because the labels are, at their core, merely cells in a table and, unlike most 12-year-olds, Word has no problem setting a table.

Normally, I wouldn't write about labels, but over the years I've received lots of fan mail regarding Word's ability to print labels. Therefore, way back here in the shadowy part of the book, I offer you a chapter on Word and its label-making abilities.

The Label Thing

Word isn't a label-making program. Although it has the ability to produce labels, as shown in the sections that follow, it's not your best choice. I highly recommend that if you plan on printing labels, you get a label-design program, one specifically geared to print labels — perhaps even some type of database program that lets you manage simple lists as well. That said:

Word prints on labels just as it prints on any sheet of paper. Basically, Word puts a table on the page, with each cell the same size as the sticky labels. It then fills the cells with information, which fits snugly on each label. When the sheet emerges from the printer, you have a bunch of labels for your peeling-and-sticking pleasure.

✔ Labels can be found wherever office supplies are sold. Labels come in packages thin and thick, with various label layouts and designs.

✔ Ensure that you buy labels compatible with your printer. Laser printers need special laser printer labels. Some inkjet printers require special, high-quality paper to soak up the ink.

✔ Of all the label brands available, I recommend Avery. Its stock numbers are standard. So, if you buy Avery stock number 5160 or something similar, your software and printer know which type of label you have and which format it's in.

Here's a Sheet of Identical Labels

One of the things Word does easily and reliably is to print a sheet of identical labels. Just follow these steps:

1. Click the Mailings tab.

2. Click the Labels button (in the Create group).

The Envelopes and Labels dialog box appears, with the Labels tab ready for action, as shown in Figure 29-1.

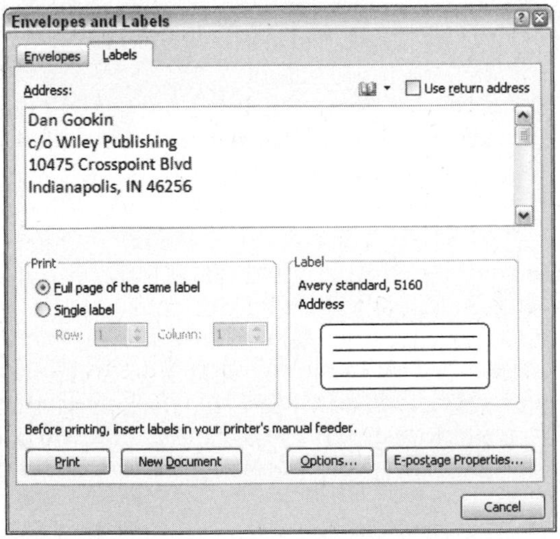

Figure 29-1:
The Labels side of the Envelopes and Labels dialog box.

```
Envelopes and Labels                                    ? ×

  Envelopes | Labels

  Address:                              📖 ▼  □ Use return address

  Dan Gookin                                                  ▲
  c/o Wiley Publishing
  10475 Crosspoint Blvd
  Indianapolis, IN 46256                                      ▼

  ┌Print──────────────────────┐  ┌Label────────────────────┐
  │ ⦿ Full page of the same label │  │ Avery standard, 5160    │
  │ ○ Single label             │  │ Address                 │
  │    Row: 1 ▲  Column: 1 ▲  │  │   ┌─────────────────┐   │
  │                            │  │   │                 │   │
  └────────────────────────────┘  │   │                 │   │
                                   │   └─────────────────┘   │
                                   └─────────────────────────┘
  Before printing, insert labels in your printer's manual feeder.

  [ Print ]  [ New Document ]   [ Options... ]  [ E-postage Properties... ]

                                              [ Cancel ]
```

3. Use the Address box to type what you want printed on the label.

Keep in mind that you have only so many lines for each label and that each label is only so wide.

Press the Enter key at the end of each line.

You can apply some simple formatting at this stage: bold, italic, underlining. If you right-click in the Address box, you can choose Font or Paragraph from the pop-up menu to further format the label.

4. **In the Print section of the Envelopes and Labels dialog box, select the Full Page of the Same Label radio button.**

5. **In the Label section, choose the type of label you're printing on.**

   If the stock number displayed doesn't match up, click the sample label to display a Label Options dialog box, from which you can choose the proper stock number or design of your labels.

6. **Click the New Document button.**

   By placing the labels in a new document, you can further edit them, if you like. You can also save them to disk so that you can use the same document in case you need to print a batch of labels again.

7. **Print the labels.**

   Ensure that the sheet of labels is loaded into your printer, proper side up. Use the Ctrl+P command to print the labels as you would any document.

I have a whole folder on my hard drive full of label documents I print from time to time. For example, one document is my return address, and another has my bank's address. They come in quite handy.

- ✔ When you elect to save the labels to a new document, avoid the temptation to mess with the table because it's perfectly aligned to the labels. Also don't adjust the page's margins or paragraph formatting.

- ✔ You can edit the labels. Sure, they all look the same, but if you like, you can type a few new names or other information in several of the little boxes.

Print That Address List

Word has the ability to take a list of names and addresses and print them all, or a selected few, on a sheet of labels. This is more of a mail-merge thing than a true label-making ability; therefore, I highly recommend that you check out the mail-merge process in Chapter 28 before proceeding with the following steps:

1. **Start a blank, new document in Word.**

2. **Click the Mailings tab.**

   All the action in the remaining steps involves command buttons on the Mailings tab.

3. **From the Start Mail Merge button's menu, choose Labels.**

   A Label Options dialog box appears.

4. **Choose the product number representing the sheet of labels upon which you're printing.**

   For example, to print on a sheet of standard Avery address labels, use Avery catalog number 5160.

5. **Click OK.**

   Word builds a table on your document, one with cells perfectly aligned to match the labels on the sheet you selected. (The table's gridlines may be hidden, but it's still there.)

   Do not edit or format the table! It's perfect.

6. **From the Select Recipients button's menu, choose either Type New List to create your own list of names for the labels or Use Existing List to take advantage of lists you've already created.**

   Please refer to Chapter 28 for information on creating an address list.

   Word fills in all but the first cell (label) with the <<Next Record>> field. That field is how Word can duplicate the label layout from the first label onto the remaining labels on the page. Before that can happen, although, you need to build the first label.

7. **Use the Insert Merge Field button to insert fields to help create and format the first label.**

   Clicking the Insert Merge Field command's menu button displays a list of fields associated with the address list you chose in Step 6. Choose a field from the list, such as First Name. Then type a space and insert the Last Name field from the list. Use the fields, as well as your keyboard, to build the first label. Figure 29-2 shows an example.

8. **Check the layout.**

   Ensure that you have spaces between those fields that need the spaces, and also commas and other stuff.

9. **Click the Update Labels button.**

   Word populates the remaining cells in the table with the same fields. This is why I had you check the layout in Step 8; if you find a mistake now, you have to fix every dang-doodle label rather than a single label.

10. **Choose the proper command from the Finish & Merge button's menu:**

    To save the document and print, choose Edit Individual Documents.

    To just print, choose Print Documents.

11. **Select which records to print, or just keep the All option chosen in the Merge To dialog box.**

12. **Save. Print. Whatever.**

   If you're presented with a new document, save it to disk. You can then use it over and over and print it any time you like.

   When you've chosen to print the labels, click OK in the Print dialog box to start printing. (Be sure that the printer is loaded with as many sheets of labels as you need.)

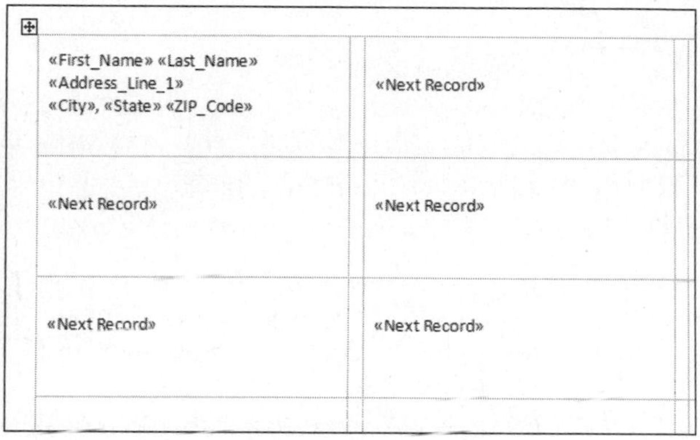

«First_Name» «Last_Name» «Address_Line_1» «City», «State» «ZIP_Code»	«Next Record»
«Next Record»	«Next Record»
«Next Record»	«Next Record»

Figure 29-2: The first label dictates how the other labels are formatted.

A Label Trick with Graphics

It's possible to add a graphical image to the mailing label. This can be done to a sheet of labels that are all identical or when you're merging names from an address list. I recommend reviewing Chapter 23 on using graphics in Word before you proceed.

To stick a graphical image into your list of labels, work through Steps 1 through 5 from the preceding section. What you do next depends on whether you're merging an address list or just making a sheet of identical labels.

✔ When you're merging in an address list, follow Steps 6 through 8 from the preceding section.

✔ When you're creating a sheet of identical labels, simply type and format the label you want in the table's first cell, such as your own name and address to be used for return address labels.

After making your label, either from an address list's Merge fields or by just typing plain text, you're ready to add the graphical image: Click the Insert tab and use the Picture button to insert the image — or use any of the techniques covered in Chapter 23 for sticking graphics into a Word document.

This is important! Click the image and choose Square as the text-wrapping option. Resize and position the image so that it's completely within the first cell in the table, as shown in Figure 29-3.

Figure 29-3:
Creating a
label with
an image.

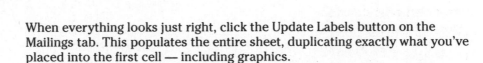

George Washington
1600 Pennsylvania Ave.
Washington, DC 20500

When everything looks just right, click the Update Labels button on the Mailings tab. This populates the entire sheet, duplicating exactly what you've placed into the first cell — including graphics.

Unfortunately, because this graphical trick involves fooling Word's mail-merge function and before you can save or print your document, you need to get rid of those <<Next Record>> fields. Here's my suggestion:

1. **Carefully select the text <<Next Record>>, including the angle brackets on either side.**

   You have to select the whole thing; clicking just the field turns it gray. That's not selecting! Drag the mouse over the entire thing to select it.

2. **Press Ctrl+C to copy that text.**

3. **Press Ctrl+H to conjure up the Find and Replace dialog box.**

4. **Click the mouse in the Find What box and then press Ctrl+V to paste.**

   This step pastes the text <<Next Record>> into the box.

   Leave the Replace With box blank.

5. **Click the Replace All button.**

   At this point, Word may replace only the selected text. That's fine: Click the Yes button to continue replacing throughout the entire document.

   Also click the Yes button if you're asked to continue searching at the beginning of the document.

   Click OK when the search-and-replace operation has been completed.

6. **Close the Find and Replace dialog box.**

   And all those annoying <<Next Record>> things are gone from the labels.

Now your labels are ready to save and print.

Chapter 30

Customizing Word

In This Chapter

▶ Using the Zoom command

▶ Configuring the status bar

▶ Working with the Quick Access toolbar

▶ Customizing the Quick Access toolbar

▶ Restoring the Quick Access toolbar

What you see is not what you have to put up with. Word 2007 offers fewer chances to customize things than earlier versions of Word, but that doesn't mean that you utterly lack ways of modifying Word's appearance. This chapter covers a few things you can do to make Word your own, by customizing its look and interface to match the way you use the program. *Paint an inch thick!*

All the Better to See You, My Dear

Since computers went graphical some 15 years ago, just about every program has a Zoom command. Like the zoom lens on a camera, the Zoom command is used to make the stuff you work on appear larger or smaller. So, if you have a difficult time seeing your document, you can zoom in. Or, to help get the big picture, you can zoom out.

The main Zoom control is found on the status bar, as shown in Figure 30-1. The percentage value is the approximate ratio between the size of your document on the computer's monitor versus how big it will be when printed.

Figure 30-1:
The Zoom tool.

✔ To make the document appear larger, slide the gizmo to the right (toward the plus sign).

✔ To make the document appear smaller, slide the gizmo to the left.

You can also zoom about by using the commands found in the View tab's Zoom group.

Clicking the Zoom button displays the Zoom dialog box, which contains custom controls for setting document magnification, as shown in Figure 30-2.

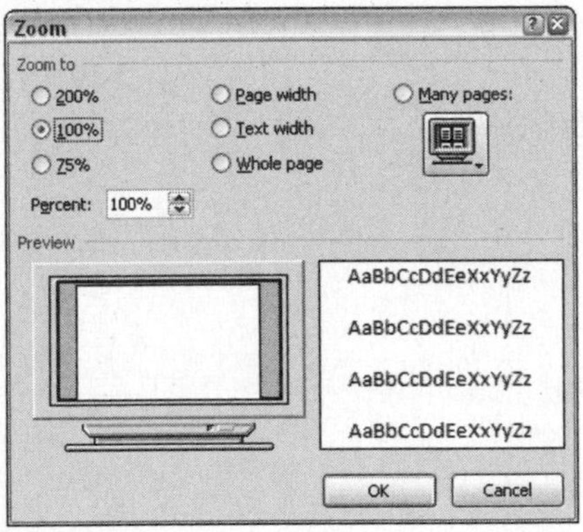

Figure 30-2:
The Zoom
dialog box.

The Whole Page command zooms out so that you can see the entire page on the screen. The text is very tiny, but — amazingly — you can still edit (if you're nuts).

Like the One Page command, the Two Pages command zooms out and shows two pages on the screen at one time. You can see more than two pages at a time by using the Many Pages button in the Zoom dialog box. (Refer to Figure 30-2.)

The Page Width command sets the zoom level so that you see your entire document from its left to right margins; it's my favorite setting.

✔ You can also display the Zoom dialog box by clicking the zoom percentage (100%) on the status bar.

✔ When zooming takes you too far out, your text changes to shaded blocks, called *greeking*. Although it's not keen for editing, zooming out that far gives you a good idea of how your document looks on the page before printing.

✔ If you have a Microsoft IntelliMouse (or any other wheel mouse), you can zoom by pressing the Ctrl key on your keyboard and rolling the wheel up or down. Rolling up zooms in; rolling down zooms out.

The Status Bar Configuration Menu

Word's status bar is an extremely useful strip of informative tidbits and controls, lurking at the bottom of Word's screen. Chapter 1 introduces the status bar, but only hints at its potential. Now it's time to reveal all: Right-clicking the status bar produces the helpful Status Bar Configuration menu, shown in Figure 30-3.

Customize Status Bar	
Formatted Page Number	1
Section	1
✓ Page Number	1 of 1
Vertical Page Position	1"
Line Number	1
Column	1
✓ Word Count	0
✓ Spelling and Grammar Check	No Errors
Language	
Signatures	Off
✓ Information Management Policy	Off
✓ Permissions	Off
Track Changes	Off
Caps Lock	Off
Overtype	Insert
Selection Mode	
Macro Recording	Not Recording
✓ View Shortcuts	
✓ Zoom	100%
✓ Zoom Slider	

Figure 30-3: The Status Bar Configuration menu.

The Status Bar Configuration menu does two things. First, it controls what you see on the status bar, informational tidbits as well as certain controls. Second, it lets you turn on or off some Word features. Here are my thoughts:

✔ Choosing an item from the menu doesn't cause the menu to disappear, which is handy. To make the menu go away, click the mouse elsewhere in Word's window.

✔ The menu's options are on when a check mark appears next to them.

✔ The top eight items on the menu display information about your document. You can also choose to have that information displayed on the status bar by choosing one or more of those options.

✔ The options from Caps Lock down through Macro Recording are used to turn off or on those features. (Selection Mode is the F8-key thing, as covered in Chapter 7.)

✔ This book doesn't cover Word's macros.

✔ The last three items on the menu control whether the View or Zoom shortcuts appear on the status bar.

The Quick Access Toolbar

If you used Word back in the old days, you may or may not have known that you could customize the toolbars, or even create your own. Few people did. That may change with the new Ribbon interface. Despite the Ribbon's quicker nature than the toolbars of old, you may find yourself pining for certain commands that used to be immediately available on a toolbar and are now buried deep somewhere within the Ribbon.

To satisfy your customization desperation, Word comes with the Quick Access toolbar, which can be customized to your heart's content. This section explains.

Finding the toolbar

The Quick Access toolbar is preset to dwell above the Ribbon, just to the right of the Office Button, shown in Figure 30-4. Three command buttons reside on the toolbar: Save, Undo, and Redo. Beyond the toolbar's curved right end, you find its menu button, illustrated in the figure.

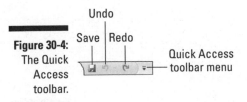

Figure 30-4: The Quick Access toolbar.

Moving the toolbar

Like many creatures, the Quick Access toolbar can be found in two habitations. The ocelot exists in both North and South America. The peregrine falcon can be found in both Eastern and Western hemispheres. The Quick Access Toolbar can be found either above or below the Ribbon.

Use the toolbar's menu to set where it calls home.

- ✔ Choose the Show Below the Ribbon command from the toolbar's menu to lodge the toolbar beneath the Ribbon.

- ✔ Choose the Show Above the Ribbon command to domicile the toolbar back on top.

There's no need to evict the toolbar from its top perch unless it's growing so many command buttons that it crowds over onto the title bar.

Adding command buttons to the toolbar

You're free to add command buttons to the Quick Access toolbar: popular commands you use often, commands missing from the Ribbon, or commands that add a festive and tasteful touch to Word's interface, ideal for those who enjoy decorating on a budget.

There are two ways to add a command to the Quick Access toolbar. The easiest way is to right-click a command button on the Ribbon (or just about anywhere in Word) and choose Add to Quick Access Toolbar from the shortcut menu.

The second way to add a command to the Quick Access toolbar is to use its menu. The top several items in the menu are common commands that most folks would enjoy having on the Quick Access toolbar. To add a command, simply select it from the menu.

Not all the commands in Word are listed on the Quick Access toolbar's menu. But that doesn't mean that those commands are excluded. Simply choose the More Commands item from the menu and you see the Word Options dialog box appear, as shown in Figure 30-5. You can use the Customization area in that dialog box to add commands to the toolbar.

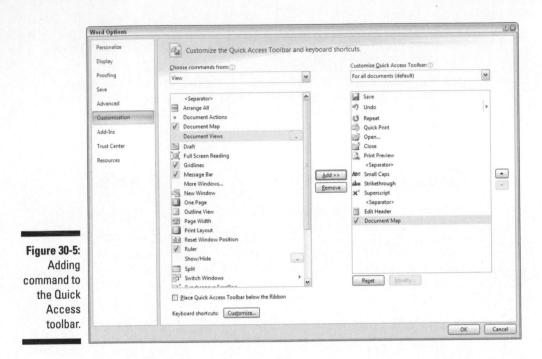

Figure 30-5:
Adding
command to
the Quick
Access
toolbar.

When you're done making additions, click the OK button to close the Word Options dialog box and return to Word. There, you can view and treasure your new Quick Access toolbar.

✔ Word remembers which commands you add to the toolbar. Those same commands will be there the next time you start Word.

✔ Not all the commands on the Quick Access toolbar are available for use.

✔ Choose the All Commands item from the Choose Commands From menu to view every possible command in Word. Sometimes, a missing command that you think could be elsewhere ends up being available in the All Commands list.

✔ Some commands place buttons, and others place drop-down menus or text boxes on the toolbar.

✔ When your command list gets long, consider organizing things. Use the `<Separator>` item to help group similar commands. The `<Separator>` appears as a vertical bar on the Quick Access toolbar.

✔ Yes, some of the items lack specific graphics on their buttons; they show up as green spheres. And sometimes the button graphics don't really make any sense.

✔ My personal Quick Access toolbar contains these commands: Save, Open, Close, Print Preview, Quick Print, (Separator), Undo, Redo, Edit Header, Show/Hide, (Separator), Strikethrough, Small Caps, Subscript, and Superscript.

Removing commands from the toolbar

The easiest way to remove a command from the Quick Access toolbar is to right-click its button. From the pop-up menu, choose Remove from Quick Access Toolbar.

Mass removal can also take place in the Word Options dialog box. (Refer to Figure 30-5.) Choose a command from the right, and then click the Remove button.

I wouldn't recommend removing the Undo or Redo commands from the toolbar, unless you've really committed the Ctrl+Z and Ctrl+Y keyboard shortcuts to memory.

Restoring the Quick Access toolbar

Clicking the Reset button in the Customization portion of the Word Options dialog box, as shown in Figure 30-5, restores the Quick Access toolbar to the standard way it comes with Word. After you click Reset, you see a confirmation dialog box: Click Yes to restore the toolbar as it once was.

Part VI
The Part of Tens

The 5th Wave   By Rich Tennant

"Needlepoint my foot! These are Word fonts.
What I can't figure out is how you got the
pillow cases into your printer."

In this part . . .

The Guinness folks list only the world's records, which is an extensive list but with only one item in each category. That's a list of one. My grandmother loved to say that things come in threes. When you're listing mystical things, however, seven seems to be the key number, as in the Seven Wonders of the Ancient World. Ancient pantheons came in twelves, a six-pack each of male and female gods. I prefer lists of tens, such as the Ten Commandments. Ten is handy because humans carry around their own list of ten: ten fingers! It's also very trendy in that the Roman numeral for ten is X.

At this point in the book, I present The Part of Tens. Each chapter that follows contains a list of ten items, all related to some aspect of Word. It's my way of drawing this fat, fact-filled book to a fun and fancy finish.

Chapter 31

The Ten Commandments of Word

. . . .

In This Chapter

▶ Thou shalt remember to save thy work

▶ Thou shalt not use spaces unnecessarily

▶ Thou shalt not press Enter at the end of each line

▶ Thou shalt not neglect thy keyboard

▶ Thou shalt not manually number thy pages

▶ Thou shalt not use the Enter key to start a new page

▶ Thou shalt not press OK too quickly

▶ Thou shalt not forget thy Undo command

▶ Honor thy printer

▶ Thou shalt have multiple document windows before thee

. . . .

Despite this book's girth, there are still some very simple rules I would recommend to anyone using a word processor. These rules are nothing new; even the biblical Ten Commandments include basic moral codes embraced by most civilizations. So, despite being written about elsewhere in this book, these rules are worth repeating. I call them my Ten Commandments of Word.

Thou Shalt Remember to Save Thy Work

Save! Save! Save! Always save your stuff. Whenever your mind wanders, have your fingers wander to the Ctrl+S keyboard shortcut. Savest thy work.

Thou Shalt Not Use More Than One Space

Generally speaking, you should never find more than one space anywhere in a Word document. The sign of two or more spaces in a row is a desperate cry for a tab. Use single spaces to separate words and sentences. Use tabs to indent or to align text on a tab stop.

✔ Refer to Chapter 13 on setting tabs.

✔ Refer to Chapter 20 for creating tables, which is a great way to organize information into rows and columns.

Thou Shalt Not Press Enter at the End of Each Line

Word automatically wraps your text. As you type and your text approaches the right margin, the words are automatically advanced to the next line. Therefore, there's no need to press the Enter key unless you want to start a new paragraph.

✔ For one-line paragraphs, pressing the Enter key at the end of the line is okay.

✔ When you don't want to start a new paragraph but need to start a new line, use Shift+Enter, the *soft* return command.

Thou Shalt Not Neglect Thy Keyboard

Word is Windows. Windows is a graphical operating system. Graphics means using the mouse. So, although you can get lots done with the mouse, some things in Word are done faster by using the keyboard.

For example, when I'm working on several documents at once, I switch between them with Alt+Tab. Stab the Ctrl+S key combo to quickly save a document. Ctrl+P to print works better than fumbling for the mouse. You don't have to learn all the keyboard commands, but knowing those few outlined in this book helps.

Thou Shalt Not Manually Number Thy Pages

Word has an automatic page-numbering command. Refer to the section in Chapter 14 that talks about where to stick the page number.

Thou Shalt Not Use the Enter Key to Start a New Page

When you need to start text at the top of a new page, you use the *manual page break* command. The keyboard shortcut is Ctrl+Enter. That's the best and most proper way to start a new page. Also see Chapter 14.

The worst way to start a new page is to brazenly press the Enter key a couple of dozen times. Although that may look okay, it doesn't guarantee you anything; as you continue to edit your document, the page break moves back and forth and ends up looking ugly.

Thou Shalt Not Click OK Too Quickly

Word has many Yes/No/OK-type questions. If you click OK or Yes without thinking about it (or press Enter accidentally), you can delete text, delete files, or perform a bad replace operation without meaning to. Always read your screen before you click OK.

Some dialog boxes have a Close button rather than an OK button. These buttons are typically used when you make some choice or reset some option and you don't want to continue with the command. For example, you can change printers in the Print dialog box and then click the Close button to continue without printing.

Thou Shalt Not Forget Thy Undo Command

Just about anything that happens in Word can be undone by choosing the Undo command from the Quick Access toolbar or pressing the popular and common keyboard shortcut Ctrl+Z.

Honor Thy Printer

The biggest printing problem anyone has is telling Word to print something when the printer isn't on. Verify that your printer is on, healthy, and ready to print before you tell Word to print something.

Never (or at least try not to) keep using the Print command over and over when a document doesn't print. Word tries to print once every time you use the Print command. Somewhere and sometime, those documents will print, unless you do something about it.

Thou Shalt Have Multiple Document Windows Before Thee

In Word, as in most Windows applications, you can work on more than one document at the same time. In fact, you can have as many document windows open as you can stand (or until the computer runs out of memory). Word even lets you view a single document in multiple windows. Refer to Chapter 25 to see how things are done.

✔ You don't have to close one document to open and view another document.

✔ You don't have to quit Word to run another program either. In Windows, you can run multiple programs at a time. So don't quit Word when you plan on starting it again in just a little while.

Chapter 32

Ten Cool Tricks

In This Chapter

▶ Saving automatically

▶ Using keyboard shortcuts

▶ Creating fractions

▶ Setting electronic bookmarks

▶ Checking document security

▶ Creating a drop cap

▶ Using the Document Map

▶ Creating and printing envelopes

▶ Sorting paragraphs

▶ Hiding your text

*W*hen it comes down to it, just about everything that Word does can be considered a cool trick. I still marvel at *word wrap,* or how you can change margins after a document is written and all the text instantly jiggles into place. Everything in this book could be considered a cool trick, but when it came down to the wire, I found ten cool tricks not really mentioned anywhere else and stuck them in this chapter.

Automatic Save with AutoRecover

Word's AutoRecover feature will save your butt someday. What AutoSave does is to periodically save your document, even when you neglect to. That way, in the event of a computer crash, Word recovers your document from a safety copy that it has secretly made for you. That's a blessing.

Ensure that AutoSave is activated: From the Office Button menu, choose Word Options. In the Word Options dialog box, choose Save on the left. On the right side of the window, ensure that there's a check mark by the item Save AutoRecover Information Every 10 Minutes. Click OK to close the window. Whew! You're safe.

Most of the time, you never notice AutoRecover. But when there's a computer crash and you restart Word, you see a Document Recovery task pane displayed that lists any files you didn't save before the crash. To recover a document, point the mouse at the document name. Use the menu button that's displayed to open and recover the document.

✔ If the power is unstable at your home or office, enter **5**, **3**, **2**, or even **1** minute as the AutoRecover backup interval.

✔ The best way to avoid accidentally losing your stuff is to *save now* and *save often!*

Keyboard Power!

Windows and its programs, including Word, reside in a graphical kingdom. As such, the mouse is your primary means of making things happen. But don't forget the keyboard! You can also use the keyboard in Word to do just about anything that the mouse can do. Specifically, you can use the keyboard to work the Ribbon interface.

Each tab on the Ribbon has its own keyboard shortcut. To see the shortcut, you need to press one of two magical keys: Alt or F10. After you press either key, a tiny bubble appears, telling you which key to press next to choose a tab on the Ribbon.

After you press a tab's shortcut key, additional shortcut keys appear for each command or group on the tab. Sometimes one character appears as a shortcut, and sometimes two characters appear. Either way, pressing those keys one after the other activates the command or displays further keyboard shortcuts.

For example, to change the page orientation to Landscape mode, you press Alt, P, O to display the Orientation menu and then press the down arrow key to choose Landscape. Press Enter to choose that menu item.

After you press Alt or F10 to activate keyboard control over the Ribbon, your keyboard is used to manipulate the Ribbon, not to write text. Press the Esc key to cancel this mode.

Build Your Own Fractions

Word's AutoCorrect feature can build common fractions for you. Actually, it doesn't really build them as much as it pulls them from a set of existing fraction "characters." Sadly, there are only a few of those fraction characters. When you need your own, specific fraction, such as ³⁄₆₄, you can create it this way:

1. **Press Ctrl+Shift+= (the equal sign).**

    This is the keyboard shortcut for the superscript command.

2. **Type the *numerator* — the top part of the fraction.**

    For example, type **3** for ³⁄₆₄.

3. **Press Ctrl+Shift+= again to turn off superscripting.**

4. **Type the slash.**

5. **Press Ctrl+= to turn on subscripting.**

6. **Type the *denominator* — the bottom part of the fraction.**

7. **Press Ctrl+= to turn off subscripting.**

There's your fraction.

Electronic Bookmarks

Word allows you to stick electronic bookmarks into your document. They not only help you set your place in a document, but they also can be used to flag specific tidbits of text for other commands, such as Go To, or the Browse buttons. Bookmarks can prove quite handy — better than trying to use the Find command to locate stuff in your text.

To set a bookmark in your document, observe these steps:

1. **Put the insertion pointer where you want to place the bookmark.**

2. **Click the Insert tab.**

3. **Click the Bookmark button in the Links group.**

    The Bookmark dialog box opens, listing any current bookmarks but also allowing you to create a new bookmark.

4. **Type a name for the bookmark.**

    Be clever! The name reminds you of where you are in your document, but it cannot contain spaces. (Use underlines rather than spaces.)

5. **Press Enter or click the Add button.**

    You don't see anything on the screen, but the bookmark is there, invisibly lurking in your text.

Of course, bookmarks mean nothing unless there's a way to find them. That's where the Go To command comes in handy:

To jump to a bookmark anywhere in a document, press the F5 key. It summons the Go To tab in the Find and Replace dialog box. Choose Bookmark from the Go To What list, and then select a bookmark name from the drop-down list on the right side of the dialog box. Click the Go To button to visit that bookmark's location. (Close the Find and Replace dialog box when you're done with it.)

Document Inspection

Stories in the media a few years ago disclosed that the typical Word document contains more than just the text you see on the screen. Occasionally, some personal data would slip out with a Word document, allowing anyone reading it to trace that document back to whoever wrote it or at least figure out on which computer it was written. Some people consider this a security flaw. I agree!

To help protect your document from snooping eyes, you can perform a Document Inspection. Here's what I do:

1. **Save your document to disk.**

   Do this step a final time before inspecting. And, yes, this step assumes that your document has already been written.

2. **From the Office Button menu, choose Prepare⇨Inspect Document.**

   Mr. Document Inspector appears, listing suspicious things it looks for inside a document.

3. **Click the Inspect button.**

   Any suspect items found in your document are flagged in the Document Inspector window. To fix the items, click the Remove All button(s).

4. **Click the Reinspect button to scan your document again, if you feel the need.**

   Go to Step 3 if you choose to reinspect.

5. **Click the Close button.**

The Drop Cap

A *drop cap* is the first letter of a report, article, chapter, or story that appears in a larger and more interesting font than the other characters. Figure 32-1 shows an example.

> I was born in a log cabin I built myself using mud and clay. My parents couldn't afford to have a child right away, so it wasn't until I was 9-years-old that I was finally born. Because I was so old, the other children teased me a lot. This continued well beyond my childhood and into my adultery.

Figure 32-1:
A drop cap.

Here's how to add a drop cap to your document:

1. **Select the first character of the first word at the start of your text.**

   For example, select the *O* in "Once upon a time."

   It also helps if this paragraph is left justified and not indented with a tab or any of the tricky formatting discussed in Part III of this book.

2. **Click the Insert tab.**

3. **Choose a drop cap style from the Drop Cap button's menu.**

   The first option, None, isn't a drop cap at all. The Dropped style is second, and the In Margin style is third. I prefer the Dropped style myself. To select the style you prefer, click in that box.

   The final menu option, Advanced, summons the Drop Cap dialog box, from which you can select a font or make other, specific drop cap adjustments.

You can undo a drop cap by clicking it and then choosing Drop Cap⇒None.

Drop caps, like other fancy elements in your text, show up best in Print Layout view.

The Document Map

The Document Map feature is there to help you see the big picture, especially if you use Word's heading styles. Click the View tab and put a check mark by Document Map in the Show/Hide group. A special task pane opens to the left side of your document, listing a quick summary of the various heading styles used.

I find the Document Map useful in getting a quick overview of how my document is structured. Also, by clicking a heading inside the map, you can instantly jump to that part of your document.

Remove the check mark by Document Map to close that special view of your document.

Add an Envelope to Your letter

A quick way to print an envelope with every letter you create is to attach the envelope to the end of the letter. After typing your letter, click the Envelopes button in the Mailings tab. When your document already has an address in it, Word magically locates that address and places it in the Delivery Address box in the Envelopes and Labels dialog box. Click the Add to Document button, and you're done.

If Word doesn't find the address, you can manually type it in the Envelopes and Labels dialog box. Remember to click the Add to Document button to return to your document.

It may not be obvious on the screen, but the first page of your letter is now an envelope. When you're ready to print the letter, the envelope is printed first and then the letter. All you have to do is stuff the letter into the envelope and seal it and then apply the ever-increasing postage.

✔ Most printers prompt you to manually enter envelopes if that's what they want you to do. After doing so, you may have to press the Ready, On-line, or Select button for the printer to continue. (My LaserJet printer just says "Me Feed!" and, for some reason, it knows when I insert the envelope because it just starts going!)

✔ Check the envelope as you insert it into your printer to ensure that you didn't address the backside or put the address on upside down — as so often happens to me.

✔ If you have trouble remembering how the envelope feeds into your printer, draw a picture of the proper way and tape it to the top of your printer for reference.

Sort Your Text

Sorting is one of Word's better tricks. After you understand this feature, you go looking for places to use it. You can use the Sort command to arrange text alphabetically or numerically. You can sort paragraphs, table rows, and columns in cell tables and in tables created by using tabs.

Save your document before sorting. It's just a good idea.

Sorting isn't that difficult. First, arrange what needs to be sorted into several rows of text, such as

```
Arthur
Richard
Martin
Pat
Isaac
Tanya
```

 Word sorts by the first item in each paragraph, so just select all the lines as a block. Then click the Sort button in the Home tab's Paragraph group. Mess around in the Sort Text dialog box if you wish, but most of the time clicking OK is all you need to do to sort your text alphabetically.

Text That Doesn't Print

One of the stranger text formats is *hidden text*, which seems bizarre until you discover how useful it can be. For example, rather than cut something, you can just hide it, maybe to revive it later.

Hiding text is done by first selecting the text and then choosing the Hidden attribute from the Font dialog box. To display the Font dialog box, click the Dialog Box Launcher in the lower-right corner of the Font group on the Home tab. Choose Hidden from the list of effects in the Font dialog box.

Hidden text is made invisible in your document. There's no blank spot where the text was; things just appear as though the text was never written. But you can make the text show up anyway:

1. **Choose Word Options from the Office Button's menu.**

2. **Choose Display from the left side of the Word Options dialog box.**

3. **On the right side, put a check mark by Hidden Text.**

Completing these steps allows hidden text to appear with a dotted underline in your document. Ta-da! You can see the hidden text.

Hidden text normally doesn't print. You can direct Word to print it. Simply repeat these steps for showing hidden text, except in Step 3 choose Print Hidden Text from the Printing Options area.

Chapter 33

Ten Odd Things

In This Chapter

▶ Inserting pretty equations

▶ Making basic math calculations

▶ Defending your document (or not)

▶ Hyphenating text

▶ Setting document properties (or not)

▶ Beholding the Developer tab

▶ Making a cross-reference

▶ Avoiding Smart Tags

▶ Disabling click-and-type

▶ Keeping Word separate from the Internet

*I*f Word were only about word processing, this book would have been over by Chapter 18. Fully half the book talks about things I would consider to be along the lines of desktop publishing or even graphics, tasks that can be done far better with other applications. But beyond those strange abilities are things I consider even more strange and unusual. Welcome to the *Twilight Zone*, the chapter where I list ten of the oddest things I've found in Word.

Equations

Here's a feature that everyone needs, as long as everyone graduated from college with a degree in astrophysics or mathematics. It's Word's Equation tools, which you need whenever you're desperate to stick a polynomial equation into your document and don't want to go through the tedium of building the thing yourself.

You can pluck a pre-made equation from the Insert tab's Equation button menu, providing that the equation you need is shown there. Otherwise just click the button by itself (not the menu triangle) and two things happen. First, an equation *control* is inserted into your document at the insertion pointer's location. Second, the Equation Tools Design tab appears on the ribbon, shown in Figure 33-1. Creating equations was never easier! Well, creating them is easy, but knowing what they mean is a different story altogether.

No, Word won't solve the equation.

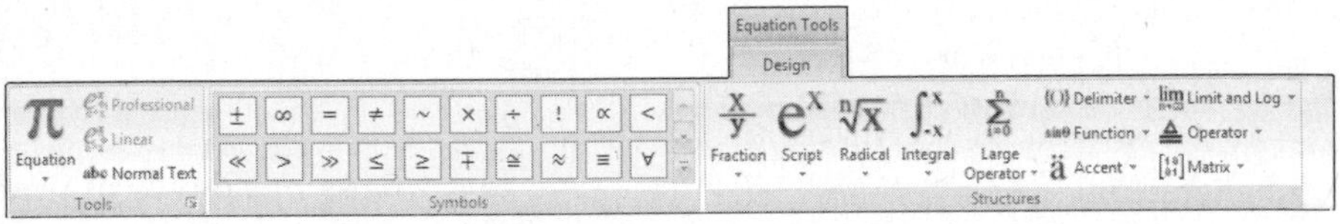

Figure 33-1:
Somewhere
in here is
the formula
for artificial
gravity.

Math

Equations are merely graphical decorations in your text. But when you really want Word to do math for you, it can — not the "Taylor series expansion of *e* to the *x*" type of equations, although some simple math isn't beyond Word's reach.

f Formula   Word's math is primarily done in tables, and it's basically a subset of some simple math formulas found in Excel worksheets. After creating a table, click the Table Tools Layout tab and locate the Formula button in the Data group. Clicking that button displays a Formula dialog box, from which you can paste into the table various functions that do interesting things with numbers in the table.

For example, to calculate the total of a column of numbers, click in the bottom cell in that column, choose the Formula command, and insert the =SUM(ABOVE) function. Word automatically calculates the total. If the values change, right-click in the cell and choose Update Field from the pop-up menu.

Document Defense Options

There are several places in Word where you can protect your document from being modified. The aptly named Protect Document command button on the Review tab is one of them, as are certain commands on the Prepare submenu on the Office button's menu. Both these places offer tempting options that I strongly recommend you avoid. They can lead to trouble.

Yes, there's an advantage to protecting your document. Yes, it's possible to lock up anything you create with Word so that only you can open it. Don't do it. That's because when (not *if,* but *when*) you lose the password or forget how to open the locked document, *you are screwed.* No one can help you. Not Microsoft. Not myself. No one. That's why I believe it's better just not to mess with those options.

There's a difference between protecting a document in Office and having a Word document flagged as read-only in Windows. Read-only in Windows is a *file attribute.* It can be set or removed by using the file's Properties dialog box: Right-click the file icon and choose Properties from the pop-up menu. That's not the same as protecting a document in Word, which cannot be so easily undone.

Hyphenation

Hyphenation is an automatic feature that splits a long word at the end of a line to make the text fit better on the page. Most people leave this feature turned off because hyphenated words tend to slow down the pace at which people read. However, if you want to hyphenate a document, click the Page Layout tab, Page Setup group, and choose Hyphenation⇨Automatic.

Hyphenation works best with paragraph formatting set to full justification.

Document Properties

When your company (or government agency) gets too big, there's a need for too much information. Word happily obliges by providing you with a sheet full of fill-in-the-blanks goodness to tell you all about your document and divulge whatever information you care to know about who worked on what and for how long. It's called the *document properties.*

To eagerly fill in any document's properties, click the Office button and choose Prepare⇨Properties to summon the Properties task pane. Fill in information as you see fit. The information can be used to track the document or used in the document itself: From the Insert tab's Text group, choose Quick Parts⇨ Properties to insert various property text information tidbits into a document.

The Developer Tab

Word's advanced, creepy features lie on a tab that's normally hidden from view: the Developer tab. To display the Developer tab, follow these steps:

1. **Choose Word Options from the Office Button menu.**

2. **Choose Popular from the list on the left in the Word Options dialog box.**

3. **Click to put a check mark by the option labeled Show Developer Tab in the Ribbon.**

4. **Click OK.**

The Developer tab is aptly named; it's best suited for those who either use Word to develop applications, special documents, and online forms or are hell-bent on customizing Word by using *macros*. A discussion of these subjects is well beyond the scope of this beginner's book.

To hide the Developer's tab, repeat the preceding steps and remove the check mark in Step 3.

Cross-References

The References tab sports a bunch of features that I don't touch on in this book, not the least of which is the Cross-Reference button in the Captions group. The Cross Reference command allows you to insert a "Refer to Chapter 99, Section Z" type of thing into your document. This feature works because you absorbed excess energy from the universe during a freak lightning storm and now you have an IQ that would make Mr. Spock envious. Anyway, the Cross-Reference dialog box, summoned by the Cross-Reference command, is the place where cross-referencing happens. Page 653 has more information about this feature.

Smart Tags

The Smart Tags feature was introduced back when literally four people were clamoring for such a feature. Fortunately, it now comes disabled in Word. When it's enabled, though, it underlines names, dates, places, and similar contact information with a dotted purple line. Pointing the mouse at any text underlined with purple dots displays a Smart Tag icon, from which you can choose a menu full of options that work only when you have Microsoft Outlook (not Outlook Express) on your computer and everything is configured by an expert.

Enabling Smart Tags involves some clever decision-making processes in the Word Options dialog box, in both the Advanced and Add-In areas. On the remote chance that you're in an office situation where Smart Tags can make a difference in your life, odds are that the thing is already configured and ready for you to use. Otherwise, I've wasted as much text as I care to on the silly subject of Smart Tags.

Click-and-Type

A feature introduced with Word 2002, one that I don't believe anyone ever uses, is *click-and-type*. In Print Layout mode, on a blank sheet of paper, it allows you to click the mouse anywhere on the page and type information at that spot. *Bam!*

I fail to see any value in click-and-type, especially when it's easier just to learn basic formatting. But click-and-type may bother you when you see any of its specialized mouse pointers displayed; thus:

I≞   I≞   I≞   ≞I

That's click-and-type in action, with the mouse pointer trying to tell you the paragraph format to be applied when you click the mouse.

The best news about click-and-type is that you can disable it: Choose Word Options from the Office Button menu. In the Word Options dialog box, choose Advanced from the left side. On the right side, in the Editing Options area, remove the check mark by Enable Click and Type. Click the OK button to rid yourself of this nuisance.

Word and the Internet

Microsoft went kind of kooky in the 1990s when Bill Gates suddenly realized that his company was behind the curve on the Internet. In response, many Microsoft programs, including Word, suddenly started to bud various Internet features, whether the features were relevant to the software's original intent or not. For example, Word has — even to this day — the ability to create Web pages or send e-mail.

Word is a great word processor. Word is a lousy e-mail program. Word is even worse at creating Web pages. Still, these features exist, and even more were added in Word 2007, including the ability for Word to be used to help you create an online Web log, or *blog*. Word also sports tools for collaborating with others on the same document by using some Internet let's-work-together feature that's really more a part of Microsoft Office than of Word itself.

Yes, I cover none of that stuff in this book. This book is about *word processing*. If you want software for e-mail, making Web pages, using an Internet fax, creating a blog, or finding pictures of famous celebrities in compromising poses on the Internet, you just have to look elsewhere.

Chapter 34

Ten Avuncular Suggestions

In This Chapter

▶ Keeping yourself supplied

▶ Using real-world references

▶ Organizing your files

▶ Knowing Windows

▶ Backing up your work

▶ Using AutoCorrect

▶ Memorizing keyboard shortcuts

▶ Exploring new ways of doing things

▶ Putting Word to work

▶ Relaxing your 'tude

I just can't let you leave this book without checking on a few things first. Just like Mom wouldn't let you run off to school without ensuring that you wore a sweater (especially when she was cold) and had your books, homework, lunch, and money for milk, I don't want you to leave this book without at least ten more pieces of loving, Word-friendly advice. This chapter is where that advice is found.

Keep Printer Paper, Toner, and Supplies Handy

The electronic office is a myth. Along with your word processor, you need some real-world office supplies. Keep them stocked. Keep them handy.

✔ When you buy paper, buy a box.

✔ When you buy a toner cartridge or printer ribbon, buy two or three.

✔ Keep a good stock of pens, paper, staples, paper clips, and all other office supplies handy.

Get Some References

Word is a writing tool. As such, you need to be familiar with, and obey, the grammatical rules of your language. If that language just happens to be English, you have a big job ahead of you. Even though a dictionary and a thesaurus are electronic parts of Word, I recommend that you keep a few references handy:

- ✔ Strunk and White's *Elements of Style* (Allyn & Bacon) is also a great book for finding out where apostrophes and commas go.

- ✔ Any good college or university dictionary is helpful. If the bound copy comes with a computer disc, all the better.

- ✔ Get a good thesaurus. (I love a good thesaurus. The one I use is from 1923. No electronic thesaurus I've seen has as many words in it.)

- ✔ Books containing common quotations, slang terms and euphemisms, common foreign words and phrases, and similar references are also good choices.

If you lack these books, visit the reference section of your local bookstore and plan on investing some good money to stock up on quality references.

Keep Your Computer Files Organized

Use folders on your hard drive for storing your document files. Keep related documents together in the same folders. Properly name your files so that you know what's in them.

One of the biggest problems with computers today is that millions of people use computers who have no concept of basic *computer science*. You can get a good dose from my *PCs For Dummies* (Wiley), but also consider taking a class on computer basics. You'll enjoy your computer more when you understand how to use it.

Know a Little Windows

Along with file organization, try to make an effort to learn a bit more about your computer, especially its operating system, Windows. For example, I highly recommend learning how Windows can help you find files on your computer. Unlike previous versions, Word 2007 no longer has a file searching command; you're expected to use Windows to do that.

Back Up Your Work

You should have two copies of everything you write, especially the stuff that you value and treasure. There's the original copy you keep on the computer's hard drive; this book tells you how to save that copy. A second copy, or backup, should also be made, one that doesn't live on the same disk drive as the original.

To back up your work, use a CD-R, DVD-R, USB thumb drive, flash drive, or network drive. You can back up files by simply copying them in Windows, though using a traditional backup program on a schedule is the best thing. Refer to my book *PCs For Dummies* (Wiley) for more information.

Use AutoCorrect

As you work in Word, you soon discover which words you enjoy misspelling the most. These words appear on the screen with a red zigzag underline. The common thing to do is to right-click the word and correct it by choosing a proper replacement from the pop-up list. I suggest that you go one step further and choose the AutoCorrect submenu and *then* choose the replacement word. With your oft-misspelled word in the AutoCorrect repertoire, you never have to fix the misspelling again. Well, either that or just learn how to spell the dumb word properly in the first place!

To quickly insert things you type over and over, like your name and address, use an AutoText entry. Type your entry once, and then define it as a glossary entry under the Edit menu. Then use the shortcut key to zap it in whenever you need it. See Chapter 8 for more about AutoText.

Use Those Keyboard Shortcuts

You should have a repertoire of keyboard shortcuts, representing many of the commands you use often. This book's Cheat Sheet, inside the front cover, lists a few, but also check in this book for shortcuts related to commands you use often. Though it may not seem so at first, using the keyboard is much faster than getting by with the mouse.

Try New Things

In Word, as in life, people get into habits and do things the same way over and over. Rather than fall into that trap, consider trying new things from time to time. For example, consider using a table rather than tabs to organize your stuff. If you're an ancient Word user from days gone by, try out some of the Quick Styles or mess around with a theme. Try to explore as much of Word as possible. You may learn a new trick or discover a faster way to get something done.

Let Word Do the Work

Word does amazing things. In fact, any time you feel that you're doing too much work in Word, there's probably an easier, faster way to get the same job done. Use this book's index or the Word help system to peruse the various tasks you undertake. You may be surprised that a shortcut exists, one that saves you time and makes your stuff look good.

Don't Take It All Too Seriously

Computers are really about having fun. Too many people panic too quickly when they use a computer. Don't let it get to you! And please, please, don't reinstall Word to fix a minor problem. Anything that goes wrong has a solution. If the solution isn't in this book, consult your computer guru. Someone is bound to be able to help you out.

Index

• Symbols •

* (asterisk), in searches, 69
^# (caret hash mark) searches, 71
^p (caret p)searches, 71
^? (caret question mark) searches, 71
^t (caret t) searches, 71
— (em) and – (en) dashes
  adding to documents, 303
  as special characters, 241
¶ (paragraph mark) in documents, 71
? (question mark), in searches, 69

• A •

accepting revisions, 337
Add to Dictionary command, 98
Add to Quick Style List, 221
address lists
  labels, 354
  mail merge, 340, 345–346
alignment. *See also* document formatting;
    paragraph formatting
  for documents on a page, 248
  multiple images, 300
  paragraphs, 157–158, 168, 170–174
  tab stops for, 168, 170–174
  text in table cells, 272
All Programs menu start up, 13–14
Alt key, 26
Alt+Ctrl+D key combination, 287
Alt+Ctrl+F key combination, 287
Alt+Ctrl+Shift+S key combination, 216, 220
Alt+H,K key combination, 166
Alt+P, P, S key combination, 188
Alt+Shift+# key combination, 327
Alt+Shift+- key combination, 327
Alt+Shift++ key combination, 327
Alt+Shift+1 key combination, 327
Alt+Shift+2 key combination, 327

Alt+Shift+A key combination, 327
Alt+Shift+D key combination, 245
Alt+Shift+→/← key combinations, 325, 327
Alt+Shift+T key combination, 245
Alt+Shift+↑/↓ key combinations, 326, 327
Alt+Tab key combination, 312
Any Character, Any Digit, Any Letter
    searches, 70–71
Apply Styles task pane, 218
Arrange All button (View tab), 313
Arrange group
  Bring to Front/Send to Back options, 299
  Position Command button, 296
  Rotate menu, 299
arrow keys
  document navigation, 50
  with outlines, 325, 327
  table navigation, 269
asterisk (*), in searches, 69
At least line spacing (Paragraph dialog
    box), 160
Attach Template dialog box, 236
AutoComplete, 34
AutoCorrect
  accessing, 243
  adding entries, 102–103
  benefits of using, 387
  building fractions using, 372–373
  enabling/disabling, 243–244
  how it works, 101
  icon for, 103
  indentation using, 162
  undoing corrections, 103
AutoFormat
  borders, 242
  disabling, 243–244
  features and uses, 239–240
  numbered lists, 241–242
  undoing formatting, 242–243
automatic hyphenation, 381

automatic page numbering, 190, 369
automatic startup, 13
Automatically Update Document Styles
    option, 236
autoproofing, 98
AutoRecover, 371–372
AutoShape
  accessing and using, 292–293
  inserting pictures or text into, 293–294

• B •

back to front printing, 130
back ups, 387
background colors, 194–195, 259–260
Backspace key, 27, 30, 56
Balloons menu
  Show All Revisions Inline option, 333
  Show Revisions in Balloons option, 333
bar tabs, 178
Behind Text wrapping option, 295
blank area of window, 17, 19–20
Blank Document option (Office Button
    menu), 113
blank pages
  inserting at end of documents, 192–193
  inserting within documents, 193–194
  removing, 132
Blank Template document form, 234
Block Text style, 215
blocks of text
  copying, 87
  defined, 80
  deleting, 58
  deselecting, 86
  Highlighting mode, 335
  linked copy, 90
  moving, 88, 90–91
  printing, 134
  selecting, 80–85
blue underlines, 34
blue zigzag underlines, 33
bolding text, 142
Book Title style, 215
Bookmark dialog box, 373–374
bookmarks, electronic, 373

Border command button/menu, 254–255
borders
  AutoFormatting feature, 242
  features and uses, 253–254
  horizontal lines, 256
  line size options, 256
  margin settings, 256–257
  page borders, 258–259
  removing, 259
  in tables, 270–271
  title boxes, 257
Borders and Shading dialog box
  accessing, 255
  creating line rules, 256
  Page Border tab, 258
  Shading panel, 260
Breaks menu. *See also* sections, section
    breaks
  accessing, 199
  creating new sections, 200
Bring to Front/Send to Back options, 299
Browse Up/Browse Down buttons, 52–53, 67
browsing palette, 52, 53
bulleted lists
  automatic creation, 242
  creating, 280
  line spacing, 161
  styles for, 212
Bullets menu access, 279

• C •

capitalization
  Caps Lock key, 27
  case changes, 151
  drop caps, 374–375
Caption style, 215
Captions group, 382
caret hash mark (^#) searches, 71
caret p (^p) searches, 71
caret question mark (^?) searches, 71
caret t (^t) searches, 71
case changes, 151
Categories list (fields)
  Document Information, 246
  Numbering, 245

NumPages, 247
PrintDate, 247
cells
   aligning text in, 272
   defined, 262
   deleting, 271
   merging, 270–271
   resizing, 268
   splitting, 271
center alignment
   for documents on pages, 248
   paragraph formatting, 157
Center command, 154
center tab stop, 173–174
Change Back to . . . option (AutoCorrect),
   103
Change Styles button, 219
Changes group, 337–338
characters
   deleting, 56
   with diacritical symbols, 302–303
   forbidden, 118
   index code, 284
   nonprinting, hiding/showing, 168
   searches using, 69, 71
   special, keyboard shortcuts for, 71
   special, viewing, 70–71
   styles for, 212–213
Choose a SmartArt Graphic dialog box, 307
Clear All button
   clipboard, 93
   tabs, 182
clear formatting
   command button for, 219–220
   keyboard shortcut for, 150
click-and-type, 20, 383
clip art
   deleting, 294
   locating and inserting, 205, 291–292
Clip Art task pane, 291–292
Clipboard
   cleaning, 93
   copying and pasting using, 87, 92–93
   task pane, 91–93
Close command
   for documents, 23–24, 44
   keyboard shortcut, 24

closing Word program, 22–23
collating documents, 135
color
   adding to SmartArt, 308
   in backgrounds, 194–195, 259–260
   colored text, 34, 146–147
   in themes, 228, 230
Column breaks, 200, 277
Columns dialog box
   accessing, 274
   format options, 275–276
   This Point Forward option, 276
columns (documents)
   aligning numbers in, 177
   columned lists, 170–171
   ending within document, 277
   full justification, 158
   landscape mode, 186
   overview and tips, 273–275
   removing, 277
columns (tables)
   creating, 263–266, 268
   deleting, 271
   deleting or inserting, 271–272
   formatting, 274–276
   Mail Merge fields as, 346
   overview, 262
   resizing, 272
command buttons
   Quick Access toolbar, 361–363
   in Word window groups, 18
commands deleted from Word 2007, 2
comments
   adding to documents, 331–333
   Comments command access, 331
   deleting, 334
   hiding/showing, 333
   printing, 334
   reviewing and navigating, 333–334
   viewing in balloons, 333
Comments group, 333
comparing documents
   Compare Documents dialog box, 336
   comparison process, 336–337
   reviewing changes, 337–338
content controls, 245
Continuous section breaks, 200

Control AutoCorrect Options, 103
Convert Table to Text dialog box, 267
Convert Text to Table dialog box, 266
copying
  character formatting, 249
  Clipboard for, 91–93
  text blocks, 87
Cover Page menu
  layout options, 201
  tips for using, 202
Create button, 37–38
Create New Style from Formatting
    dialog box
  accessing, 221
  Style for Following Paragraph list, 222
  Style Type list, 223
cropping images, 298–299
Cross-Reference feature, 382
Ctrl key, 26, 27
Ctrl+@+a key combination, 302
Ctrl+,+c key combination, 302
Ctrl+= key combination, 143, 150
Ctrl+- key combination, 303
Ctrl++ key combination, 143
Ctrl+↓ key combination, 51
Ctrl+← key combination, 51
Ctrl+→ key combination, 51
Ctrl+↑ key combination, 51
Ctrl+/+o key combination, 302
Ctrl+`+vowel key combination, 302
Ctrl+^+vowel key combination, 302
Ctrl+:+vowel key combination, 302
Ctrl+'+vowel key combination, 302
Ctrl+~+a, o, or n key combination, 302
Ctrl+0 key combination, 166
Ctrl+1 key combination, 159, 166
Ctrl+2 key combination, 159, 166
Ctrl+5 key combination, 159, 166
Ctrl+A key combination, 85, 155
Ctrl+Alt+PgDn key combination, 52
Ctrl+Alt+PgUp key combination, 52
Ctrl+B key combination, 150
Ctrl+C key combination, 87
Ctrl+E key combination, 154, 157, 166
Ctrl+End key combination, 51, 132
Ctrl+Enter key combination, 192

Ctrl+G key combination, 53
Ctrl+Home key combination, 51
Ctrl+I key combination, 140, 150
Ctrl+J key combination, 158, 166
Ctrl+L key combination, 154, 157, 166
Ctrl+M key combination, 163
Ctrl+N key combination, 322
Ctrl+O key combination, 121
Ctrl+P key combination, 129
Ctrl+R key combination, 157, 166
Ctrl+S key combination, 119
Ctrl+Shift+= key combination, 143, 150, 373
Ctrl+Shift+> key combination, 145
Ctrl+Shift+< key combination, 146
Ctrl+Shift+- key combination, 302
Ctrl+Shift+A key combination, 150
Ctrl+Shift+C key combination, 249
Ctrl+Shift+D key combination, 150
Ctrl+Shift+E key combination, 338
Ctrl+Shift+F8 key combination, 201
Ctrl+Shift+H key combination, 150
Ctrl+Shift+M key combination, 166
Ctrl+Shift+N key combination, 327
Ctrl+Shift+spacebar key combination, 302
Ctrl+Shift+T key combination, 166
Ctrl+Shift+V key combination, 249
Ctrl+Shift+W key combination, 150
Ctrl+Shift+Z key combination, 148
Ctrl+spacebar key combination, 148,
    150, 219
Ctrl+T key combination, 154, 162–163
Ctrl+Tab key combination, 269
Ctrl+U key combination, 143, 150
Ctrl+V key combination, 87
Ctrl+W key combination, 120
Ctrl+X key combination, 88
Ctrl+Y key combination, 61, 63
Ctrl+Z key combination, 61
Current Page option (print options), 133
cursors
  with Backspace key, 30, 57
  cursor-movement keys, 26, 50–52, 274
  with Delete key, 57
  with find and replace, 69
  insertion pointer, 17, 28
  paintbrush, 249

text block selection using, 84
when typing, 38
Custom Margins button, 186
CUSTOM.DIC dictionary file, 100–101
customizing Word
overview, 19
Quick Access toolbar, 360–363
Status Bar Configuration options, 359–360
Zoom tool, 357–359

• D •

Data Source file (mail merge), 346
dates
adding to headers or footers, 205
content controls, 245
current, inserting in documents, 247
Date & Time dialog box, 247
decimal tabs, 177–178
defaults
fonts, 149
margin settings, 186
NORMAL.DOTM, 237
paste options, 89
style sets, 219
tab stops, 181
Delete key, 27, 30, 56
demoting outline topics, 324–326
deselecting text blocks, 86
Design tab, 205
desktop publishing (DTP), 274, 275
desktop shortcut to Word 2007, 13–14
Developer tab, 382
diacritical symbols, characters with, 302–303
dictionary (spell checker)
adding words to, 98–99
removing words from, 100–101
Different First Page option (headers), 207
disks, saving documents to, 117
dividers, text, 178
document formatting. See also page
numbers; styles; themes
columns, 273–277
cover pages, 201–202
graphics placement options, 294

headers and footers, 202–209
numbering text lines, 281
overview, 38–39, 192
page alignment, 248
placing graphics in, 294–296
Quick Styles, 214–216
sections, 197–201
styles overview, 211–212
templates, 230–237
themes, 227–230
document information, 17, 246
Document Inspection, 374
Document Map view, 375–376
document properties, 381–382
Document Recovery task pane, 19, 372
Document Showing Markup option (Print
dialog box), 334
Document Views group, 322
documents. See also document formatting;
editing text; typing
adding new blank pages to, 193–194
closing after saving, 23–24
closing without saving, 120
comparing versions, 335–338
creating tables from tabbed text, 266
current date and time displays, 247
defined, 15
deleting pages from, 57, 59
as files, 112
hard page breaks, 192–193
inserting fields into, 244–245
insertion pointer, 28
inspecting, 374
multiple, viewing and using, 311–314
navigating, 51
new from Blank Document, 37, 113–114
new from templates, 114–115
nonprinting characters, enabling/
disabling, 33
in non-Word file formats, 317–318
in older Word file formats, 319–320
opening existing documents, 120–122
opening in a single window, 37
opening in multiple windows, 314–315
outlines, 322–328
page break indictors, 32–33

documents *(continued)*
    paper size options, 184–185
    previewing before printing, 42, 126–128
    printing options, 128–130, 132–133
    proofing, 42, 104–105
    protecting, 381
    removing blank pages from end of, 132
    saving, 39–41, 115–118, 119–120
    selecting entire document, 85
    size of, 113
    spell checking, 96–101
    splitting, 315–316
    updating and resaving, 118–119
    view options, 32–33
    viewing names of, 15, 41
    viewing styles used in, 218–219
    watermarks, 195–196
    word wrap, 29
    zigzag underlines in, 33–34
Documents folder, 15–16
Draft view
    comments in, 332
    footnotes and endnotes, 287
    function, 19–20
    page break indictors, 32
    section breaks in, 200
dragging. *See also* mouse
    elevator buttons, 48
    mouse cursor, 82–83
drag-move/drag-copy features, 90
Draw Borders group, 270–271
Draw Table window, 264–266
Drawing Tools menu, 296
drop caps
    Drop Cap dialog box, 375
    uses for, 374–375
DTP (desktop publishing), 274, 275

• E •

editing graphics. *See also* graphics
    cropping, 298–299
    resizing images, 298
    rotating images, 299
    WordArt text, 305

Editing group
    accessing from Ribbon, 65
    command buttons, 66
    Find button, 66
    Home tab, 66
editing text. *See also* text blocks; text
        formatting
    address lists, 346
    deleting, 55–59
    joining, 60
    mail merge recipients list, 346
    marks and conventions for, 33–34
    mouse pointer shape, 20
    selection options, 85
    in SmartArt inserts, 308
    splitting, 59
    text wrap points, 296
    Undo and Redo commands, 60–61
    words in custom dictionaries, 101
electronic bookmarks, 373–374
elevator button (scroll bars), 48
em (—) dashes
    adding to documents, 303
    as special characters, 241
e-mail messages
    mail merging, 340
    using Word for, pros and cons, 384
Emphasis style, 215–216
en (–) dashes
    adding to documents, 303
    formatting, 241
Encarta dictionary access, 108
End key, 51
endnotes
    adding to documents, 286–287
    deleting, 287
Enter character, 60
Enter key
    locating, 27
    in table navigation, 269
    when to use, 28–29, 368, 369
envelopes, printing, 376
equations, 379–380
Eraser command (Draw Borders), 270–271
Esc key, 27
Even Page/Odd Page section breaks, 200

Exactly line spacing (paragraphs), 160
Excel (Microsoft) spreadsheets, copying text from, 90
exiting Word program, 22–23
exporting styles, 226
extended selection mode, 84

• F •

F1 key, 21
F2 key, 91
F4 key, 63
F5 key, 374
F8 key
  marking text, 84–85
  when deleting a page, 59
F9 key, 245
fields, document
  adding to headers or footers, 205
  adjusting/managing, 246
  inserting into documents, 244–246
  updating, 246
  uses for, 244
fields, mail merge
  adding and deleting, 344
  assigning to documents, 343–345
  filling with records, 346
  function, 340
  inserting into main document, 347
  for labels, 354
file attributes, 381
file formats, filename extensions
  for documents, 118
  for graphics, 291
  non-Word file formats, 317–318
  older Word files, 319–320
  PDF/XPS files, 318
  templates, 231
  viewing, 317
  Word 2007 documents, 39–40
File Name box, 116
files. *See also* documents
  inserting graphics from, 290–291
  inserting text from, 123
  locations for, 116–117
  overview, 111–112

Files of Type drop-down list, 317
Fill palette, 260
Find and Replace dialog box
  accessing, 66
  Any Character, Any Digit, and Any Letter searches, 70–71
  Find All Word Forms (English) option, 69
  Find Next button, 66–67
  Find What box, 66–67, 72–73
  Find Whole Words Only option, 68
  finding formatting, 72–73
  font selections, 73
  Go To tab, 53
  replacing formatting, 76–77
  replacing text, 74–75
  Search Options area, 68–69
  with selected text and text blocks, 81
  Sounds Like (English) option, 69
  Special button, 70–71
  Superfind features, 67–70
  using, 66–67
  White Spaces searches, 71
Finish & Merge button (mail merge)
  document merges, 349
  label merges, 354
Font group
  basic text formatting, 140–141
  Change Case command, 151
  character formatting, 142–143
  Clear Formatting command, 148
  Font dialog box access, 148–149
  Highlighting mode, 335
  Home tab, 140–145, 335
  Text Highlight button, 335
  Write tab, 141
fonts
  color, 146–147
  size options, 144–146
  style options, 141
  in themes, 228, 230
  viewing list of, 141–142
Fonts group, 141–142
footers
  adding to documents, 203–204
  deleting, 209
  with document sections, 207–209

footers *(continued)*
 editing, 204–206
 footnotes versus, 202
 odd and even, 206–207
 removing, 209
footnotes
 creating, 286–287
 deleting, 287
 footers versus, 202
foreign languages, special characters in,
  302–303
Format dialog box, 224
Format Painter, 249
Format tab
 Arrange group, 296, 299
 Drawing Tools menu, 296–297
 Insert Shapes group, 294, 306
 Shape Styles group, 293
 Text Wrapping menu, 295–296
formatting. *See also* document formatting;
  paragraph formatting; text formatting
 AutoFormat, 239–244
 fields, 244–247
 Find and Replace for, 72–73, 76–77
 Format Painter, 249
 new features in Word 2007, 1–2
 special content indicators, 245
 styles, 211–225
 tables, 270–272
 templates, 230–237
 themes, 227–230
fractions
 creating custom, 372–373
 formatting options, 240
Full Page of the Same Label button, 353
Full Screen Reading view, 328–329
function keys, 26. *See also* keyboard
  shortcuts

• *G* •

Go to Header/Go to Footer commands, 204
Go To tab, 53–54
Gookin, Dan (*PCs For Dummies*), 7, 41,
  112, 126
grammar checker, 104

graphics
 adding to headers or footers, 205
 adding to mail labels, 355–356
 AutoFormat feature, 292–294
 clip art, 205, 291–292, 294
 cropping, 298–299
 deleting, 294
 editing tools, 297
 framing using AutoShapes, 293–294
 inserting from file, 290–291
 linking and unlinking to text, 296–297
 moving, 296
 moving within documents, 296
 multiple images, managing, 299–300
 overview, 289
 placing in documents, 290, 294
 resizing, 298
 rotating, 299
 shape-drawing tools, 292–293
 in themes, 228
greeking, 358
green zigzag underline, 33, 104
gridlines
 in tables, 270
 for viewing graphics, 300
groups, 18
Grow Font command, 145
gutter (columns), 277

• *H* •

handles
 border and line management, 256
 for resizing images, 296, 298
 for rotating images, 299
 wrap points, 296
hanging indents, 154, 162–163
hard page breaks, 192–193
Header & Footer group, 190–191, 203–209
headers
 adding to documents, 203–204
 deleting, 209
 for document sections, 207–208
 editing, 204–206
 headings versus, 202
 odd and even, 206–207

removing, 209
showing/hiding on first page, 207
headings
  headers versus, 202
  Heading 1/Heading 2 styles, 215–216
help system, 17, 21–22, 388
hidden text, 150, 377
highlighter tool, 334–335
Home key, 26, 51
Home tab
  Font group, 335
  paragraph formatting commands, 155
  Paragraph group, 377
  Styles group, 214, 219
Horizontal Line command (Border
    command button/menu), 256
horizontal scroll bar, 49
HTML Web pages
  copying text from, 90
  horizontal line tags, 256
hyperlinks, formatting options, 240
hyphens
  disabling autohyphenation, 381
  inserting in documents, 301–302

• I •

icons
  AutoCorrect, 162
  AutoFormat, 241
  browse buttons, 52
  Browse Up/Browse Down buttons, 67
  character formatting, 142
  Demote command, 325
  Demote to Body Text button, 326
  for expanded and collapsed topics, 327
  for files, 112
  font color, 146
  Format Painter, 249
  Full Screen Reading view, 328–329
  Move Up/Move Down, 326
  Paste Options, 88–89
  Position Command, 296
  printer, 136
  Promote command, 325
  Reveal Formatting, 219

for reviewing and navigating comments,
    333–334
Rotate menu, 299
on the Ruler, 165, 169
Save, 119
strikethroughs, 143
subscripts and superscripts, 143
Table Layout tab, 271–272
text attributes, summary, 150
Top button/Bottom button, 256
underlining text, 143
undoing formatting, 148
whole paragraph indents, 163
Zoom tools, 358
Ignore All command (spell checker),
    98–100
Illustrations group
  AutoShape feature, 293
  Clip Art task pane, 291–292
  Insert Picture dialog box, 290
  SmartArt feature, 307–308
images. *See* graphics
importing styles, 226
In Front of Text wrapping option, 295
In Line With Text wrapping option, 295
indenting paragraphs
  automatic increasing/decreasing, 163
  first line indents, 161–162
  hanging indents, 162–163
  tab key for, 168
Index code, 284
Index dialog box, 285–286
indexes
  creating, 285–286
  overview, 283
  selecting and marking, 283–284
  updating, 286
in-line graphics placement, 290
Insert Footnote/Insert Endnote command,
    287
Insert mode, 62
Insert Picture dialog box, 290
Insert Shapes group, 294, 306
Insert tab
  Drop Cap dialog box, 375
  Field dialog box, 244–246

Insert tab *(continued)*
  Header & Footer group, 190, 203–207, 209
  Illustrations group, 290–293, 307–308
  Links group, 373–374
  Pages group, 201–202
  Quick Parts feature, 205, 244, 245
  Symbol menu, 303
  Text group, 123, 247, 305, 306
Insert Table dialog box, 263–264
inserting text from files, 123
insertion point, pointers. *See also* cursors
  extended selection mode, 84
  impact of scrolling on, 49
  moving using keyboard, 50–51
  moving using mouse, 50
  pasting text, 87
  returning to original position, 53
  splitting text using, 59, 60
inspecting documents, 374
instant previews, 1
Intense Emphasis style, 215
Intense Quote style, 215
Intense Reference style, 215
italicizing text, 140, 142–143

• *J* •

joining text, 60
justifying paragraphs, 157

• *K* •

Keep Source Formatting paste option, 89
Keep Text Only paste option, 89
keyboard
  document navigation, 50–52
  keys and layout, 26–27
keyboard shortcuts
  accessing bookmarks, 374
  benefits of using, 368, 372, 387
  case changes, 151
  characters with diacriticals, 302–303
  Clear Formatting command, 219–220
  Close command, 24
  closing documents without saving, 120
  content controls, 245

copying character formatting, 249
copying text, 87
creating shortcut keys, 224–225
demoting/promoting topics in outlines, 325
em or en dashes, 303
footnotes and endnotes, 287
growing and shrinking fonts, 145–146
hanging indents, 162–163
italicizing text, 140
line spacing, 159
moving text, 88
navigating documents, 50–52
new blank document, 322
new page break, 192
nonbreaking spaces and hyphens, 302
opening documents, 121
outlines, 327
Page Setup dialog box, 188
paragraph formatting, 33, 154, 157–158, 166
PgUp/PgDn keys, 51–52
printing documents, 129
rearranging outline topics, 326
redo command, 63
Replace command, 75
returning to last edited spot, 53
Reveal Formatting command, 219
save command, 41
saving documents, 119
selecting entire documents, 85
selecting text and text blocks, 81
Show/Hide command, 201
soft returns, 60
special characters, 71
Style task pane, 216
subscripts and superscripts, 143
for switching between documents, 312
table navigation, 269
text formatting, 150
Track Changes tool, 338
Undo and Redo commands, 61
undoing formatting, 148
viewing, 225
whole paragraph indents, 163
Word Help access, 21

• L •

labels
  adding graphics to, 355–356
  identical, printing sheets of, 351–352
  mail merge approach, 353–354
Labels and Envelopes dialog box
  accessing, 352
  Label section, 353
  Print section, 353
landscape mode, 185–186
Layout tab (page setup), 248, 267
leader tabs, 180–181
left alignment (paragraphs), 157
Left justified command, 154
left tab stop
  for lists, 170–171
  setting, 168–170
  for tab-tab paragraphs, 172–173
letters
  Mail Merge for, 339–350
  printing envelopes for, 376
Line Numbers menu, 281
line spacing options
  custom settings, 159–161
  summary, 166
  traditional line spacing, 158–159
lines
  borders versus, 253
  margin settings, 256–257
  removing from documents, 259
  removing from tables, 270
  text dividers, 178
  thick, drawing around text, 256
  title boxes, 257
lines of text, selecting/deleting, 57, 58
linked copy, 90
linked style, 212
Links group, 373–374
List Paragraph style, 215
lists
  bulleted, 280
  combining right and left stops, 175–176
  decimal tabs for, 177–178
  numbered, 241–242, 280
  right tab stops in, 176–177
  styles for, 212
  tabbed entries for, 170
  tab-tab paragraphs, 172–173
locked scrolling, 314

• M •

macros, 231, 236, 382
mail merge
  address lists, 340, 345–346
  data source file, 346
  fields, 340, 343–345
  inserting fields into main document, 347
  for labels, 353–355
  main document, 339, 341–342
  previewing and running results, 348–350
  process overview, 339–341
Mail Merge Recipients dialog box, 346
Mail Merge task pane, 341–350
Mail Merge Wizard, 341
Mailings tab
  Envelopes and Labels dialog box, 352, 376
  Preview Results group, 348
  Select Recipients menu, 343
  Start Mail Merge menu, 343, 346–347,
    353–354
main document (mail merge)
  assigning fields, 343–345
  creating, 341–342
  function, 339
  inserting fields and data, 347
Manage Styles dialog box (Styles task
    pane), 226
margin settings. *See also* alignment
  for lines and borders, 256–257, 258
  page margins, 165, 186–189
  for paragraphs, 163–164
  previewing before printing, 127–128
  using the Ruler, 18, 165
Margins tab
  accessing, 186
  Pages area, 188
  settings, 188–189
  Whole Document option, 189
Mark Index Entry dialog box, 283–284
markup area, showing/hiding, 333

Match Case option (find and replace), 68
Match Destination Formatting (pasting), 89
math and calculation tools, 380
Maximize button, 16
Merge To dialog box, 354
merging cells in tables, 270–271
Microsoft Excel spreadsheets, copying text
from, 90
Microsoft Office Button menu
accessing, 18
Blank Template form, 234
Close command, 23, 44
Exit Word command, 22–23
New command, 37, 113–114
Open dialog box, 120–121, 317, 320
Prepare tab, Inspect Document, 374
Print command, 42–43, 131, 136
Print Preview command, 42–43
proofing tools, 100, 106
Quick Print feature, 131
Save As dialog box, 40, 116, 233, 317
Save command, 40
viewing recently opened files, 122
Word Options command, 85, 168, 243, 377
Microsoft Outlook, copying addresses
from, 340
Mini Toolbar
Highlight button, 335
paragraph-formatting buttons, 156
quick formatting using, 98
showing/hiding, 82
text-formatting buttons, 141
Minimize button, 24
Minimize Ribbon command, 19
misspelled words. *See also* spell checking
tools
common, 100
correcting using AutoCorrect, 101–103
correcting using right-clicking, 97
More Layout Options (Text Wrapping
menu), 296–297
mouse
deleting text, 58
managing tables, 267–268
managing wrap points, 296
moving images, 296

moving insertion pointer, 50
moving text, 90
rearranging outline topics, 326
scrolling using, 49
selecting text, 82–83
zooming, 359
mouse pointer
click-and-type mode, 20
during copy and move actions, 90
in table-related operations, 268
during text entry, 20–21
when choosing objects, 20
multiple documents
switching between, 312–313
using, 311–312, 370
viewing simultaneously, 313
Multiple line spacing, 160
multiple windows, viewing documents in,
314–315

• *N* •

naming. *See also* file formats, filename
extensions
custom styles, 221
documents, 15, 22, 39–40, 118
mail merge fields, 345
templates, 233
navigating documents
browse buttons, 52–53
footnotes and endnotes, 287
in Full Screen Reading view, 329
Go To command, 53–54
moving insertion pointer, 50–52
scrolling, 48–49
navigating tables, 268–269
New Address List dialog box, 345–346
New command, 37, 113–115
New Comment button, 332
New Document window
Blank Document option, 113–114
Create button, 37–38
New from Existing option, 115
placing labels in, 353
template options, 114–115
new page break, 192

New Style button, 221
New Window button, 314–315
No Formatting button (find and replace), 72
No Spacing style, 215
nonbreaking spaces, 301–302
nonprinting characters, 33, 168
non-Word file formats
  loading documents using, 317–318
  saving documents using, 319
  viewing, 317
Normal style
  accessing and using, 215–216
  reapplying, 220
  template for, 231, 236–237
Num Lock key, 26, 51
numbered lists
  AutoFormatting for, 241–242
  creating from Numbering menu, 280
Numbering field, 246
numbering text lines, 281
numbers. *See also* page numbers
  decimal tabs, 177–178
  fractions, 240, 372–373
  math and calculation tools, 380
  numeric keypad, 26
  ordinals, 240
  searches using, 71
NumPages field, 247
NumWords field, 247

• O •

Object command, 123
odd and even headers/footers, 206–207
Office Button menu
  accessing, 18
  Blank Template form, 234
  Close command, 23, 44
  Exit Word command, 22–23
  New command, 37, 113–114
  Open dialog box, 120–121, 317, 320
  Prepare tab, Inspect Document, 374
  Print command, 42–43, 131, 136
  Print Preview command, 42–43
  proofing tools, 100, 106

Quick Print feature, 131
  Save As dialog box, 40, 116, 233, 317
  Save command, 40
  viewing recently opened files, 122
  Word Options command, 85, 168, 243, 377
office supplies, 385
Open dialog box
  Convert to Word 2007 option, 320
  opening Word 2007 documents, 120–121
  viewing non-Word file types, 317
opening documents
  inside another document, 122–123
  using Open dialog box, 120–121
  using recently opened files list, 122
ordinals, formatting options, 240
Organizer dialog box, 226
orienting text
  for printing, 185–186
  in table cells, 272
Outline view
  enabling/disabling, 323
  Show Level list, 327–328
outlines
  creating new outlines, 322
  demoting topics, 325
  expanding and contracting, 326–328
  keyboard shortcuts summary table, 327
  main topics, 323–324
  printing, 328
  promoting topics, 325
  rearranging topics, 326
  subtopics, 324–325
  text topics, 326
Outlook (Microsoft), copying addresses
    from, 340
Overtype mode, 62

• P •

Page Background group
  Page Color command button, 194
  Watermark menu, 195–196
page borders, 258–259
Page Color command button, 194
page count feature, 247

Page Layout tab. *See also* Page Setup
 dialog box
 Breaks command button, 199
 Margins menu, 186
 Page Background group, 194
 Paragraph After command, 160–161
 paragraph formatting commands, 155
page numbers
 adding to headers or footers, 205
 adding using fields, 246
 automatic, 190, 369
 customizing, 190–191
 document sections, 198–199
 removing, 192
 Roman numerals, 192
Page Range section (printing), 133–134
Page Setup dialog box
 accessing and using, 188–189, 248, 267
 Center from the Vertical Alignment
  list, 248
 Columns button, 274
 Line Numbers menu, 281
 Margins tab, 186
 orientation settings, 185
Page Up/Page Down (PgUp/PgDn) keys,
 26, 51–52
Page Width command, 358
Pages area, 188
Pages group, 201–202
pages, deleting from documents, 57, 59
pagination. *See* page numbers
paper
 for printing, 130
 size options, 184–185
 text orientation, 185–186
Paragraph button, 33
Paragraph dialog box
 accessing, 156
 Indentation area, 161–164
 Line Spacing, 158–159
 the Ruler, 164–165
 Spacing area, 159–160
paragraph formatting
 alignment options, 157–158
 bar tabs, 178
 borders, 253–255

bullets and numbers, 177–178, 280
center tab with, 173–174
commands and shortcuts, 155–156, 166
custom styles, 221–222
drop caps, 374–375
Format Painter, 249
indenting lines, 168
indenting whole paragraphs, 163
line spacing options, 158–161
margin settings, 163–164
overview, 153–155
Quick Styles for, 215
space between paragraphs, 160–161
styles overview, 211–213
tab-tab paragraphs, 172–173
Paragraph group
 command buttons, 155–156, 254
 Home tab, 33, 145, 155–156, 377
 Page Layout tab, 163–164
 Sort Text dialog box, 377
 Write tab, 150, 160–161
paragraph mark (¶) in documents, 71
paragraph symbol (^p) searches, 71
paragraphs. *See also* paragraph formatting
 defined, 154
 deleting, 57, 58
 soft returns, 60
 widows and orphans, 194
Paste Options icon, 88–89
Paste Special dialog box, 89–90
pasting text
 special pasting, 89–90
 text blocks, 87
PCs For Dummies (Gookin), 7, 41, 112, 126
PDF (Portable Document Format) files, 318
PgUp/PgDn (Page Up/Page Down) keys,
 26, 51–52
Picture button, 205
Plain Text style, 215
poke-and-point text selection method, 83
portrait mode, 185–186
Position Command button, 296
Preview Results command button, 348
previewing
 documents before printing, 42, 126–128,
  203, 277

fonts, 142
mail merge results, 348
Print Background Colors and Images
    option, 195
Print command
  accessing, 42–43
  canceling print jobs, 136
  Print Preview mode, 42–43
  Quick Print feature, 131
Print dialog box
  Document Showing Markup option, 334
  Page Range section, 133–134
  Properties dialog box options, 130
  Selection item, 134
  viewing and selecting printers, 131–132
Print Layout view
  function, 19
  for graphics, 290
  hard page breaks, 193
  header and footer displays, 203
  mount pointer in, 20
  page break indictors, 32–33
  previewing lines and borders, 257, 258
  viewing document columns, 275
  when making comments, 331
  for working with tables, 262
Print Preview mode
  benefits of using, 42
  viewing columns using, 277
  viewing documents, 126–128
  viewing headers and footers, 203
PrintDate field, 247
printers
  canceling print jobs, 136
  preparing for printing, 125–126
  turning on, 370
  viewing and selecting, 131–132
printing documents
  adding print date, 247
  back-to-front printing, 130
  canceling print jobs, 135–136
  color printing, 195
  comments in, 334
  envelopes, 376
  highlighted text, 335
  labels, 353

multiple copies, 134–135
outlines, 328
overview, 42–43
page ranges, 132–134
previewing before printing, 126–128
printing options, 129
text blocks, 134
watermarks, 195–196
whole documents, 128–130
proofing documents
  customizing proofing options, 106
  entire documents at one time, 104–105
  grammar checking, 104
  importance of, 42
  Research task pane, 108–109
  spell checking, 96–101, 105
  Spelling and Grammar button, 105
Proofing group/tools
  Custom Dictionaries, 100
  customizing proofing options, 106
  Spelling and Grammar button, 105
Properties task pane, 381–382
Protect Document feature, 381
pull quotes, 306
purple dots, 34

• Q •

question mark (?), in searches, 69
Quick Access toolbar
  adding command buttons, 361–363
  customizing, 19
  finding, 360–361
  moving, 361
  removing command buttons, 363
  restoring/resetting, 363
  Save icon, 119
Quick Launch Toolbar, 14
Quick Parts feature
  Field option, 205, 244
  Properties command, 245
Quick Print feature, 131
Quick Styles
  accessing, 214
  format names, 215

Quick Styles *(continued)*
  with pre-Word 2007 documents, 216
  using, 213
quotation marks, formatting options, 240
Quote style, 215

• R •

range of pages, printing, 133–134
read-only files, 381
recently opened files, viewing, 122
records (mail merge), 345–346
red zigzag underlines, 33, 96–98
Redo command, 61–62
reference materials, 386
References tab
  features and uses, 281
  Footnotes group, 286–287
  Index group, 283–286
  Table of Contents menu, 282–283
rejecting revisions, 337
Repeat Typing command, 62–63
repeated words, 99
replacing text, 74–75
resaving documents, 118–119
Research task pane, 108–109
Reset to Theme from Template option, 229
resizing. *See* sizing
Reveal Formatting task pane, 219
reverse printing, 130
Review tab
  Changes group, 337
  Compare group, 336
  New Comment button, 332
  Proofing group, 105
  Track Changes button, 338
  word count feature, 109
revising documents, 335–338
revision marks, 34
Ribbon system
  Editing group, 65, 66
  hiding/viewing Ribbon, 19
  keyboard shortcuts, 372
  Quick Access toolbar, 360
  Table view tabs, 262
  Word 2007 interface, 1, 16

right alignment, 157
right clicking
  deleting comments, 334
  grammar corrections, 104
  marking text with similar formatting, 149
  for pop-up menus, 14
  removing changes, 337
  on the Ribbon, 19
  spelling suggestions, 97–98
  Status Bar Configuration menu, 359–360
  for synonyms, 107–118
right tab stop, 174
rotating images, 299
rows (mail merge), 346
rows (tables)
  adding and deleting, 271
  creating, 263–266
  overview, 262
  resizing, 272
the Ruler. *See also* tab stops
  paragraph formatting using, 164–165
  setting tab stops, 168–171
  viewing on window, 18

• S •

Save As dialog box
  for templates, 233
  viewing non-Word file types, 317
  when to use, 40, 116
Save As Type option, 317
Save command, 40
Save Selection as New Quick Style option, 222
saving documents
  AutoRecover feature, 371–372
  first time saves, 115–117
  first time versus subsequent saves, 23–24, 39–41
  importance of, 367
  keyboard shortcut, 41
  before printing, 128
  saving to disk, 117
  status bar information, 31
screen. *See* Word window

scrolling
  horizontal scroll bar, 49
  impact on insertion pointer, 49
  mouse for, 49
  in multiple documents, options for, 314
  vertical scroll bar, 47–49
Search drop-down list, 69–70
Search Options area, 68–69
searching. *See also* Find and Replace
      dialog box
  find and replace basics, 65–67
  Superfind features, 67–70
sections, section breaks
  for columns, 277
  creating, 199–200
  deleting, 201
  features and uses, 198–199
  headers and footers with, 204, 207–208
  for indexing, 286
  using, 200
  viewing, 200
security settings, 374
Select Outlook Contact, 343
Select Recipients drop-down menu
  for labels, 354
  for mail merge documents, 343
selecting pages
  for deletion, 59
  for printing, 132–134
selecting text
  entire documents, 85, 155
  F8 key for, 84–85
  mouse pointer shape, 20
  for printing, 134
  in tables, 267
  text blocks, 80–81
  using keyboard, 81–82
  using mouse for, 82–83
Selection option (printing), 134
sentences, deleting, 57, 58
Set Default Paste, 89
shading, 260
Shape Styles group, 293
Shift keys
  locating and using, 26–27
  selecting text and text blocks, 81

  using with mouse, 83
  when resizing images, 298
Shift+Ctrl+T key combination, 154
Shift+Enter key combination, 60, 269
Shift+F1 key combination, 219
Shift+F3 key combination, 151
Shift+F5 key combination, 53
Shift+Tab key combination, 269
shortcut icons on Desktop, 12–14
shortcut keys, creating, 224–225. *See also*
      keyboard shortcuts
Show All Revisions Inline option, 333
Show Level drop-down list, 327–328
Show Markup option, 333
Show Notes button, 287
Show Revisions in Balloons option, 333
Show/Hide command, 201
Shrink Font command, 146
size
  of documents, 113
  of fonts, 144–145
Size pop-up list (find and replace), 73
sizing
  columns in documents, 275–277
  graphic images, 298
  table cells, 268
  tables rows and columns, 272
  Word window, 16–17
smart quotes, 240
Smart Tags, 383
SmartArt feature, 307–308
soft returns, 60
sorting feature, 376–377
Sounds Like (English) option, 69
spacebar
  location, 27
  when to use, 29–30
spaces, single, 368
Special button (find and replace), 70–71
special characters
  diacritical symbols, 302–303
  em or en dashes, 303
  index code, 284
  nonbreaking spaces and hyphens,
      301–302
  upper case characters, 303

spell checking tools
  common misspelled words, 100
  dictionaries, spell check, 98–101
  proofing entire documents, 105
  red zigzag underlines, 96–98
Spelling and Grammar button, 105
splitting cells in tables, 271
splitting documents, 315–316
splitting text, 59
Square text wrapping option, 295
Start Mail Merge menu
  Label Options dialog box, 353–354
  Labels option, 353–354
  Mail Merge Recipients dialog box, 346–347
  Mail Merge Wizard, 341
  Select Recipients menu, 343
Start menu
  adding Word icon to, 14
  startup from, 12–13
starting Word
  automatic startup, 13
  from Quick Launch Toolbar, 14, 15
  from Start menu, 12–13, 14
  using Desktop shortcut, 13–14
  from Word Documents folder, 15–16
Status Bar Configuration menu, 359–360
status bar (Word window)
  document information on, 18, 41
  features and uses, 31
  View buttons, 18
  word counts in selected text, 81
  Zoom thing (Word window), 18
Step by Step Mail Merge Wizard, 341
StickyKeys, 31
Stop Automatically Correcting . . . option, 103
strikethroughs, 143
Strong style, 215–216
Style for Following Paragraph drop-down list, 222
Style Inspector, 219
Style Type drop-down list, 223
styles
  Apply Styles task pane, 218
  applying to tables, 270

  autoswitching feature, 222
  custom, creating from existing text, 220–223
  custom, naming, 221
  deleting, 225
  identifying in documents, 218
  importing/exporting, 226
  managing, 225–226
  modifying, 223–224
  overview, 211–212
  Quick Styles, 213, 214–216
  removing, 219–220
  switching style sets, 219
  for table of contents, 282–283
  templates for, 222
  types of, 212–213
  using, 213
Styles group (Home tab)
  accessing, 214
  Change Styles button, 219
  Quick Styles gallery, 214
Styles task pane
  deleting styles, 225
  displaying, 216–217
  Manage Styles button, 226
  modifying styles, 224
  Styles Inspector, 218–220
subscripts, 143
Subtitle style, 216
Superfind features, 67–70
superscripts, 143
Switch Windows menu, 312
symbols, locating and inserting, 303–304
Synchronous Scrolling button, 314
synonyms, locating in the Thesaurus, 107–108

• T •

tab characters
  hiding/showing, 168
  searches using, 71
Tab key, 27
  function and use, 168
  in table navigation, 269

tab stops. *See also* the Ruler
  center tab, 173–174
  combining right and left stops, 175–176
  decimal tabs, 177
  function, 18
  right tab stop, 174
  setting using Tabs dialog box, 179–180
  setting using the Ruler, 168–171
  tab-tab paragraph formatting, 172–173
  traditional left tab stops, 170
  unsetting, 182
  viewing, 168
tab symbol (^t) searches, 71
Table group, 267
Table Layout tab
  adjusting row and column size, 272
  aligning text, 272
  deleting cells, columns or rows, 271
  deleting tables, 272
  inserting columns or rows, 271
Table menu
  Convert Text to Table dialog box, 266
  Insert Table dialog box, 263–264
  Insert Table menu, 263–264
table of contents (TOC), 282–283
Table Tools Design tab, 269–270
Table Tools Layout tab, 267
Table view, 262
tables
  adding text to cells, 268–269
  creating from tabbed text, 266
  creating using Draw Table, 264–266
  creating using Insert Table, 263–264
  deleting cells, columns, or rows, 271
  deleting tables, 272
  design tools, 269–270
  moving table elements, 268
  navigating, 269
  overview, 262–263
  selection options, 267
  styles for, 212, 270
  table to text conversions, 266–267
  uses for, 261–262
Tables Tools Layout tab, 267
Tabs dialog box
  accessing, 179
  Clear All button, 182

default tab stops, 181
  leader tabs, 180–181
  setting tab stops, 179–180
task panes
  Clip Art, 291–292
  Clipboard, 91–93
  Document Maps, 375
  Document Recovery, 19, 372
  Mail Merge, 341–350
  Properties, 381–382
  Research, 108–109
  Reveal Formatting, 219
  Styles, 213, 216–220, 224–226
  in Word 2007, 19
technical assistance, 7
templates
  attaching to documents, 235–236
  cautions using, 115
  creating from existing documents,
    231–233
  creating from scratch, 234
  defined, 114, 230–231
  features and uses, 114–115, 231
  filename extensions for, 231
  modifying, 234–235
  naming, 233
  NORMAL.DOTM, 236–237
  saving, 233–234
  saving styles as, 222
  unattaching, 236
Templates and Add-Ins dialog box,
    235–236
text
  deleting single characters, 56
  deleting single words, 57
  searching, Superfind features, 67–70
  unlinking graphics from, 297
text blocks
  copying, 87
  defined, 80
  deleting, 58
  deselecting, 86
  Highlighting mode, 335
  linked copy, 90
  moving, 88, 90–91
  printing, 134
  selecting, 80–85

Text Box menu, 306
Text Box Tools Format tab, 294, 306
text boxes
  creating using AutoShapes, 294
  inserting in documents, 306
Text Direction button (tables), 272
text formatting
  adding color, 146–147
  adding lines and borders, 255
  bar tabs, 178
  basic commands, accessing, 140–141
  bolding, 142
  case changes, 151
  centering, 173–174
  combining formats, 144
  drop caps, 374–375
  fonts, 141–142, 148–149
  Format Painter for, 249
  fractions, 240
  Highlighting mode, 335
  italics, 142–143
  linking graphics to, 296
  overview, 38–39, 139–140
  pasted text, 88–89
  Quick Styles, 215
  special characters and symbols, 301–304
  strikethroughs, 143
  styles for, 211–212
  subscripts and superscripts, 143
  tab keys, 168
  tabbed lists, 170–171
  in tables, 272
  text boxes, 306
  text size, 144–146
  underlining, 143
  undoing, 147–148
  using Quick Styles for, 214–216
Text From File option, 123
Text group
  Date and Time button, 247
  inserting documents using, 123
  Object command, 123
  Text Box menu, 306
  WordArt Gallery dialog box, 305
Text Highlight button, 335

text sorting, 376–377
text wrapping
  automatic, 29
  breaks for, 200
  with labels, 356
  wrap points, 296
  wrapping options, 295–297
themes
  applying to documents, 228–229
  applying to graphics, 297
  custom, creating and managing, 229–230
  features and uses, 227–228
  modifying or creating, 229–230
  removing from documents, 229
Themes menu
  applying themes to documents, 228–229
  color themes, 229–230
  font themes, 229–230
thesaurus, 107–108
This Point Forward option
  columns, 276
  margins, 189
This Section option (margins), 189
Through text wrapping option, 295
Tight text wrapping option, 295
time stamps
  in documents, 247
  in headers or footers, 205
time-sensitive content controls, 245
title bar (Word window), 18
title boxes, 257
Title style, 215–216
TOC (table of contents), 282–283
Top and Bottom text wrapping option, 295
topics (outlines)
  expanding and contracting, 326–328
  main-level topics, 323–324
  promoting, 325
  rearranging, 326
  text topics, 326
Track Changes button, 338
Two Pages zoom command, 358
Type New List option, 343
typewriter keys, 26

typewriter keys versus computer keyboards, 30–31
typing. *See also* text; text formatting; word processing basics
  AutoComplete feature, 34
  Backspace key, 30
  Enter key, 28–29
  keyboard versus typewriter, 30–31, 38
  Insert versus Overtype modes, 62
  insertion point, 28
  repeat typing feature, 62–63
  spacebar, 29–30
  status bar features, 31
  underlines and colored text, 33–34
typos, removing, 30

• *U* •

Undo commands, 60–61, 369
Update Field command, 246
updating documents, 118–119
Use Existing List mail merge option, 343
Use Wildcards option (find and replace), 68–69

• *V* •

versions of documents, comparing, 335–338
Vertical Alignment drop-down list, 248
vertical scroll bar, 48, 52–53
View buttons (Word window), 18
View Ruler button, 18, 171
View tab
  Full Screen Reading view, 328
  New Window button, 314–315
  Split button, 315
  Switch Windows menu, 312
  View Side by Side option, 314
views. *See also* Draft view; Print Layout view
  Document Map, 375–376
  Full Screen Reading, 328–329
  Outline, 322–328
  Table, 262

• *W* •

Wambooli Forums Web site, 7
watermarks, 195–196
Web page addresses, 34
Web pages, 384
When Selecting Automatically Select Entire Word option, 85
white space searches (find and replace), 71
Whole Document margins, 189
Whole Page zoom command, 358
Widow/Orphan control, 194
wildcards in searches, 68–69
Windows taskbar, 19
Word 2007. *See also* Ribbon system
  exiting from, 22–23
  first-time set up questions, 16
  new features, 1–2
  opening, 12–16
word counts, 81, 109–110, 247
Word Equation tools, 379–380
Word Help system, 17, 21–22, 388
Word Options dialog box
  AutoCorrect options, 243
  click and type feature, 383
  Custom Dictionaries, 100
  Developer tab, 382
  Display Hidden Text option, 377
  Editing options, 85
  nonprinting characters, 168
  Proofing tools command, 100, 106
  Templates and Add-Ins dialog box, 235–236
  When Selecting Automatically Select Entire Word option, 85
word processing basics. *See also* Word window
  AutoComplete feature, 34
  closing Word program, 44
  formatting documents, 38–39
  help systems, 21–22
  keyboard keys and layout, 26–27
  mouse pointer, 20–21
  previewing documents, 42–43
  printing documents, 42–43

word processing basics *(continued)*
   process overview, 36
   proofing documents, 42
   typing process, 28–31, 38
word searches. *See* Find and Replace
   dialog box
Word window
   blank area, 19–20
   layout and features, 17
   Maximize button, 16
   maximizing, 16
   Minimize button, 24
   Office Button, 18
   Ribbon system, 19
   the Ruler, 18
   size of, 16–17
   status bar, 18–19
   tabs, 18

task panes, 19
title bar, 18
Windows taskbar, 19
word wrapping. *See* text wrapping
WordArt Gallery dialog box, 305
WordPerfect documents, 319
wrap points, 296. *See also* text wrapping
Write tab, 141–142

• X •

XPS (XML Paper Specification) files, 318

• Z •

zigzag underlines, 33–34
Zoom dialog box, 358
Zoom tool, 18, 357–359

SPORTS, FITNESS, PARENTING, RELIGION & SPIRITUALITY

0-471-76871-5

0-7645-7841-3

Also available:
- Catholicism For Dummies
  0-7645-5391-7
- Exercise Balls For Dummies
  0-7645-5623-1
- Fitness For Dummies
  0-7645-7851-0
- Football For Dummies
  0-7645-3936-1
- Judaism For Dummies
  0-7645-5299-6
- Potty Training For Dummies
  0-7645-5417-4
- Buddhism For Dummies
  0-7645-5359-3

- Pregnancy For Dummies
  0-7645-4483-7 †
- Ten Minute Tone-Ups For Dummies
  0-7645-7207-5
- NASCAR For Dummies
  0-7645-7681-X
- Religion For Dummies
  0-7645-5264-3
- Soccer For Dummies
  0-7645-5229-5
- Women in the Bible For Dummies
  0-7645-8475-8

TRAVEL

0-7645-7749-2

0-7645-6945-7

Also available:
- Alaska For Dummies
  0-7645-7746-8
- Cruise Vacations For Dummies
  0-7645-6941-4
- England For Dummies
  0-7645-4276-1
- Europe For Dummies
  0-7645-7529-5
- Germany For Dummies
  0-7645-7823-5
- Hawaii For Dummies
  0-7645-7402-7

- Italy For Dummies
  0-7645-7386-1
- Las Vegas For Dummies
  0-7645-7382-9
- London For Dummies
  0-7645-4277-X
- Paris For Dummies
  0-7645-7630-5
- RV Vacations For Dummies
  0-7645-4442-X
- Walt Disney World & Orlando
  For Dummies
  0-7645-9660-8

GRAPHICS, DESIGN & WEB DEVELOPMENT

0-7645-8815-X

0-7645-9571-7

Also available:
- 3D Game Animation For Dummies
  0-7645-8789-7
- AutoCAD 2006 For Dummies
  0-7645-8925-3
- Building a Web Site For Dummies
  0-7645-7144-3
- Creating Web Pages For Dummies
  0-470-08030-2
- Creating Web Pages All-in-One Desk
  Reference For Dummies
  0-7645-4345-8
- Dreamweaver 8 For Dummies
  0-7645-9649-7

- InDesign CS2 For Dummies
  0-7645-9572-5
- Macromedia Flash 8 For Dummies
  0-7645-9691-8
- Photoshop CS2 and Digital
  Photography For Dummies
  0-7645-9580-6
- Photoshop Elements 4 For Dummies
  0-471-77483-9
- Syndicating Web Sites with RSS Feeds
  For Dummies
  0-7645-8848-6
- Yahoo! SiteBuilder For Dummies
  0-7645-9800-7

NETWORKING, SECURITY, PROGRAMMING & DATABASES

0-7645-7728-X

0-471-74940-0

Also available:
- Access 2007 For Dummies
  0-470-04612-0
- ASP.NET 2 For Dummies
  0-7645-7907-X
- C# 2005 For Dummies
  0-7645-9704-3
- Hacking For Dummies
  0-470-05235-X
- Hacking Wireless Networks
  For Dummies
  0-7645-9730-2
- Java For Dummies
  0-470-08716-1

- Microsoft SQL Server 2005 For Dummies
  0-7645-7755-7
- Networking All-in-One Desk Reference
  For Dummies
  0-7645-9939-9
- Preventing Identity Theft For Dummies
  0-7645-7336-5
- Telecom For Dummies
  0-471-77085-X
- Visual Studio 2005 All-in-One Desk
  Reference For Dummies
  0-7645-9775-2
- XML For Dummies
  0-7645-8845-1